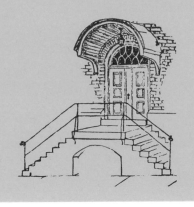

SHAKESPEARE'S OPPOSITES

The Admiral's Men is the acting company that staged Christopher Marlowe's plays while its companion company was giving the first performances of Shakespeare. Unlike the Shakespeare company, there is a great deal of evidence available telling us what the Admiral's company did and how it staged its plays. Not only do we know far more about the design of its two playhouses, the Rose and the Fortune, than we know of any other playhouse from the time, including the Globe, but we have Henslowe's *Diary*. This recorded everything the Admiral's company performed from 1594 to 1600 and after, what the company bought to stage its plays, who performed which parts, who wrote which plays, and even how much they were paid. The first history to be written of the Admiral's Men, this book tells us not only about the company's own work, but also much about how the Shakespeare company operated.

ANDREW GURR is Emeritus Professor of English at the University of Reading. As chief academic advisor, he was a key figure in the project to rebuild Shakespeare's Globe Theatre in London. His many publications include *The Shakespearean Stage, 1574–1642* (Cambridge, fourth edition 2009), *Playgoing in Shakespeare's London* (Cambridge, third edition 2004) and *The Shakespearian Playing Companies* (1996). Professor Gurr regularly contributes articles on Shakespeare to publications ranging from *Shakespeare Survey* to the *Times Literary Supplement*.

SHAKESPEARE'S OPPOSITES

The Admiral's Company 1594–1625

ANDREW GURR

CAMBRIDGE
UNIVERSITY PRESS

CAMBRIDGE UNIVERSITY PRESS
Cambridge, New York, Melbourne, Madrid, Cape Town, Singapore, São Paulo,
Delhi, Dubai, Tokyo

Cambridge University Press
The Edinburgh Building, Cambridge CB2 8RU, UK

Published in the United States of America by Cambridge University Press, New York

www.cambridge.org
Information on this title: www.cambridge.org/9780521869034

First published 2009
Reprinted 2010

Printed in the United Kingdom at the University Press, Cambridge

A catalogue record for this publication is available from the British Library

Library of Congress Cataloging-in-Publication Data
Gurr, Andrew.
Shakespeare's opposites : the Admiral's company, 1594–1625 / Andrew Gurr.
p. cm.
Includes bibliographical references and index.
ISBN 978-0-521-86903-4
1. Admiral's Men (Theater company)–History.
2. Theatrical companies–England–London–History–17th century.
3. Theatrical companies–England–London–History–16th century.
4. Repertory theater–England–London–History–17th century.
5. Repertory theater–England–London–History–16th century. I. Title.

PN2599.5.T54G87 2009
792′.09421–dc22

2008054458

ISBN 978-0-521-86903-4 hardback

HERE'S TO THE ADMIRAL'S MEN
(Adrian Fennyman, alias Tom Wilkinson, *Shakespeare in Love*)

Contents

Acknowledgements

For the illustrations in this book, my thanks are due to the British Library (1, 4, 9, 15, 16, 17), Dulwich College (2, 7), the Photographic Survey, the Courtauld Institute of Art (3), Records of Early English Drama (Subhash Shanbhag, 5), Penguin Books (6), the Museum of London (8 and 13), the Royal Library, Stockholm (10). Jon Greenfield (11), and the Library of the Rijksuniversiteit Utrecht (12 and 14).

A multitude of other thanks go to my advisers and helpers, above all my scholarly friends who have read drafts and advised me to make changes, John Astington, Susan Ceresano and Grace Ioppolo. To Julian Bowsher I owe a particular debt for showing me, sharing with me and arguing over some of the multitude of remnants from the Rose now identified and secured in the Museum of London's depot in Islington. I owe unspecifiable debts to my fellow-members of the Rose Theatre Trust, who share with me the hope that on some remote day enough money will be made available to resume the all-too abruptly truncated archaeological scrutiny of the Rose's remains. To Sarah Stanton of Cambridge University Press, as always, I owe the constant pleasure of her help and encouragement. Finally, I owe a comprehensive debt to all those friends, colleagues and enemies whose consistent preoccupation with Shakespeare pushed me into this quest for his shadow in the Admiral's Men.

Illustrations

The company's unique features

For six years from May 1594 the English government gave two acting companies the exclusive right to entertain Londoners. We know little about what one of the companies did to fulfil that privilege, except for Shakespeare's plays, about which we otherwise know a great deal. About the other company we know a lot, more in fact than about any other of the playing companies of the Shakespearean period. We even know more about its two playhouses, the Rose and the Fortune, than about any of the other twelve or more playhouses built between 1567 and 1629. The other company, generally known as the Admiral's Men, is the subject of this book.

Between 1594 and 1600 the Shakespeare company staged an unknown number of plays. Of those that survive we have evidence for only four besides the nineteen of Shakespeare's up to *Hamlet*. On the other hand we know that the Admiral's Men staged 161 plays up to the end of 1600, twenty-two of which still exist in print. The survival rate of plays by both companies is similar, but the history of the Shakespeare company, the Chamberlain's Men, gives no indication of the 140 or so other plays they are likely to have staged to match those performed by the Admiral's. Since the two companies ran in parallel for those six years as the dominant force in English theatre, a history of the Admiral's career can show a great deal of what in the Shakespeare company's long life still lies in shadow.

The Admiral's Men found their own distinctive way to cope with the unique demands laid on them by the exclusive access to professional playing in London that they were granted in 1594. Once they had settled into their daily routine of performing a different play each day to much the same body of customers, they invented a device that enhanced each performance in ways the Shakespeare company, so far as we know, seems to have ignored almost completely. They faced the fact that the same familiar faces had to appear on stage each playing a different role every afternoon, as successively, say, Tamburlaine, Faustus, Hieronymo or Barabbas, alongside the equally familiar faces of their fellows in each play.

To cope with this the company developed a trick that exploited precisely the audience's familiarity with their faces. While the lesser players doubled their bit parts, the company gave their leads plays involving quick-change disguises. In one play of 1595 their leading player Alleyn took four parts, three of them in disguise parodying his more famous roles in other plays, notably Tamburlaine and Barabbas. It was a trick they sustained for decades. Sam Rowley, a long-term sharer in the company, wrote a play about Henry VIII that included scenes where the king disguises himself to walk anonymously among his people. The tradition reached its apotheosis in 1611 with *The Roaring Girl*, a play about a well-known Londoner, who was persuaded at one performance to appear on stage in person and sing a song, setting her own reality up against the company's representation of her. The company's long history shows that metatheatrical trickery of this kind was basic to its activities.

It may well be that such tricks were far more basic to all Elizabethan theatre than can readily be recognised from readings of Shakespeare. We know he gave disguises to the boys playing Portia in *Merchant of Venice* in 1596 and Rosalind in *As You Like It* in 1599. We also know that *Measure for Measure* uses the old trick of the disguised governor fashionable at the time, and we know that Henry V disguises himself to talk to his humble soldiers, but otherwise the Shakespeare canon gives us little sense of the intimacy that prevailed in the original conditions of performance. With the multitude of different outlets in the media for modern entertainment that we enjoy today we find it difficult to imagine the effect of having the choice restricted to one of the only two venues and companies open daily in the 1590s. In a city of perhaps two hundred thousand people, Philip Henslowe's records suggest that in 1594 the average playgoer went to a play as many as twenty times every year, once a fortnight. No other playing company could have had such a close familiarity with its audiences. Those audiences standing crammed together in broad daylight around the stage had a familiarity with what they were experiencing that no modern audiences can create.

May 1594 was the greatest growth-point in English theatre history. An appalling epidemic of bubonic plague which killed over ten thousand Londoners had stopped the performing of any plays from June 1592 to April 1594 except for only two short stints in the frozen months of January 1593 and January 1594 when for a while the plague was latent. During that long break from acting Shakespeare turned to writing his two great poems, *Venus and Adonis* and *The Rape of Lucrece*, which his friend from Stratford Richard Field published in spring 1593 and 1594. *The Rape* was entered in the Stationers' Register on 9 May 1594. In that same month two Privy Councillors, Henry Carey the Lord Chamberlain, who was responsible for the regulation of playing, along with his son-in-law Charles Howard the Lord Admiral, succeeded in setting up a deal with the Lord Mayor of London designed to achieve a compromise between the mayor, who insisted that all plays be banned from his city, and the two Council members, who wanted playing to flourish. They identified two playhouses in the suburbs of the city where a pair of fresh companies made up from the most outstanding players in the land could stage their plays.[1] The deal they forged creating the new playing companies must have been a decisive factor in turning Shakespeare back to the play-writing that he had forsaken while the plague raged and he looked for a sponsoring lord. He had composed and published his two epyllions on Field's presses with letters of dedication that showed his growing hope of reward from the Earl of Southampton. We can only guess how willingly he went back to his former work as a player in the Lord Chamberlain's new company during that momentous month.

The Privy Councillors as they saw it had a duty to entertain the queen with the best new plays every Christmas. In the event their two new companies could (and did) provide this service exclusively for the next six years. Carey's and Howard's plan had an obvious precedent, the major company set up eleven years before in 1583 with the queen herself as its patron.[2] Entitled the Queen's Men, it took the best two or three players from each of the companies then competing for attention at court, and received the exclusive right to perform at inns and other places inside the city and to take their plays round the country.[3] In May 1594 Carey and Howard took the extra precaution of setting up not one but two new companies, and appeased the Lord Mayor by agreeing to ban all playing at the city inns where plays had been staged regularly in the past. Instead they allocated their companies to playhouses out in the suburbs, both of which belonged to people with whom the two Councillors already had long contact. James Burbage, builder and owner of the Theatre in Shoreditch, had been a servant to Carey for the last ten years. Edward Alleyn,

---

[1] The idea behind this scheme, with its brilliant resolution of the problem of running plays in a city whose mayor and aldermen were opposed to playing, is only a hypothesis, but it gives by far the best explanation of the available evidence, which is deficient chiefly because the Privy Council papers between 1593 and 1595 have disappeared. For a full account of the situation and the hypothesis, see Gurr, 'Henry Carey's Peculiar Letter', *Shakespeare Quarterly* 56 (2005), 51–75.

[2] Howard rather than the unsubtle Carey seems to have been the grey eminence behind the establishment of the two new companies in 1594, though the key executive figure must have been the Master of the Revels. Howard is thought to have been sponsor of Edmund Tilney's original appointment as Master of the Revels in 1578, since they were related by blood.

[3] The story of this venture is given by Scot McMillin and Sally-Beth MacLean, *The Queen's Men and Their Plays*, Cambridge University Press, 1998.

son-in-law to the builder and owner of the Rose playhouse on Bankside, Philip Henslowe, had worn Howard's livery for a similar period.

Each company took up players from a variety of former groups. The Chamberlain's Men took Richard Burbage, son of the Theatre's owner, along with others who had been in the Earl of Pembroke's Men, almost certainly including Shakespeare. They also took several players from the recently deceased Lord Strange's, later the Earl of Derby's Men, and one former Queen's Men's player. The Admiral's took a mix including one Queen's man, two from the old Admiral's, now a travelling group, and several players from other companies. For their repertory Carey's company were given some of the old Queen's Men's plays, including several that Shakespeare eventually rewrote for them: the first *King John*, an ur-*Hamlet* and *King Leir*. They also acquired all of Shakespeare's earlier plays, including the first histories he had written or shared the writing of up to the hugely popular *Richard III*, along with his early comedies and his one tragedy, *Titus Andronicus*. Howard's group, the Lord Admiral's Men, took all the Marlowe plays that Alleyn had made his name with, the two *Tamburlaines*, *Faustus*, *The Jew of Malta* and *The Massacre at Paris*, along with *The Spanish Tragedy* and a variety of plays that Alleyn had purchased over the years from Robert Peele and other writers.

The Admiral's Men were Shakespeare's opposites, the other half of this adroit scheme that sponsored and limited all playing in London from May 1594 till 1600. The two companies quickly developed quite distinct identities, which is half the reason for this book. While the Shakespeare company was always a team of sharers taking equal parts even in the playhouse they built, the Admiral's Men, led by the most famous and venturesome actor of the time, eventually became the first playing company to be controlled by an impresario. Alleyn ran it along with his father-in-law for most of its thirty years. The two companies also gradually diverged in their general policy and in the audiences they aimed at. The Burbage company tried to use their outdoor venue only in the summer, while hoping to secure a different venue indoors for each winter.[4] By contrast the Alleyn company proved ready or at least willing to use its outdoor playhouse throughout the year. This difference in their preferences meant that by the end of their long life the Admiral's company catered chiefly for the mass of 'citizen' playgoers at the cheaper outdoor playhouses, whereas their opposites, the King's Men, fed and chiefly lived off the richer playgoers at the indoor Blackfriars.

---

[4] This story has often been told recently, initially in Gurr, 'Money or Audiences: The Choice of Shakespeare's Globe', *Theatre Notebook* 42 (1988), 3–14.

As impresarios Alleyn and his father-in-law Henslowe live now in Shakespeare's shadow. That is unfortunate because not only do we have so much more knowledge of their work through their first six years than we have for the Shakespeare company but their work ran in radically distinct ways which the Shakespeare shadow all too readily obscures. Henslowe has left us the unique and invaluable *Diary* of his dealings through the 1590s, and equally valuably we now have archaeological evidence of his first playhouse, the Rose, in similarly unique detail. Amongst Henslowe's and Alleyn's papers we even have a builder's contract for the playhouse, the Fortune, that replaced the Rose in 1600 and remained in use staging *The Spanish Tragedy* and Marlowe's *Tamburlaine* and *Faustus* regularly until 1642.

The stories of the two companies interact remarkably, even though for their first six years they marched in parallel lines, the sort that never meet. Their playhouses, the Rose with its replacement the Fortune, and the Theatre with its successor the Globe and later the Blackfriars, featured in different ways in the early careers of what are now known with good reason as the duopoly companies, the Admiral's and their opposites the Chamberlain's. The term 'duopoly' suits them because for the six years from May 1594 thanks to Carey and Howard the two companies held an almost exclusive share of performances in London. Their founders, Carey and Howard, set them up as a pair with the same purpose but the forms their enterprise led them to diverged from the start. They had different repertories and different players, and for all the similarity of function their activities diverged as much as Shakespeare's plays differ from Marlowe's. Just as the Chamberlain's worked as a team of equal sharers whereas Alleyn controlled the Admiral's repertory, so Shakespeare wrote plays that invited a more equal sharing of roles for the players than did Alleyn's great dominating roles. The eponymous King Richard II shared his role in Shakespeare's first history play for his new company with the 'silent king', Bullingbrook, whereas Alleyn's Tamburlaine conquered and ruled everybody in his plays. In *The Blind Beggar of Alexandria* Alleyn delivered almost three-sevenths, more than one-third, of all the lines in the play, as we shall see below. The radical difference between divided authority in *Richard II* and the absolute dominance of the hero in *Tamburlaine* is an almost parodic representation of the roles the leading actors played in each company.

Whereas we know of only the nineteen or so Shakespeare plays plus just a few others in the Chamberlain's repertory up to 1600, for the Admiral's Men we have the titles, or their approximations, for 229 plays staged at the Rose and then at the Fortune between May 1594 and the summer of 1625. Of that total, thirty-five have survived in early printed texts, with varying levels of reliability. We also have manuscripts for two plays, one of them,

John a Kent and John a Cumber, written in the author's own hand, with
another, *Jugurtha*, in an incomplete mid-seventeenth-century transcript,
and a third in five different hands which seems to have been prepared for
a revival in 1601 but never got past the censor. That play, *Sir Thomas More*,
stands outside the repertory considered in this book and is therefore
examined separately from the rest. Considering that the titles of the plays
staged at the Rose and the Fortune are only comprehensive for the first
three years of their existence, and that nearly two hundred plays from the
later years after 1600 have probably been lost forever, it is even more
regrettable that we have perhaps less than one in twelve of the total of plays
that we know were rehearsed and prepared through the usual three-week
preparation schedule at the Rose before being tried out in the playhouse.[5]

[5] This book so far as possible cites plays in facsimile editions. The lists given here are by author, starting
with plays by unknown writers. MSR = Malone Society Reprints, Oxford, which appear in type
facsimiles. EEBO = Early English Books Online. A few are taken from other editions. Anon., *George
a Greene, the Pinner of Wakefield* (Q 1590) MSR 1911; Anon., *A Knack to Know an Honest Man*
(Q 1595) MSR 1910; Anon., *Look About You* (*Disguises?*) (Q 1600) MSR 1913; Anon., *Thomas Stukeley*
(Q 1605) MSR 1970 (see also George Peele, *The Stukeley Plays*); William Boyle, *Jugurth* (Bodleian
MS.Rawl.poet.195, 1660?); George Chapman, *The Blind Beggar of Alexandria* (Q 1598) MSR 1928
[ed. Lloyd E. Berry] in *The Plays of George Chapman: The Comedies*, Urbana, 1970, earlier editions by
R. H. Shepherd (1873), and T. M. Parrott, *Comedies* (1914); George Chapman, *An Humorous Day's
Mirth* (Q 1599), MSR 1937 [1938] [ed. Allan Holaday in *The Plays of George Chapman: The Comedies*,
Urbana, 1970]; Henry Chettle, *Hoffman* (Q 1631) MSR 1950 (1951); Henry Chettle and John Day,
1 The Blind Beggar of Bednall Green (Q 1657) facsimile edition, Uystpruyst, 1902; Thomas Dekker,
Old Fortunatus (Q 1600), in *The Dramatic Works of Thomas Dekker*, ed. Fredson Bowers, 4 vols.,
Cambridge, 1956–62, Vol. 1; Dekker, *The Shoemaker's Holiday* (Q 1600) ed. Bowers, Vol. 1; Dekker,
Henry Chettle, William Haughton, *Patient Grissill* (Q 1603), ed. Bowers, vol. 1; Dekker and Thomas
Middleton, *1 The Honest Whore* (Q 1604), ed. Bowers, Vol. 2; Thomas Dekker, *The Whore of Babylon*
(Q 1607) ed. Bowers, Vol. 2; Thomas Drue, *The Duchess of Suffolk* (Q 1631) EEBO; Robert Greene, *Friar
Bacon and Friar Bungay* (Q 1594) MSR 1926; William Haughton, *Englishmen for My Money* (Q 1616)
MSR 1912; William Haughton, *The Devil and His Dam* (*Grim the Collier of Croydon*) (Q 1662), reprinted
in *A Choice Ternary of English Plays* Gratiae Theatrales, ed. William M. Baillie, New York, 1984;
Haughton and John Day, *Two Lamentable Tragedies* (Q 1601) EEBO; Thomas Kyd, *The Spanish
Tragedy* (Qq 1592, 1599, 1602) MSR (1592), 1948 [1949], MSR (1602), 1925; Christopher Marlowe,
1 Tamburlaine (1587, Q 1590), *2 Tamburlaine* (1587, Q 1590), *Doctor Faustus* (Qq 1604, 1616), *The Jew of
Malta* (Q 1633), *The Massacre at Paris* (O 1594?) [in *The Complete Works of Christopher Marlowe*,
ed. Bowers, 2 vols., second edition, Cambridge, 1981]; Middleton and Dekker, *The Roaring Girl*
(Q 1611) in *The Dramatic Works of Thomas Dekker*, ed. Bowers, Vol. 3, ed. Paul Mulholland, The
Revels Plays, Manchester, 1987; Middleton, *No Wit/No Help Like a Woman's*, ed. John Jowett, in *The
Collected Works of Thomas Middleton*, ed. Gary Taylor and John Lavagnino, Oxford, 2007; Anthony
Munday, *John a Kent and John a Cumber*, ms 1595, MSR 1923; Munday, *The Downfall of Robert Earl of
Huntingdon* (Q 1601) MSR 1964 [1965]; Munday, *The Death of Robert Earl of Huntingdon* (Q 1601) MSR
1965 [1967]; Munday, Michael Drayton, Robert Wilson, Richard Hathway, *1 Sir John Oldcastle* (Q 1600)
MSR 1908; George Peele, *The Battle of Alcazar* (Q 1594) MSR 1907 [*The Stukeley Plays* (*The Battle of
Alcazar* and *The Famous History of the Life and Death of Captain Thomas Stukeley*), ed. Charles Edelman,
The Revels Plays, Manchester, 2005]; George Peele, *The Love of King David and Fair Bethsabe. With the
Tragedie of Absalon* (Q 1599) MSR 1912; Peele, *Longshanks* (*King Edward the First*) (Q 1593) MSR 1911;
Henry Porter, *The Two Angry Women of Abingdon* (Q 1599) MSR 1912; Samuel Rowley, *When You See
Me, You Know Me* (Q 1605) MSR 1952.

For centuries now we have revelled in Shakespeare's plays because we have them in print and can linger on their wonderful use of language. In playhouses his theatrical brilliance has been deployed to more variable effect, although in recent years a more generous acknowledgement of his genius in playmaking comparable to his genius with language has grown in public awareness. Theatrical brilliance is of course less easily registered than verbal genius because it is far more difficult to put on record. This difficulty puts the company opposite to Shakespeare's at an even greater disadvantage, because their skills were in theatre and their surviving play-texts reward close study on paper much less readily. The evidence set out in this book argues that for the six years while they partnered the Shakespeare company in sharing the monopoly of playing for Londoners they proved more inventive in exploiting the resource the new duopoly gave them. By their nature such skills are not easily reproducible, for reasons set out in the second chapter here. But the fact that the story of the Admiral's Men is on record in far more detail than that of their opposites means that it repays careful scrutiny as the mirror to the other great theatrical success story of those fertile years.

A broad mosaic of tangible if fragmentary evidence survives in the Rose's financial and repertory records from those first hectic years. Even more tangibly, the Admiral's company was lodged in the only one of the ten open-air amphitheatres built through that key period that survives today in an almost complete set of foundations and a mass of associated remains. The third of these great escapes from the usual processes that destroy historical records is the builder's contract for the company's second playhouse, the Fortune. Putting the three together gives us more substantial evidence about the Admiral's Men and their two main theatre venues than for any other company or playhouse of that unique theatrical era.

Yet for all the wealth of shadowy presences and the crowds of nameless participants in the theatre of the Shakespeare period there is a real danger of making overconfident deductions from the fragments of evidence. It is dangerous because such plentiful pieces of the mosaic tempt us into making tenuous connections that we would like to be stronger than they really are. The first comment ever made about the earlier Admiral's company to which Marlowe sold his *Tamburlaines*, an anecdote in a letter by Philip Gawdy, illustrates the dangers of connecting these riches too tightly.

Gawdy, born in 1562, was a younger son of Norfolk gentry with little income and no prospect of ready employment. Ostensibly a law student at Clifford's Inn, he mostly hung around the court. At the age of 29, in 1591, he ventured out to sea. His ship was the soon-to-be-famous *Revenge*, commanded by Sir Richard Grenville. He was on it in the Azores when they confronted a Spanish battle fleet of fifteen warships sent out to safeguard the treasure ships from South America that were bringing home their annual delivery of bullion which the English fleet was after. The English ships were too far away to help the *Revenge*, which was captured after a ferocious battle, patriotically celebrated by Tennyson in his famous ballad.[6] Grenville was wounded and taken prisoner along with sixty other English seafarers including Gawdy. While they waited to be ransomed, they were imprisoned in Lisbon Castle. Gawdy was one of the last to be released because his captors overestimated his social status and his financial backing. One of his letters to his elder brother sent from Lisbon on 9 February 1592 begins, understandably in the circumstances, by proclaiming his low social status and his lack of resources. He was released that autumn in exchange for a Spanish prisoner at a cost to his brother of £200.

The letter that concerns us, however, was written some years before his seafaring misadventure, on 16 November 1587. Addressed to his father in Norfolk, it is full of cheerful chat about his current activities in London. One of his stories is about a disaster that struck the first company of Admiral's Men while they were performing at a suburban playhouse:

My L. Admyrall his men and players having a devyse in ther playe to tye one of their fellows to a poste and so to shoote him to deathe, having borrowed their callyvers one of the players handes swerved his peece being charged with bullet missed the fellowe he aymed at and killed a child, and a woman great with child forthwith, and hurt an other man in the head very soore.[7]

In 2002, Charles Edelman, a leading expert on Elizabethan military technology, pointed out that calivers, long-barrelled muzzle-loading firearms, were unlikely for the sake of the actors to have been loaded with bullets, and the players could not have used blanks, which did not then exist. So the caliver that killed the young playgoers must have had gunpowder in its chamber to make the noise of a shot, but only wadding should have been fired from the barrel. Citing similar precedents, Edelman argued that the projectile doing the damage must have been the broken-off tip of a scouring rod.[8] Prompted by this explanation, Julian Bowsher, the

[6] 'At Flores in the Azores Sir Richard Grenville lay . . .' *The Revenge. A Ballad of the Fleet*, in *The Poems of Tennyson*, ed. Christopher Ricks, Longman, London, 1969, pp. 1241–45.
[7] I. H. Jeayes, ed. *The Letters of Philip Gawdy*, London, 1906, p. 23; BL MS Egerton 2804, fo. 35.
[8] Charles Edelman, '"Shoot at him all at once": Gunfire at the Playhouse, 1587', *Theatre Notebook* 57 (2003), 78–81.

Figure 1. A caliver being scoured, an engraving from Jacob de Gheyn, *The Exercise of Armes*, 1608. It accompanies the order 'Draw your skowringe-stick out of your Musket'.

archaeologist, then engaged in cataloguing the 40,000 fragmentary remains dug up at the Rose site in 1989, was able to identify an obscure piece of bent iron found in the Rose's yard as the broken tip of a scouring rod.[9] Gawdy's fatal engine appeared to be identified.

Gawdy's anecdote is seductive, drawing us into the temptation such fragments can engender when we try to connect one piece of evidence with another. His account is thought to refer to a performance of the second *Tamburlaine*, published in 1590 as an Admiral's company play. In the first scene of its final act, Tamburlaine's soldiers shoot at the captured

[9] See Julian M. C. Bowsher, and Patricia Miller, *The Rose and the Globe – Playhouses of Tudor Bankside, Southwark: Excavations 1988–1991*, Museum of London, London, 2009.

Governor of Babylon while he hangs from the city walls. Edelman's
conjecture offers seeming proof that both *Tamburlaines* were on stage by
late 1587, and that they were first staged at the Rose, built in that year. Thus
it seems that the first Admiral's Men, with Edward Alleyn starring as
Tamburlaine, were performing there more than four years before Philip
Henslowe started his famous *Diary* in 1592.

It is regrettably not such a firm connection. The *Diary* records day by
day all the performances by Strange's Men with Alleyn as their leader
from February 1592, and yet *Tamburlaine* gets no mention until August
1594. Gawdy specified the company involved in the incident but not the
playhouse. Partly on the evidence of an assertion by Thomas Middleton
in 1603 about *Faustus*, that a character 'had a head of hayre like one of my
Divells in Doctor Faustus, when the olde Theater crackt and frighted the
Audience',[10] it is now thought that the chief playing-place in London of
the early Admiral's Men when they first staged *Tamburlaine* and *Faustus*
was not the Rose but the Theatre. Middleton may or may not be right in
naming the location for his *Faustus* anecdote. He was too young to recall
anything but a legend from the 1580s, so the Admiral's company really
might have been at the newly built first Rose rather than the bigger
Theatre. But it must be conceded that nothing tangible connects
2 Tamburlaine with the early Rose. The small piece of curved iron found
in the Rose's yard is not necessarily the murderous fragment figuring
in Gawdy's tale and Edelman's deduction. We have to treat this cross-
connection of the fragmentary pieces of evidence as no more than a
seductive possibility. Early English theatre and everything to do with
Shakespeare even when he is only an opposite is full of such temptations.

This book tries to be the biography of a company, telling how it came
into being, followed by its long and distinguished career of thirty-two
years until the great plague epidemic of 1625–26 forced its closure. As a
biography it ought to treat the team of players which is its subject in the
singular, a collective, as teams are sometimes thought to be. But the
endeavours of the many individuals who worked for it demands use of
the plural, so from here on the company will be 'they' or 'them'. After a
summary history and an account of some features of their repertory that
contrasts in striking ways with the more familiar Shakespearean one it will

---

[10] T. M., *The Black Booke*, Middleton, *The Collected Works*, ed. Gary Taylor and John Lavagnino,
Clarendon Press, Oxford, 2007, p. 209. I hope that at least through this book readers will
pronounce the Marlowe hero's name as Henslowe did, 'fostes', or 'forstus', and not with the
German pronunciation immortalised much later by Goethe.

examine the design of the two playhouses the company used and the distinct staging they both generated before returning to the plays, still the most tangible evidence. When they were first formed in 1594 the Admiral's Men first ran 'old' plays that came ready-made to the company, the work of Marlowe and Kyd. Next came specific kinds of play they bought to keep their repertoire fresh. Besides the distinctive species of comedy using disguises which we will look at in the second chapter these include the company's invention of the comedy of 'humours', stories of magic and devilry, examples of English history in the so-called 'chronicle' plays that developed into the Foxean 'Elect Nation' plays, plus special categories such as classical and biblical stories. Their gradual move in later years towards the traditional repertory of the 'citizen playhouses' completes this survey of what the company developed at the Fortune between 1600 and 1625. Regrettably, there is far less information available about these later years than for the rich period of the 'duopoly' phase, either of the plays themselves or their titles, so it is inevitable and perhaps misleading to see the company's last twenty years as a period of continuity or conservatism compared with the enterprise and social advance of the King's Men. That was the judgement of the time, however, and there is not much evidence to gainsay it.

During their thirty-two years the company's membership stayed remarkably stable, although they had three different patrons and therefore three names at different times. From 1594 till the end of 1603 they were technically the servants of the Lord Admiral, later Earl of Nottingham. In 1603 King James made his elder son, Prince Henry, their patron. When Henry died in 1612 he was replaced as patron by his sister Elizabeth's new husband, Lord Palsgrave, who became Frederick V the Elector Palatine, and for a few days in 1619 the King of Bohemia. None of these patrons took any direct interest in the company that used their name, so the central element in this collective biography is the special history of its two great managers and entrepreneurs, Philip Henslowe and Edward Alleyn, and their social and commercial climb to the top of their respective ladders.

Tall, strong and distinguished-looking, Alleyn was already the most celebrated actor in England when Shakespeare reached London. In 1592 Thomas Nashe picked Alleyn out as the pre-eminent player of the time. Ben Jonson wrote a verse eulogy to him published with his *Epigrams*, a handsome tribute, presumably composed a little before 1603, when Alleyn finally retired from playing and Jonson had only recently stopped writing for Henslowe.

If Rome so great, and in her wisest age,
Feared not to boast the glories of her stage,
As skilful Roscius and grave Aesop, men
Yet crowned with honours as with riches then,
Who had no less a trumpet of their name
Than Cicero, whose every breath was fame:
How can so great example die in me,
That, Alleyn, I should pause to publish thee?
Who both their graces in thyself hast more
Out-stripped, than they did all that went before;
And present worth in all dost so contract,
As others speak, but only thou dost act.
Wear this renown. 'Tis just that who did give
So many poets life, by one should live.[11]

Alleyn became an impresario of sorts surprisingly early, buying playbooks that he liked to perform in from 1590 onwards. Acting for roughly the same number of years that Shakespeare worked in London his management of players, his investments in plays, playhouses and, perhaps most distinctively, his running of the Bear Garden and its activities particularly for the court made him immensely wealthy by the standards of the day.[12] Born in 1566, two years after Shakespeare, Alleyn was an actor before he was fifteen, retiring (finally) at the end of 1603, when he was thirty-six and his long-term patron Howard was replaced by Prince Henry. Physically powerful in appearance and in personality,[13] with a wry capacity for self-mockery over his strutting parts that shows up in some of the plays, he died at the age of sixty in 1626. A few months after he started playing at the Rose in February 1592 he married Joan Woodward, Henslowe's step-daughter. She died in 1622, and soon after he took a new wife, Constance, a young daughter of the Dean of St Paul's, John Donne. Both marriages reflected his status at the time.

His early career emerges surprisingly strongly out of the few records surviving from the 1580s. The youngest of five sons, his father was an

---

[11] Quoted in his *Poems*, ed. Ian Donaldson, Oxford, 1975, p. 46. Much later Jonson wrote with more characteristic scorn that Alleyn's roles had 'nothing in them but the *scenicall* strutting and furious vociferation' (in his notebook *Discoveries, Works*, ed. Herford and Simpson, 11 vols., Oxford, 1925–52, VIII, 587).

[12] The wealth accumulated from his impresario work was what allowed him to make his major gift to posterity, the College of Christ's Gift, now known as Dulwich College. The College was given ownership of the Fortune playhouse (by the ancient statute of Mortmain), and loyally kept many of his papers, including his father-in-law's folio-size workbook now known as *Henslowe's Diary*, with its uniquely rich record of playhouse receipts and company documents from the 1590s.

[13] For his physical presence, see Susan Cerasano, 'Tamburlaine and Edward Alleyn's Ring', *Shakespeare Survey* 47 (1994), 171–79.

innkeeper and property owner in the parish of St Botolph's, Bishopsgate, not far from where the Theatre and Curtain were built in 1576–77 and where Shakespeare lodged in the 1590s. Alleyn's father, who was porter to Queen Elizabeth, died when Edward was four, leaving enough money for his widow Margaret to raise the five boys comfortably. She, however, remarried twice, taking a second husband in 1571 only four months after husband Alleyn died. The second husband died in 1578, and eighteen months later she married a Westminster haberdasher, giving young Edward at the difficult age of thirteen a second stepfather.[14] Whether that helped to drive Margaret's youngest away we do not know. Within a few years, possibly thanks to the new playhouses now operating in the outer suburb of Shoreditch nearest Bishopsgate, he had begun his great career as a player.

By January 1583, aged sixteen, he was acting with Worcester's Men. This company, patronised by the third earl, is on record as touring extensively through the 1580s, performing in towns such as Coventry, Nottingham, Leicester, Stratford-upon-Avon, Norwich and Ipswich. The Leicester clerk copied down one of the first provincial references made to the authority of the Master of the Revels, Edmund Tilney, as licenser of plays. In doing so he named the Worcester's company leader as George Haysell. On 6 March 1583 he supplied the names of the whole company, in Haysell's absence, as 'Robert Browne, James Tunstall, Edward Allen, William Harryson, Thomas Cooke, Rychard Johnes, Edward Browne, Rychard Andrewes'. Some of these names recur eleven years later in the Admiral's company of 1594. The mayor of Leicester paid them not to play, but they did, which is what prompted the clerk to record their names. They had to apologise, and were allowed to resume playing provided they would declare that they were licensed to do so by the mayor.[15]

Soon after this Alleyn and several other Worcester's players[16] became the first company known as the Lord Admiral's Men. Howard was briefly Lord Chamberlain in 1584 before he handed the role to his father-in-law Henry Carey. His first overt declaration of an interest in plays, most likely when he relinquished the Chamberlainship for his more exacting role as

---

[14] This information comes from S. P. Cerasano, 'Edward Alleyn's Early Years: His Life and Family', *Notes and Queries* 232 (1987), 237–43. See also her *NDNB* entry for Alleyn.

[15] See E. K. Chambers, *The Elizabethan Stage*, 4 vols., Clarendon Press, Oxford, 1923, II. 221–24. The mayor may have been reasserting his old power to authorise performances in his town against Tilney's new regime.

[16] Edward Browne, Richard Jones and James Tunstall were Admiral's Men along with Alleyn, most probably in the early company as well as the new one of 1594.

head of the Admiralty, appeared when he decided to found a new playing company. As Chamberlain and responsible for playing he seems to have thought it wrong to have his own company. Carey was patron of a playing company and made James Burbage his servant just as Howard around the same time made Alleyn his, but neither man gave their patronage to a whole company while they served as Lord Chamberlain until they founded their two new companies as the duopoly of 1594. Alleyn certainly drew attention with the first Admiral's. Christopher Marlowe sold his two *Tamburlaine* plays and most likely *Doctor Faustus* in 1587–88 to the company with Alleyn. It was ordered to perform at court before the queen in the Christmas season of 1585–86, an early mark of pre-eminence. In 1588–89 with the Marlowe plays in their repertory they and the Queen's Men each performed twice, while Paul's Boys under John Lyly gave three plays. In the next season they performed once, the Queen's Men twice, and Paul's Boys three times. In 1590–91, after the boy company had been suppressed, the Queen's Men performed at court five times and a new group, Lord Strange's plus Alleyn retaining Howard's livery, played twice.

This new grouping, Strange's Men headed by Alleyn in his Admiral's livery, was noted in the court records on 27 December 1590 and 16 February 1591 under the name of Lord Strange's Men but payment for the shows was officially made to the Lord Admiral's. Clearly Alleyn himself was still using his title as Howard's man while working as the new group's leader. For him to retain that allegiance while performing with a company under another lord's patronage was unique, and there is nothing to explain it other than a personal bond between Alleyn and Howard. The company's patron was Ferdinando Stanley, Lord Strange, younger brother of the Earl of Derby. To retain another man's livery while working as Lord Strange's servant was an unprecedented act of dual loyalty. The peculiarity of this new group's formation was openly acknowledged by the Privy Council including Howard himself in a letter dated 6 May 1593. A document authorising the company to play, it specified 'the bearers hereof, Edward Allen, servaunt to the right honorable the Lorde Highe Admiral, William Kemp, Thomas Pope, John Heminges, Augustine Phillipes, and Georg Brian, being al one companie, servauntes to our verie good the Lord the Lord Strainge'.[17] In 1594 the five named in the letter as Strange's Men all entered the opposite company.

For the next two years this group of players in Strange's livery, their leader wearing Howard's, dominated performances at court. In 1591–92

[17] Chambers, *Elizabethan Stage*, II. 123.

they performed six times for the queen, in a season accompanied by a single play from each of the Queen's, Sussex's and Hertford's Men. In the shorter season of 1592–93 they played three times in between two by a new group, Pembroke's Men.[18] In 1593 the very lengthy interruption to playing in London because of plague meant that several companies including Pembroke's folded, while others disappeared because their patrons died. The sole court performance that winter was given by the Queen's Men. As we have seen, in large part Howard and Carey's setting up their new companies in 1594 was an attempt to resolve the troubles the Lord Chamberlain had undergone through this long-running epidemic of disruptions. The two Privy Councillors, and especially Carey whose responsibility it was, needed professional companies of high quality that could be relied on to keep the queen entertained through future Christmas seasons.

This they certainly did. From 1594 no other company graced the festivities at Court until 5 February 1600, when Derby's Men supplemented the other pair's five shows with a single performance. Besides their official choice as the prime performers at court, the duopoly companies fulfilled their promise with what we can now easily see were their most distinctive features, Alleyn's established repute as a player and the plays of two great writers, Marlowe and Shakespeare.

One promise is recognisable in Thomas Nashe's praise of Alleyn and the popularity of playgoing in 1592 in *Pierce Penilesse*. After registering the emotional impact that patriotic plays about English history were having on London audiences in wartime, Nashe went so far as to claim that 'Not *Roscius* or *Aesope*, those admired tragedians that have lived ever since before Christ was borne, could ever performe more in action than famous *Ned Allen*'.[19] That promise was easily fulfilled. The other was realised by the allocation of all the existing Shakespeare plays to one company and all the available Marlowes to the other.

That was not so easy. Alleyn's fame lay chiefly in his Marlowe roles, as Faustus, Tamburlaine and Barabbas. However, so long as he was playing for Lord Strange, the first three plays, his most famous Marlowe parts, seem to have been in the hands of the residual Admiral's touring the country.[20] The two *Tamburlaines* and *Faustus* did not return to Alleyn

---

[18] See John H. Astington, *English Court Theatre 1558–1642*, Cambridge, 1999, Appendix pp. 233–34.
[19] The full passage is quoted in Chambers, *Elizabethan Stage*, IV. 241–2.
[20] See Gurr, 'The Great Divide of 1594', in *Words that Count: Essays on Early Modern Authorship in Honor of MacDonald P. Jackson*, ed. Brian Boyd, Associated University Presses, 2004, pp. 29–48.

Figure 2. Edward Alleyn in his maturity, from the portrait at Dulwich College.

until some months after the new Admiral's was set up in 1594. Although he certainly had bought other plays, evidently he had not bought the first three Marlowe's for himself. They must have belonged to the sharers in the first Admiral's company, who the 1590 *Tamburlaine* title-pages acknowledged as the performers. Presumably in 1587–88 Alleyn lacked the cash that he had a few years later when he bought playbooks from Peele. There is a whiff of evidence from the sequence of contemporary comments on the plays that both *Faustus* and the *Tamburlaines* were absent from London between 1592 and 1594 because they were on tour with the first Admiral's Men.[21] Perhaps Alleyn thought the establishment of the new company might be a device to give him back his two most famous parts. He was certainly playing them again at the Rose by August 1594. Most likely the three playbooks for *Tamburlaine* and *Faustus* came to the new Admiral's through James Tunstall and perhaps Richard Jones of the old company, who became the first sharers along with Alleyn in the new Admiral's. Alleyn does appear to have bought the later Marlowes for himself, notably *The Jew of Malta* and *The Massacre at Paris* and some other plays, selling them to Christopher Beeston in 1625 during that lengthy plague closure.[22]

Alleyn started engaging in what must be seen as entrepreneurial activities along with his elder brother John quite early. A deed dated 3 January 1589 when he was in the first Admiral's records his purchase for £37 10s from Richard Jones of 'all and singuler suche share parte and pocion of playinge apparrelles, playe bookes, instruments, and other commodities whatsoever belonginge to the same'.[23] Jones cannot have sold him the Marlowe playbooks at this time. This was when he also bought some of George Peele's playbooks, probably including *The Battle of Alcazar* which appeared in the later Admiral's repertory, *Longshanks* (*Edward I*), and possibly later Antony Munday's *Wise Men of West Chester*. Throughout his career he kept the ownership of a number of playbooks, selling some and retaining others to himself once he acquired the Fortune, a practice he continued in the impresario role of his last twenty-five years from 1601 onwards. The set of inventories in Henslowe's *Diary* all date from about March 1598, and may well reflect Alleyn's own desire, once he had retired from playing at the end of 1597, to assess the total assets that he, his father-in-law and the company had in common at the Rose. They may also mark a shift in his thinking in 1598 from player into impresario and controller of the company's resources. That shift became more clearly apparent in

[21] The complex story of the ownership of playbooks, and especially of the copies authorised for performance by the Master of the Revels, is told in Gurr, 'Did Shakespeare own his own Playbooks?', *Review of English Studies* 59 (2008).

[22] The existence in print of some of these playbooks might be seen as providing alternatives to the 'allowed book' in manuscript with the authorising signature of the Master of the Revels. In later years printed playbooks were used instead of the signed books. But the Dulwich remains do not include any printed playbooks that Alleyn might have owned.

[23] *Henslowe Papers*, ed. W. W. Greg, London, 1907, p. 31.

1601–02, when he was back playing at the Fortune and sold off several of his old playbooks to the company.

Charles Howard was Alleyn's patron from when he joined the first Admiral's Men in 1586 or so until Prince Henry replaced Howard as company patron at the end of 1603. In 1584, a year after the Queen's Men was founded, Howard was made Lord Chamberlain in charge of playing before he became Privy Councillor and Lord Admiral in charge of the navy. In this he followed his father, who held both roles. He was an efficient administrator with a consistent enthusiasm for theatre, or at least for its control by the Privy Council. Most of the Privy Council's letters about playing between 1584 and 1603 have his signature on them. His place at court was always secure, because his wife, Katherine Carey, was the queen's closest friend. In spite of that advantage he had to wait patiently for a long time to get promoted to the posts his father had held before him under Henry VIII. When he became Lord Admiral in 1584 the chamberlainship went to his father-in-law and close ally on the Council, Henry Carey, who had an interest in playing and gave his livery to James Burbage. Both men were consistent while holding the chamberlainship in not making themselves patrons of any playing company until they introduced their great change of 1594. As soon as he gave up the chamberlainship to become Lord Admiral in 1584 Howard did give his patronage to a company, and soon had Alleyn on its staff. He knew what he was doing, and where playing quality lay. Through the turbulent years that followed while he prepared the English navy to withstand the Spanish Armada Howard remained loyal to Alleyn, as did Alleyn to his master.[24] In all, Alleyn wore Howard's livery as his player-servant for twenty years, at a time when the companies performing in London were under maximum pressure from the Lord Mayor's hostility. The allegiance of Burbage and Alleyn to the two Privy Councillors that began ten years before they devised their celebrated compromise that resolved the running conflict with the Lord Mayor over playing shows someone's long-term percipience. I like to think it was the efficient administrator Howard who conceived the duopoly of 1594.

Setting up two companies sharing pre-eminent players and repertory, with the exclusive right to perform in London's suburbs, and licensed to perform in the two best playhouses outside the city walls, called for a lot

---

[24] The link was strikingly durable. It may have been helped by Edward's brother John, also a player, who was said in a letter of 1589 to be living in Howard's household (Chambers, *Elizabethan Stage*, II. 138).

Figure 3. Charles Howard, Lord Admiral, attending the queen in 1595. He is the greybeard
parading second from left. On his right is George Carey, Henry Carey's son, the
second Lord Hunsdon, his successor as the Chamberlain's Men's patron from 1596.
From a painting (School of Robert Peake), known as the 'Procession Portrait'
of Queen Elizabeth.

of political muscle. As it happened Howard was Lord Lieutenant of
Surrey, where the Rose stood, and chairman of the magistrates for
Middlesex, where the Theatre was located. It must have been Howard
who, besides giving his name as patron, handed the leadership of his new
company to his loyal follower, backed by his father-in-law Henslowe.
Both of the duopoly companies were based on a tight family alliance.

From 1594 till 1600 Alleyn shared with Henslowe the roles of playhouse
manager and company impresario. On stage he was the star of his
company with its Marlovian repertory for their first three years. Late in
1597 he retired to pursue other interests, not the least of which was the
construction of a new playhouse for the Admiral's Men in place of the
Rose. Late in 1597 he must have felt that the arrival of several new players
into the Admiral's from the collapsed Pembroke's freed him from his
former responsibilities as the company's star player. At least part of his
time away in 1598–99 was spent developing the impresario side of
his interests. On 22 December 1599, roughly six months after the Globe

had opened only fifty yards from the Rose, he leased the site of the
Fortune and paid for its construction, acquiring its freehold in 1610. After
the new playhouse opened in 1600 he gave Henslowe half, while the
vacated Rose was allocated to another company, Worcester's Men. When
the new Fortune opened he resumed his role as the company's star on
stage, allegedly as we shall see by order of the queen herself. After she died
he retired from the stage at the age of thirty-six, by which time he had also
taken charge of the animal-baiting house near the Rose, and ran baiting
shows for the court and for the people.

By then Alleyn was so renowned as an orator that he was chosen to
deliver the main speech to King James at London's long-postponed
welcome of the king to the city on 15 March 1604. Through the years
that followed his many investments in property, theatre and baiting
meant that by 1614 he could afford the ten thousand pounds that
founding Dulwich College is said to have cost him.[25] Such an amount
was amazing riches for the time. It compares with the equivalent sum
Howard allegedly gained annually from the privateering, de facto piracy,
that as Lord Admiral he licensed in the attacks on Spanish shipping in the
1590s, or the forty thousand pounds that the Earl of Southampton spent
in five years of his wild and extravagant youth in the 1590s.[26] Howard and
Southampton were rich aristocrats, with vast properties in land. Alleyn's
wealth came in large part from his investments as an impresario in plays
and bears, though as a property owner his income from rents of various
kinds was also considerable. His fame as an actor started him on his
way, but through more than half his working life he was a model citizen
entrepreneur.

Alleyn's part in London's welcome to the Scottish royal family is
notable because his celebrity as a speaker made him the obvious choice
to represent 'the Genius of the City'. In *The Magnificent Entertainment*,
Dekker's account of his and Jonson's composition for the welcome, the
figures present on the first arch, at Fenchurch Street, are described.
Dekker added:

Of all which personages, *Genius* and *Thamesis* were the only Speakers: *Thamesis*
being presented by one of the children of her Majesties Revels: *Genius* by Master

[25] He officially founded the college in 1619, but was buying the land in Dulwich for some years
before that.
[26] Southampton's wife and steward recouped these staggering losses while he was in the Tower in
1603–04, largely by selling his Bloomsbury estates to developers. See Lawrence Stone, *Family and
Fortune*, Oxford, 1973, pp. 217–19.

Figure 4. Alleyn is the figure on the right, waving his garland from the arch depicting London, at the formal welcome of King James in 1604. From Stephen Harrison, *The Arches of Triumph*, 1604, Illustration 3, p. 10.

Allin (servant to the young Prince) his gratulatory speech (which was delivered with excellent Action, and a well tun'd audible voice) being to this effect:

That *London* may be prowd to behold this day, and therefore in name of the Lord *Maior* and *Aldermen*, the *Councell*, *Commoners* and *Multitude*, the heartiest Welcome is tendered to his Majesty, that ever was bestowed on any King, &c.[27]

No less a figure than Howard himself was ready to assert that Alleyn's acting found favour with Queen Elizabeth, though he had his own reasons for doing so. His Privy Council letter of 8 April 1600 to the Justices of Middlesex demanded that they agree to the construction of the Fortune, specifying that it was the queen's own wish, 'haveinge been well pleased heretofore at tymes of recreacion with the services of Edward Allen and his Companie Servantes to me the Earle of Nottingham'.[28] As an actor Alleyn has been reputed as being loud in speech and flamboyant in his physical

[27] Dekker, *Dramatic Works*, ed. Bowers, II. 260–61.
[28] See below, p. 136.

appearance, the kind of figure that Hamlet scorned for his strutting and bellowing. It is true that 'stalking and roaring' were the terms used of Alleyn in his most famous roles,[29] but that was part of his act. Underneath he had a sharp and self-deprecating sense of humour, fully capable of mocking his own public image. A letter in the Henslowe papers, sent when the company was on tour and ostensibly written by his boy 'pyg' to Alleyn's wife in London but actually composed by Alleyn himself, included jokes about his reputation. At the end it declares 'I gott on to wright it m^r doutone & my m^r knows nott of it'. Alleyn, who wrote it, was 'my master', Thomas Downton a leading player in the company who took over Alleyn's famous roles when he retired from acting at the end of 1597.[30] In the same letter Alleyn makes 'pyg' swear 'by the fayth of a fustian king', a derisive term for Alleyn's kind of role in the company's plays.[31]

An even stronger image of Alleyn's capacity to send up his own fustian roles can be found in the first play the company bought from George Chapman early in 1595, *The Blind Beggar of Alexandria*. First staged as 'ne' or new on 12 February 1595, then playing another seventeen times to the end of 1596 and revived when Alleyn came back to the stage in 1600, it was a short and extremely popular farce using the new device of metatheatrical disguise. Very largely featuring Alleyn himself, he appeared as the hero and in three distinctive disguises, two of them making him out to be a character parodying his more serious leading roles from the Marlowe plays. Out of the 1611 lines in the Malone Society reprint[32] Alleyn's four roles gave him 674 of them to speak, well over a third of the entire script. A wonderfully fast-moving farce, it is an early example of the remarkable set of plays exploiting disguise that the Admiral's inaugurated in its first years settled at the Rose, of which more will be said in Chapter 2. Chapman's play also set up an early example of the comic 'humours' tradition that he helped the Admiral's to develop more strongly later.

In the play Alleyn as the banished Duke Cleanthes first appears in Alexandria disguised as Irus, the blind beggar and seer of the title. Next he appears dressed as the frantic or 'humorous' courtier Count Hermes, wearing

---

[29] Jonson's parody of Alleyn as Histrio in *Poetaster* cites him as a 'player, rogue, stalker' (3.4.122–23), growing rich as a 'two-penny teare-mouth' with '*fortune*', and summoning the stalking Moor and his queen Calipolis from Peele's *Battle of Alcazar*, which had recently been revived at the Fortune.
[30] According to the *Diary*, p. 93, in 1598 Downton took on Hercules for the popular two-part play.
[31] Quoted in *Diary*, pp. 282–83.
[32] George Chapman, *The Blind Beggar of Alexandria 1598*, ed. W. W. Greg, The Malone Society Reprints, Oxford, 1928. Line references (TLN = Through Line Numbers) and quotations are taken from this edition.

an eye patch. Thirdly he disguises himself as Leon the usurer, who 'hath a great nose' (TLN 627), and finally he appears as his heroic self, the banished Duke, general of the Alexandrian army. All these disguises are explained to the audience immediately. At the outset for instance he appears as the blind seer, immediately declaring himself to be the disguised Cleanthes.

> See Earth and Heaven where her *Cleanthes* is,
> I am *Cleanthes* and blind *Irus* too,
> And more then these, as you shall soone perceave,
> Yet but a shepheardes sonne at *Memphis* borne.   (104–7)

The plot is simple, the disguises the play's chief entertainment before Cleanthes has to resume his military role to save Egypt from its invaders. The humble origin that Cleanthes announces here affirms his affinity with Tamburlaine, and Marlovian echoes abound in his speeches as the heroic General.[33] His 'humour' and the game of disguising he announces in a declamatory speech at 323–40.

> And so such faultes as I of purpose doe,
> Is buried in my humor and this gowne I weare,   (334–5)[34]

Visited as the seer Irus by the princess and two of her court ladies he prophesies to the princess who loves Cleanthes and then to her ladies how each of them will meet their future husbands. Meeting the two ladies subsequently, disguised in the ways he foretold them their husbands would appear, he marries each of them, as well as the princess.

The game of disguising involved some very quick changes of costume. In Scene 4 as the usurer Leon with his great nose he exits to return only five lines later as the roistering Count with pistol and eye mask (761–66). Later in the same scene he changes from Count Hermes back to Irus while offstage for only six lines (804–10). This one scene required him to make three rapid changes, probably including the use of a reversible gown. At 1304–7 his change from Hermes to Leon has him saying

> But here must end *Count Hermes* strange disguise,
> My velvet gowne my pistol and this patch,
> No more must hide me in the countes attire,
> Now will I turne my gowne to Usurers Cotes.

---

[33] According to Millar MacLure, *George Chapman: A Critical Study*, University of Toronto Press, 1966, it 'was obviously designed to remind the spectators continually of Marlowe and especially of Tamburlaine . . . The language is frequently a travesty of Marlowe's style.' (pp. 84–5).

[34] This phrase was memorable enough on stage for Edward Pudsey to jot down in his commonplace book, Bodleian Sum. Cat. MSS. 30049: Eng. Poet. d.3.

The Count's eye-patch might echo a similar part from another play, because as Leon the usurer his great nose, which gets him called at 1180 'the bottle-nosd knave your husband', must have reminded the first audiences of Alleyn playing Barabbas in *The Jew of Malta*.[35] As the heroic Duke Cleanthes, his inflated speech parodies his own Tamburlaine. In-joke allusions to Alleyn's other roles were integral to the farcical comedy of the play.

The Blind Beggar's type of disguising game was a device the company developed early, once the duopoly system laid its uniquely heavy pressure on the two companies. Having only the two companies performing intensified the need for variety already familiar to both groups from the eleven months when several of the players from both companies played continuously at the Rose as Strange's Men. Performing at a fixed play-house needed an incredibly versatile repertory system with a different play every afternoon. As we saw above, from 1594 the new system for the first time gave audiences only the two choices of playhouse, so playgoers came to know only too well the faces of the players taking their different role each day.[36] The Admiral's Men soon learned to exploit their audiences' expectations of familiarity with their games of disguise. That trickery, sadly, can never be renewed now. The intimacy of the Rose audience's reactions is a feature of the Admiral's plays that has helped them to be grossly down-rated by 'literary' critics in the last century. This unique side-effect of the duopoly system will be examined more closely in the next chapter.

The second major individual to feature in this biographical history of the company is its father-figure, Philip Henslowe. He stands out for us partly because his son-in-law preserved the working papers he used as theatre landlord and financial controller, especially the giant folio jotter of 242 leaves known nowadays as his *Diary*. More significantly, though, his enthusiasm for theatre and all it brought him can be found in much more than his jottings and figures about the Admiral's and other playing companies. He did not build the Rose purely for profit, and even his long and rewarding engagement with bear-baiting shows signs of the pleasure as well as the profits he took from his deployment of the means to provide public entertainment. I have commented before on one name that crops up,

---

[35] See below, p. 159.
[36] The famous moment in *Hamlet* where Polonius claims to have played Julius Caesar and been killed by Brutus, alias Hamlet, is almost the only acknowledgement of this feature of early playing to be found in the Shakespeare company repertory.

perhaps in error, in the *Diary* (p. 88), Sir Piers of Exton.[37] Henslowe used it as the title of a play for which he paid Wilson, Dekker, Drayton and Chettle forty shillings on 30 March 1598. Chambers (*Elizabethan Stage*, II. 167) thought it was a mistake for 2 *Earl Godwin*, since that sum would complete the otherwise not recorded payments for the play. That may be so, but either way it shows that Henslowe had in mind a play that would develop a feature of Shakespeare's *Richard II*, which makes Exton, an otherwise almost unknown historical figure, into Richard's murderer. Even if it was a slip of the mind, Henslowe's use of the name indicates that he was alert to possible subjects for new plays, and that he had been at the opposition's playhouse and picked up the idea there. The fact that we have little besides his accounts to show his mind should not make us assume he was merely a grey suit behind the Admiral's venture.

Henslowe was born around 1555, of a family that had status in the south, his father being Master of the Game for the royal forest of Ashdown in Sussex. Ashdown had substantial mineral deposits that his brother mined, to considerable profit as the country armed itself for the war with Spain. As a teenager Philip went to London, where he started work in Southwark apprenticed to a dyer. He was perhaps thirty-two when he built the Rose in 1587, thirty-seven when he allied himself with England's most celebrated actor Alleyn, who was only ten years younger (though Philip immediately began calling him his 'son'), and thirty-nine when he and Alleyn set up the Admiral's company which is the subject of this book.[38] He ran a number of profitable businesses, collecting rents from nearly thirty properties in the vicinity of the Rose. In 1593 he became a courtier as Groom of the Chamber, was raised to the status of Gentleman Sewer in 1603 and became a Court Pensioner in 1606. With such elevated status he busied himself on the fringes of the royal court while making himself the first true impresario of London's entertainment world. He always lived in the Liberty of the Clink, becoming in 1608 a churchwarden at the parish church St Saviour's, now Southwark Cathedral.

For Henslowe to finance and build the Rose in 1587 was a remarkable adventure and a major financial investment. Henslowe's father at Ashdown

---

[37] Gurr, 'Intertextuality in Henslowe', *Shakespeare Quarterly* 39 (1988), 394–98, pp. 396–97.

[38] See S. P. Cerasano, 'Revising Philip Henslowe's Biography', *Notes and Queries* 332 (1985), 66–71, pp. 70–71, and 'Henslowe, Forman and the Theatrical Community of the 1590s', *Shakespeare Quarterly* 44 (1993), 145–58, especially p. 153, where she argues that Henslowe was born in 1555–56 and married at 24. Simon Forman in his notebook wrote in 1597 that he was then 'of 42 years'.

Forest gave him a status and family connections that helped him in a variety of ways. Apprenticed to the Southwark merchant and dyer Henry Woodward, he married Woodward's widow two months after her husband died in January 1579, when Philip was aged about twenty-four. His brother Edmund also prospered as a London merchant, becoming a servant to Henry Carey, the Lord Chamberlain. It may have been this connection that helped Philip gain a place at court, although Edmund died in 1591, two years before Philip became a Groom of the Chamber. We do not know when their father died, but the family's eminence in Sussex must have helped Philip to make his presence known in London and especially at court.

To finance the Rose at the end of 1586 Philip enlisted the help of a Southwark grocer, John Cholmley, who apparently put up a proportion of the cost in return for the right to sell food and drink there to the visiting public. Cholmley probably owned the cottage then standing on the corner of Maiden Lane and Rose Alley on the south-western flank of the site. Nothing is known of Cholmley's· participation in the venture after he co-signed the contract for catering at the Rose on 10 January 1586.

Building London's third open-air theatre was an anomaly for Henslowe as much it was a new mercantile venture. The first of the theatres on Bankside (apart from an older venture built in 1575 a mile south of the river at Newington Butts), the Rose was the first playhouse to be built in London's suburbs for ten years, after the two ventures in the northern suburb of Shoreditch, the Theatre and the Curtain. The Newington Butts playhouse had existed for the same length of time but was too remote from the city to ever be a popular venue for plays. The Rose was ideally situated, no distance either from the riverbank where ferries could deliver customers or from London Bridge where the citizenry could walk across the river. Moreover it adjoined the Bear Garden, already a resort for the London crowds seeking entertainment. Henslowe's venture may have been influenced by the Bear Garden's proximity and its crowds, although its adjacent kennels produced noise and smells that cannot have made good neighbours. It was a fairly waterlogged piece of ground – when the old London Bridge with its narrow arches a little downriver was finally demolished the water table at the Rose and Globe sites dropped by as much as three feet. But at least it was near London's only bridge across the river, in a suburb that seemed to tolerate the crowds who sought entertainment there.

How well the Rose did through its first five years we do not know, because almost nothing survives to say what was staged there. Through its first seven years it had to compete with its plays against the northern playhouses and the city's inns and innyards. Philip Gawdy's anecdote of 1587 about the Admiral's Men shows how tenuous the evidential connections between playgoing events and particular playhouses could be. But the Rose was evidently successful enough to justify the major enlargement that Henslowe undertook when Alleyn and his company arrived at the beginning of 1592. Not until that February, when Alleyn's team of Lord Strange's Men started there and Henslowe began his *Diary*, is there any tangible record of what activities the Rose could provide. The *Diary* reveals an immediate transformation. With such an eminent company coming into residence Henslowe laid out a major sum of money to enlarge his five-year-old playhouse. The company opened on Saturday 19 February, Henslowe noting seventeen shillings and fourpence as his share of the takings for 'fryer bacone', Greene's well-known play. The amount Henslowe recorded was half the money gathered from playgoers sitting in the galleries, the standard rent for use of a playhouse at the time.

From then on for six afternoons every week he took his share, while also paying for the alterations he had commissioned. One of the many mysteries in the *Diary* is how the company managed to perform while the enlargements to the Rose were going on. The work was extensive and expensive. It entailed breaking up and dismantling the timber frame of the five northernmost bays from the fourteen in the Rose's polygon where the stage and tiring house stood, and rebuilding it all a little over six feet further back. This extended the three levels of galleries on each side by over six feet while enlarging the space occupied by the stage and tiring house just a little. The alteration did not produce much change to the shape of the stage itself, which was a broad hexagon with three angles in the *frons scenae*, each with a doorway, and a lengthy front edge with sides angled back to the flanking bays of the *frons*.[39] It was an elaborate and awkward reshaping, rapidly done but carefully planned.

Unless the enlargement had been completed, painted and ready for use before 19 February 1592, when Alleyn and his fellows opened there, we have to envisage the builders suspending their labours each afternoon while the plays were performed on temporary scaffolding. Henslowe did not pay the bills for the materials or the wages of the craftsmen used for the rebuilding until March and April 1592. His costs included hiring barges and wharfing to land the timbers, bricklayers' and carpenters' wages, the purchase of nails, lime for the plastering, along with charges

---

[39] The precise shape of the Rose and its stage will be looked at in more detail in Chapter 4.

at the end for painting the plastered walls. So unless Henslowe paid all these charges well in arrears Strange's Men at first had to perform in the chaos of a building site. It would be nice to believe that Henslowe prepared his playhouse's enlargement for Alleyn and Strange's arrival well in advance, but if he did so his builders only got their wages a long time after they did all the work. Henslowe's habit of making his payments far in arrears after the work was done may be the first lesson we can take from a careful reading of the *Diary*.

The book's first entries for performances show that Strange's Men played daily from 19 February until 22 June 1592, when a mayoral protest following complaints of riots in Southwark, plus the onset of the summer plague epidemic that began a drastic season of deaths, caused the closure of all the playhouses and inns used for playing. Strange's Men went on tour. On 29 December they reopened at the Rose for a month, but the dreadfully extended period of plague closures and consequent fretful touring soon resumed. On 27 December 1593 after Lord Strange's death a new group, Sussex's Men,[40] restarted at the Rose, and various other companies made brief use of it before the duopoly Admiral's with Alleyn began their long reign on 14 May 1594. After a short run of a week alternating with the other new company, the Chamberlain's, in the south at Newington Butts their wonderfully prosperous first sequence of unbroken performances that ran for the next three years and more began at the Rose on 15 June. That is where the *Diary* starts its uniquely valuable record of the Admiral's company's daily activities and expenditures up to 1603.

While the *Diary* is a uniquely rich record of theatre activities from 1592 till 1603, it has huge gaps in the evidence it supplies us with. Essentially it exists as a record of two different types of business activity. The first, running from 1592 when Henslowe began it with Alleyn's arrival at the Rose as the leader of Strange's Men, ends early in 1597, when a complex of events altered his relationship with the Admiral's, by then three years into their settled duopoly role. The second is the record of what his relationship with the company grew into. From 1597, some time before Alleyn withdrew from the company, Henslowe seems to have no longer served just as its landlord at the Rose but as its banker and financier. Consequently what appear to be the daily lists of the landlord's share from the takings for each performance disappear and the record of what was played

---

[40] It has recently been suggested, with some justification, that Alleyn may have starred in this new company, conceivably along with Richard Burbage and even Shakespeare. He has not been identified anywhere else before May 1594.

turns into payments to the writers and theatre personnel and notes of the
money spent by the company to buy clothing and other 'thinges' for their
staging. Both kinds of record are punctuated by Henslowe's money-lender
activities, so far as they affected his playing business, chiefly loans made to
the company for its expenses and sometimes to individual players in the
company.

Apart from this evident change in the system of recording payments for
performances, there are several places in the *Diary* where the entries seem
seriously deficient. Such gaps may explain why it does not record full
payments for plays such as *The Shoemaker's Holiday, Englishmen for My
Money, Troilus and Cressida*, and *Agamemnon*, all of which we know were
performed at the Rose and which we must therefore assume were fully
paid for. The most obvious of these gaps are in the autumn of 1597 and
the spring of 1603. The recorded payments for Dekker's *Phaeton* in 1597
amount to a mere eighty shillings, or four pounds, less than the normal
total, and in 1603 only the first advances appear for *The Siege of Dunkirk, 2
The London Florentine*, and Chettle's *Hoffman*. Other gaps seem to exist
from June to December 1600, where there is a single payment for a playbook, *Fortune's Tennis*, but several for its apparel and other staging costs
which indicate that it did reach the stage.[41] What seem to be incomplete
payments are also apparent for such lost plays as *William Longsword*
(Jan. 1598), *Truth's Supplication to Candlelight* (Jan. 1599), *The Tragedy
of Orphenes* (Nov. 1599), *Owen Tudor* (Jan. 1600), *2 Fair Constance of
Rome* (June 1600), *Robin Hood's Pennyworths* (Dec. 1600), *Too Good to
Be True* (Nov. 1601), and *Malcolm King of Scots* (April 1602).[42]

The reason for these gaps is unclear. Susan Cerasano has suggested that
Henslowe had to be away from the Rose whenever he attended the court,
and at such times might have left the business of recording payments
to other people such as Robert Shaa or other company sharers.[43] Some
of the obvious gaps most likely signifying his absences at court include

[41] See S. P. Cerasano, 'The Geography of Henslowe's Diary', *Shakespeare Quarterly* 56 (2005), 328–53,
especially p. 339.
[42] Roslyn L. Knutson, 'The Commercial Significance of the Payments for Playtexts in *Henslowe's
Diary*, 1597–1603', in *Medieval and Renaissance Drama in England* 5 (1991), 117–63, suggests that
several plays for which the full price was only forty shillings must have been old scripts, since that
was what Alleyn and Martin Slater received for their old playbooks, whereas the usual price for
a new play was five or six pounds. She thinks (pp. 117–18) that this applies to several plays among
the Admiral's play-titles, *The Cobbler, The Miller, The Conquest of Brute, Mulmutius Dunwallow,
Vayvode, Bear a Brain, Tristram de Lyons, Phillip of Spain*, and *The Four Sons of Amon*. All the
Admiral's play titles recorded in the *Diary* are listed in sequence in Appendix 1.
[43] Use of the *Diary* by other people does suggest that Henslowe saw the book as an official record of
his company transactions, a point to be considered further in Chapter 3.

12 September to 11 November 1600, perhaps even till 14 December.
Cerasano also proposes that batches of theatrical receipts were entered
in bunches as copies from another list, perhaps made by Alleyn, and after
1597 by the company sharers Shaa and Thomas Downton. William
M. Baillie, editor of *Gratiae Theatricales* (1662), which includes an edition
of *Grim the Collier*, noted (pp. 273–74) that Henslowe's single advance of
five shillings to Haughton on 6 May 1600 'in earneste of a Boocke wch he
wold calle the devell & his dame' was subsequently crossed out, and no
further entries relate to this title. He adds, however, that the recorded
advances to Haughton 'for his *Englishmen for My Money* total only about
one-third of the customary £6 price, though that play was certainly
completed and performed' (p. 274). Deficiencies in the payment records
for the latter half of 1600 may conceal the final payments for these plays.

These are only the more recognisable gaps. Other obvious deficiencies
include entries made in the wrong column, where the dates go askew.
Some of the day-by-day records seem to show plays performed on
Sundays, and in at least two instances Henslowe had to re-line or correct
the dates. Worse, from 24 January 1597 until the daily entries stopped on
5 November he introduced a new system with five columns of entries
which has defied scholarly attempts to explain.[44] More about the *Diary*'s
variable accounting systems will be said in the analysis of finance and
other matters in Chapter 3. The chief omissions are often surprising, most
notably the absence of payments to individuals such as Alleyn himself.
He owned playbooks that the company used, but nothing says that he
took any money for loaning them to the company. What the *Diary* does
not enter may have gone into another account book belonging to the
company which has not survived. Other routine expenses that may have
appeared in a different book are entries such as the weekly payments to
the hired men. These must have been company matters that were not
Henslowe's business. Through the whole period from 1597 onwards there
are uncertainties about what was or was not a company expense that
might have been recorded elsewhere than in the *Diary*. This uncertainty is
compounded by the different entries for payments and for loans to the
company.

Sticking for the moment to the biographical record, after the *Diary*
stops Henslowe's career is on record more patchily, chiefly in surviving
items of his correspondence. The duopoly system collapsed after 1600
under pressure from other companies finding places to perform in

---

[44] The editors of the *Diary* give their best explanation on pp. xxxiii–xxxvi.

London, and Henslowe helped that by renting the vacated Rose to Worcester's Men, the third company that muscled its way in to join the older two. It later became Queen Anne's Men at the Red Bull, and eventually matched the Fortune company with its 'citizen' repertory. The notorious *Complaint* written by Lady Elizabeth's Men in 1615, a year before Henslowe died, registers their grievances about his impresario role stretching far beyond his planting them at the new Hope among the stinks of the bears and dogs kennelled nearby. It is not even clear quite how Henslowe divided his work with Alleyn to run the old Rose, the new Fortune, the old Bear Garden and the new Hope.[45] When he died his estate was contested, and accusations were made against Alleyn that he wrongly pre-empted a large part of Henslowe's property for his own uses.[46] That seems more like a charge made out of jealous greed than truth, since while alive the two men shared their interests happily. The only formal divisions they made were of the various properties their business led them to buy.

No playing company ever stands alone. Consideration of its audiences and the competition from other companies along with its location and its repertory is integral to its biography. Most historians of early theatre in London assume that the need to attract large audiences meant that each company saw the others as competition. In *Playing Companies and Commerce in Shakespeare's Time*, Roslyn Knutson, however, issued a reproof for such an oversimplification. In it she maintains that the licensed companies had a shared interest not unlike those merchants, members of the great livery companies, who protected the monopolisation of their markets with their own 'companies' and a mass of statutes to regulate how each of them would work and trade. The government supported monopoly control, since such a system backed its own authority, especially in the case of the potentially troublesome activities like printing or the price of food and clothing. Monopoly companies, and

---

[45] For one speculation about Henslowe's activities in this period, see Gurr, 'Bears and Players: Philip Henslowe's Double Acts', *Shakespeare Bulletin* 22 (2004), 31–41. John Day, one of the poets paid to write for the Admiral's, has a set of dialogues surviving in manuscript (Lansdowne MS 725), including one about a Fenerator or Usuring Bee which may satirise Henslowe's activities. The Bee is a 'broaker' who 'takes up' clothes, like Henslowe, and 'Most of the timber that his state repairs, / He hew's out o' the bones of foundred players / They feed on Poets braines, he eats their breath.' The *Complaint* makes similar charges. See Chambers, *Elizabethan Stage*, II. 248–50.

[46] The accusations were initially made by Henslowe's nephew, who accused Alleyn of forcing Henslowe to alter his will. The charges describe a deeply complex history of the two men's shared business investments. While financial self-interest is all too evident in the claims made on both sides, the truth of the matter may never be properly identifiable.

perhaps especially from 1594 to 1600 the two theatre companies licensed to perform plays on the flanks of London, were always careful to protect the shared interests of the groups working within their sphere of influence.

Henslowe's contributions to the company's work supply a good record of this basic feature of the company's life through the earlier years. The other duopoly company has no comparable personality except for James Burbage, who died in March 1597. Of course the two playing companies, unlike the companies of merchants in London, had no overarching livery company to protect them. They did pay the Master of the Revels, who upheld their exclusive right to perform specific plays and who protected their playhouses through the Privy Council. But they had no authority to prevent the start of new companies, as happened at the Swan in 1596, at the Boar's Head in 1600, and at the Rose when the Admiral's moved to the new Fortune. Keeping the number of playing companies down was for the Privy Council to do, a body taking little concern for the day-by-day regulation of such private enterprises. Henslowe and the Admiral's certainly regarded the Pembroke's Men at the Swan as dangerous rivals in 1596, and quickly swallowed their leading players when at last the Privy Council was moved to suppress them. Whether they also saw their opposites the Chamberlain's company as colleagues or as rivals we have no direct way of knowing. Building the Globe in 1599 within fifty yards of the Rose has certainly been seen as a challenge and an affront to the Admiral's. It has also been claimed that the owners of the Rose may have planned their move to the north as early as 1597, and the switch that took place in 1599–1600, with the northern company moving to Bankside and the Bankside company then moving north, could be viewed as an adroit renewal of the original plan of 1594 to locate one company on each side of the City.[47] But there is no evidence of such a co-operative attitude. When a third company established itself in London Henslowe installed it at the Rose and promptly gave them *Sir John Oldcastle* with its solemn correction of new neighbour Shakespeare's misleading image of Sir John Cobham as Falstaff. That at least suggests that the two companies had rather more a competitive than a casual or fraternal relationship.

None the less, so long as only the two companies regularly offered plays, what was written for each of them to stage had to take note of what the other was doing. They knew of each other's legal and public problems,

---

[47] See S. P. Cerasano, 'Edward Alleyn's "Retirement"', *Medieval and Renaissance Drama in English* 10 (1998), 98–112.

even bearing witness in one another's contracts and lawsuits. Given the limited forms of public entertainment then available, regular attendance by the same people at the suburban playhouses where the two companies performed was inevitable. The reception by such self-renewing audiences of the plays at each of the only two venues invited cross-reference, both implicit and explicit. The plays written for the two companies up to 1600, especially the Admiral's, give ample notice that writers and players alike expected a majority of their listeners to be familiar with the plays appearing on the other side of the city. The membership of the two companies and the joint origin of many of them in Strange's reflects just such a kinship.

Besides Alleyn himself, whose career shows an intriguing gap between his time with Strange's and his reappearance at the Rose as leader of the new Admiral's, the players who joined the Admiral's in May 1594 were experienced men from a variety of former groups. Richard Jones was a former Admiral's man just returned from playing abroad. James Tunstall came more directly from the old Admiral's, which according to the *Records of Early English Drama* (*REED*) from mid-1591 toured the country without ever playing in London. Tunstall may have brought *Tamburlaine* and *Faustus* with him from the old company, though their first appearance after more than two months of playing suggests some other difficulty with their acquisition. Thomas Downton came to the new Admiral's from Strange's, unlike most of the other ex-Strange's Men who went to the other company. John Singer probably came from the Queen's Men, of which he had been a founder member. Both companies drew their players from a similar range of former companies. They were among a brotherhood of players.

In the new Admiral's the key individual players, particularly those who had the status of sharers, are not at first easily distinguishable from the *Diary's* scribbled array of names.[48] An initial list appeared in December 1594, in two columns. The longer column is headed 'E A' for Alleyn, with below it in succession 'J singr / R Jonnes / T towne / m^r slater / Jube / T dowten / donstone'. A shorter column to the left has 'same / Charles / alen'. Those entered under Alleyn's initials are thought to have been the sharers, John Singer, Richard Jones, Thomas Towne, Martin Slater, Edward Juby, Thomas Downton and James Tunstall, all of whom continue to appear through the later years of the *Diary*. That would make eight

---

[48] A short biography of each player known to have performed for the new Admiral's or its successors is given in Appendix 2.

sharers in all, comparable to the number who started the Chamberlain's. The left-hand column may have been non-sharers, and has been read as referring to Sam Rowley, Charles Massey and Richard Allen. The first two of these were with the company for the next thirty years, both of them writing plays for the company. A few years later, in October 1597 after the Pembroke's players had joined the company, Henslowe made a note saying 'A Juste a cownt of All suche money as I have layd owt for my lord admeralles players begynyng the xi of actobre whose names ar as foloweth borne gabrell shaw Jonnes dowten Jube towne synger & the ij geffes'. Without Alleyn the sharers now seem to have been ten in number: William Bird, Gabriel Spencer, Robert Shaa (more rarely spelled 'Shaw'), Richard Jones, Thomas Downton, Edward Juby, Thomas Towne, John Singer, and the brothers Humphrey and Antony Jeffes, who joined the company after the Pembroke's troubles of 1597.[49] The 'plot' of *Frederick and Basilea* written in 1597 names Richard Allen along with Alleyn, Juby, Slater, Towne, Tunstall, Massey, Rowley and some others.[50]

Surviving 'plots' name more players, but the next significant listing of the company's sharers was the patent for Prince Henry's Men, issued in 1606. It names Bird, Towne, Downton, Rowley, Juby, Humphrey Jeffes, Massey and Antony Jeffes. A book listing Prince Henry's household in 1610 added the names of Edward Colbrand, William Parr, Richard Price, William Stratford, Francis Grace and John Shank, who a few years later went to the King's Men. A subsequent patent for Palsgrave's Men in January 1613 names twelve of this fourteen, omitting Towne, who had died, and Antony Jeffes, who left and became a brewer. In their places appear William Cartwright and Richard Gunnell. A few years later the city of Cambridge, expelling the company (*Acta Curiae*, 25 March 1616), named them as 'Thomas Dounton, Edwarde Jubey, William Byrde, Samuel Rowle, Charles Messey, Humphry Jeffe, Franck Grace, Willyam Cartwright, Edward Colebrande, Willyam Parrey, Willyam Stratford, et alii'.[51] Most of these men, plus Richard Fowler and Andrew Cane, were still with the company in 1622. The durability of the major names is a remarkable record of company loyalty.

For different reasons the year 1597 was the first period of turmoil for both duopoly companies. The Chamberlain's lost their playhouse and the

---

[49] This is noted in the *Diary*, p. 84.
[50] This play demanded huge numbers on stage. The 'plot' even specifies 'gatherers' to do walk-on parts in the most crowded scenes. A modernised text of the 'plot' is reprinted by Carol Chillington Rutter in *Documents of the Rose Playhouse*, Manchester, 1984, pp. 111–13.
[51] *REED Cambridge*, I. 552–53.

Admiral's suffered its biggest shake-up with its trouble over Pembroke's Men playing nearby and Alleyn's retirement. New competition had already arrived on Bankside. A group calling themselves Pembroke's Men based at the nearby Swan took Downton, Jones, Slater and perhaps others from the Rose company that year. When the wrath of the Privy Council was turned on the Swan and its players in July, most of them returned. Downton came back immediately, bringing with him Bird, Shaa and Spencer. The others returned once they were released from prison where the Privy Council injunction put them. Henslowe got them to sign bonds on their return declaring that they would only play in London at the Rose. More significant than these changes, however, was Alleyn's departure from the company that November, once the Pembroke's imports had settled in. His departure led to substantial changes in the repertory. New play titles appeared in the *Diary*, and new names as sharers started signing for company payments and guarantees. In the new configuration Shaa and Downton became the leading figures, signing for the purchase of playbooks and costumes.

It was around this time that Henslowe's function shifted from just being the company landlord to being their banker. As a financier his money-lending practices had always been available to individuals in the company. Richard Jones on 2 September 1594 paid him £3 for 'A manes gowne of Pechecoler In grayne' (*Diary*, p. 35), to be paid off at five shillings a week. On 27 August 1594 James Tunstall bought 'a manes gowne of purpell coller cloth faced wth conney & layd on the sleves wth buttenes for xxxxiij s iiij d to be payd xx^{s} in hand & xxiij iiij d at mychellmase next cominge', that was one pound immediately and the remaining twenty-three shillings and fourpence by the end of September. On 3 December 1596 another company loan was to Alleyn, 'unto my sonne to by the saten dublet wth sylver lace' (*Diary*, p. 50). These were for the players to use on stage. Simpler loans were one pound to William Bird (Borne) on 12 December 1597 and on 19 December another thirteen shillings. The first was witnessed by Shaa, Downton and Alleyn, and the second by 'Thomas dowten biger boye whom fecthed yt fore hime'. On 24 February 1598 Henslowe lent Bird another pound 'for A wascotte wraght wth sylke', which Bird repaid in four instalments of two shillings and sixpence a week until he had to borrow another three pounds on 3 April. A more spectacular loan, with some personal edge to it, came three years later, 'Lent unto mrs Birde alles Borne the 26 of November 1600 in Redye money to descarge her husband owt of the kynges benche when he laye upon my lord Jeffe Justes warrant for hurtinge of a felowe w^{ch}

browght his wife a leatter.' Getting the company's players out of prison was essential if they were to continue appearing at the daily performances.

The company's rate of production did not vary significantly through these busy years. In the company's first stint between 15 June 1594 and November 1597 they staged eighty-three different plays.[52] Fifty-four of them Henslowe marked as 'ne', probably to indicate that they were new at least in that production, a rate of one fresh play every two or three weeks. Through the first three and a half years the company performed at least 689 times at the Rose, besides special occasions when they played at court or at private celebrations. Henslowe took more than two hundred and fifty pounds a year from his rents, while the income of Alleyn and the other sharers, despite the inferences we might draw from Henslowe's loans to individual players, cannot have been very far behind. Late in 1597, however, Alleyn withdrew from playing and went away with his wife into Sussex for several months. This may have been when he started planning the Fortune. He may have taken some of the plays he owned off with him too, because his absence led the company to modify its repertory quite distinctly, while they probably took on several plays from the Pembroke's repertoire. Most of the old plays Alleyn had made famous disappeared and were replaced by new ones.

A few that Alleyn had been renowned for did continue, with Downton now assuming his former roles. The company revived *Hercules* (1598) and *Old Fortunatus* (1599), but his most spectacular roles disappeared. Between 1598 and 1600 for instance there is no sign of *The Jew of Malta* or *Doctor Faustus*. Other old plays like *Bellendon* (*Belin Dun*) likewise disappeared, and unlike the Marlowe plays were never revived. Not until Alleyn returned to the Fortune stage in 1600–03 did the old favourites reappear, often in revised or augmented form. Through this new Alleyn period revivals included *The Spanish Tragedy*, *Friar Bacon and Friar Bungay*, *The Blind Beggar of Alexandria*, *Mahomet*, *Tasso*, and *Vortigern*. In these years he sold the company his playbooks of *The Massacre at Paris*, *The Wise Men of West Chester*, and *Tamar Cham* along with others that the company kept reviving.

Up to the end of 1597 Henslowe's records suggest that the Admiral's company was markedly more inventive than their opposites at the Theatre, so far as we can tell from the extremely limited number of Chamberlain's plays surviving. They started their run of disguise plays in 1595, with *The Wise Men of West Chester*, *Look About You* (*Disguises*) and *The Blind*

---

[52] The sequence of plays by title is given in Appendix 1.

Beggar of Alexandria. Even the play with which they probably launched
their new role as Prince Henry's Men, Sam Rowley's *When You See Me
You Know Me*, relating Henry VIII's achievement of a male heir to James's
two healthy sons, advertised its game of disguise in its intricate title and
used Henry's own disguised adventure among his citizens as the play's
central feature. They developed the comedy of 'humours', too. Chapman's
second play for the company, *An Humorous Day's Mirth*, first staged in May
1597, enlarged the 'humorous' Count Hermes of *The Blind Beggar* into a
whole play of humours characters. It was a surprising success, taking more
each day during its first six performances. That June John Chamberlain
wrote to his friend Dudley Carleton in Holland about it. 'We have here a
new play of humors in very great request, and I was drawn alonge to yt by
the common applause, but my opinion of yt is (as the felowe sayde of the
shearing of hogges) that there was a great crie for so little wolle.'[53] The wry
Chamberlain may not have seen its innovatory quality, but Ben Jonson,
then writing for Henslowe, soon picked the idea up and gave *Every Man
in His Humour* to the other company. Chapman's second comedy for
the Admiral's was the play that came to mark the term 'humours' or
'humorous' as a standard concept for a comedy. The earlier title-pages to
the printed Admiral's plays simply called their comedies 'pleasant', as in
An Humorous Day's Mirth itself (printed in 1599), *Englishmen for My
Money* (1616), *Look About You* (1600), *Old Fortunatus* (1600) *The Two
Angry Women of Abingdon* (1599) and others. But the title-page for the last
of these also hailed 'the humerous mirthe' of its two clowns, as did *The
Blind Beggar of Alexandria*, printed in 1598. *The Shoemaker's Holiday*
(1600) similarly noted its feature element as 'the humorous life of Simon
Eyre' in its title.

Like the disguise games, the 'humours' idea came early and strongly.
Alleyn as Irus in *The Blind Beggar of Alexandria* makes the point moralis-
tically, saying: 'The faultes of many are bueried in their humour.' Nor was
it single-mindedly satirical. *An Humorous Day's Mirth*, set in rural France,
announces its 'humorous companions' at the outset, and plays up their
idiosyncrasies in games of adroit farce. One semi-final joke in Chapman's
play is about the King's 'instrument of procreation' being cut off. At 1614–20
in Scene 13 the humorous courtier Lemot tells the Queen that the King
is enamoured of another lady, and tells her: 'Another lord did love this
curious ladie, who hearing that the king had forced her, as she was
walking with another Earle, ran straightwaies mad for her, and with

---

[53] *Letters of John Chamberlain*, ed. N. E. McClure, 2 vols., Philadelphia, 1939, I. 132.

a friend of his, and two or three blacke ruffians more, brake desperately upon the person of the King, swearing to take from him, in traitorous fashion, the instrument of procreation.' On their way to find the deprived King they meet another of the 'humours' characters in pursuit of his own revenge, swearing: 'Ile geld the adulterous goate, and take from him the instrument, that plaies him such sweet musicke' (1694–95). They meet the King with the virtuous lady Martia, and Lemot extends the scam, claiming that the lady was his intended instrument of procreation. He told the Queen, he says, that the would-be gelder wanted the lady, 'and what was that now, but *Martia* being a fayre woman, is not shee an instrument of procreation, as all women are' (1727–29). In the end of course the Queen renews that role with the King and all is sorted out comfortably.

Interaction between the duopoly companies meant they soon began to share the 'humours' game. Both started to use comic catchphrases, sometimes deliberately echoing each other's. In Porter's *Two Angry Women of Abingdon* Nick Proverbs, the servant whose humour is always to quote proverbs (paroemiology), keeps using a particular variety of the catchphrase that the Chamberlain's company had initiated in 1597 with *2 Henry IV*, Nym's iteration of 'And there's the humour of it'. There were many such intertextual exchanges. It did not long outlast the century, but was easily capable of revival, as Middleton did at the Fortune in 1611 with *No Wit / No Help Like a Woman's*. The recorder at court when it was staged there in 1616 retitled it *The Almanac* after its most 'humorous' character.

A more substantial innovation in the Admiral's repertory for 1597 was the introduction of contemporary London as a setting for comedy. A couple of years before that the Chamberlain's staged a tragedy set in London, *A Warning for Fair Women*. Based like *Arden of Faversham* on a story told by Holinshed, it claimed 'truth' as the justification for its readiness to specify London localities. A year or two later Falstaff's scenes at a London inn started appearing. The Admiral's copied *A Warning's* London tragedy in 1599 with similar stories of English murders in *Cox of Collumpton* and *Two Lamentable Tragedies*. Both of these were plainly journalistic accounts of sensational murders in London. But the first play to be set explicitly and entirely in London as a comedy was William Haughton's *Englishmen for My Money*, staged at the Rose in February 1598 soon after Alleyn left, and less than a year after Falstaff and Prince Hal appeared at an Eastcheap tavern making fun of the tapster Francis.

Haughton made Alleyn's absence a feature of his play. Copying Barabbas in the Marlowe play now out of use, *The Jew of Malta*, its central figure

Pisaro begins like Barabbas by counting up his ships and wealth, as a Portuguese merchant settled and married in London. Like Barabbas and his parody Leon in *The Blind Beggar of Alexandria* he has a false bottle nose (TLN 250–51). The play emphasises its London location to comic effect throughout. Pisaro meets the Dutch, French and Italian suitors for his daughters at the Exchange (229) and invites them to his house in Crotched Friars. On the way there they are said to go through Leadenhall and Tower Street, and while groping in the dark of London's fog they bump into two posts – 'It is so darke, I know not where I am' (1685). The play also makes fun of two of the other repertory's hits, leaving the Dutch wooer dangling in a buck-basket when he tries to haul himself up to his beloved on her balcony. The play concludes with another trick from the disguise tradition, where the daughters' English lovers dress themselves as women (2256), which is what Robin Hood does in *Look About You* (*Disguises*) and *Downfall*, the first of Munday's two Huntingdon plays, which also featured in the company's 1598 repertory.

The *Downfall* and its sequel *The Death of Robert Earl of Huntingdon* offered another feature of the Admiral's repertory that they shared with their opposites. Plays set in English history were consistently popular through the 1590s, possibly beginning with Peele's *Edward I* (*Longshanks*), which Alleyn bought from its author in 1590. The Admiral's used historical settings for comedies like *Look About You* as they did for Munday's elaborate rewrites of the Robin Hood stories long familiar in folk-myth entertainments at country festivals. Other plays from English history along with classical dramas about Caesar and other Roman heroes featured regularly, judging by the titles Henslowe put on record.

The point that plays should educate as well as entertain underlay much of the Admiral's repertory. The Queen's Men had staged their history plays on the slightly specious argument that truth was more honest than fiction.[54] Thomas Heywood, who wrote regularly for the Admiral's from 1598, reiterated his similar view of the educational value of history in the 'Epistle to the Reader' of his translation of Sallust's *Histories* published in 1608.

History ought to be nothing but a representation of truth, and as it were a Map of mens actions, sette forth in the publicke view of all commers to bee examined; And therefore the predescanting opinion of the writer cannot but bring much discredite to the Action, in that hee presumeth to prepossesse the

---

[54] See Scott McMillin and Sally-Beth MacLean, *The Queen's Men and Their Plays*, Cambridge, 1999, p. 33.

minds of Artists with imaginarie assertions, seeming to teach those, who knew better then himselfe what belongeth to such affaires, to the wiser sort, who will not be deceived (for that he cometh to Counsel before he be called) he seemeth verie suspitious.[55]

His Sallust translation covers two stories from which plays were made for the Henslowe enterprise: the Catiline conspiracy, for which Wilson and Chettle were commissioned in 1598, and William Boyle's *Jugurtha* in 1600, of which a late and incomplete manuscript exists. Heywood's faith in the value of presenting historical 'Action' on stage appears in his own history plays written for Worcester's at the Rose in 1602 and the Red Bull in 1605. What he might have thought about the 'predescanting opinion' and Foxean[56] bias that determined the plotting of such stories we do not know. His translation of Sallust declared that he was presenting 'THE TWO MOST WORTHY AND NOTABLE HISTORIES WHICH REMAINE UNMAIMED TO POSTERITY: VIZ. THE CONSPIRACIE OF CATELINE, UNDERTAKEN AGAINST THE GOVERNMENT OF THE SENATE OF ROME, AND THE WARRE WHICH JUGURTH FOR MANY YEARES MAINTAINED AGAINST THE SAME STATE, BOTH WRITTEN BY C. C. SALUSTIUS.' They were of course 'unmaimed' because they were free from 'predescanting opinion'. Heywood's insistence on the value of the assertions of truth in historical stories is very close to the claim that Melpomene makes about truth in the Chamberlain's Induction to *A Warning for Fair Women*.

Alleyn's return to the stage in 1600 was part of a deal that let the company move from the Rose to the new Fortune. Charles Howard had made his long-acting servant's presence on stage an undertaking in his letter of 8 April 1600 as Privy Councillor ordering the Middlesex magistrates to allow its construction to go ahead. He wrote to them affirming that because 'her Majestie (in respect of the acceptable Service, which my saide Servant and his Companie have doen and presented before her Highenes to her great likeinge and Contentment, aswell this last Christmas

---

[55] SALLUST. THE CONSPIRACY OF CATILINE AND THE WAR OF JUGURTHA translated into English by THOMAS HEYWOOD anno 1608, Alfred A. Knopf, New York, 1924, p. 16.

[56] For the 'Elect Nation' concept, see Judith Doolin Spikes, 'The Jacobean History Play and the Myth of the Elect Nation', *Renaissance Drama* n.s. 8 (1977), 117–49, and Mark Bayer, 'Staging Foxe at the Fortune and the Red Bull', *Renaissance and Reformation* 39 (2003), 61–94. Richard Helgerson, *Forms of Nationhood. The Elizabethan Writing of England*, University of Chicago Press, 1994, p. 240. argues that 'The situation of the citizen and the Protestant—both figures who identify strongly with the nation and its ruler but both of whom are intent on keeping some part of themselves and their community free from the encroachment of national power—is central to the Henslowe version of English history. Neither of these figures is of much interest to Shakespeare, at least not in the strongly favorable way characteristic of the Henslowe plays.'

as att sondrie other tymes) is gratiouslie moved towards them, with a speciall regarde of favor in their proceedings', the Fortune must be built.[57] It would of course be fanciful to see the restoration of the old repertory at the Fortune as thanks to Queen Elizabeth's enduring liking for Alleyn's Marlovian roles, but Alleyn did renew many of his parts from before 1597. His return was marked not only by the revival of his most famous roles[58] but by new history plays, including two about Cardinal Wolsey and a pair of new sequels to a revival of *The Blind Beggar of Bethnal Green*.

The most conspicuous innovation of his return, though, was a series of plays based on stories from the Bible. Biblical subjects had been tried before to judge by titles such as *Nebuchadnezzar* (1596), but in 1601 a whole flurry of new biblical plays arrived. They include Bird and Rowley's *Judas* (1601), *Pontius Pilate* also in 1601, then Munday and Dekker's *Jephtha* (possibly taking their cue from Hamlet's comment to Polonius), along with two by Chettle, *Samson* and *Tobias*, plus Rowley's *Joshua*, all in 1602. Robert Shaa bought *The Four Sons of Amon* for the company, the last of the series, in December 1602. Mostly they were purchased by a single full payment of £2, which suggests that they were old plays acquired for the company from various sources. Their introduction may mark a new fashion that prompted them to find old playbooks and revise unfinished ones like Haughton's *Judas*. It is tempting to think that the impulse came from Alleyn wishing to assert his Christian credentials.

The death of Elizabeth in March 1603 followed by an extremely lengthy stoppage for plague was a major disruption for the company, and under King James no attempt was made to stage any new biblical plays. Dramatisations of the Bible have been a long-running feature of English culture, although the Reformation had cut down markedly on the use of Christian rituals on stage. Their presence at the Rose when Alleyn was playing there goes back to *Hester and Ahasuerus* and Peele's *David and Bethsabe* before 1594. The first of the new Admiral's plays on biblical topics, *Julian the Apostate*, staged as 'ne' on 29 April 1596, was a post-biblical story, though intimately concerned with the rise of Christianity in Constantinople. The seven stories in the company plays taken directly from the Bible

[57] Chambers, *Elizabethan Stage*, IV. 326.
[58] Knutson, 'The Commercial Significance of Payments', notes that: 'Between December 1600 (*Phaeton*) and December 1602 (*Bacon*), audiences at the Fortune were treated to revivals of as many as seventeen of the Admiral's old plays' (p. 129).

ran through 1601–02, all of them while Alleyn was back on the stage. Conceivably he was already starting to think of his great donation, the College of God's Gift, and wanted to set out shows on stage that might counter the fuss about his most famous roles, 'that atheist Tamburlaine' and his revivals of *Faustus*.[59]

Titles do not usually tell us much about the central topic of a play. Bible stories were told frequently in churches and cited and recited in printed sermons and tracts even more often. Weekly church-going made every child familiar with stories from the Bible. In fact the problem the theatre writers had with the best-known tales such as those of Judas, Pontius Pilate or Samson was that they were already too familiar. Judas Iscariot's story might have been linked with the extensive myths about the Wandering Jew, but his essential act, the kiss that betrayed Jesus for thirty pieces of silver, could hardly have sustained much in the way of an original plot. The story of Judas Maccabaeus, the alternative possibility for a play called *Judas*, might have made possible a more elaborate retelling. His wars against the Syrians, his purification of the temple and his death in war might have warranted some inventive elaborations. Similarly, the story of Jephtha and the daughter he has to sacrifice together with his invention of the famous password 'shibboleth' had good tragic possibilities. The story of Amon, King of Judah, and the murder of his eldest son Josiah to appease the Assyrians would similarly have suited a dramatisation that reached beyond routine moralising. The *Apocrypha*'s story of Tobias, the son of Tobit in the Book of that name, was a much more obvious subject then than it is now, since it was popular enough to be used in paintings by, among others, Botticelli, Titian and Rembrandt. Tobit's son travelled on his father's business with help from the angelic guide Raphael, who uses magic and arranges Tobias's marriage with a kinswoman called Sarah. In paintings it was usually presented as a simple moralised tale where virtue leads to riches.

All these were familiar at the time, and one success on stage might readily have led to others. It seems to have been *Judas* that triggered the seven plays on biblical subjects in 1600–02. Haughton was given a single payment of ten shillings 'in earnest' for a play by that name in May 1600, but no further payments to him were recorded. Then more than eighteen months later, in December 1601, Bird and Rowley received £5 'in fulle payment' for a play of the same name, and on 3 January 1602 Antony

---

[59] It is worth remembering that he played Faustus wearing a cross round his neck, a truly Christian safeguard against the real devils that some thought might be present among the stage demons.

Jeffes took thirty shillings to buy cloth for its staging. Nine days later Dekker was paid for writing a prologue and epilogue for another play possibly already in the repertoire, *Pontius Pilate*. Writing a special introduction to and exit from the plays not only shows that biblical subjects were in particular favour at this time, but suggests a degree of awkwardness behind the staging, particularly when the company was setting out on such well-known subjects.

One distinctly deviant accompaniment to the plays based on Bible stories was the arrival in 1600 of a first comedy about the Devil. As with *Judas* it was Haughton, who also started the comedies set in London, who seems to have started the fashion for devil comedies at the Rose. *Grim the Collier of Croydon* (*The Devil and his Dam*), first noted by Henslowe in May 1600, was based on a 1593 pamphlet *Tell-Trothes New-yeares Gift* using Machiavelli's novella *Belfagor*. Much as *The Blind Beggar of Alexandria* sent up Alleyn's Marlovian roles, so *Grim the Collier* parodies *Faustus*. The Devil, pretending to be the Spanish Castiliano, is made a fool much as he was a year or two later in the Chamberlain's *Merry Devil of Edmonton* and later still in their 1616 play by Jonson, *The Devil is an Ass*. The mode was also taken up in *Wily Beguiled* (Q 1606, probably by Paul's), which proved popular enough to go through seven quartos before 1642. The Admiral's play was certainly Haughton's, according to William M. Baillie,[60] who identifies him as the author by linguistic tests that compare it to *Englishmen for My Money*, Haughton's only other unassisted play. He also affirms the date as 1600.

It is possible that the devil comedies, along with the lost play or plays about St Dunstan from the company's earliest years, may show some wish to counter the effects of *Faustus*, since it is Dunstan who counters the Devil's evil in *A Knack to Know a Knave*, acted at the Rose by Strange's between June 1592 and January 1593, the title-page of which proclaimed it 'as it hath sundrye tymes bene played by ED. ALLEN and his Companie. With Kemps applauded Merrimentes of the men of Goteham, in receiving the King into Goteham.' That helps to make it likely that Alleyn had St Dunstan as well as Dr Faustus in his mind when he prompted the company to stage its biblical plays in his first years at the Fortune.[61]

---

[60] 'The Date and Authorship of *Grim the Collier of Croydon*', *Modern Philology* 76 (1978), 179–85.
[61] It may be worth renewing here the point that Elizabethans spoke of Dr Faustus as if his name was pronounced 'forstus', or 'fostes', which is how Henslowe wrote it. The original German pronunciation, now universal, did not enter English until Goethe's work had its not insubstantial impact.

These first years at the Fortune settled a number of the company's main features, most notably its role in London playmaking and its repertory. As we have noted, by 1600 the duopoly was facing competition. Three earls had companies trying to match the Chamberlain's and Admiral's with a base in London. Their joint success made competition inevitable. The old Earl of Pembroke died in 1599 and his remnant company was taken up by the young and ambitious Earl of Worcester, while both Oxford and Derby were writing plays themselves and sponsoring companies to perform them. Moreover, the choristers of St Paul's had been revived as a company of boy players in 1599 at their small playhouse in the St Paul's precinct. They were soon joined by a second boy company that opened at the Chamberlain's indoor Blackfriars, which like Paul's was in a liberty over which the Lord Mayor had no control. Both boy companies performed only weekly instead of daily, claiming to run 'private' performances that kept them out of the reach of the Master of the Revels. In an edict to the magistrates of Middlesex and Surrey dated 31 December 1601 the Privy Council tried to insist on the duopoly, but by 31 March 1602 they had to concede the presence of a third company combining Oxford's and Worcester's Men and playing at the Boar's Head. This was the group that used Henslowe's Rose for a while, and eventually became the third adult company under King James, given the name of Queen Anne's Men. Having three adult and two boy companies performing regularly in London not only broadened the scope for playgoing but demanded increasingly tight specialisation of their repertories by the five companies as they had to focus on narrower sections of the spectrum of audience tastes.

In this new situation, when the Admiral's became the Prince's Men and Alleyn retired from acting, they continued to run much of their older repertory but with a few notable innovations. This twenty-year period is far less well documented than the duopoly years, but it does seem possible to identify a few of the more innovatory plays that extended the old repertory. Two of the company's more celebrated plays, both published, had titles based on paradox, and both were about the morality of womanhood, *The Honest Whore* (1604) and *The Roaring Girl* (1611). Dekker's and Middleton's collaborative play about a 'good' courtesan, rather like Webster's later *White Devil* for the Red Bull, had a title inviting its audiences to question their standard thinking about whores and female schemers. In 1611 *The Roaring Girl* celebrated one of London's current scandals, the cross-dressing Mary Frith, also known as Moll Cutpurse. In *1 The Honest Whore* and later in *The Roaring Girl* Middleton showed a new kind of sympathy for the role of women that is not often evident in the company's other plays.[62] Middleton's whores, consistently called courtesans, have a lot to say for themselves. The heroine in *No Wit / No Help*, Middleton's next play for the Fortune company after *The Roaring Girl*, uses the old game of disguise to control the plot and win her rights by posing as a young gallant. Later in *A Trick to Catch the Old One* for Lady Elizabeth's two leading courtesans end up back in society married and wealthy. *The Roaring Girl*'s heroine, for all her masculine bravado, works consistently to better the characters she meets and to improve their social lot, as does the heroine of *No Wit*.

After the death of Elizabeth the growing nostalgia for Tudor plays based on English history produced its own changes. In 1605 and 1606 the Prince's Men converted the history play tradition of truth-telling into new 'Foxean' plays flaunting an overtly Protestant view of English history. The company sharer Sam Rowley's *When You See Me* matched Heywood's two-part *If You Know Not Me* in this form, and in 1606 Dekker celebrated the Armada victory in *The Whore of Babylon*. Displays of patriotism on stage seem to have played their part in moving the company towards the 'citizen' role and audience that they are thought to have maintained for the rest of their working life. Evidence for the Fortune becoming a 'citizen' playhouse, however, is limited except for a number of audience testimonies which claimed that the older plays and their style continued to dominate the outdoor playhouse repertory. After the complex (and deeply self-interested) celebration of London shoemakers in Dekker's play of 1599 a few specifically citizen-celebrating plays did appear in 1611, but nothing at all survives in the records after that apart from one late contribution to the Protestant history play tradition, *The Duchess of Suffolk* in 1624. The lack of evidence about the company's new plays through this period, truly a dearth after the amount known up to 1603, lasts until the final three years when a flood of new plays came to replace the stock lost in the Fortune's midnight inferno in the winter of 1621.

---

[62] In his *Amends for Ladies* (*c*.1611), an apology for the rudeness of his previous play, *A Woman is a Weathercock*, Nathan Field wrote a scene with Moll in it. A cancel title-page of the 1618 quarto advertised the play as 'WITH THE HUMOUR OF RORING', and the 1639 quarto actually identified it 'With the merry prankes of Moll Cut-Purse: Or, the humour of roaring'. The play uses a shop in the city, tobacco, and other London features, including cross-dressing with lots of disguises, and references to going to Blackfriars and the Fortune. The reference to Moll's appearance from *The Roaring Girl* comes in 2.1 when she enters to the shop with a letter. She roars, and the wife Grace says (in verse, p. 177) 'I know not what to tearme thee man or woman.' She roars again, and leaves. The moment has no function besides its allusion to the Fortune play and character. In 3.4. the tavern drawer tells the roarers (p. 201) 'I have beene at *Besse Turn-ups*, and she swears all the Gentlewomen went to see a Play at the Fortune, and are not come in yet, and she beleeves they sup with the Players.' It glances back at the 'humour of roaring' as a stock comic device.

The years after 1615 were also when the Fortune and Red Bull companies lost their access to playing at court. The fact that nothing got into print in those years is an absence that will be related in the final chapter to the Fortune's redefinition as a 'citizen' playhouse.

Becoming known as a playhouse for citizens rather than gentry did not really develop until well after the King's Men were established at the Blackfriars and Christopher Beeston had established his Cockpit in Drury Lane. Orazio Busino, chaplain to the Venetian ambassador, is said to have visited the Fortune in 1617 when he was impressed by the gentility of the audience.[63] Knowing no English, he could only comment on 'so much nobility in such excellent array that they seemed so many princes, listening as silently and soberly as possible'. Such respect contrasts with John Melton's view four years later about a performance of *Faustus*, when he wrote that 'men goe to the *Fortune* in *Golding-Lane*, to see the Tragedie of Doctor *Faustus*. There indeede a man may behold shagge-hayred Devills runne roaring over the Stage with Squibs in their mouthes, while Drummers make Thunder in the Tyring-house, and the twelve-penny Hirelings make artificiall Lightning in their Heavens.'[64] Such noisy staging can hardly have been aimed at silent and sober princes. The enduring popularity of *Faustus* at the Fortune, given its age and its fireworks, is certainly the mark of a 'citizen' reputation. In 1612 the young Richard Norwood, leaving an unfinished apprenticeship with a London fishmonger before he spent two years at sea, lived through that summer haunting the Fortune, seeing plays and writing his own. He had been first attracted to theatre when, aged fourteen, he played a woman's part in a play at his home town, Stony Stratford. At the Fortune *Faustus* especially gripped him. It later also caught Francis Kirkman, who wrote about how 'the Consideration of that horrible end did so much terrifie me, that I often dreamed of it'.[65]

Faustus's fiery end must have been in the thoughts of many Londoners on 10 December 1621. Early that Monday morning Alleyn noted curtly in his diary: 'this night att 12 of ye clock ye fortune was burnt'. John Chamberlain reported more graphically: 'On Sonday night here was a great fire at the Fortune in Golding-lane the fairest play-house in this towne. Yt was quite burnt downe in two howres and all their apparel and

[63] Bentley (*The Jacobean and Caroline Stage*, VI. 151–3) gives a version of this story, expressing doubt that it could have been at the Fortune. On his contempt for the 'citizen' playhouses see Chapter 4.
[64] John Melton, *Astrologaster*, 1620, E4.
[65] Quoted in Charles Whitney, *Early Responses to Renaissance Drama*, Cambridge, 2006, p. 176. On pp. 170–85 he analyses Norwood's mentality in detail.

play-bookes lost, wherby those poore companions are quite undon.'[66]
The players suffered the loss of more than their resources in plays and
properties, because in 1618 Alleyn had copied the arrangement whereby
the King's Men took shares in their playhouses by setting up a contract
giving the leading Palsgrave's Men shares in a lease of the Fortune. When
the Globe burned down in 1613 the King's Men could use their other
playhouse at Blackfriars, a back-up not available to the Palsgrave's.
Moreover, the Globe caught fire during a performance, so they could
salvage their playbooks and apparel, including the sixteen Shakespeares that
did not appear in print until 1623. Not so the Fortune company in 1621.
The lease of 31 October 1618 had listed ten of them, 'Edward Jubye william
Bird alias Bourne Franck Grace Richard Gumnell Charles Massie
william Stratford william Cartwright Richard Price william Parre and
Richard Fowler' as signatories to the deal. Subsequently, Alleyn had the
Fortune rebuilt in brick, but his backing now came from financiers, not
the players. For the next three years Rowley, Gunnell and Thomas Drue
are on record as writing several new plays for them, Gunnell's his only
recorded writing efforts. Henry Herbert, the new Master of the Revels,
licensed the company fourteen new plays in 1623 and 1624, of which the
only text to survive is the player Drue's revival of a story from Foxean
history, *The Duchess of Suffolk*. That the company kept going at all is a
testimony to their faith in their collective resources. They did not close
finally until they suffered from the massive plague epidemic that killed
25,000 Londoners, a tenth of the population, in 1625–26. That appalling
epidemic began, like the earlier one of 1603–04, with the death of the
monarch. Many changes to London theatre accompanied the arrival of
the new king.

The arrival of Charles I led amongst many other things to a new
theatrical regime. James's system of giving all the licensed companies to
himself and his family could not survive under a newly-wed king who had
only himself and his queen as possible patrons. The companies using the
two indoor playhouses thrived, and new or re-formed companies moved
into the other playhouses. A third indoor playhouse opened in 1629.
At the cheap open-air venues the new companies revived the old repertory, although periodically some did switch from one sort of playhouse to
the other, presumably taking their plays with them. A residue of the
Palsgrave's played on at the Fortune as the King and Queen of Bohemia's
Men, taking their former patron's shortlived claim to be King of Bohemia

---

[66] Both quotations are in Bentley, *Jacobean and Caroline Stage* VI. 153.

for their title. They lasted till 1631, after which different companies shifted between the two 'citizen' venues, the Fortune and the Red Bull.

In the Caroline years two players in particular helped sustain the Fortune's 'citizen' reputation. Both were enlisted in the Palsgrave's during its last decade, when they seem to have been trained in the Alleyn tradition. From 1618 Richard Fowler renewed Alleyn's stalking and roaring in his Marlovian roles. Andrew Cane became the most famous clown of the last years, above all for doing jigs in the barnstorming style that many reporters noted. Fowler, who continued at the Fortune after 1625 as a member of the King and Queen of Bohemia's company, was named in Thomas Rawlins's *The Rebellion* (1639) as the notoriously strident player of *The Spanish Tragedy*'s Hieronimo ('Marke if I doe not gape wider than the widest Mouth'd Fowler of them all'). A 1664 pamphlet has an anecdote about his vigour in sword and buckler or target fights.[67] Open-mouthed roaring and the noisy banging of broadswords on metal shields became a main feature of both Fortune and Red Bull plays under Charles.

I have tried to base the bulk of this chapter on such facts as are on record rather than on speculation. Features of the Gawdy anecdote do cast their opaque shadows, though, and it all remains a story, whether history or biography. The next chapters will spend more time on that other kind of tangible evidence, the *Diary* and the surviving plays rather than the players, and the conditions in which the plays were performed, because we still need to cling to the written text as the most substantial form of what survived from this period, however gratifying may be the material multitude of cherry stones and other objects found by the archaeologists at the Rose. Even tangible relics like the broken-off tips of scouring sticks still need illuminating with whatever we can find about their verbal context.

---

[67] Both stories about Fowler are quoted in Bentley, *Jacobean and Caroline Stage*, II. 440. The comic anecdote about Fowler's 'Conquering parts' is quoted here in Chapter 5, p. 172.

2

Disguise and travel

Imagine a team of fifteen or more stage-players, all of them well trained and familiar with the long-running business of taking a half-dozen plays round the country. The team are all London-bred, but playing in London is only available to the best, and no playing group had any experience of performing non-stop for a year or more at one venue until after June 1594. The Lord Strange's Men stayed at the Rose for six months in the spring and early summer of 1592, not long before their best player married the step-daughter of the man who owned their playhouse. But plague and other troubles stopped that run. So when the Admiral's new company started playing non-stop at the Rose in 1594 their horizons were enlarged. For the first time they could expect to use a licensed playhouse with some real chance of sticking to it for years on end. It gave them a wholly novel security of tenure. Within a year they were thinking of ways to exploit this unprecedented durability of their foothold in London.

We cannot say whether the Chamberlain's Men did anything with their share in this novel security, but a study of the first plays written for the Admiral's tells us that they were exploiting it by the end of their first year. In London they had to run a uniquely exhausting schedule, staging a different play every afternoon from Monday to Saturday, almost always to much the same audiences. When travelling or switching from one London venue to another they could expect strange faces to confront them, but not now at the Rose. The playgoers who regularly went to one of the only two sites in London open for plays saw the same players pretending to be somebody new, often by doubling assuming more than one character in the same play. Every habitual London playgoer at the Rose could recognise the same player as somebody different. On each visit seeing Alleyn as Hieronymo, Tamburlaine, Barabbas, Faustus, or Muly Mahamet soon became a familiar experience barely mitigated by the expectation of a new role in a new play every week or two. In the third week of August 1594, for instance, on Monday the 17th they saw Alleyn as Marlowe's

Lord High Admiral of France, on Tuesday as Tasso, on Wednesday as King Henry I confronting the clown Belin Dun, on Thursday he was the hero of *The Ranger's Comedy*, on Friday Galiaso and on Saturday he stalked as the heroic Cutlack. They would just as easily have recognised Richard Jones, Edward Juby, Thomas Towne and the others in their various parts. Metatheatrical awareness that each player was in a different disguise every day was a vital feature of the endless run of shows at the Rose.

One immediate effect of this new knowledge about how familiar the recurrent members of the Rose's audiences became as they recognised the double identities of the different characters on stage was in the variety of clothing the players needed to wear. We can easily be shocked by how much the company and individual players spent on their doublets, cloaks and gowns compared with the price of a new playbook. A play usually brought its three or four writers six pounds while the cost of clothing and 'thinges' for new plays could easily run to twice that. New clothing as well as new plays was a constant drain on player funds. Between 7 April and 15 June 1598, when Alleyn's absence demanded new stock for the repertory, Henslowe laid out £35 on plays, seven of them to Martin Slater for the five plays he sold the company when he left, and £21 10s 8d on clothing and other 'thinges'. In one expensive week at the end of July he paid out £43 on plays and £13 10s 8d on clothing. This was not long after Henslowe and Alleyn drew up their inventories of the clothing stored at the Rose, showing the enormous resources they had and could re-use. Given the regular tailoring of worn clothing with 'fripperies'[1] it was not difficult by then to satisfy the need for new and colourful attire on stage every day.

Yet the novelty of such attire was in constant contrast to the familiar faces wearing them every day. A new doublet or gown would enhance the newness of the character on show, but while the new garb could offset the familiar faces wearing them it only intensified audience awareness of the metatheatricality inherent in the occasion. In conventional thinking clothes did not make the player, any more than they made the man. On stage the robes and furred gowns that King Lear said 'hide all' were a business of self-conscious artifice that highlighted the pleasures of being entertained by the expected deceptions that playgoers went to the Rose for.

Nobody had encountered this situation before 1594, having to cater for a captive audience already completely familiar with the team of players they came to see daily. Indeed it was a novelty they would never experience

---

[1] On the use of 'fripperies' in Elizabethan tailoring, see Peter Stallybrass and Annie Jones, *Renaissance Clothing and the Materials of Memory*, Cambridge, 2000.

again. Not only were the playgoers affected by the challenge this new situation threw up, but so were the players by the need to keep the throng of familiar faces entertained with fresh experiences. The need to stage a different play every day and a new one every week or so kept the company on their toes, but the other novelty in the business of playmaking, that audiences came to know their faces as well as or better than they knew their plays, came to present a further and much more complex challenge. The other monopoly company had their Shakespeares. What the Admiral's did now was commission their own writers to create a new kind of play that would satisfy the demands of an audience that was beginning to get used to seeing the same faces in so many different roles. Their answer was brilliantly simple. By late 1595, a little more than a year after they first settled into the pattern of regularly playing at the one playhouse, they were prompting their writers to give them plays that exploited the most obvious feature of the whole business of acting, disguise. Their customers were getting used to seeing the players change their dress daily. Now they could exploit that expectation with new games.

Through disguise in the play's plot, an almost momentary change of gown or cloak could make a face familiar in one role re-enter in another. Alleyn needed only five lines of dialogue while he was offstage in *The Blind Beggar* to change his character The experienced audience knew who each player was, and could watch the game of trickery through disguise without any risk of being conned in the way that the plots would in fooling their gullible stage characters. Donning a new gown or furred robe did not alter the face or the character showing itself over the new guise. Even the hat an actor wore might be recognisable from another play. Alleyn as Barabbas in *The Jew of Malta* objects to Ithamore mocking his headgear by saying "Twas sent me for a present from the great *Cham*', an obvious in-joke about the hat he had worn for *Tamar Cham*.[2] Recognising the tricks being played with quick-change disguises made audiences feel comfortably superior. They connived with the players in their trickery while admitting the whole process of deception through disguise as an integral part of the larger trickery, the metatheatrical entertainment they had paid to view.

In the middle of their trickiest disguise play, one that I think Henslowe chose to register in his *Diary* simply as '*Desgysses*', the writer took care to insert a pause in the heart of the intricate plot in order to explain to

---

[2] *The Complete Works of Christopher Marlowe,* ed. Fredson Bowers, 2 vols., Cambridge, 1973, I. 322 (*Jew of Malta*, 4.4.70). The extant text dates from 1633; the allusion may have been a late addition.

anyone who had not managed to keep up with the story all the disguising
that had gone on in the play so far. Few of the regular playgoers would
have needed such a concession. To appreciate the plays of this company,
especially in their most creative period from 1594 till 1600, we need to
maintain a delicate sense of the jokes and the tricks that were inherent in
such localised and heavily conditioned theatricality, and to look out for
the metatheatrical games that the company began to exploit and regularly
use in their new plays. The immediacy of the local and particular occasion
that inspired such brilliant farces as *The Wise Men of West Chester* and *The
Blind Beggar of Alexandria* needs carefully tactful reconstruction.

Distinctive features from the Admiral's long tenure at the Rose and the
Fortune are of course, like those of any long-gone theatre company,
inherently elusive. Alleyn's notoriety with his 'stalking and roaring' in
the first years gained him a reputation that Richard Fowler came to
maintain at the Fortune up to 1642. Yet his fame at quoting Marlowe in
a loud voice as he strode round the stage has to be set against not just his
recognisable skills in burlesquing his own roles but the evidence set down
in the company's playhouse 'plots' like *Tamar Cham* and *The Battle of
Alcazar*. They record not just his quick shifts of costume but a series of
bloody spectacles where gruesome entrails were flaunted for shock effect,
creating appallingly realistic images of the carnage inherent in such
stories. That has made it easy for us to accept Neil Carson's differentiation
between the early 'theatre of enchantment', with its blood and its magical
shows, compared with the more sophisticated 'theatre of estrangement'
of other companies after his strutting and roaring became a stock feature
of the Rose plays, where boys playing men could automatically assume a
metatheatrical alertness in the audiences at all of their performances. Boys
playing adult men or boys playing girls generate their own metatheatrical
anti-realism, just as would a familiar player appearing in a new gown in a
new play. Carson's distinction is a truism that seems to position the
Admiral's on the less sophisticated 'enchantment' side of this divide.[3]
It presupposes a more innocent audience at the Rose compared with the
Blackfriars, a crowd of the kind that would not grasp the subtleties of
Shakespeare's late plays.

But it is not easy to reconcile the simple graphic realism set out in the
Admiral's 'plots' as the dominant mode with the wonderfully elaborate
farce of disguise and thoroughgoing self-mockery when Alleyn parodied
his own Marlovian roles in *The Blind Beggar of Alexandria*. Nor could

---

[3] See Neil Carson, 'John Webster: the Apprentice Years', *Elizabethan Theatre* 6 (1978), 76–87.

Alleyn and his successors have continued through the years to play
The Spanish Tragedy while completely ignoring the mocks and burlesques
it attracted. How the gruesome realism of the *Alcazar* dumbshows was
accommodated at the Rose and Fortune is a question demanding a
cautiously complex view of the kind of playing that seems to have evolved
at the Rose through the 1590s. The main subject of this chapter is how the
players learned what they could do to develop and enhance relations with
their regular audiences, in a highly complex and thoroughly localised
pattern of tragedy and comedy.

We still find it far too easy to think of sixteenth-century acting as ruled
by the stage realism that cinema has made it so easy for us to expect now.
The camera, in its privileged position peering up the nostrils of a modern
actor, gives us a quite different experience from what early playgoers
witnessed, where an actor's whole body was in motion on a platform that
you clustered round while you viewed him from amongst a crowd of your
peers as tangible to you as the players on stage. At the Rose or the Globe
self-awareness in audiences was almost axiomatic. In broad daylight, fully
conscious of the audience pressing and shuffling around you, it could
never have been easy to lose yourself in the realism of the shows as modern
cinema now expects us to do. Then you were aware of being part of a
crowd, developing the collectively intensified feelings you shared with
everyone else in your responses to the play. The end of the performative
process which is theatre needs to take very carefully into account how such
a crowd, visible as the Elizabethans always were, interacted with the
players on the stage. For the player, speaking to a crowd invites an
averaging-down effect since the speaker has to allow for a wide range of
interests and expertise. But that downward trend is offset and uplifted by
the intensity of the crowd responses and the way the individuals in the
crowd infect each other. Too little has been attempted in recent years to
discover how the collective crowd responses in theatre audiences differ
from individual reactions, because audiences are now too easily seen as
aggregates of individuals, without the strong yet intangible aggregative
feeling that being part of a crowd generates. Theatre crowds tend not to
riot as readily as sporting and political crowds, with the result that their
more subtle and complex shared responses have been overlooked (not that
group feelings are ever easy to identify as a unit).

Early modern theatre used innumerable devices, many of them deliberately antagonistic to stage realism. Quite apart from the popular tradition of using boys to play adults and in the adult theatre boys to play
women, the use of verse for dignified speech was inherently, and I think

knowingly, anti-realistic. The formality of verse counteracts the normal prose idioms of ordinary speech. Social divisions in early adult theatre gave verse to the 'gentle' folk and comic prose to the rude mechanicals, quite unlike what writers supplied for the boy companies. Almost all the boy company plays from Lyly's onwards were written as prose, to be delivered swiftly and wittily but as not as verse, however euphuistic the language might be. I strongly suspect that boys could afford to speak normal prose because being boys they ran less risk of being thought of as truly the adults they were pretending to be. Fear of illusion as the work of the devil was constantly harped on in the pulpits of the time. Shakespeare's player kings must have been well aware not only that they made themselves a motley to the view but that they were deceitfully professing a status of nobility that their clothes asserted yet their work denied. Artificial speech in verse, along with asides to the audience that other players were not supposed to hear, concealments that did not conceal, disguises that the audience had to see through, all these were routinely non-realistic features of early staging.

And then there was the jig that ended the play, always the traditional ending of a performance at the Rose and the Fortune. A farcical piece of clowning designed to send the audience away happy, in later years jigs became one of the most distinctive features of the 'citizen' playhouse repertories. The Shakespeare company seems to have abandoned them by 1612, when the Middlesex magistrates issued an order banning jigs at the Fortune in response to complaints 'that by reason of certayne lewde Jigges songes and daunces used and accustomed at the play-house called the Fortune in Goulding-lane divers cutt-purses and other lewde and ill disposed persons in great multitudes doe resorte thither at th'end of everye playe many tymes causing tumults and outrages wherebye His Majesties peace is often broke and much mischiefe like to ensue thereby.'[4] There is no doubt that jigs to conclude even tragedies had been standard at the Globe previously, if only on Thomas Platter's testimony from 1599. The non-English-speaking Platter recorded his pleasure at the dance by two players in men's and two in women's clothing at the end of *Julius Caesar*. I have a strong suspicion that there was also a jig at the end of the Globe's hit of the following year, *Hamlet*, because that play is the only one of Shakespeare's histories or tragedies to leave a group of corpses on stage at the end with no instruction to carry them off. Hamlet is carried off like a dead soldier, on Fortinbras's order, but Claudius the king, Gertrude

[4] Bentley, *Jacobean and Caroline Stage*, VI. 146.

the queen and Laertes are all left lying there. Could Shakespeare have
expected them to get up and start the jig? Hamlet had contemptuously
dismissed Polonius's liking for jigs in the theatre: 'He's for a jig or a tale
of bawdry or he sleeps.' To end such a theatre-conscious play with a jig
would be a wonderfully neat metatheatrical final twist. We now find jigs
unthinkable at the end of tragedies but there was certainly one at the end
of the original *Julius Caesar*. Perhaps we sink too easily into expectation
of emotional realism to admit the chance that other and earlier audiences
might take the deaths lightly enough to want a jigging conclusion to
the afternoon's entertainment. If the Fortune continued to stage jigs at
the end of *The Spanish Tragedy* or *Tamburlaine*, as seems to be the case,
we need to adjust our thinking about how the audience participated in the
play event's interactions.

The Admiral's company practices are alien to twenty-first century
theatre in a multitude of ways. By modern standards they had an
unbelievably demanding repertoire. In their first twelve months from
June 1594 they staged as many as thirty-seven different plays, twenty-
one of them new or 'ne' texts.[5] In the second year they staged thirty-eight
plays of which seventeen were new, and in the third twenty-nine plays of
which fourteen were new. Each day they had to offer a different play.
At least once every fortnight they mounted a new play, which took three
weeks to go from purchase of the completed playbook to its first appearance on the Rose's stage. In the course of a year the repertory always
had at least thirty current plays on hand. A new play would run for up to
a dozen performances over six months, the most popular lasting for as
long as eighteen before they were retired. Revivals would usually be laid
on two or three years after the first run. Some plays were always popular.
Marlowe's *Tamburlaine* and *Faustus* and *The Spanish Tragedy* ran on
at the Fortune well beyond the last years of the Palsgrave's Men. When
Alleyn returned to the stage to open the new Fortune three years after
retiring from the Rose in 1597 he revived as many as seventeen of his
old favourites. Some of these old favourites stayed in the repertory for
more than fifty years at the heart of what came to be called the citizen
playhouses.

For the other company set up in 1594 very little besides Shakespeare's
plays remain to tell us what its repertory contained. From what evidence
besides the Shakespeare plays we have, the opposite company's outlook

---

[5] For a comment on the varied interpretations of Henslowe's designation of plays as 'ne', see below,
pp. 92–94.

seems to have been fairly conservative. By contrast the Admiral's responded far more positively from the outset to the riches they gained from having a steady location at a licensed playhouse on the fringes of London and daily performances. The Shakespeare company seems never to have copied the Admiral's brilliant games of disguise, for instance. Both companies ran plays demanding a large number of roles, well beyond the usual eight or ten speaking parts with a similar number of mutes or walk-ons. The need for the sharers to double their roles by taking other parts in the same play on stage became a feature in almost every play, whether it demanded the forty-three parts of *Henry V* or the even larger number for *Titus Andronicus* and the two *Tamburlaines*. Not even the hired men could always provide the required number of mutes on stage. For the plot of *Frederick and Basilea*, acted by the Admiral's in 1597, the plotter twice calls for the addition on stage of 'gatherers', the collectors of gate money, at Scene 9 and at the finale. Presumably by Scene 9 when they were halfway through the play not all the gatherers were needed to continue guarding the entrance-ways where customers paid for access.

What the Admiral's first new plays at the Rose make clear is that they soon learned to exploit the now guaranteed stability of their playing location. The idea of exploiting disguise must have come from the players themselves as much as from the writers like Munday and Chapman who wrote the innovatory ideas into their manuscripts. The players well knew the risk of such games causing confusion, so, as we shall see, their writers took care to announce each disguise in advance to the audience. In the play that I think is the company's *The Wise Men of West Chester*, the manuscript known as *John a Kent and John a Cumber*, disguise in one scene (TLN 1200) involves John a Kent disguised as John a Cumber meeting John a Cumber disguised as John a Kent. It was a joke that could not work unless the audience knew which player was pretending to be which wizard. Such tricks became a major element in the constant process of generating audience complicity.[6]

As early as October of their second year the Admiral's Men started running plays using tricks with disguise that expected a complicit audience. We have already noted that Chapman's first comedy for them, *The Blind Beggar of Alexandria*, featured Alleyn, famous for his looks,

---

[6] Many Elizabethans were fascinated by the question of vision and the illusions that could be generated by misuse of the eye, of which the game of disguise was obviously one. For a wide-ranging conspectus of the issues relating to vision and illusion, see Stuart Clark, *Vanities of the Eye: Vision in Early Modern Europe*, Oxford University Press, 2007.

his speech and his stature, as a star trickster using several parodic disguises to develop the plot. Chapman's play was printed in 1598, in a fairly good copy. Its plot is quite deliberately farcical.[7] Irus's initial prophecies to the ladies bring three wives to Alleyn's main role, Cleanthes, one wife for each of his roles other than Irus. As himself, the Alexandrian General, brought back from his ostensible exile to rescue Egypt from its invaders, he marries the princess. Her two ladies he also marries, one while posing as Leon the usurer and the other as the roistering Count Hermes. Both of these wives he declares in his role as Cleanthes at the end are 'widows', Leon and Count Hermes having both disappeared and been declared dead. He therefore re-marries them off to two of the four kings who have submitted to his success as general of the Egyptian forces, having returned from his ostensible banishment to defeat them. The four kings are led by 'Blacke *Porus*', king of Ethiopia, a colour reaffirmed at the end (TLN 1592), when he is made husband to one of the ostensible widows. (More will be said about the use of characters in blackface on the Rose stage in Chapter 4). The disguise game flaunts these remarriages. The question of the hero's bigamy by the replacement husbands is coolly avoided by the fiction that Leon and Hermes are dead. The play is a brilliant but unrepeatable farce, entirely dependent on the audience's recognition of the way it sends up Alleyn's own 'fustian' roles. Modern audiences, lacking such localised knowledge, cannot appreciate the extent of Chapman's ingenious farce.

Another early disguise play I believe to be the one that appears in Henslowe's record under the generic title '*Desgysses*'. No play under that title is known, but one appeared in print in a rather less competent edition than Chapman's in 1600 under the title *Look About You*. It was printed as an Admiral's play but with a title that appears nowhere in the *Diary*. In the absence of any other candidate I believe the play Henslowe gave the name 'disguises' to must be the play printed as *Look About You*. Both this play and Chapman's comedy can be presumed to have gone to the press as a result of their popularity once they dropped out of the standard repertory. *Look About You*, if it really was the play Henslowe called '*Desgysses*', was performed 'ne' on 2 October 1595. It was popular, appearing another five times up to 10 November, two months before Chapman's *Blind Beggar*. Chapman's farce may well have been inspired in its use of disguises for Alleyn by the success of this play.

---

[7] Chapman's farcical plot did not please earlier critics. Millar MacLure says that the modern reader 'will have cause to reflect grimly (as every reader of minor Elizabethan drama must) on the curious tastes of our ancestors' (p. 84).

What is most significant as evidence for the company's adventurousness at this early stage in their long career is the prevalence of disguise in the company's repertory in 1595 and long after. If, for instance, the hugely popular *Wise Men of West Chester* really was the play that survives in manuscript under the name *John a Kent and John a Cumber* its comic success was equally due to its exploitation of disguise. The surviving manuscript seems to date from 1595, in Munday's hand, which is the right date for an early disguise play.[8] *John a Kent*, which Henslowe called *The Wise Men of West Chester* (the name *John a Kent* never appears in the *Diary*) gained that name chiefly because it is set at a castle near Chester, at 'noble Chesters Courte' (TLN 4). The two Johns are both wise men who compete with their magic like Friar Bacon against Friar Bungay in Greene's play, which preceded Munday's by several years. There is still not a serious consensus that Munday's manuscript does give us the text of the *Diary*'s greatest hit, but his presence in 1594–95 as a writer for Henslowe and its disguise theme that year makes it very likely. Munday's manuscript, more-over, has in it the hand of the same book-keeper which appears as 'Hand C' in *Sir Thomas More*, also a company play. The same man wrote the 'plots' of *2 Seven Deadly Sins* of 1591 and the Admiral's *Fortune's Tennis* in 1598.[9] *John a Kent*'s extensive use of disguise for its magical tricks gives it only a loose kind of association with the Admiral's repertory, but does augment the likelihood that *John a Kent* should be identified with the notable hit of 1595 that *The Wise Men of West Chester* certainly was according to Henslowe.

What Henslowe first transcribed as "*the wise man of chester*", making it "weschester" and "weaschester" in later entries, was a play that first appeared as a 'ne' entry for 2 December 1594.[10] The two wise men use magic to support their rival parties, a form of witchcraft that in this case amounts to no more than setting up illusions of disguise. The plot is

[8] The date is debatable. I. A. Shapiro read it as 1590, altered to 1596, but Peter Beal now reads it as 1595. See Grace Ioppolo, *Dramatists and their Manuscripts in the Age of Shakespeare, Jonson, Middleton and Heywood: Authorship, Authority and the Playhouse*, Routledge, London, 2006, p. 101.
[9] The usual association of the *2 Seven Deadly Sins* 'plot' with Strange's in 1591–92, which would make sense of Hand C moving on to work for the post-1594 Admiral's, was questioned in 1989 by Gary Taylor and Scott McMillin, who suggested that it was more likely to have been made for a play revived by the Chamberlain's Men in 1598. David Kathman, in 'Reconsidering *The Seven Deadly Sins*', *Early Theatre* 7 (2004), 13–44, recently revived the idea, arguing that the play might date not from 1590–91 but from 1598, when it would have been prepared for the Chamberlain's Men. That theory has to ignore the real puzzle over how a plotter, Hand C, could have been working with Alleyn in the early 1590s and in 1601–02, and in between could shift his loyalties to work for the Chamberlain's in 1597–98. Gurr, 'The Work of Elizabethan Plotters, and *2 The Seven Deadly Sins*', *Early Theatre* 10 (2006), 67–87, argues for the original dating in 1591.
[10] *Diary*, p. 26.

about rival pairs of lovers for the two ladies of the Earl's castle and the neighbourhood of Westchester. The pair that John a Kent supports are the true lovers, while their opponents are favoured by the Earl, who is father and uncle of the two ladies. The aspirant pair of lovers swear to each other that 'spight of Chesters strong inhabitants / Thorow west chester' they will 'lead my Sidanen and your Marian, / while both our Rivalles, and their following trayne, / Sheeplyke stand shivering at our wrathfull lookes' (TLN 54–58). Henslowe's titles, including his occasional plural for the wise men, do fit Munday's play very precisely.

The plot allows each John to appear disguised as his opposite, to the point where one complains that the other is pretending to be him, saying 'he hath tane my shape' when in an obvious double bluff he actually is the other. John a Cumber's chief magical trick is to parade in front of the main characters four 'antiques' in the figures of their rivals (TLN 1213). In the end John a Kent tricks John a Cumber by making him think the four real characters are the 'antiques' he created earlier. These magical disguises must have been fairly tricky for the audience to follow. At TLN 1277 John a Cumber exclaims 'how now? Whats this? My shaddowes taught to speak, / that to my face, they should unto my foe?' But the magic is simple to stage so long as the audience can follow which of the two is the real John a Kent and which the real John a Cumber, and similarly which are the 'antiques' or 'shaddowes' and which the real characters they imitate. John a Cumber loses when he mistakes the real people for his own magic shadows. One hopes the audience would not have been similarly confused.[11]

If *John a Kent* is indeed *The Wise Men of West Chester* it must have planted a feeling about the value of disguise in the company's minds, a feeling well developed soon after by Chapman with *The Blind Beggar of Alexandria*. The text of *Look About You*, staged ten months after the *Westchester* play, takes the game even further. A 'pleasant' comedy, as the title-page calls it, its frame came from English history but its plot is weirdly original. It has been ignored by almost every critic, partly I suspect because its author is almost completely unidentifiable (see 39, Appendix 1),

---

[11] It may be worth noting that the 'plot' of *The Dead Man's Fortune*, of uncertain date, and with Burbage's name in it (a possible Admiral's name there too may be Sam Rowley, as 'b. samme'), also makes frequent use of disguise. At 2.6 it specifies 'validore passeth ore the stage disguised', at 3.3 'Enter *Tesephon* allgerius at severall dores disguisd with meate', and at 4.6 'Enter aspida & validore disguisd like rose wth a flasket of clothes to them rose wth a nother flasket of clothes'. A marginal note to the climactic scene, 5.2, specifies that the formerly disguised Tesephon and Algerius should '*enter w^t out disguise*'.

a point that Peter Hyland has made.[12] Printed in 1600 'As it was lately played by the right honourable the Lord High Admiral his servaunts', it lacks an author's name and survives only in a rather rough text with quite a few obvious omissions, mostly of exits and entrances but perhaps also of some dialogue. Its story derives vaguely from the history material that Munday later drew on for his two Robin Hood plays performed by the company early in 1598. The first of Munday's Huntingdon plays, *The Downfall*, makes similarly good use of disguises – in the first Act Queen Elinor tries to exchange clothes with Maid Marian, telling her 'But get thee in, and shift of thy attire', adding suggestively 'My roabe is loose, and it will soone be off.'[13] Robin Hood, since he is a fugitive, also appears in disguise, though not as the lady he pretends to be in *Look About You*. The anonymous play's tricks with disguise are fairly routine except for their extraordinary quantity, but are used with outstanding inventiveness. Summarising the plot is the most banal form of critical analysis, but for such a well-crafted farce it is worth listing the constant twists and turns to show what this remarkable play does with all its disguising tricks.

Set in the time of Henry II and Elinor of Acquitaine, its characters include the three princes, Henry the eldest, Richard and John, plus the Earls of Gloucester (spelled Gloster), Lancaster and Leicester, and Sir Richard Faukenbridge, whose wife Prince Richard tries to seduce.[14] Robin Hood appears as the young Earl of Huntingdon, while at the play's centre is a trickster and disguiser called Skinke. OED records a 'skink' as a small lizard, so named by Philemon Holland in his *Pliny* (1601) and by Topsell in 1608. It could also mean a sausage, while as a verb it meant to pour or serve drink like a tapster, and sometimes the drink itself.[15] The first of these meanings, if applied to a chameleon, would certainly fit Skinke in the play, though at one point he does disguise himself as a tapster.

---

[12] See Peter Hyland, '*Look About You*, Anonymity, and the Value of Theatricality', *Research Opportunities in Medieval and Renaissance Drama* 44 (2005), 65–74.

[13] At TLN 411–12 of the Malone Society Reprint edition (1964).

[14] Prince Richard's seduction of Faulconbridge's wife is the origin of the Bastard in Shakespeare's *King John*, written a little before *Look About You*. Named Margaret she had previously featured as bearing Richard's child in the Queen's Men's *Troublesome Raigne of King John*. This more virtuous wife might have been designed as a corrective to the Queen's Men's and Shakespeare versions, though it is equally likely that her plot function as subject to a jealous husband left that issue (so to speak) on the sideline.

[15] In *The Pilgrimage to Parnassus*, a Cambridge play of 1599, the Italian Madido (wet) speaks of 'our poore englishe skinkers', meaning drawers of liquor (*The Three Parnassus Plays*, ed. J. B. Leishman, London, 1949, p. 103).

The historical basis is a royal conflict familiar to early audiences, when Prince Henry and his quarrelsome brothers deprive old King Henry of his crown. In the opening scene Robin Hood, ward to Prince Richard, learns from Skinke, who is disguised as a hermit and prophet, that a villain (actually Skinke himself) has poisoned Rosamond, the old king's lover, and is to appear at the royal court to be defended by Richard and John, where with the frustrated Queen Elinor's support her eldest son Prince Henry will take the crown from his father. Apart from Skinke John is the play's worst villain, along with his French mother Elinor. Faukenbridge is the chief gull, the galloping clown Redcap another, while Prince Richard appears as something of a hero, supporting the boldly outspoken Gloster, the central hero, who has to become a fugitive in disguise when he objects to Prince Henry's usurpation. Gloster is the good disguiser, Skinke the lower-class trickster. Richard is a gallant though ultimately unsuccessful lover of Lady Faukenbridge, who is Gloster's sister, giving Richard an ulterior motive for helping Gloster when he is in flight from the usurping Prince Henry.

Scene 2 is the first of two major confrontations at the royal court, one at each end of the play. In this scene Prince Henry takes over from the old king on the ground of his lechery and disloyalty to his queen, Henry's mother. The boisterous Gloster becomes a victim when he strikes Prince Henry for rewarding Skinke with his lands. This show of taking sides is counterbalanced by the second confrontation, the court scene that ends the play and results in general accord, when Prince Henry decides to restore old Henry as king and himself retreats to a life of penance. These two framing court scenes are the only ones in the play where nobody adopts a disguise.

All the disguises are made quite obvious to the audience. Mostly they are quick offstage changes of identifiable clothing, simply donning nobles' or ladies' gowns, cloaks and hats to conceal more normal attire, or adding the identifying features of a trade like a tipstaff's rod, a tapster's apron or a falconer's lure. Two identical sets of false beards 'and hayre' are also used, one for the first disguiser, Skinke, while he plays the hermit in his monk's gown with hood and beads, all put on several times by Skinke, and a duplicate set used later by the fugitive Gloster. Inevitably they both disguise themselves as the hermit at one point and confront each other as mirror images.

The stage directions specify the disguises throughout. The play opens, as does *The Blind Beggar of Alexandria*, with the chief disguiser dressed as a hermit. To him comes 'Robert Hood, *a young Noble-man, a servant with*

him, with ryding wandes in theyr handes, as if they had beene new lighted.
Robin tells his servant:

> Goe, walke the horses, wayte me on the hill,
> This is the Hermits Cell, goe out of sight:
> My business with him must not be reveal'd,
> To any mortall creature but himselfe.[16]

The business is a letter from Prince Richard asking the hermit for his
help as a seer and magician. As soon as Robin has delivered the letter and
left, the hermit tells the audience how he magically knew Robin – he
recognised him from the court – and what he will do with Richard's
letter, which tells him to make sure that Skinke will appear at court
tomorrow, where Richard and John will defend him for poisoning
Rosamund.

From his first appearance as the hermit Skinke shows himself a masterly
disguiser. In subsequent scenes he becomes the clownish tipstaff Redcap,
then Gloster, then Prince John, the hermit again, and a falconer (*'Enter
Skinke with a patch on his face, and a Faulconers lure in his hand'*, 2008–09).
His opposite Gloster when he escapes from the court also uses quick-
change disguises including Skinke's own as the hermit (*'Enter Gloster in
the Hermits gowne, putting on the beard'*, 2071–02). The third notable
disguiser is Robin Hood, who spends the middle of the play dressed as
Lady Faukenbridge while she in turn disguises herself as a merchant's
wife. Her disguise is to help her get good advice from the hermit, after
Robin tells her that Richard has promised to save her brother Gloster if
she will sleep with him. Her husband Faukenbridge has already overheard
Richard trying to seduce her, so this sub-plot interlocks with Gloster's
escape.

The comic characters also adopt disguises. The clown Redcap, a tipstaff
marked and mocked for his stammer and his constant running across the
stage, involuntarily helps Skinke, who at one point exchanges clothes with
him ('there's my cloake and hat to keep thee warme', 518). Skinke then
pretends to be Redcap even to the clown's own father, who is Porter of the
Fleet prison where Gloster is held. Disguised as Redcap he also confuses
Gloster. To keep free by playing his own game of disguise, Gloster takes
Redcap's clothes from Skinke, leaving his nobleman's coat behind, saying

---

[16] I have used the Malone Society Reprints edition of *Look About You*, edited by W. W. Greg and
published by Oxford University Press in 1913, and its through-line numbering. These lines are at
TLN 5–8.

'Ile leave my gowne, change is no robbery' (819). Prince John enters with the Porter, and Gloster, now disguised as Redcap and imitating his stammer, directs him to Skinke. John speaks to Skinke, who is now pretending to be Gloster in his gown. In a gesture of false friendship John offers to play Gloster at bowls, but then goes off for a word with his cousin Morton, also in the Fleet, leaving his own cloak, rapier, and hat with the disguised Skinke, who puts them on and departs as John. The real Redcap then appears, bemusing his father who had just said goodbye to Skinke disguised as Redcap, and John returns, now reluctantly dressed '*in Gloster's gowne*'. He orders the Porter to be held in prison for letting Gloster escape.

Skinke's original disguise in the hermit's 'weedes' with 'false hayre and beard' (2076) explains why he knows so much about the political situation, and his own reason for, like Gloster, using so many disguises. He confides to the audience that as hermit he has been consulted by 'all the faction / That take the young Kings part against the old . . . The olde Kings part would kill me being stain'd, / The young Kings keep me from their violence.' (64–70). This role is amplified in the sixth scene, when Prince Henry enters to formal trumpets, now holding court as king. His brother John enters wearing Gloster's gown, and Henry and Richard both assume he is Gloster until he discards his 'case' (1066), a neat contrast to the more deliberate disguisings. John curses Gloster, reckoning rightly that he must now be disguised as John. Prince Henry orders search parties sent out to kill Gloster in John's gown, while the old king sends Richard and Faukenbridge to save him and catch Skinke. The old king tells them 'If ye finde Skinke see that you apprehend him', adding with unconscious irony,

> I heare there is a wizard at blacke heath,
> Let some enquire of him where Skinke remaynes.   (1109–1111)

The magical powers of the 'wizard' at Blackheath are cited as the most likely means to find them both, an idea with more truth than any of the folk on stage know.

Scene 7 sets out the sub-plot. Lady Faukenbridge asks Robin Hood 'will you agree / To be the Lady Faukenbridge one day?' (1142–3) so that she can go in disguise to the hermit's cell and learn her future. Before she sets off her servant enters '*bleeding*' along with Gloster, who is still in disguise not as Prince John but as Redcap. The servant is sent away and the lady recognises her brother. She offers to re-disguise him as her husband, 'with beard & hayre' that she got from Prince Richard when

he came 'in a maske' (1195). He does so. As soon as he is dressed as
Faukenbridge Redcap arrives with a constable in pursuit of Gloster,
grieving over his father's punishment. They leave, Gloster now posing
as Faukenbridge, and Lady Faukenbridge sets off for Blackheath.

The next scene thrives on a flurry of confusions. Skinke enters '*like
Prince John*' and meets the real Faukenbridge, who thinking him John has
no problem entrusting him with a gold chain, and leaves. Five lines later
Gloster enters dressed as Faukenbridge, meeting Skinke disguised as John.
Both are confused. Skinke assumes Faukenbridge has returned for his
chain, though with remarkable haste, and worries that he must be suspi-
cious about Skinke's disguise. So believing he faces the real Faukenbridge
he breaks the chain in half and gives one part to the disguised Gloster.
Skinke as John then leaves, and five lines later the real John enters along
with Prince Richard and the Sheriff in pursuit of Gloster, who is onstage
disguised as Faukenbridge. John first speaks with hostility to Gloster,
thinking him to be the real Faukenbridge, a supporter of the old king
and Gloster. But when the pretend Faukenbridge says he knows Gloster's
whereabouts John embraces him, which makes Richard curse him. Gloster
then takes Richard aside and reveals who he really is: 'Prince Richard at
this corner make your stand: / Know I am Gloster and not Faukenbridge'
(1347). He then tells John and the Sheriff that Gloster will come there
'in a russet cloake / And must attend me like a servingman' (1357–58).
John gives him his sword and Gloster leaves. Eight lines later the real
Faukenbridge enters and asks John for his chain. John asks him about
Gloster to no avail, and in response to his question about the chain points
out that he, Faukenbridge, has John's sword. This Faukenbridge denies
(Gloster disguised as Faukenbridge went off with it). They quarrel until
Richard admits that the man who just left was not the real Faukenbridge.
They all agree to look for the truth at a nearby tavern. In a final tweak,
Richard says that the trickster was Skinke, whereas John claims it was
Gloster. Both of course are right.

For Scene 9, '*Enter Gloster like Faukenbridge with a Pursevant, Gloster
having a paper in his hand, the Pursevant bare*' (1463–64). The paper is the
old king's reprieve for the Porter. They talk in a tavern called the
Salutation, where Gloster gives the Pursuivant, who has taken his hat
off out of respect for Lord Faukenbridge, a drink plus sugar to make him
sick so he can steal 'your warrant and your boxe' (1510). He has decided on
another disguise, saying 'Gloster wil be a proteus every houre'. They leave
the tavern, whereupon '*Enter Skinke like Prince John*' (1527). Skinke asks
the tapster to fetch him some pig's blood and takes the tapster's apron,

handing him John's cloak, hat, and sword. To the aproned Skinke as tapster enter the real John, Richard, the real Faukenbridge, the Sheriff and officers, all hunting for Gloster. Applying the blood to himself Skinke tells them that Prince John assaulted him. John reckons the culprit must have been Gloster whereas Richard thinks it must have been Skinke in disguise. They go off to search the tavern, and Skinke slips away. The pursuers return dragging with them the boy tapster with John's clothing. The sick Pursuivant is also brought in, accusing the real Faukenbridge of drugging him. The tapster gives confirmatory details, a story that Richard identifies in an aside as Gloster's kind of joke. The Pursuivant complains to Faukenbridge about his stealing his box with the warrant, but Faukenbridge denies the theft. This time it is John who declares that the culprit must have been Skinke, whereas Richard says it must have been Gloster. They all leave, Faukenbridge setting off with John to Blackheath to find the hermit while Richard goes off to woo Lady Faukenbridge. His object is to help her save her brother Gloster's life in return for her love, an act that anticipates Angelo's blackmailing offer to Isabella in *Measure for Measure*.

Scene 11 begins '*Enter Robin Hood in the Lady Faukenbridges gowne, night attire on his head*' (1747–48). After some byplay with a page and the stammering Redcap, '*the Porter with his cloake muffled*' (1810) – Redcap's innocent father, now freed from prison – appears. He is also concealing his identity, though he is not actually in disguise. Speaking as the lady, Robin predicts that the old man will become better than a porter in the future. Richard's arrival to woo her is then announced and Robin leaves to speak with him. But Richard's wooing has to wait until the real lady has launched her own disguise, so the next scene starts with Skinke entering once again '*like a Hermit*' (1844), followed by '*Ladie Faukenbridge in Merchants wives attire*' (1851). Skinke sees through her disguise when she asks him about Gloster, but John and her husband who soon join them do not. Both pursuers, deceived by her disguise, praise her beauty, and Faukenbridge gives her his ring as a token of his love, starting the process that will get his wife revenge for his possessive jealousy. In his turn Skinke quietly decides to rob both John and Faukenbridge.

It is at this point that a short dialogue explains the main disguisings for anyone who might still be confused, and reminds the more alert of the many shifts they have already enjoyed. John asks Skinke where Gloster is, 'That in my cloathes brake prison in the Fleete?' (1910). 'No, it was Skinke', replies Skinke as the hermit, and tells him what happened.

Knowe thrise honour'd Prince, that Skinke did cousen Redcap of his cloathes.
Gloster did couzen Skinke, and so escapt.   (1917–19)

'Twas Skinke in Glosters gowne, whome you did visit,' he adds, 'That
playd at bowles and after stole your cloths.' (1923–24). The disguised
Skinke offers just as much of the truth as is in his own interest.

Lady Faukenbridge's disguise is also working well. John underlines the
chronic lechery of the royal family by proposing that the two of them
should go out onto the heath where, he says, 'ile venter for a baby' (1966).
She agrees and suggests they meet at the Hinde tavern. In an aside she says
that she will send the 'princess' to John in her place, hinting at a bed trick.
Skinke tells Faukenbridge that the hermit has told him it was Skinke who
escaped them at the Salutation Inn and who had the chain. Moreover,
he prophesies, in half an hour Skinke will attempt a robbery on the heath.
The text here gives us no exit for Skinke, John or Faukenbridge, though
they must depart somehow, leaving the lady alone to go into the hermit's
cell. First Skinke emerges from it *with a patch on his face, and a Faulconers
lure in his hand* (2008–09) in pursuit of John and Faukenbridge.
He heads off and the lady enters his cell, where she finds 'a beard?
A counterfeited hayre? / The Hermits portes? Garments and his beades?'
(2020–21). She worries that the 'murderer (as I ges him one)' (2024) will
attack Faukenbridge and Prince John, but reckons that they can defend
themselves, and so flees. Disguised as a falconer Skinke meets John and
Faukenbridge, claiming to have just lost his hawk to a thief. John says
'There are caves hereabout good fellow are there not?' and Skinke replies
'Yes sir, tread the ground sir, & you shal heare their hollowness, this way
sir this way' (2043–45). John and Faukenbridge fall down the stage trap
and Skinke forces John to throw his purse up to him before running
off. The victims climb out and concluding, rightly for once, that the
hermit who tricked them must have been Skinke they set off back to his
cell for revenge.

The danger of assuming that the hermit must be Skinke is heralded in
the next scene, which opens with *'Gloster in the Hermits gowne, putting on
the beard'* (2070–71). Disguised as the pursuivant he has found the cell
after his sister fled, concluding, quite reasonably, 'Sure he that keeps this
Cell is a counterfeit, / Else what does he here with false hayre and beard?'
(2074–75). Skinke enters and finds Gloster in the distance wearing his own
disguise and walking 'devoutly like my counterfeit' (2084). Announcing
that he has a second gown he leaves by one door as John and Faukenbridge
enter by another. They see Gloster walking meditatively. From the posture

and the book Gloster is carrying they conclude that the new hermit cannot be Skinke, 'he is a learned reverend holy man' (2095). John tells the disguised Gloster as holy man that they would have thought him a thief, since he (actually Skinke) had told them they would soon meet a robber. The disguised Gloster tells them it was Gloster who took Faukenbridge's chain and John's sword and saved the porter. When John curses Gloster the pseudo-hermit defends him, making a pious prediction that Gloster will soon appear before John's father the king. John chooses to ignore the political implications of that assertion and thanks him for his prophecy, promising to build him a shrine where he will be worshipped. The two angry men head off to Stepney, while the disguised Gloster goes off in search of the other fake hermit.

Scene 15 returns to Prince Richard's wooing of the lady, opening as Richard enters '*with musicke*' to sing a serenade he has penned for Lady Faukenbridge. As the lady Robin Hood begs him to send the musicians away without performing. Knowing what was in Richard's mind, he/she begs Richard to save her brother Gloster, promising sex in return. Richard asks if she knows where Robin Hood has got to and Robin replies that she sent him off 'Upon some business of import for me' (2220). He/she promises Richard to 'be your bedfellow, and from that hour / Forsweare the loathed bed of Faukenbridge' (2228–29), if only he will save Gloster. In the opening lines of the play Robin had told Skinke 'I am [Richard's] ward, his Chamberlaine & bed-fellow' (30), so it was not a false promise. When Richard leaves in joyful anticipation Robin expresses his gratitude at 'this devise', because 'He would else have tyred me with his sighes and songs' (2236–37).

Lady Faukenbridge returns to Robin still dressed as a merchant's wife and they exchange their news. She asks him to stay disguised as her because her husband, now hotly pursuing the person he thinks is the merchant's wife, is 'almost at the gate'. On his arrival, hearing that the merchant's wife has already arrived Faukenbridge protests his innocence to Robin, thinking he is excusing himself to his wife. His real wife, still in the merchant's dress, he accuses of telling his wife about his offer. She denies it: 'I tel your wife? Thinke ye I am such a beast?' (2285). So to his apparent wife, the disguised Robin, Faukenbridge embarks on an excuse that he promised the merchant wife's husband 'some two thousand pound: or more perchance' (2292) in a secret business deal. He then asks her to leave him alone with the merchant's wife to sort the matter out. When Robin expresses doubt Faukenbridge scorns what he says is her jealousy and tells her he knows Prince Richard has been

her guest. Robin leaves and Faukenbridge says to the lady who he thinks is
not his wife

> Ah wench content thee, I must bear her hard,
> Else she'l be prining into my dalliances:
> I am an olde man sweet girle I must be merry,
> All steele, al spright, keep in health by change,
> Men may be wanton, women must not range.   (2313–17)

His disguised wife says that is good counsel for wives and gives him his
ring back. Still trying to get her consent he protests that she had told him
her husband was 'an unthrift', which she admits is true. 'Indeed my
husband is a bankrout, / Of faith, of love, of shame, of chastity, / Dotes
upon other women more then me' (2324–26), she says, truth in disguise.
He says such a truth must mean that her husband is ripe for cuckolding
and asks if he is old or young. She replies, again with perfect truth, that he
is 'About your age'.

The trick runs in that vein for another hundred lines, Robin returning
to quiz Faukenbridge about what he would do if his wife were to adopt
the policy he had just announced. When the real wife reveals the two
impersonations and exposes his pretences Faukenbridge first tries Falstaff's
trick, pretending that he knew all along who she really was. Ridiculed,
however, he is finally made to swear that he will be loyal to her and never
be jealous again. The scene ends with Robin riding off to the hermit's cell
at Blackheath in pursuit of Gloster. Faukenbridge proposes that they play
the same trick on Prince John that he has just undergone, reaffirming the
bed-trick idea his wife proposed much earlier.

In Scene 16 Gloster, still as the hermit, after sending Redcap running
off to search for the missing Gloster meets Richard, dressed '*like a Serving
man*' (2465), followed by Skinke in a similar hermit garb to Gloster's.
'Hath got his other sute since I went foorth', says Gloster (2471), of
Skinke, who runs away. Richard has to decide which of the two hermits
he will ask about Gloster's whereabouts, making the obvious choice of the
one who did not run away and is now 'at his beades'. But when he
approaches the new hermit Gloster reveals a buckler and a 'bilbowe blade'
under his gown (2492), and seeing Richard only as 'some lover' (2489)
demands his purse. They fight three lengthy bouts, each learning to
respect the other's skill, until Robin Hood arrives. A stage direction
specifies the last bout: '*Fight. Enter Robin Hood, they breath, offer again*'
(2517–18). At first failing to recognise Richard, Robin offers to fight in
defence of what he thinks is the older man, Gloster, still in his hermit's

disguise. But he and Gloster identify Richard at the same moment as a friend, and they are reconciled. Gloster, for all his disguise as a false prophet, then predicts the final court scene where the old king is expected to be humbled as Prince Henry's cup-bearer.

Richard and Robin leave Gloster, who meets his ally Lancaster, who tells Gloster he has also been beaten and robbed by Skinke, so Gloster resolves to rob the thief. A break in the text at line 2600 then puts Skinke on stage, with Gloster in the background. The clown Redcap enters, and Skinke resolves to rob him. The two men both dressed as hermits then confront Redcap, each accusing the other of being a counterfeit. Redcap strikes with his cudgel at Gloster, who trips him and pushes Skinke into his place. The fracas is stopped by the entry through opposing doors of two nobles, Leicester who backed young Henry in the first court scene, and Lancaster who backed the old king, each with their followers. Both hermits renew their claims that the other is the counterfeit, until Redcap says Skinke has a sword and buckler under his gown, and Lancaster finds that his own stolen possessions are there too. Gloster then tries to attack Skinke with his sword, and both hermits are arrested, identified (at last) as their real selves, and taken off to the court for judgement.

In Scene 17 Robin Hood and Lady Faukenbridge tell Prince Richard of the trick played on him, Robin declaring 'twas I in her attire that promist you' (2714). They make peace until Faukenbridge enters '*in his hose and doublet*', ready for Prince John's revels at a city tavern where the bed trick will be played using John's princess. In the brief Scene 18 that follows John, Richard and Faukenbridge with John's Isabel receive from Redcap the news of the capture of Gloster and Skinke, and after demanding the Porter be brought there too they all rush to the court for the finale.

The final scene, 19, opens with a sennet and a procession of the crowned princes with the royal regalia, followed by '*Henry the elder bareheaded*' (2823). There are no disguises here. Instead a comparable service is done by the symbolic ceremonials of the chair of state and the crowns and coronets. '*Henry the elder places his Sonne, the two Queenes on eyther hand, himselfe at his feete, Leyster and Lancaster below him.*' From the royal seat Prince Henry asks why Gloster is not wearing his coronet. Gloster's answer is abrupt: 'Because his Soveraigne doth not weare a Crowne' (2851–52). For the same reason Gloster sits on the ground, not amongst the other nobles (2864). An explanatory dialogue follows with Redcap, Skinke and Gloster all telling their stories of disguise and trickery. As king Prince Henry forgives Skinke, and orders Gloster's right hand struck off, despite Lady Faukenbridge's pleas. Richard objects, but John angrily counters him. Queen Elinor urges 'Harry off with his hand, then with his head' (3042). Prince Henry orders his bareheaded father to fill the official cup with wine for him: 'To day your Office is to beare our cupp' (3048). To Gloster's outspoken outrage King Henry kneels to his son. Young Henry orders Leicester to give Gloster wine, but Gloster throws it in Leicester's face. Some fuss follows about who should execute Gloster, until out of the blue Prince Henry reverses his position, embraces Gloster, and orders the princes to kneel to his father and 'cast your Coronets before his Crowne' (3134).

This reversal brings the framing pseudo-history to an end. Queen Elinor's and John's fury is quelled by Prince Henry, who renounces the world.

> Off with these silkes, my garments shall be gray,
> My shirt hard hayre, my bed the ashey dust,
> My pillow but a lumpe of hardned clay:
> For clay I am, and unto clay I must,
> O I beseech ye let me goe alone,
> To live, where my loose life I may bemone.   (3165–70)

Like Shakespeare's Mowbray in *Richard II* Prince Richard announces that he will go to Palestine as a soldier of Christ. Gloster, backed by Skinke of all people, announces that he will fight the Moors in Portugal.

Short of identical twins the author makes use of just about every twist in the disguise game to be found anywhere in this sort of drama. Composed by someone utterly at home with the Rose repertory, it exploits the playhouse's open-stage features to the full. The central opening is the hermit's cell, Skinke makes Faukenbridge and Prince John fall down the stage trap (2044–47), and the court ceremony with trumpets, the centrally-positioned chair of state and regal crowns and coronets adorn the framing scenes. Scene 2 where the split within the court is set out deploys the rituals of royalty that are to be defaced and then set right in the last scene. All but Gloster are positioned there according to their rank (76–98). The play maintains traditional blocking with the central opening serving both as the *locus* for royal entrances and parodically as the fake hermit's cave whence truth emerges in contorted forms.[17] At the end of the first court scene royal discord is marked by separate exits through the opposing doors on each side of the stage, '*Exeunt with Trumpets two*

---

[17] For the symbolic function of the *locus*, see Robert Weimann, *Author's Pen and Actor's Voice. Playing and Writing in Shakespeare's Theatre*, Cambridge University Press, 2000, pp. 67–68 and elsewhere.

waies', whereas in the finale, the happy ending that confirms the old King's authority, they all walk off in harmony together through the central opening.

In all, the play has sixteen disguisings. Five of them are Skinke's, four Gloster's, two by Lady Faukenbridge and Robin Hood, two by the clowns, and one involuntarily by Prince John in Gloster's gown. The Pursuivant and Prince Richard appear in simpler disguises. Sixteen of the nineteen scenes have one or more tricks of disguising, the only exceptions the major confrontations at the royal court. Disguise utilises all the familiar games, false prophesying, robbery, overhearing the truth in disguise, a bed trick, eavesdropping to discover information, and the exposure of uxorious pretence.

The steeplechase of a plot shows a writer who knew exactly what sort of story he could expect the players to exploit and just what devices the players could use to make it all work. The nineteen scenes introduce twenty-seven characters, with unspecified walk-ons playing the watch, sheriffs and officers and huntsmen, plus two heralds with trumpets and one or more people who enter in Scene 15 to play 'Music'.[18] There is no obvious need to double any role. Each of the two major court scenes, 2 and 19, has the same thirteen speaking characters. The final scene has sixteen people on stage, four of them boys playing women, of whom three speak. Lady Faukenbridge's part is substantial. Two of the other boys, Queen Elinor and the younger Henry's wife, have very small parts, while the fourth, John's Isabel, is silent throughout. The play was designed for the company with considerable precision. The working title for the play must have been what Henslowe called it, 'Desgysses'. It is mildly regrettable that, coming as it does from the early phase when Henslowe did not note any payments to his writers, there is little to say who wrote it.

Throughout the 1590s the company's known writers kept inventing new forms. One of the major innovators whose credentials have hardly ever been recognised was William Haughton. He started the run of comedies set in London with *Englishmen for My Money*, and the idea of comedies about the Devil with *Grim the Collier of Croydon* (more will said in Chapter 5 about both plays). Haughton had an acute ear for novelty, possibly adding the London horror story *Two Lamentable Tragedies* to his London-set comedies, working with Chettle and Dekker on *Patient Grissill*, and very likely launching the company's series of biblical plays

---

[18] The stage direction has Richard entering '*with musicke*'. The speech heading for the one line he or they speak gives only '*Musi*', but the exit line says '*Exeunt Musicke*'.

with *Judas* in 1600. But isolating the skills and the special contributions of particular writers is not a central function of this company history.

A point that is more relevant along with the emphasis on disguise is the prevalence of features of staging that needed little in the way of major properties. Spectacle was a feature in some of the surviving play-texts but in general few properties other than costumes were called for by the principal repertory. If we knew more about the hundreds of lost plays it might be possible to make a distinction between the many plays needing little more than costumes and small disguise features like false noses, which were therefore easy to take on tour, and those like Greene's *Friar Bacon* and Marlowe's *Jew of Malta* at the Rose or *The Duchess of Suffolk* at the Fortune which demanded major properties or features such as a trapdoor if they were to be properly staged. What was written for the company settled at the Rose would not necessarily be easy to take on tour, which the company did with some of its repertory in most years. For all its need of a trap to take Faustus down to hell at the end, Marlowe's second great opus seems to have been toured in both of the surviving versions. *Faustus* was surprisingly portable provided the players had fireworks for their devils and carried with them Faustus's false head and similarly small devices for the clowning scenes. *Tamburlaine*, for all its need of a two-wheeled chariot, was also certainly taken on tour, both before 1594 and in later years by the Fortune company. The *Diary's* inventories give us long lists of properties used on stage, but the number of items that can be identified as features of specific surviving play-texts staged in London is surprisingly small.

Staging tricks like disguise were a direct consequence of the company playing as one of the only two licensed to perform for Londoners. That, however, did not stop them from doing what had been everyone's routine practice before May 1594. The profits that came in various forms from the company's assured base in London never stopped them from continuing to take a selection of their plays around the country. However well settled they felt at the Rose they went on tour almost every summer, much more frequently than their opposites the Chamberlain's Men, and even in most winters through the time when London closed all playing down for the forty days of Lent. In early 1597 they seem to have registered the strength of their position at their London base by continuing to play through part of Lent, at least in March (*Diary*, p. 56). Generally, though, they chose to break up their long year of daily performances every summer. The Privy Council's closure orders because of plague applied mostly to the warmer months, but even when there were no orders to close the London playhouses they seem to have enjoyed travelling for up to three months through the summer. Taking only three or four plays, each staged once at every stopover, was a holiday of sorts after the hectic daily changes in London. From very early on they learned to rely on their audiences at the Rose to give them the constant feedback that helped to establish not just their repertory but their best stage practices. How easy they found it to take the Rose plays on a holiday tour testifies to the flexibility of their staging practices as much as it does to the professionalism of their teamwork.

Mostly their travels took them to the west and south, but they did on occasion go as far north as Coventry and Leicester. Access by water seems to have been a major determinant in their choice of routes for touring.[19] Coastal shipping could take them as far north as Newcastle, where they played in April 1597. That was one of the many ports that served their travels. In several winters during the Lent closures in February and March they toured the Kentish towns. Indeed, if we include Kentish ports such as Faversham, which along with Rye and Folkestone joined Hastings, Hythe, New Romney, Sandwich and Dover as the 'cinque ports' in those years, records of their visits to the port towns greatly strengthen the likelihood that they normally travelled by water with their plays, personnel and props from London rather than by road. Even allowing for the fairly good condition of the Tudor highways between, say, the port of Bristol and inland Shrewsbury, where Alleyn journeyed with Strange's Men in August 1593, there were major advantages to transporting a company by water. The twelve or more adult players travelling with their boys and stagehands (that was the number Cambridge barred from performing in 1616) could be accommodated more easily and probably more cheaply on a boat than on carts and horseback.

The ports they visited besides Bristol and the Kentish cinque ports included Southampton, Lyme Regis, Exeter, Plymouth, Barnstaple, Bridgwater, Gloucester, Norwich, Ipswich, Dunwich, York and Newcastle. During the long plague closure of 1603–04 they went up to York, readily accessible from the North Sea by boat as John Taylor the Water Poet demonstrated in 1622.[20] The visit to Newcastle in 1597, which the early

---

[19] A full list of the records retrieved by the *Records of Early English Drama* is printed in Appendix 3.

[20] Taylor travelled all over England and parts of Scotland, publishing his travelogues in doggerel verse. In 1622 he took a battered London wherry, propelled by two oars and a sail, from London to York, sailing first up the North Sea to Cromer, the northernmost cinque port, then inland by river through Lincolnshire to Hull, including one day when they rowed a hundred miles to get across the Wash to Boston, and thence to the River Ouse and York. His lively account of the voyage (along with a much more succinct report of the return on horseback) was issued in 1622 as *A Very Merry*

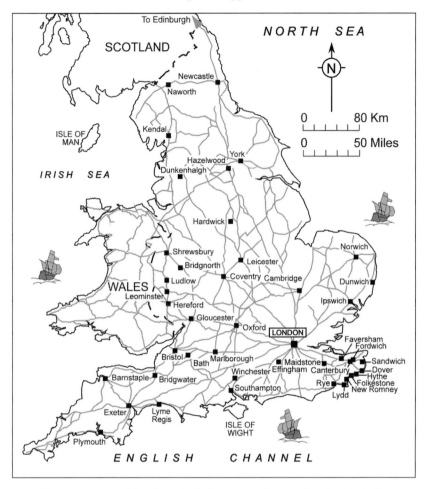

Figure 5. A map of the places, including country houses, that the Admiral's
and Prince's Men are known to have visited between 1594 and 1625. Drawn from
the *REED* evidence by Subhash Shanbhag.

Admiral's had visited in 1593, might well have been part of a longer tour
inland through the north that started from the port. In all they are on
record as visiting twenty-two ports compared with fifteen inland towns,
most of which, like Shrewsbury and Canterbury, had their own good
access by river.

Wherry-Ferry-Voyage: OR Yorke *for My Money: sometimes Perilous, sometimes Quarrellous, Performed
with a paire of Oares, by Sea from* London, *by John Taylor, and Job Pennell.* 1622.

Four great houses appear on the map of their recorded travels, including the Lord Admiral's own titular estate of Effingham, although there is no clear evidence that his company ever attended him there with their plays.[21] His consistent support for playing in London appears to have been stimulated more by the desire to entertain his queen than to enjoy the plays for himself.

The choice of plays to take on tour must always have been simple: those that did not demand too much elaborate staging and those which had already secured a good reputation. It seems unlikely they would have taken very many of their disguise plays, which depended on an audience already familiar with the players' faces. Nor do they seem to have travelled with *The Jew of Malta*, which lays down heavy demands for staging its finale, when Barabbas is made to fall down from the upper stage into the hellish cauldron that he had been seen and heard contriving on the stage balcony. His own visible carpentry specified in the 1633 edition's stage directions preludes the eventful staging, '*with a Hammar above, very busie*' (5.5.0 sd) followed by his appearance below in the cauldron – '*the cable cut, a Caldron discovered*' (5.5.62 sd). But evidence for which plays went on tour is almost non-existent. It is a great pity that local officials in the towns never bothered to note play titles. Alleyn does mention travelling with *Harry of Cornwall* at Bristol, but that was when he was with Strange's in February 1593. The only clear evidence for a play the company might have taken with it comes from Ludlow in Shropshire in 1620. In that year at least two local boys were christened with the outstanding and quite exceptional name of the hero from the company's Marlowe repertory. Tamburlaine Davies (1620–1685) later became High Bailiff of Ludlow. His fellow mercer Tamberlane Bowdler was also born there in 1620.[22]

---

[21] In apparent contrast to Howard, his father-in-law Henry Carey may have helped the other duopoly company with extra work at Christmas. The famous *Gesta Grayorum* with its report about the Prince of Purpoole, and the 'Night of Errors' when the Lord Chamberlain's Men performed *A Comedy of Errors* for them was far from their only evening trip to a Westminster Inn of Court to entertain the lawyers. John Manningham wrote in his diary about *Twelfth Night* at the Candlemas feast in Middle Temple Hall in February 1602, and later records from the Inns show regular professional performances at their Candlemas and All Saints festivities. The Christmas invitation to Gray's Inn in December 1594 possibly resulted from the fact that Carey as new patron of the Chamberlain's was a member of Gray's Inn. Either he suggested the idea to that year's Prince, or the Prince thought it a nice compliment to a senior member of the Inn to invite the new company of which he was patron to perform. The absence of evidence from the *Diary* showing Charles Howard doing similar things for his new company says nothing about his personal interest in plays. The Palsgrave's staged a play at the Middle Temple at Candlemas 1616, when Juby received £12 for the company in payment (*REED Westminster*, ed. Alan H. Nelson, forthcoming), but that was long after Howard had given up his patronage.

[22] Rick Bowers, '*Tamburlaine* in Ludlow', *Notes and Queries* 243 (1998), 361–63.

Such extraordinary baptismal names indicate the impact the play must have had on their parents. The *REED* volumes note a visit in that year by the Palsgrave's company to Leominster in Herefordshire, only twelve miles south of Ludlow.

It seems that the old tradition of travelling was a far more routine and frequent activity than on the occasions when the Privy Council stopped London playing. The contract Henslowe made out for Richard Jones when he returned to the company after the 1597 closure of Pembroke's at the Swan was explicit about that. He was to play 'in my howsse only knowne by the name of the Rosse & in no other howse a bowt London publicke & yf Restraynte be granted then to go for the tyme into the contrey & after to retorne agayne to London'.[23] The entire company travelled together, and did not, as is usually assumed, send out only a limited party of players. We know that from the list of Palsgrave's Men the Cambridge authorities wrote down in 1616 in their order to ban them from playing.[24]

Money was a constant need. The other time of year when the company customarily travelled was in the worst of winter, during February and March. This must have been a direct consequence of the frequently renewed ban on any playing in London through Lent. Leaving London at such a time is distinctive because when Henslowe started to get his players to sign contracts to play at the Rose in 1597 he always made their contracts run from the day they signed until Shrove Tuesday a year or more following. Shrove Tuesday, once called Pancake Day, when the remnant fats from the meat-eating that was banned for Lent were consumed, heralded the beginning of the forty days of Christian fasting up to Easter. Henslowe must have expected that playing would have to stop at the Rose on that day, making it the best time for any reorganisation of the company's membership.

Travelling through Lent certainly became one of the company's distinctive routines. The earlier Admiral's are known to have played at Ipswich in February 1586, and at Shrewsbury in February 1593, though this second visit was during that year's seemingly endless closure for

---

[23] *Diary*, pp. 239–40.

[24] The old delusion that the 'bad' quartos must represent texts cut for touring with reduced casts has been well disproved. The odds are that, particularly in the earlier years, all the playbooks used were routinely trimmed in length for performance on stage in London itself. The relatively high proportion of Admiral's plays that survive in shortened versions of less than 2,000 lines is a testimony to their theatrical origins but certainly not evidence for their use by the company only when travelling.

plague in London. The new Admiral's certainly played at Faversham in February 1596 and in March 1602, and the company was recorded at Fordwich in March 1614, at Cambridge in March 1616, at Coventry in March 1617, and at Sandwich, Fordwich and Dover through February and March 1621. The *Diary* (p. 130) has a note dated 6 February 1600 for Robert Shaa to buy a drum 'when to go into the contry'. The Admiral's were by no means the only company to take their plays on tour through Lent, so it must have been a standard way of keeping up a company's income. It seems only London was firm in enforcing the official closure for Lent.[25]

The clerks of most towns and parishes across England kept records in their archives of the payments their mayors or councils made to the companies that visited and played in their region. These records appear in the many volumes of the *Records of Early English Drama*, a work still in progress. Sadly, this huge archive has very few notes about one of the more intriguing features of the London companies on their travels, their visits to great houses to entertain the families and servants of rich land-owning lords. Summer was the time when most of the rich left London for their country estates, some of them to avoid the plague and others because the royal court and the law courts were out of session. That, along with the greater pleasure of travelling in warm weather on dry roads or by water, was a good reason for the London companies to make their own tours in summer. The Chamberlain's Men, for instance, seem to have quite frequently visited Shropshire, where Henry Herbert, the second earl of Pembroke, had his official residence as Lord President of the Welsh Marches. Some of the Chamberlain's players had very likely been in a company under Herbert's patronage in 1592–93. In later years his two sons William and Philip, the third and fourth earls, both of whom came to serve the king as Lord Chamberlain, also received company visits at Ludlow in Shropshire and at their main residence at Wilton in Hampshire. They were co-dedicatees of the first Shakespeare Folio. The Admiral's Men had a much shorter distance to travel to serve their own lord but there is nothing to say he ever summoned them either to his London house or to his estate at Effingham. Many other rich dignitaries, however, might

---

[25] Knowledge of the Lenten closure for players was certainly in the Mayor of Canterbury's mind in 1636, when he wrote a complaint to Archbishop Laud about a London company causing trouble in a week of performances 'especially in this tyme of abstynence' during Lent. The archbishop took the point, and punished them for them breaking the Lenten order. See Gurr, 'The Loss of Records for the Travelling Companies in Stuart Times', *Records of Early English Drama Newsletter* 19 (1994), 2–19, p. 15.

have called on their services through the summer. Up to now, though, information about the Admiral's company going to such destinations is minimal. A slightly grumpy note in the *Diary* (p. 88) records three shillings paid to a carrier 'for carrying & bryngyn of the stufe backe agayne when they played in fleatstreat pryvat & then owr stufe was loste', an irritating extra charge for a visit presumably to perform at a lord's house in Westminster. The only other tangible evidence for the company fulfilling such commissions is a record that on Candlemas 1616, the same festive day in February that the Chamberlain's Men played *Twelfth Night* for the Middle Templars, the Palsgrave's were invited by the same party of young lawyers to perform an unspecified play there. Edward Juby signed a receipt for the twelve pounds the company was paid for its show.[26]

From the few records that have survived, travelling to a great house does not seem to have offered very high financial returns, but a major country estate would of course offer bed and board to its visitors on a fairly grand and handsome scale. The level of profit from travelling and the size of the payments made to London companies on tour have proved almost impossible to identify, not just because of the dearth of evidence from great house records but because the town and parish archives usually noted only what the mayor gave the companies for performances at the local guildhall and not whatever else the gatherers might secure at that or any other useable site in town. The Leicester clerks routinely noted the payments made by the council as 'more than was gathered' by the company, or as New Romney put it, the town's payment was 'for the benevolentes of the touneship'. Sometimes the clerks also noted payments made in kind, such as food and drink, or wine with sugar, as Gloucester did when the Admiral's played there in 1595–96. The main income from the towns visited must have come from commercial performances presented to the townsfolk at large. In later years, when the Master of the Revels took over the censorship that town mayors used to exercise, companies no longer had to perform before the mayor and most guild-halls closed their doors on the players. As a result they used courtyards of inns such as the Swan at Norwich, for which no financial and few other records survive.

Plague closures in London usually directed the company to parts of the country that were not oppressed by the current epidemic. But summer

---

[26] The information about this visit will appear in the Inns of Court volume of the *REED* papers, edited by Alan H. Nelson. I am grateful to Alan H. Nelson for his paper 'Professional Performances at the Inns of Court', which outlines all the known evidence.

tours were so popular with the players that tours were organised even when the lists of deaths from plague in London's 126 parishes did not reach a level high enough to warrant the Privy Council's closure orders. In 1595, their full first summer after starting at the Rose, the Admiral's company set off out of London in June. This excursion was not prompted by any closure order from the Privy Council, although the Council did express concern over apprentice riots in London on 13 June at Southwark market and on 23 June at Billingsgate market. These disturbances, which the Lord Mayor complained were hatched at the playhouses, may have been what prompted the company to make a tactful departure. They are on record that summer as playing at Bath and Maidstone, but started back at the Rose on 25 August. In the next year, 1596, the Privy Council did issue an order restraining playing on 22 July, and the Admiral's promptly left London, returning to the Rose on 27 October (payments to the company by Henslowe restarted two weeks before that). In 1597 another Privy Council ban came on 28 July, this time the notorious order to pull down all the playhouses. Henslowe records that again the company kept away from London between 28 July and 27 October.[27] The latter date, Michaelmas, seems to have been the usual time for the Privy Council to allow playing to resume after a summer suspension.

In the summer of 1598, their first without Alleyn, the company for once played at the Rose throughout, but in 1599 Henslowe recorded no receipts between 3 June and early October. This either indicates a plague closure, in spite of the fact that there were actually very few recorded deaths from the plague that summer, or more likely the company's wish to take its usual summer holiday. They seem to have gone on tour again early in February 1600, shortly before the usual Lent closure, since on 6 February Henslowe noted that they bought 'a drome to go into the contry'. A note dated 10 February was about payments 'sence we left playing'. That was at the Rose. Some time that November they opened at the Fortune, after a summer which must have once again been occupied with touring. Henslowe has no payments for the month up to 14 August, and the company is on record as playing at Canterbury and Bath. Early in November, shortly before they opened at the Fortune, they went north to perform for the Cavendish family at Hardwick Hall.

---

[27] The *Diary*, p. 236, notes an undated loan of 40s to Alleyn to lend to John Singer and Thomas Towne 'when they went into the contrey'. A marginal note adds 'at ther last comynge', which may signify the 1597 travels. The preceding note, a loan of £3 for Edward Dutton, is dated 14 March 1597.

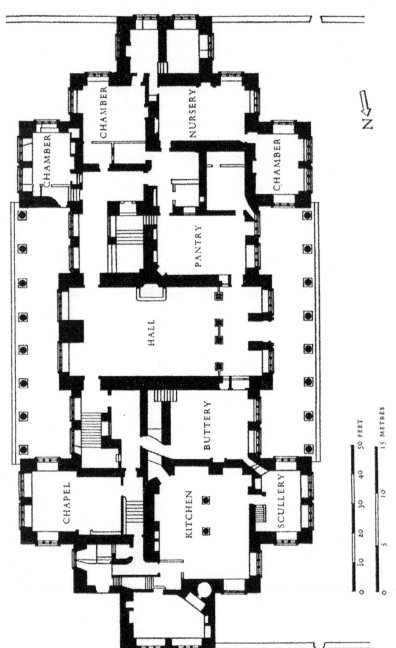

Figure 6. A plan of Hardwick Hall, ground floor, showing the central hall with its great fireplace and the posts upholding the gallery. On a winter visit (November), the players would most likely have used the space opposite the fireplace as their stage. The plan is from John Summerson, *Architecture in Great Britain 1530 to 1830*, Penguin Books, 1953, p. 34.

For the years from 1601 up to the great plague epidemic that followed Elizabeth's death in March 1603 Henslowe's records of the Fortune company mostly concerned 'ther privet deates' for Bird, Shaa, Jones and Downton, notes about payments to the writers for new plays, and occasional payments for new attire for the plays. The *REED* records show travels to the Kentish ports but not to any more distant places. During the long closure of 1603–04 the travels were much more extensive, taking them as far north as York. Henslowe has a note of the totals due to him dated 5 May 1603, the day, he says, 'when we leafte of playe now at the kynges cominge'. Probably they stayed in London until then hoping for an early renewal of playing. By the new year they were back at the Fortune. On 15 March 1604, when London could at last celebrate James's arrival with a formal entry into the city through five arches erected for him to pass under from his start at the Tower, Alleyn was chosen to stand and make a speech to the king from the centre of the arch in Fenchurch Street called Londinium (Illustration 4). By then, however, he had made his second and final withdrawal from playing, so his absence on his arch did not discomfort the company if they performed that day.

These first two chapters have tried to give a rough outline of the company's thirty-two-year history, patchy though it has to be in so many ways. We have considered some of the more distinctive features, including individual biographies, the repertory innovations and the company's tours in some detail, however inadequately. It now remains first to look a little more closely at what more can be gleaned from the all too often enigmatic entries in the *Diary*, before going into detailed analysis of the Rose and Fortune's structures as the company's principal venues along with some analysis of the staging there of the surviving play-texts. Almost the only record of the company's career after 1603 lies in the regrettably few of its plays that got into print. The general tag of 'citizen' repertory that came to attach itself to the Fortune by 1615 marks out a series of plays that seem less inventive than those of its first decade, but that do show a fairly consistent allegiance to the London citizenry and the handicraft artisans and apprentices who were celebrated so tongue-in-cheek by Dekker with *The Shoemaker's Holiday* of 1599. A closer look at this repertory is in Chapter 5. The first challenge though is to examine some of the complications inherent in the material information of Henslowe's accounts, and then some of the more striking features of the company's accomplishments as they appear in print and manuscript from the company's extant play-texts.

3

Henslowe's accounts and the play-texts

Henslowe's Diary is not the sort of book that a modern auditor would enjoy going through. In no way is it an account book, although it had some sort of official status since Henslowe used it to record the signatures of witnesses to loans that he made. Of his notes about his loans to the players Neil Carson says: 'These scattered records do not look like the accounts of a professional money-lender; they have more the appearance of the rather casual efforts of a man to keep track of his personal loans.'[1] They are personal to the extent that, for instance, the records of his dealings with the Admiral's come to an end when they moved to the Fortune. He had a financial interest in the Fortune but seems to have left its accounts together with those of its resident company in his son-in-law's hands from 10 July 1600, when the *Diary* has an entry that seems to mark a summing-up. Certainly he started a new set of accounts with Worcester's in it from 28 October when they began to play at the Rose, and even after that date he continued to enter the loans he made to the Admiral's, although, fatally for auditing purposes, he made no entries of any repayments. Only in the most rudimentary way does the *Diary* record Henslowe's full accounts for his theatre business.

Out of the chaos of the *Diary*'s throng of jottings Bernard Beckerman[2] tried to impose order by identifying four phases in Henslowe's relationships with the various playing companies. The first, which he calls the 'early Rose' period from before 1592 when the *Diary* starts until Alleyn's 'retirement' at the end of 1597, involved him acting largely as theatre landlord. This was when he recorded what he took daily from the performances as his rental income. The second, the 'later Rose–Fortune' period, from 1598 to 1603 or so, shows him in a more direct financial and

---

[1] Neil Carson, *A Companion to Henslowe's Diary*, Cambridge University Press, 1988, p. 10.
[2] Bernard Beckerman, 'Philip Henslowe', in *The Theatrical Manager in England and America*, ed. Joseph W. Donohue Jr., Princeton, 1971.

managerial role. This was what Beckerman calls his 'banker' time, when he recorded mainly the loans and payments made in his dealings with the Admiral's. Towards the end of this period he seems to have left most of the Admiral's Men's business with Alleyn at the Fortune while he concentrated first on the new company using the Rose near his house and then on his Bear-master role at the Bear Garden. That led to the third period, his 'Bear Garden' time, when he and his son-in-law chiefly made their fortunes from the bears. The final period was his most managerial, what Beckerman calls the 'Hope' period from 1613, when he built the Hope as a dual-purpose theatre and baiting-house. That was a not insignificant change since, after eight years without any playhouse on Bankside to manage, he signed the contract for it within a month of the adjacent Globe's burning down in July 1613.

It was in the third and fourth periods, according to the *Complaint* by the Lady Elizabeth's Men, that he worked as theatre impresario, running and then dismantling up to five acting companies through the period between about 1604 and his death in 1616. This is distinctly odd because throughout that period he had no playhouse to use.[3] For the sake of the Admiral's history, though, questions should focus chiefly on the second of Beckerman's four periods, when he argues that Henslowe made the transition from landlord to financier and became England's first theatre and company manager and impresario. The difficulty with that is identifying the effect of this change in roles and what ought to be a consequent change in the accounts he noted. In the first phase he should have been entering his own expenditure and profits. As the company's banker, however, he should have moved on to recording not his own but the company's expenditure and income. Later still, as impresario, he should have returned to recording just his own outgoings and income. The main challenge in interpreting his figures is to identify which role he was in when he made each entry.

Finding how and when Beckerman's transitions from landlord to manager and from financier to impresario took place needs other evidence than Henslowe's papers. What would have been the most valuable single relic is the company's own records, or at least the separate account-book that Alleyn must have kept. Some outline of the company's own financial transactions that did not appear in Henslowe's book, a guesstimate of

---

[3] For the speculative idea that he might have staged plays at the Bear Garden, see Gurr, 'Bears and Players: Philip Henslowe's Double Acts', *Shakespeare Bulletin* XXX (2004), 31–41.

their likely income and expenditure, is given below, but it wholly lacks the precision and the extraordinary detail of the *Diary*.

Alleyn certainly took on management of the Admiral's / Prince's Men at the Fortune, and retained some control over their operations till 1625. He gave up acting for the second time at the end of 1603, I think in favour of the rewarding business of company and bear management and property acquisition and control. His name is not on the company list of February 1602 yet he was still named as the payee for their court performances until January 1604. It is easiest to see him, even though he continued to live in Southwark, as running the company at the Fortune in Clerkenwell near the Revels Office while Henslowe ran the Rose players and the bears in his home parish on Bankside. After the Rose closed, some time before its lease expired in 1605 and up to the time when Henslowe and Alleyn built the Hope in 1614 (while the Bankside's only other playhouse was rebuilding after its 1613 fire), Henslowe had no playhouse to manage. The Fortune was run by Alleyn. This must mean that Henslowe was operating rather as an impresario and financier than as theatre landlord, the role he started with.

From 1598 to 1603 the *Diary* seems to testify that the management system and Henslowe's relations with the Admiral's did not change significantly, and indeed that the players maintained their authority over their playbooks and the acquisition of new plays throughout the period until the end of 1600 when the Fortune and Rose became joint yet separate exercises. Roslyn Knutson has provided a meticulous analysis of the Admiral's play-buying process through that period.[4] It seems that through such a time of major expansion and investment the players routinely bought their own playbooks. Nothing suggests that Henslowe himself then owned any of the company's stock of plays. This was when Alleyn sold his playbooks to the company, so Knutson's evidence strongly implies the Admiral's Men's autonomy in this period. And yet there are the inventories, including a list of playbooks, drawn up over roughly the same period largely by Alleyn in March 1598,[5] and there is also the

---

[4] Roslyn Lander Knutson, 'The Commercial Significance of the Payments for Playtexts in *Henslowe's Diary, 1597–1603*', *MRDE* 5 (1991), 117–163. The Appendix (pp. 134–63) lists the nineteen or twenty plays paid for in each of those years.

[5] Alleyn has one inventory in his own hand, *Diary* pp. 291–4. It probably dates from his years running the Fortune, or at least after he returned to acting in 1600. He may have been imitating Henslowe's practice in 1598 of making inventories of costumes, properties and playbooks, now that he was running affairs on his own in Finsbury. Some of the items reproduce those in the earlier lists, such as 'will somers cote', and 'pryams hoes'. It also includes new items for old plays, such as 'faustus Jerkin his clok'.

underlying fact that the company's base at the Rose and later at the Fortune guaranteed the necessary and mutually beneficial continuing relationship between the team of sharers in the playing company and their landlord and banker Henslowe. It was a relationship calling for the kind of regular day-to-day exchanges that make one wonder just what place Cuthbert Burbage had with the Chamberlain's Men as a co-owner of the Globe and the Blackfriars but not a company player.

One factor that is worth bearing in mind if we are to see the playhouse landlords turning into impresarios in these years is how ready Alleyn was to share the ownership of the Fortune with the company. Like Richard Burbage's kinship to his father and brother, Alleyn's alliance with 'father' Henslowe must have divided his loyalties. There is a draft lease of 1608 (day and month not filled in), probably drawn up during that long plague closure when the company's opposites, the King's Men, took shares in their new indoor playhouse at Blackfriars. The lease says that for £27 10s Alleyn was to make the player Thomas Downton the holder of a one-thirty-second share in the Fortune for thirteen years along with its income and expenditure proportionately. This must be a mark of Alleyn's desire to integrate the playing team with the financial controllers, an arrangement not unlike what was being developed at the same time by the company sharers at the Globe and Blackfriars.[6] In the event no new sharing deal for the Fortune was executed, but the idea recurred ten years later at the insistence of the players. On 31 October 1618 Alleyn had the leading company sharers to dinner and drew up a bond for all ten of them to pay £200 a year, plus a rundlet of sack and one of claret every Christmas, in return for a 31-year lease of the Fortune. This they were to regret three years later when it burned down along with all their playbooks and properties. But the deal shows that Alleyn was never the hands-on controlling impresario that later businessmen like Beeston and Heton became. And whereabouts in that range of control was Henslowe?

Many questions are thrown up by the incompleteness of Henslowe's *Diary* jottings. Susan Cerasano's view that it contains entries made in batches suggests that its owner thought of it as a formal book of record, but that he allowed or employed other hands to tot up the totals it records.[7] As she asserts, the lengthy periods he spent at court would necessitate the use of assistants in that way. Taking as an example just

[6] See Gurr, *The Shakespeare Company 1594–1642*, Cambridge University Press, 2004, pp. 87–9.
[7] S. P. Cerasano, 'Philip Henslowe and the Elizabethan Court', *Shakespeare Survey* 60 (2007), 49–57, p. 52.

one sort of financial transaction, which I think is potentially as revealing as the marketing of the company's plays to the press, his records of his payments to the Master of the Revels for various licences very likely included payments for plays as well as for his theatre, even in the first Rose period. Edmund Tilney, the Master of the Revels appointed in 1578, who managed the growth and establishment of the professional playing companies for their first thirty years, was a man who seems to have been genuinely devoted to his labours, not least his fees and his duty of censorship. He must have been one of the minds who conceived and enacted the first two major controlling orders in the early history of the London playing companies, the establishment of the Queen's Men as a monopoly in 1583 and then of the Chamberlain's and Admiral's as a duopoly in 1594. Sadly, almost nothing that shows his personal interest in his work survives apart from the remarks he wrote on the manuscript draft of *Sir Thomas More* when he was censoring it.

We have rather more information about Tilney's relative and successor as Master, Sir George Buc, who took on the Mastership in 1610 when Tilney died, having introduced himself to the work by starting to censor printed playbooks some years before. While he held the reversion of the Mastership, Buc wrote a book, now lost, about court revels partly based on his visit to the Spanish court in the wake of the peace treaty of 1604. He also collected play quartos. On the title-pages of several of the copies he bought he wrote notes with guesses about their anonymous authors. He bought a copy of *George a Greene, the Pinner of Wakefield*, for instance, probably when it was first printed in 1599. His purchase survives slightly truncated in the Folger Shakespeare Library.[8] The quarto does not name any author on its title-page, but Buc must have wanted to know whose work it was. He asked two men who he thought might know, one from each of the duopoly companies, and noted their replies on the title-page of his copy. His note says

> Written by . . . . a minister, who ac[ted]
> the pinners part in it himselfe. Teste W Shakespea[re]
> Ed Juby saith that the play was made by Ro. Gree[ne].

The difference between the two responses he noted impartially, and at the different times they came to him. Shakespeare, who had been a player well before the Chamberlain's was set up in 1594, was the obvious person to

[8] See Alan H. Nelson, 'George Buc, William Shakespeare, and the Folger *George a Greene*', *Shakespeare Quarterly* 49 (1998), 74–83.

turn to in that company for his memories of who wrote what, and Juby, who along with Sam Rowley and Robert Shaa was the chief intermediary between Henslowe and the writers from 1598 to 1602, was an obvious choice for the other company. Buc was clearly interested in the plays he was eventually to 'allow', including the older ones from the 1580s and 1590s. Another story about him, registering his long memory of London playgoing, is given here at the beginning of Chapter 5.

The *Diary* records Henslowe's regular payments to the Master of the Revels, mostly amidst the dates noted for performances. On 6 November 1595, for instance, alongside a note of his income from *The Wise Men of West Chester* is a small note 'm^r pd'. The same note appears on 18 December alongside the note of payment for *1 Hercules*. His records of payments to the Master are thorough, one of the more consistent items among his various outgoings. From February to May 1592, and up to March 1595 he made a regular payment of five shillings a week to the Revels Office. This later became six shillings and eightpence (one mark, or one-third of a pound), and later still a monthly payment of ten shillings a week. He was far better at making these payments than the Burbages, who Tilney took to court in 1606 for more than a decade of failing to pay him. But just what the payments were for needs consideration. Were they on behalf of the companies for play licences or were they the owner's licences for the Rose itself? If they were for the plays Henslowe did the company's job from remarkably early on, since they mostly owned their own plays and should have made their own payments to get their playbooks licensed. It is conceivable that Henslowe did own some plays himself from early on, and paid for them, most likely the ones that recur in the tenure of different companies, up to and after May 1594. Since *The Jew of Malta* seems to have posed too many difficulties with staging its final act to be worth taking on tour he perhaps kept it at the Rose and paid the Master to license it. That would explain why it recurs in the *Diary* as played first by Strange's in 1592, then by the Queen's and Sussex's in early 1594, and then the Admiral's from May–June 1594 onwards. Its eventual sale to Christopher Beeston for use at the Cockpit in the 1630s must be a consequence of Henslowe passing it on to Alleyn, who sold it to Beeston some time before he died. The same thing must have happened to *Friar Bacon and Friar Bungay*, which also lays heavy demands on staging. Marlowe's *Massacre at Paris* went from Strange's to the Admiral's, too, though probably for a different reason (I suspect it was Alleyn's property) since Strange's had closed and it along with other plays moved to the Admiral's in 1594.

There are far too many similar and equally unanswerable questions about the *Diary*. As a banker Henslowe seems to have charged no interest, so where did his profits come from? Did he take money in ways that do not appear in the *Diary*? What was Alleyn's share, and did Alleyn keep a set of records which has not survived from his estate as his father-in-law's did? When did Alleyn stop taking his share as a player and turn into a manager of players? He resumed acting at the Fortune in 1600 when the new playhouse needed an initial boost. Did he resume his income as a company sharer at the same time as he took on the landlord role with the Fortune? If so his function was truly ambivalent, though it was not unlike Richard Burbage's 'housekeeper' role at the new Globe in 1599 and later with the Blackfriars which he inherited in 1597. Many questions about the identity of the *Diary* entries relate to the same set of questions. Did the loans of the second period from 1597 onwards come out of Henslowe's own pocket or did they come from the cash that he held as banker for the Admiral's? What were the relations between Henslowe's finances and those of his son-in-law? It was Alleyn who bought the Bear Garden in 1594, and both of them were engaged in running baiting from 1600 while Henslowe was in charge in Southwark and Alleyn was at Clerkenwell. Perhaps the most searching question is what did Henslowe as impresario use for a playhouse after the Rose was demolished. The Lady Elizabeth's were expected to run at the newly built Hope, but where did they and their predecessors perform before 1614?

When, or indeed if, Henslowe turned from landlord into impresario or theatre manager is another question to which no ready answer can be found. From Beckerman's fourth period, the time of the 'Articles of Agreement' and the notorious '*Complaint*' by the Lady Elizabeth's, there are signs that Henslowe had developed a tighter managerial function than he maintained at the turn of the century. If we believe the Lady Elizabeth's they report that Henslowe and his baiting partner Jacob Meade had 'raised' the companies, specifying that 'Fower or Five Sharers' be appointed for them as company financiers/managers to deal with. If Henslowe and Meade took the initiative in 'raising' the companies, whatever that means, they were doing more than acting passively as company bankers. The evidence up to 1603 indicates that Henslowe had a standard procedure for the Admiral's Men, serving as banker and financier but never as controlling impresario. The Lady Elizabeth's complaints speak of a degree of control that can only be called managerial, even exploitative. We have little of Henslowe's own story for the intervening Bear Garden years. It is possible to believe that his outlook hardened as the years and the companies rolled on.

But with the Admiral's his behaviour always seems to have been fair, scrupulous and never noticeably exploitative, for all the profits the company's long residence at the Rose brought him.

The payments to the Master of the Revels need a closer look, if only because they should be of two kinds. As we have noted one was a pattern of regular payments, the same amount each week and later each month, which would fit the idea they were for Henslowe's recurrent licensing of the playhouse. The other must therefore have been a series of banking entries for payments he made to the Master on behalf of the company to license their plays. The weekly payments of five shillings begin in February 1592:

> Itm pd vnto mr tyllnes man the 26 of febreary 1591. . . . . . .vs. (repeated 4 March, 10 March, 17 March, 24 March, etc., to 10 May).
> Itm pd vnto mr tyllnes man the 13 of maye 1592. . . . . .xijs. (followed by three more weekly payments of 6s 8d).

Then, in a list of daily play receipts, appears this extra note:

> 10 of marche 1594 (1595) 17 p---- Rd at the Knacke [from hence lycensed][9] xxiiijs.

Similar notes appear for 31 May, 6 November ('mr. pd'), 18 December, 30 January 1596, 26 April, 22 May, 7 June, 19 June, 5 July, and 12 July. On 27 February the final entry of a run of play receipts is followed by the note 'the master of the Revelles payd vntell this time al wch I owe hime'. This presumably matches an entry on 2 January 1595, where Thomas Stonnard from the Revels Office acknowledged the receipt from Henslowe 'in full payement of a bonde of one hundreth powndes the some of tenn powndes & in full payement of what soever is due from the daie above wrytten vntill Ashwednesdaie next ensuinge after the date hereof'. Further payments accompany the entries of play takings on 28 April, 28 May, 25 June and 16 July 1597. After that the daily lists come to a halt, though there is a final note on 26 November 'for iiij weckes the some of xxxx s'. These forty-shilling payments for 'one moneth playinge' also appear later for 2 and 22 January 1598, both received by Thomas Whittle from the Revels Office, and one on 23 February by John Carnab. Oddly, in what must have been a duplicate record or possibly another kind of payment, the 1596 fees were followed by a receipt signed by Michael Bluenson for a payment of twenty shillings: 'Rd for ij weckes paye is dew vnto the mr of

---

[9] These three words are interlined.

the Revelles frome the 12 of aprell 1596 vnto the 26 of the same month'.
Bluenson (or Blewmesone) also receipted a payment to the Revels Office
of forty shillings on 19 July 1597. On 27 June 1597 Robert Johnson had
receipted a payment of 40 shillings for that month, and on 19 July after
Bluenson's receipt for £2 appears one for £6 by Johnson, as a payment 'for
iij Monethes.ending the daie a fore.said', 19 July.

This kind of payment seems to continue, as we might expect for a
regular licensing payment. In 1599 two lots of £3 each to the Master were
recorded by Richard Veale of the Revels Office, acknowledging receipt
of the sums on 25 October and 20 November. On 9 January, 9 February,
28 April and 24 May 1600 William Plaistowe acknowledged similar payments. It is possible that this monthly £3 was the same sort of payment, plus
inflation, as the £2 (forty shillings) a month recorded in earlier years.
On 31 July Plaistowe receipted the same sum as 'one monethes paye'.
On 29 August he noted the same amount as 'this last monethts pay for the
Fortune'. Robert Hassard wrote a receipt for another £3 'for ye Fortune'
on 9 June 1601, and Plaistowe acknowledged the same amount on 8 July
1602 and again on 4 August. These payments must have been for the
licensing of the playhouses, although no more entries for the Rose appear
once the £3 a month for the Fortune begins.

The other kind of entry first appears clearly on 26 January 1598. This
one is to Thomas Downton, one of the usual payees of the Admiral's, 'for
the company to paye the mr of the Reuells for lysensynge of ij boockes
xiiij s'. Clearly this was a company payment, not Henslowe's own, and it
noted the Master's fee for 'allowing' a pair of the company's new playbooks. A similar loan to Downton appeared on 8 March. The licences for
three more plays were recorded in March as payments to the 'mr of the
Reueulles man'. This was evidently Henslowe acting as the players' banker,
not their landlord. No such entries appear before January 1598, which
suggests that till then the company paid to license playbooks out of its
own resources. Henslowe made a further entry on 28 March of 14 shillings
to license the two parts of 'Robart hoode', Munday's *Huntingdon* plays.
These must have been entered by Henslowe as company banker, not
landlord. A further note of the payment of 21 shillings for 'the lycensynge
of iij boockes' was made on 24 July 1598. Similar payments are recorded
on 3 June and in December of 1599 and January 1600. Further payments
appear later in 1600 and in September 1601.

As the Introduction to the *Diary* notes (p. xxviii) payments to license
the playhouse appear weekly at first and later fortnightly and then
monthly. Greg and Chambers reckoned they were fees for getting leave

to stage plays, though if the duopoly companies did start in May 1594 the licensing of the Rose and the Theatre as the only playhouses permitted thereafter for regular use ought to have ensured that such payments did not begin until then. The second kind of entry specifies that they are payments for licensing new playbooks. All scholars of the Revels Office, including Dutton and Bawcutt, take it for granted that the Master of the Revels required a regular fee for licensing the playhouses even though there is no record of the Rose and the Theatre having any official status with Tilney until well after 1594. When and with which playhouses the Master started his licensing we cannot say, because the Privy Council records are lost with other Council papers between 1593 and 1595. But the very regularity of the payments in time and in amount indicates that they were an official fee to the Master. Tilney must have expected similar payments to be made to him by the Burbages, Francis Langley of the Swan, and the Boar's Head and Red Bull owners. They were not payments to license playbooks for publication because that did not start until 1606, when Tilney's deputy and successor George Buc started to get a fee for it.

What all this suggests is that at the outset Henslowe made his *Diary* entries as a landlord working on his own behalf. The second set of payments to license playbooks suggests that Henslowe's banker or bank-roller function began in 1598 after Alleyn had gone off to the country, and stayed constant at least until the Rose closed. This apparent confirmation of Beckerman's division of his activities means we should ask why the *Diary* contains no entries about the purchase or licensing of playbooks before 1598. Conceivably, as other evidence suggests, at least some of the playbooks were bought and licensed by Alleyn personally through this early period and he paid for their licensing, while in other cases the sharers paid for the licences directly. Otherwise the *Diary*'s records of payments to the Revels Office include nothing to identify Henslowe as a company manager or impresario before the famous *Complaint* of 1614, though they do imply that Alleyn served as a company manager of sorts with his own accounts of income and expenditure from early on.[10]

Some of the evidence from the Revels Office payments converges on the question of who owned and who published the plays that got into print, which we will consider below. Analysis of the two sets of Revels

---

[10] In May 1598 Martin Slater sold the company five books of plays they had been acting since 1595. Between 1598 and 1602 Alleyn sold the company at least eleven 'allowed books' of the plays the company had been staging since 1594. For an overview of the ownership of playbooks, the 'allowed books' that the Master signed with his licence, see Gurr, 'Did Shakespeare Own his own Playbooks?', *Review of English Studies* 59 (2008).

entries in different sorts of document, complementing the evidence of the
Diary itself, suggests that Henslowe was always inclined, and even obliged,
to be rather more entrepreneurial than Beckerman's identification of the
changes in his functions would allow, and that his allegedly wicked
dealings with five or more playing groups in the years between 1603 and
1613 may well be not far from a fiction. That is as much of an answer as we
can find to the questions generated about this strikingly unknowable
personality who made the bulk of the entries in the *Diary* and his role
in the playmaking business.

Rather less hope of answers hangs from other *Diary* questions. Even
simple records like Henslowe's changed accounting system from 24 January
1597, when he started making his entries into five columns instead of the
previous three, still confuse us. The debate about what the five columns
were for (see *Diary*, pp. xxxiii–xxxvii) is still not over. Even the *Diary*
editors had to leave the exact origin or destination of each amount
undetermined. Nonetheless, as a whole these two runs of daily entries
do give a plenitude of evidence about such features of the company's
annual schedule as their summer tours, playing on Sundays, playing or
touring in the time of Lent, the superior level of takings on holidays,[11]
ownership of individual playbooks,[12] the cost to the company of buying
special clothing such as gowns for the boys when they played women,
and even conjectural profit and loss accounts for the company up to
1597.[13] Nothing in the *Diary* refers to the sale of plays to the press, which
happened very spasmodically, though there was a spurt of sales of the
older plays in May 1594.[14] This indicates that play manuscripts must have
been sold to the press by the company itself, selling (or transcribing)
a spare manuscript copy. The most likely origins for the printed texts of
the plays will be considered further below.

The question just what Henslowe meant when he added the term 'ne'
at the beginning of an entry for a play is another of the *Diary*'s many

---

[11] Receipts at the Fortune on holidays in 1607–8 include 25s on St Stephen's Day, 45s on St John's
Day, and 44s. 9d on Childermas Day (*Diary* p. 264).

[12] Of William Boyle's *Jugurtha*, an intriguing note says 'lent unto me Wbirde the 9 of februarye to
paye for a new booke to will: Boyle.cald Jugurth xxx^s w^c if you dislike Ile repaye it back . . . xxxs'
(*Diary*, p. 130). This was early in 1600, before Alleyn returned to the company. Was it Henslowe
who might dislike the new play, or was Bird afraid he would object to the act of purchase, since it
was Henslowe himself who normally paid his writers?

[13] See Gurr, *The Shakespeare Company 1594–1642*, pp. 99–106, especially Table 3.1.

[14] Several plays, including two 'old' plays of the Admiral's, *Friar Bacon* and *Belin Dun*, plus one about
John of Gaunt, one about Henry I and a Robin Hood story, were all entered in the Stationer's
Register on 14 May 1594. Only *Friar Bacon* and the Queen's Men's *Famous Victories of Henry V*,
also entered that day, got into print.

dangling questions. It has two main strings. One is whether it invariably meant a new play, a question that seems ultimately irresolvable, the other just what generated what were usually bigger takings for a performance so marked. The idea that double prices were charged for new plays comes from a statement by Samuel Kiechel, a German merchant visiting London in 1584. He reported that 'It may well be that they take [£10 to £12] at a time, especially when they act anything new which has not been given before and double prices are charged.'[15] If the assumption that 'ne' meant the inauguration of a 'new' play is correct, firstly it indicates that through the initial year or so of the company's operations from May 1594 its absence from the entries meant the unmarked play was a revival of an old play from some pre-existing company. That would include all the plays first staged before 1594, the Marlowes, Peeles and Kyd's *Spanish Tragedy* with some others. Secondly, we have to look into the assumption based on Kiechel and adopted by Greg and Chambers long ago that the cost of a 'ne' performance to playgoers was always doubled because of its novelty.

This may be true, but Henslowe's lists do not give a higher take on 'ne' days with the consistency that such an assumption requires. The first of the Admiral's plays marked 'ne' took only seventeen shillings at its first performance but almost four times as much, three pounds four shillings, at its second a week later. Several of the more innovative plays proved to be sleepers with returns that grew performance by performance. *The Wise Man of West Chester* took thirty-three shillings on its first afternoon, 2 December 1595, thirty-four on its second, 6 December, and £3 4s (sixty-four shillings) on its third, 29 December. *A Knack to Know an Honest Man* took forty shillings on its 'ne' performance in October 1594, forty-seven at its next and sixty-three at the third. *1 Hercules* took £3 13s on its first day, 7 May 1595, and £3 9s on the second. *Longshanks* (probably a revision of Peele's *Edward I*) took £2 at its 'ne' performance on 29 August 1595 but £3 at its second two weeks later. *The Blind Beggar of Alexandria* took £3 on 12 February 1596, not long before that year's Lent closure, and £3 6s four days later. *An Humorous Day's Mirth's* takings steadily climbed from £2 3s in May 1597 to £3 10s on 7 June, when John Chamberlain wrote about its success. *Chinon of England* took the identical amount on its first two performances in January 1596. I suspect that higher takings at first performances are much more likely to have come from the buzz of novelty raised by the playbills than from routinely doubled prices. That incidentally raises the question, also apt for the company's financial activities,

---

[15] Quoted and translated in Chambers, *The Elizabethan Stage*, II. 358.

of its use of playbills to advertise what was to be played, a matter to which we must return shortly.

Some individual plays had curious financial histories. *The Wonder of a Woman* took an almost unprecedented £4 at its 'ne' performance in October 1595, and £3 2s on the Christmas holiday, St Steven's Day. Otherwise it took only between eleven and twenty-two shillings. Some plays had only a single performance marked as 'ne', all of them with quite good takings and yet never repeated. They included *The Merchant of Emden* on 30 July 1594 (£3 8s), *The Mack* on 21 February 1595 (£3) and, less happily, *The Welshman*, 29 November 1595 (7s). Takings for the first two of these were very respectable, and leave unanswerable what could have happened at their one performance to justify the absence of any repeats.

There are other anomalies in the 'ne' entries. Only one play was entered as 'ne' twice, Martin Slater's *Alexander and Lodowick*. The dates here are peculiar, because while the first entry was on 14 January 1597 with a take of 55 shillings (repeated in a separate note as £5 for 'the fyrste time yt wasse played'), it recurred as 'ne' a month later on 11 February, taking what looks like £3 5s, ten shillings more than on 14 January. The two amounts together do total the £5 of the separate note. But its third performance was recorded as the very next afternoon, 12 February (£1 14s), which if correct was an unprecedented repeat show. These two performances in sequence were just before the Lent closedown. The additional entry giving it a 'ne' performance (*Diary* p. 51) appears in a set of payments for four new plays, *That Will Be Shall Be*, where the takings are the same as for the second performance, *Hieronimo* (*The Spanish Tragedy*) 'in parte of payment', *Alexander and Lodowick* and *A Woman Hard to Please*. The four are noted as receiving £2, £7, £5 and £4 respectively. I suspect that these were cross-payments to whoever owned the playbooks, probably Slater and Alleyn, although they were recorded as 'Rd', or receipts, not as outgoings. The more routine entries for the four performances specify respectively 42s, £3, 55s and £4, only the last identical to the one in the other set of four entries. Nothing in the *Diary* explains to any would-be auditor what these figures mean.

That is one of the many doubts generated by the entries in the *Diary*. As I have already argued, the chief is Henslowe's transition from landlord to banker and the consequent doubt about whose accounts he was noting and where the profits went. We have his records of the company's outlays, mostly as loans to individual sharers, but the great absence is the company's own notes of their costs and their takings. From other fragments we can infer the company's huge weekly outlay on wages for hired hands and boys but we do not have much note of their payments to the Revels Office nor their many other expenses that we can only guess at. Only one small entry in the *Diary* tells us much directly about the relationship of Henslowe as landlord in 1598 with the company's workers. It indicates his willingness to use the Rose for his own and their profit on days when the company was not playing, but even that raises new questions. On 4 November 1598 he noted that a fencer, James Cranwigge, had 'playd his callenge in my howsse & I sholde have hade for my parte xxxxs wch the company hath Rd & oweth yt to me' (*Diary*, p. 101). Evidently the company's gatherers were on duty and, having collected money from the audience, should now be giving forty shillings out of their takings to Henslowe. Presumably they could keep the rest for themselves, not for the company. This is an oblique confirmation that the hired men and gatherers took their wages directly from the company, not from Henslowe, but it leaves unclear just who paid the gatherers' wages, if they did not take a portion directly from their takings.

A related question, tantalising but irresolvable, is the number of gatherers at the Rose and the Fortune. We can guess who paid their wages since Henslowe's book has no entries for week-by-week payments to individuals other than occasional notes about his own boys. In the later years he copied the contractual obligations for individual hired men and boys into the *Diary* but never entered any wage payments to them. Presumably therefore it was the sharers of the company who paid the hired men, boys and gatherers. Or did the gatherers take their income directly from the cash they collected? The 'two small dores' which were all the first Globe had for access suggest that no more than two would have been required, or perhaps four, one at each entrance for the gallery-goers and one for those who went straight into the yard. But that begs a very large question about the Rose's access through its one main door, and after people had got through how the gatherers could charge the additional pennies for access from the yard into the galleries. Was there perhaps a stair turret? This is a question about the playhouse structure to be considered in Chapter 4.

It seems appropriate here to give an inevitably rough summary of the company's own likely income and expenditure, if only because like the shadow or 'opposite' company story it offsets the *Diary*'s evidence. We can calculate much of their annual income from what Henslowe tells us was the number of performances a year by adding an amount equivalent to his gallery takings to an estimate of the pennies derived from the yard. Assuming an average attendance of roughly a thousand people each day, as Middleton tells us the Fortune expected, the gross income would have been in the vicinity of five pounds a day or a little more. At an average run of more than two hundred performances a year the annual income to the company at the Rose should have been well over one thousand pounds. From that the company had to pay wages to at least twenty people, hired men including the book-keeper, gatherers and stage hands. If that was roughly ten shillings a week each in wages it came to more than ten pounds in total week by week. That took half of the minimal thousand pounds of annual income. Out of the other half the eight or ten sharers took their own cut, perhaps as much as thirty or forty pounds a year each, and paid out all the incidental expenses such as buying playbooks, properties and costumes, licences, the printing of playbills and poor relief to the parish, all the incidental costs that never appear in the *Diary*.

One of the company's expenses never recorded in the *Diary* along with all the other company charges such as wages for the gatherers and other stage attendants and the payments for poor relief to the parish was the cost of printing the playbills to advertise each day's show.[16] The printers who had the licence to produce playbills were, in succession from 1587, John Charlewood, James Roberts, and William Jaggard. Roberts and Jaggard were both also deeply involved in the printing of plays, as we shall see below, but the daily output of bills advertising the day's play which early every morning the boys had to paste on walls and posts all over the city called for a regular expenditure of six shillings or more each month. The *Diary* never records any of these recurrent company payments.

In the gradual process of evolving from company landlord to financier and banker Henslowe's entries changed in ways that are rarely obvious, and it is never clear just who owed and paid what. It was as their banker that he specified 'loans' from himself to the company for its purchases from the writers. He never records any repayments to himself, but it is rarely clear on whose behalf he made most of the payments. He seems to have paid the writers as the company's banker and purse-holder, although the two-pound payments to buy old playbooks do not seem always to have put the plays into the sharers' hands. Another vagueness is that in the earlier accounts when he was making his entries as landlord of the Rose the income from his half of the galleries was always rounded up or down. The amounts varied widely, but were never noted except to the

---

[16] For a detailed study of this practice, see Tiffany Stern, ' "On each Wall and Corner Poast": Title-pages, and Advertising in Early Modern London', *English Literary Renaissance* 36 (2006), 57–89.

nearest shilling or half-shilling. No total was entered as anything but pounds and shillings, with sometimes an odd sixpence added. We do not know whether it was the company, the gatherers or Henslowe himself who did this rounding.

Two tangible aspects of the company's finances that the *Diary* ignores bear closer analysis. One was the likely annual rates of profit and loss, the other the printing of its plays. Taking the more speculative topic first, in more detail than was given above, we can use the *Diary* to guess at something like this. Through the company's first run from 1594 till early 1597, takings for the company from the Rose's galleries came to £672 a year, the same amount as Henslowe's rents. Gatherings from the yard would have brought them perhaps £600, court performances £20, and other private shows perhaps another £20. Touring the plays might have brought in a further £30, and the sale of food and drink, if that was in the company's control rather than the playhouse owner's, another £30 or more. Henslowe's original contract with John Cholmley to pay for the building of the Rose in 1587 suggests that selling food and drink was a landlord's not a company privilege, but the absence from the *Diary* of any record of such income argues that it was the company that profited from this resource. Total income to the company over a year would have been at best £1,370. Outgoings besides the playhouse rent, half the gallery income, taken directly by Henslowe, comprised the purchase of new plays, clothing and properties, and all the incidentals such as feeding the fund for the parish poor, paying the Revels Office for licensing playbooks and printing playbills. Those costs plus wages to the hired men and other incidental expenses would have come to roughly £1,070. That left £300 profit to be divided amongst the eight sharers, or £37 10s a year each. This is guesswork, but it matches such prices as do appear in the *Diary*.[17]

The other and better-recorded matter is the first printings of the various play-texts. The issuing of such a limited number of the Admiral's company plays, a mere ten up to 1603 out of a total of 206 known titles, has its own fascination largely because it helps to identify which of its new plays the company thought were popular enough on stage to be worth making extra money from by getting them into print. Here are the ten Admiral's plays that appeared up to 1603, in the order of their appearance in print.

[17] An earlier analysis of the Admiral's likely income and expenditure is in Gurr, *The Shakespeare Company 1594–1642*, pp. 95–106.

1. *A Knack to Know an Honest Man*: performed 'ne' on 22 (23) October 1594, and 15 more times up to June 1595. It was entered to Cuthbert Burby 26 November 1595 and printed for Burby in 1596.

2. *The Blind Beggar of Alexandria*: performed 'ne' on 12 February 1596, and eight more times to April 1597, then three times in June–July 1597. It was entered in the Stationers' Register to William Jones on 15 August 1598 and printed by an unidentified press in 1598. A new costume was bought for it in 1601.

3. *An Humorous Day's Mirth*: performed 'ne' on 11 May 1597, and eleven more times in 1597. It was not entered in the Register, and printed by Valentine Sims (no publisher named) in 1599. It was listed in the stock of Admiral's books (*Diary*, p. 323) 'such as I have bought since the 3d of March 1598' (This list of twenty-nine playbooks includes the two *Huntingdon* plays).

4. *The Two Angry Women of Abingdon*: the *Diary* notes a loan of £5 to the company: 'Lent unto thomas dowton the 22 of desembre 1598 to bye A boocke of harey poorter called the 2 parte of the 2 angrey wemen of abengton'; on 31 January 1599 a loan to buy 'taffetie' for two women's gowns for 'the ij angrey wemen of abengton', and for properties on 12 February; a second loan 28 February 1599 went to Downton and Shaa to complete the purchase from Porter. It was not entered in the Stationers' Register, and printed by Edward Allde for Joseph Hunt and William Ferbrand in 1599.

5. *Old Fortunatus*: six performances January–May 1596; on 9 November 1599 Downton gave a receipt for £4 from Henslowe 'to pay Thomas Deckker in earnest of abooke cald the hole hystory of Fortunatus'; on 24 November Shaa witnessed a loan of three pounds for it to Dekker. Henslowe loaned the company £10 in early December 'to by thinges for Fortunatus'. This anticipates Henslowe and Alleyn signing the lease for the Fortune on 24 December, which would mean the play was staged as a celebration of the new playhouse. On 12 December Dekker was granted another £2 'for the eande of fortewnatus for the corte'. It was entered in the Register to William Aspley on 20 February 1600 and printed by Simon Stafford in 1600.

6. *Sir John Oldcastle*: Downton received £10 from Henslowe on 16 October 1599 to pay the four authors for Part 1, and in November Henslowe noted ten shillings as a gift to them after the opening performance. It was entered in the Register to Thomas Pavier on 11 August 1600 and printed by Valentine Sims in 1600. On 17 October

1602 at the start of his entries for Worcester's Henslowe lent the company £2 to pay Dekker for additions to the play.

7. *Look About You*: the *Diary* does not mention this play by its published title, despite its ascription to the Admiral's on its title-page. For the likelihood that it was the play Henlowe called 'Desgysses', see above, p. 57. He does note payments on 13 June and 23 July 1601 to Antony Wadeson for 'A Boocke called the life of the humeros earlle of Gloster with his conquest of portingalle', which may be a sequel to *Look About You*, since Gloster sets off for Portugal at the end of the play. It was not entered in the Register, and printed for William Ferbrand by Edward Allde in 1600.

8. *The Shoemaker's Holiday*: on 17 July 1599 Henslowe lent Downton and Sam Rowley £3 to buy the play from Dekker. It was not entered in the Register, printed by Valentine Sims 'and are there to be sold', with no bookseller named, in 1600.

9. *The Downfall of Huntingdon*: on 15 February 1598 on the Admiral's behalf Henslowe lent Munday £5 for 'the firste parte of Robyne Hoode'. It was entered in the Register to William Leake on 1 December 1600 and printed by Richard Bradock in 1601.

10. *The Death of Huntingdon*: on 20 February 1598 Henslowe lent Downton ten shillings to pay for 'his seconde parte of the downefall of earlle huntyngton', and more payments were made later. It was entered in the Register to William Leake on 1 December 1600 and printed by Richard Bradock in 1601.[18]

Several cross-linkages between the company and its publishers are indicated by this list. The booksellers who issued the plays consistently maintained links with both companies in the duopoly. Andrew Wise as publisher/bookseller and Valentine Sims as printer produced five of the Chamberlain's off-loadings through 1597–1600. Sims printed eight plays in all, and did his own bookselling for Admiral's plays in 1600–02. Ferbrand used Edward Allde to print two Admiral's plays in 1599–1600, and later a Chamberlain's play. Richard Bradock printed *A Midsummer Night's Dream* and *Every Man Out*, and later the two Admiral's *Huntingdon* plays. The flurry of play publication that developed between 1596 and 1601 was pretty largely confined to the plays of only three companies, chiefly

---

[18] All these records are based on the entries in W. W. Greg, *A Bibliography of the Printed Drama to the Restoration*, Vol. I, *Stationers' Records. Plays to 1616*. London (for the Bibliographical Society at the University Press, Oxford), 1939.

those of the duopoly along with a few from the first boy company to be resurrected in 1599, Paul's. In all, sixteen came from the Chamberlain's and ten were the Admiral's. Six plays of Paul's Boys were printed between 1599 and 1602. Otherwise in this period, according to Greg's *Bibliography*, out of a total of thirty-four only three other plays printed were ascribed to specific companies, and therefore in some way (perhaps) authorised for sale by those companies.

The most immediate question is the way taken to the press by the four out of the ten Admiral's plays that were never registered with the Stationers' Company. Their publishers were Ferbrand for *Two Angry Women* and *Look About You*, and 'anon.' for the two printed and sold by Valentine Sims. Their routes to the press certainly differed from those of the only two Chamberlain's plays not registered, *Romeo and Juliet* and *Love's Labours Lost*. Both of these were claimed on their title-pages as replacements for defective earlier printings, neither of them registered, and possibly therefore what Heminges and Condell much later alleged were 'stolne, and surreptitious copies'. Were the four unregistered Admiral's printings of that kind? The absence of any publisher or bookseller for two of them suggests that the publication process was unorthodox, rather more than simply evading payment of the extra sixpence that it cost to register a book. The publishers might have been ignorant of its consequence, which was chiefly loss of the right to control future printings. Or it may have meant that the sellers and the printers did not expect the books to sell well enough to warrant reprinting, a not unlikely expectation with these early play printings. Either way all four issues have the air of being a marginal activity. On the other hand, given the slow and perhaps casual process which usually led to the printing of such minor work their dates of issue in 1599 and 1600 may indicate that they were the first playbooks to be sold by the Admiral's or by Henslowe on their behalf. This suggests that they were chosen as notable plays, and that their sale had publicity value for the company at a time when their duopoly control was at risk of collapse.

I am inclined to think, if only because the company's name was on all the title-pages, that it was the company that sold the plays and that Henslowe did not own any of the playbooks that came into print. Their title-page ascriptions probably also indicate that none of them belonged to Alleyn or Slater. Chapman as sole author of two of the first three to get into print may have given their transmission into print an impetus, since the collaborative teams writing the others do not seem to have felt any need to advertise their collective work. The business of making such sales must have been new to the company, which might explain the unregistered printings. It is a mark of the casual and perhaps fortuitous route to the press taken by most of the published plays that James Roberts, printer of the company's playbills after John Charlewood died in 1593, took no part in their production. Another possible indication of how they came to the press is the absence in the *Diary* of any note of payments to scribes who might have copied out the playbooks for the press. Robert Yarington's signature at the end of *Two Lamentable Tragedies* marked his role as transcriber for the press, not his authorship as some commentators have assumed. The *Diary* identifies the writers who were paid for the play as Haughton and Day. The total absence of Yarington's name along with that of that of Hand C and any other 'plotter' from the *Diary* indicates that such helpers were employed and paid by the company, like the hired men and stage-hands whose pay is likewise absent. Yarington must have copied the play for the press on the company's behalf, not Henslowe's.

So what was Henslowe's policy over playbooks, and who actually owned the 'allowed' books of the plays the company performed at the Rose? I have argued that through this period from 1597 to 1600 until the Admiral's moved to the Fortune Henslowe did act as their banker. What he regularly called loans for the company's purchases either of playbooks or of clothes and other properties must have come from his holdings of the company's cash. So at least in this period we have to assume that most of the plays were owned by the company and presumably sold to the printers by the sharers just as the Chamberlain's Men's plays were similarly sold by agreement among their sharers. The chief inconsistency with this generalisation is how Henslowe came to own *Oldcastle* so that he could transfer it to Worcester's, the Rose's new resident company. Did he indeed commission it as a reprisal against the intruder company at their new playhouse? Such a hostile motive would explain his 'gefte' to the writers along with the play's explicit criticism of the neighbouring playhouse's Falstaff plays. A related question here is what was the significance of the paper in the *Diary* that listed the plays bought since March 1598. Who wrote the list, and who owned the listed playbooks?

Was Henslowe simply recording the playbooks held by the company? The published edition of the *Diary* includes a transcript made by Edmund Malone of the list, containing twenty-nine plays in all. The spelling is thought to indicate that it was originally written by Henslowe. It lists them under the heading '*A Note of all suche bookes as belong to the stocke, and such as I have bought since the 3d of March 1598*'. The full list, with his only sometimes comprehensible titling, is in two columns. The left-hand

column given here has the chronological numbering I have given each
play in Appendix 1, along with the standardised spelling of the title:
'Blacke Jonne (81, *Black Joan*), The Umers (69, *An Humorous Day's Mirth*),
Hardicanewtes (75, *Hardicanute*), Borbonne (77, *Bourbon*), Sturgflaterey
(74, *Sturgeflattery*), Brunhowlle (79, *Branholt*), Cobler quen hive (78, *The
Cobbler of Queenhithe*), Friar Pendelton (76, *Friar Spendleton*), Alls Perce
(80, *Alice Pearce*), Read Cappe (82, *Mother Redcap*), Roben Hode, 1 (85,
The Downfall of Robert Earl of Huntingdon), Roben Hode, 2 (87, *The
Death of Robert Earl of Huntingdon*), Phayeton (84, *Phaeton*), Treangell
cockowlls (88, *Triplicity of Cuckolds*), Goodwine (91, *1 Earl Godwin and
his Three Sons*)'. The right-hand column has one play fewer, and runs:
'Woman will have her will (86, *Englishmen for My Money*), Welshmans
price (90, *The Famous Wars of Henry I and the Prince of Wales*), King
Arthur, life and death (93, *King Arthur*), 1 p^t of Hercules (32, *1 Hercules*),
2 pt^e of Hercoles (33, *2 Hercules*), Pethagores (46, *Pythagoras*), Focasse (52,
Phocas), Elexsander and Lodwicke (62, *Alexander and Lodowick*), Blacke
Battman (94, *1 Black Bateman of the North*), 2 p. black Battman (98,
2 Black Bateman of the North), 2 pt of Goodwine (92, *2 Earl Godwin and
his Three Sons*), Mad mans morris (99, *The Madman's Morris*), Perce of
Winchester (102, *Pierce of Winchester*), Vayvode (106, *Vayvode*)'. The
probable dates for these twenty-nine plays fit the period after the
Admiral's absorbed some members and possibly some plays from
Pembroke's, and range from early 1595 for Slater's two *Hercules* plays to
mid-1598 for *Vayvode*.

   The meaning of Malone's transcripted heading for the list is sadly
ambiguous. Does its wording '*and such as I have bought*' mean 'including',
or does it mean 'in addition to'? Is it two groups of titles, or one? Three of
the plays it lists appeared in print. The 'Umors' must mean Chapman's
An Humorous Day's Mirth, bought and performed in May 1597 and
printed in 1599; and the sequence of two "Roben Hode" plays is identifiable as Munday's two *Huntingdon* plays, bought from the writer in
February 1598 and printed in 1601. From the evidence of their purchase
dates all three of these playbooks must have been in the company 'stocke'
before the date in the list's heading, 3 March 1598. That suggests the
heading must mean 'including such as I have bought since March 1598',
a list of all the plays then in the company's stock. But why so few, and
where are all the famous Marlowe plays and *The Spanish Tragedy*? Not all
of them were in print by 1598, which might have devalued their 'allowed
book' status. The other inventories of about the same time, listing
properties and costumes, include items that belong to many plays that

were in the current Admiral's repertory but are not in this list of play titles. So who owned them, and how did the company have the right to stage them? Does that 'I' signify Henslowe as the Admiral's banker or Henslowe the entrepreneur and impresario, collector of plays on his own behalf to be used by whichever playing company he had as his tenant at the Rose? Doubts of this kind join the other doubts over what the *Diary* has to tell. I think it most likely that Henslowe was here listing the plays owned by the company sharers but excluding all the playbooks still owned by Alleyn, including the Marlowes and Kyd, although perhaps they were still in the company's stock of useable playbooks. The list-making exercise must have gone along with the inventories, all done in the months after Alleyn retired from his work as a sharer in the company. Some of the Marlowes and *The Spanish Tragedy* do seem to have remained out of the repertory during Alleyn's three-year 'retirement' up to the end of 1600. Evidently not all the playbooks were in the collective possession of the company sharers.

The final and most intriguing issue in the *Diary* that needs consideration is what it shows about the business of play-writing. Henslowe's standard payment for a complete script through the 1590s was six pounds, usually divided among several writers. Prices must have risen later, because by 1613 Daborne was negotiating for double that rate.[19] Usually the six pounds was divided equally among the four or more writers who shared in the composition of a play, even if one of them was responsible for the original scenario, an outline of the story which the collaborators then put into speech. Sometimes writers would be paid to make additions to popular plays being revived, such as Jonson for *The Spanish Tragedy* in September 1601 and the players Bird and Rowley for *Faustus* in 1602.[20] These additions were presumably made to augment the plays when Alleyn revived them. The additions would have to pass the Revels Office at extra cost, so the company must have tried to offset such costs by advertising the revisions on its daily playbills. It was the job of the 'stage keeper' to advertise the day's play by posting up playbills. A postscript to a letter from Robert Daborne dated 1614 about the Lady Elizabeth's company asks Henslowe: 'I pray let your boy giv order this night to the stage keep

---

[19] See *Henslowe Papers*, ed. W. W. Greg, 1907, I. 76.
[20] "his adicians in geronymo", *Diary*, p. 182; "ther adicyones in docter fostes", p. 206. For Jonson's additions, see Marguerite A. Tassi, 'The Player's Passion and the Elizabethan Painting Trope: A Study of the Painter Addition to Kyd's *The Spanish Tragedy*', *Explorations in Renaissance Culture* 26:1 (2000), 73–100.

to set up bills agst munday for Eastward Hoe & one wendsday the new play.'[21] While playbills were part of the company's daily expenditure, Henslowe himself, in a uniquely valuable set of records, handled and recorded the company's outlays to the writers.

Most of the payments Henslowe made were to teams of writers working in collaboration, a point the printed texts ignored by citing only the company and no authors on their title-pages. Of the eighty-nine plays for which full payments are recorded, only thirty-four were by single authors.[22] It may not be entirely a coincidence that most of the earlier plays that got into print were single-writer texts, and we cannot discount the likelihood that writers like Chapman took a hand in seeing that play manuscripts reached the press. Mostly Henslowe paid each member of his collaborative teams the same amount, though the actual recipients of the instalments might vary from play to play, even in the process of composing a single play. Roslyn Knutson claims, rightly I think, that the company usually acquired partial drafts of plays as a mark of their writer's good intentions, and might, if a play was unfinished, pass the draft papers on to another writer.[23] That could have happened with the lost *Osric*, which was given two performances by the Admiral's in 1597 after which it probably became Heywood's *Marshal Osric* for Worcester's in 1602. The same thing might have happened to *The Italian Tragedy* for which John Day received forty shillings from the Admiral's on 10 January 1600, and 'mr smythe' (Wentworth Smith) another forty from Worcester's on 7 March 1602. Similarly, *The Devil and his Dam*, which got William Haughton a single payment of five shillings on 6 May 1600, may have been passed on for completion to other writers, though further instalments may have been paid to him in the second half of 1600 when the record has gaps. The play, or a version of it, appeared in print much later in 1663 as an old play under the name *Grim the Collier of Croydon*. In a possibly similar pattern a letter from Sam Rowley (*Diary*, p. 295) asks Henslowe to return the papers of an aborted play by Richard Hathway about John of Gaunt's conquest of Spain to the writer. Hathway wished to negotiate over his return of the initial payment for the draft. Knutson also suggests (p. 126) that Henslowe might have given the so-far drafted sheets from Haughton's aborted *Judas* to Bird and Rowley, who completed the play in 1601.

[21] Dulwich College MS 1: Article 69 (Greg, *Henslowe Papers*, Article 76, p. 71).
[22] Carol Chillington Rutter, *Documents of the Rose Playhouse*, p. 128.
[23] Knutson, 'Commercial Significance of Payments'.

The general pattern was to employ a group of writers once one of them had offered an acceptable 'plot' setting out the story scene by scene. This was not the 'plot' drawn up by the book-keeper to help with the staging and the doubling of parts, of which company manuscripts survive for seven plays, but an author's scenario.[24] The different collaborators would then divide the play scene by scene, often writing their sections simultaneously rather than *seriatim*. Usually it was in delivering their individual sections that the writers broke down. If we may judge by the payments 'lent' to the writers, and the absence of any subsequent expenditure on props or attire, quite a few plays never got beyond the early draft stage. Titles initially paid for but probably abandoned later where payments never moved from 'in earnest' to 'full payment' include Wilson and Chettle's *Catiline's Conspiracy* (1598), Rankins's *Mulmutius Dunwallow* (1598), Drayton and Dekker's *Connan Prince of Cornwall* (1598), Chettle's *'Tis No Deceit to Deceive the Deceiver* (1598), Chettle and Dekker's *Orestes Furens* (1599),[25] Chapman's *A Pastoral Tragedy* (1599), Haughton's *The Poor Man's Paradise* (1599), Chettle's *The Tragedy of Orphenes* (1599), Chettle and Haughton's *The Arcadian Virgin*, Dekker's *Truth's Supplication to Candlelight* (1599), Day, Dekker and Haughton's *The Spanish Moor's Tragedy* (1600), Chettle's *The Wooing of Death* (1600), Haughton's *The English Fugitives* (1600), the sequel to *Fair Constance of Rome* (1600), Hathway and Rankins's *Conquest of Spain* (1601), Day and Haughton's *2 Tom Dough* (1601), possibly the two parts of *The Six Clothiers* (1601) by Hathway, Smith and Haughton, Chettle's *The Danish Tragedy*, and probably others. Haughton's proposed *Judas* of May 1600 seems to have been aborted and replaced by Bird and Rowley's play of the same name in 1601. Haughton received ten shillings for it in May 1600, but nothing further is recorded until Bird and Rowley's play of the same name a year and a half later was paid for in full on 24 December 1601 and clothing bought for its staging on 3 January 1602.

On the other hand, we should note that a few plays such as Chettle's *Hoffman* were definitely completed despite the absence of any note of final payment. In *Hoffman*'s case there seems to be a lapse in the records shortly after the first payment. Breaks may exist too for other apparently uncompleted plays. We should also note that Chettle in particular ran into heavy debt with Henslowe by failing to deliver what he promised, a failure that,

---

[24] For more about the book-keeper's 'plots', see pp. 146–51 and 154–55.
[25] The play lacks any note of a final payment, but since that would have appeared in April–May 1599, when there are gaps in the *Diary*, it may be that this play was staged.

perhaps perversely, prompted Henslowe to use him for small extra tasks. Early in 1602 he was paid ten shillings for 'mendinge' a playbook written by Haughton. We must also bear in mind that collaboration between writers was not always as close and amiable a business as was sharing between the players. Twice the company lost one of its workers, each time to a belligerent writer. Ben Jonson killed the company player Gabriel Spencer in a duel in September 1598, and the writer John Day killed another of the company's writers, Henry Porter, in June 1599. It may be unwise to attribute these upsets to the absence of Alleyn's dominant and peacemaking influence on the company through those years, but it is a temptation.

The classic instance of a play written in collaboration and extensively revised but ultimately abandoned is *Sir Thomas More*.[26] One of the three company plays to survive in manuscript, its scenario was laid out by Munday, who also wrote the whole manuscript for his *John a Kent and John a Cumber*, which I believe to be the hugely popular play Henslowe called *The Wise Men of West Chester*. That single-author manuscript is a tidy work, with ample stage directions and good evidence for Munday's grasp of how the play was likely to be staged. Almost the opposite is true of the *Sir Thomas More* manuscript. It was written in five different hands, one of them that of the book-keeper known as Hand C, who also wrote the 'plot' of *2 Seven Deadly Sins* for Strange's in 1591–92 and the fragmentary 'plot' of *Fortune's Tennis* for the Admiral's in 1600–02. At some point, probably late in 1595, he wrote the title and date and some stage directions in the manuscript of *John a Kent* for the Admiral's.[27] Another of the five collaborators may have been Shakespeare. The play seems to have been first drafted in the early 1590s, but was heavily censored by Tilney, who would not give it his licensing signature. Another attempt to get it on stage seems to have come in 1602 or thereabouts, again without securing the play a licence for performance.[28]

---

[26] It is not the business of this book to study the process of collaborative writing in detail. A rewarding study of the process of creating *Sir Thomas More*, however, is Nina Levine's 'Citizens' Games: Differentiating Collaboration and *Sir Thomas More*', *Shakespeare Quarterly* 58 (2007), 31–64.

[27] Grace Ioppolo and Peter Beal contend that the date on *John a Kent* which I. A. Shapiro read as altered from 1596 to 1590 is really 1595. See Grace Ioppolo, *Dramatists and their Manuscripts in the Age of Shakespeare, Jonson, Middleton and Heywood: Authorship, Authority and the Playhouse*, London, 2006, p. 101. If it is of that date the manuscript belonged to the Admiral's Men, to whom Hand C also belonged. *Fortune's Tennis* was certainly an Admiral's play, and I believe that the *Seven Deadly Sins* 'plot', also written by Hand C, belonged to Strange's when Alleyn was with them. Hand C seems to have been a loyal worker for Alleyn through more than a decade.

[28] Largely because it is thought to include three pages by Shakespeare, the manuscript has had a lot of attention. See *Shakespeare and Sir Thomas More. Essays on the Play and its Shakespearian Interest,*

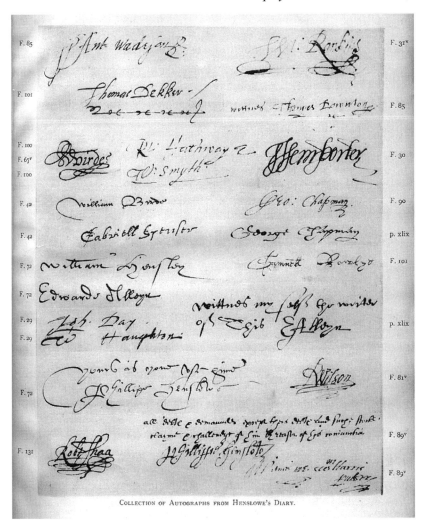

COLLECTION OF AUTOGRAPHS FROM HENSLOWE'S DIARY.

Figure 7. Signatures of writers and players including Alleyn from the Henslowe papers. This collection forms the frontispiece to Greg's transcription of the papers, London, 1907.

ed. T. H. Howard-Hill, Cambridge, 1989. In it, William B. Long, Giorgio Melchiori and Gary Taylor all agree on Hand C's contributions to the play and the plots. See also *Sir Thomas More*, ed. Vittorio Gabrieli and Giorgio Melchiori, Manchester, 1990. Since there is nothing to say it was actually staged by the company it has not had the attention in this book that it deserves. Scott McMillin wrote interesting speculations about how it might have been staged in *The Elizabethan Theatre and 'The Book of Sir Thomas More'*, Ithaca, 1987.

Two of the three manuscripts surviving from the company's earlier years, *Sir Thomas More* and *John a Kent*, show the opposite extremes of the writing process. As it stands *Sir Thomas More* is an indecipherable mess, while if we can accept the disputed dating which places it in 1595 and not either 1590 or 1596 Munday's solo manuscript of *John a Kent* is a model of single-author clarity. The third surviving company manuscript, *Jugurtha*, has defects of a different sort. Bodleian MS. Rawl. Poet. 195 is a folio volume composed of six play manuscripts, the fourth of which is entitled 'JUGURTHA, or the FAITLESS COSEN GERMAN A TRAGEDY'. References to William Boyle's play of that name appear in the *Diary*, and Henry Herbert, Master of the Revels through the company's last few years, has a note about an old play burned in Buc's time as Master (possibly in the Fortune fire of 9 December 1621), which he relicensed on 3 May 1624.[29] Thomas Heywood translated the story of King Jugurtha of Numidia in his 1608 history of Sallust. G. E. Bentley describes the manuscript as written in a late seventeenth-century hand. It was left unfinished, ending its formal numbering at Act 4.1, with a few sketched-in scenes following and after a break of three pages four smaller pages of what Bentley calls 'rough unintegrated material'.[30] Parts of it, such as the clown scene 4.1, look like pre-Restoration material incorporated into a later play. On the verso of the second folio leaf is a list of characters. Bentley concludes, sensibly, that it 'might be an incomplete and inexpert Restoration adaptation of Boyle's old play, but it does not seem much more closely related to the earlier *Jugurth* than that'. If he is right, the manuscript has little more value than have the titles for the multitude of the company's lost plays. The most we can say is that in their different ways these three manuscripts do offer evidence of the working processes the company lived with. The much bigger question, which will be looked into shortly, is how many of the surviving play-texts are authorial and how many of them came to the press after use in the theatre with evidence about how they were staged.

The thirty-five plays from the company's thirty-two years that got into print seem to reflect the whole range of manuscript origins that bibliographers find in the rest of the early drama. Old plays could easily be rewritten or added to, as were *The Spanish Tragedy* and *Faustus*. Others by contrast have a merely ghostly existence. What was most likely an early play called 'the famous historye of John of Gaunte, sonne of Kynge Edward the Third, with his conquest of Spaine and marriage of his twoo

[29] See N. W. Bawcutt, *The Control and Censorship of Caroline Drama*, Oxford, 1996, p. 151.
[30] J. C. Bentley, *The Jacobean and Caroline Stage*, III. 35–38.

daughters to the kinges of Castile and Portugale, &c.' was entered in the Stationers' Register on 14 May 1594 but apparently never published. Subsequent records suggest that Hathway and Rankins seem to have started a rewrite of this for Henslowe in 1601 but never completed it. Wherever they got their idea from, the 1601 record seems to mark a new project. The full notes in the *Diary* say: 'Lent unto m^r hathwaye & m^r Ranckens the 24 of m^{r}ch 1600 in earnests of A Boocke called conqueste of spayne some of . . . . x s at the A poyntment of Samewell Rowly; Lent unto m^r hathwaye & m^r Ranckens the 4 of Aprell 1601 in earneste of A playe called the conqueste of spayne the some of . . . v^s; Lent unto m^r hathway & m^r Ranckens the xj of Aprell in earneste of A Boocke called the conquest of spayne by John a gant some of . . . xx^s; Lent unto m^r hathwaye & m^r Ranckens the 16 of aprell 1601 in perte of payment for A Boocke called the conqueste of spayne some of . . . . iiij s.' A letter to Henslowe from Rowley, undated, says: 'M^r hynchlo I praye ye let M^r hathwaye have his papars agayne of the playe of John a gante & for the Repayemente of the money backagayne he Is contente to gyve ye a byll of his hande to be payde at some cartayne tyme as In yor dyscressyon yow shall thinke good, wch done ye maye crose it oute of yor boouke & keepe the byll, or else wele stande so muche indetted to yow & kepe the byll o^r selves. Samuell Rowlye.' Rowley as a sharer probably wrote this at Hathway's instigation, though whether because the writer wanted the manuscript back to make revisions or so he could sell it to another company is unclear. Possibly Rowley liked it well enough to want Hathway to continue rewriting it, at the cost of holding up on Henslowe's final payment.

Of the 229 plays known by their titles to have been written for and most likely performed by the company, texts for no more than thirty-seven have survived, thirty-five in print and two in manuscript. Many of the printed texts seem deficient in one way or another. It is rarely easy to identify which of them might have been printed from an author's manuscript and which from a text that had been through the sort of playhouse alterations that a company book-keeper would have inserted or cut out. Sadly the thing we can be most sure of is that none was printed from one of the 'allowed books' licensed for performance. Almost the only exceptions to that rule were the older texts of Marlowe and Kyd that were already in print and therefore available in their printed form and put to use as promptbooks or allowed books after the Fortune's fire of December 1621. One copy of a Red Bull play printed in 1620, a quarto of *The Two Merry Milkmaids* now in the Folger Shakespeare Library, seems to have been marked for use as a promptbook some time after it was first published.[31] All the post-1621 performances of *Tamburlaine*, *Faustus*, and *The Spanish Tragedy* must have used a printed copy as their promptbook. That admitted, there is still some point in identifying how the extant Admiral's play-texts got to the press, and what kinds of manuscript the printers had when they set them.

Most of the plays written specifically for the Rose appeared in a short run of years from 1599. Even with Henslowe's records of performance it is not easy to determine how quickly they moved from stage to page, but Henslowe did pay Cuthbert Burby, printer of the first of the Admiral's plays in print, *A Knack to Know an Honest Man*, and later of *Patient Grissill*, to stop the printing of the latter play ten days before it was registered with the Stationers and within little more than a month after its first staging. 'Lent unto Robarte shawe the 18 of march 1599 [1600] to geve unto the printer to staye the printinge of patient gresell the some of . . . xxx[s].' It actually reached print three years later, a fairly standard delay. By remarkable contrast from 1604 once Prince Henry's Men were back on stage at the Fortune after the long plague closure the few plays they sold to the press seem to have been got there very quickly. In 1604 Sam Rowley's *When You See Me, You Know Me* appeared from Nathaniel Butter's press within a few months of its first staging. Attitudes to printing playbooks did shift under King James, although Henslowe's and Alleyn's departure from direct involvement in the company may have been a factor in speeding the process.

The earlier history of publications by the Admiral's Men seems largely incidental to their staging. A number of the plays they inherited, *Tamburlaine*, *Friar Bacon and Friar Bungay*, *The Battle of Alcazar* and *The Spanish Tragedy*, were already in print by 1594. The new plays usually came into print slowly, the company having little reason to use publication as a means of exploiting their popularity. As we have noted, the high proportion of single-author plays getting into print hints that they were pushed into publication when their writers leant on the company, although none of them seem to have delivered their own copy to the press. In general it can be said that new plays came to the press only as incidental consequences of their staging at the Rose. The first of them, *A Knack to Know an Honest Man*, staged 'ne' in October 1594, entered in the Stationers' Register a year after its first success and only three months after it left the stage and printed soon after, went through the process with

[31] See Leslie Thomson, 'A Quarto "Marked for Performance": Evidence of What?', *Medieval and Renaissance Drama in England* 5 (1990), 225–43.

unique speed. Its title-page, dated 1596, ignored the company, simply reporting 'As it hath beene sundrie times plaied about the Citie of London'.[32] What prompted its release to the press can hardly have been its takings alone. It appeared in the bookshops shortly before the Chamberlain's began issuing their hits *Richard II, Richard III, Romeo and Juliet* and *1 Henry IV* under the company's name, adding Shakespeare's halfway through the run. The Admiral's followed their model but did not use the author's name for *The Blind Beggar of Alexandria* when Shakespeare's name started appearing in 1598, advertising it only 'As it hath beene sundry times publickly acted in London by the right honorable the Earle of Nottingham, Lord high Admirall his servantes'. Howard's title shows that the title-page was composed when it was printed. He had been elevated to the rank of earl in 1597, a promotion giving him precedence in state processions over the Earl of Essex, his explosive young colleague on the recent Cadiz expedition, delighting him and infuriating the younger man. His new eminence immediately superseded his role as Lord Admiral.

The Blind Beggar of Alexandria's 1598 quarto has careful stage directions but obvious heavy cuts, especially to the more serious romance sections, leaving a play of only 1,600 lines. The cutting was poorly done, Scene 1 including an entry by Pego when he has not left the stage. The romance between Cleanthes and Aegiale is mentioned but not shown, and Aegiale disappears early leaving Cleanthes to woo Princess Aspasia. Verse passages lapse into prose halfway through. The text has a number of apparently memorial errors, probably because it was copied from dictation. The company's third play in print, Chapman's second stage hit *An Humorous Day's Mirth*, came out a year later. It too blazoned the Admiral's company's name without the author's, although *The Two Angry Women of Abingdon* in 1599 paired Henry Porter's name with the Earl of Nottingham's company, the first company play to name its author on the title-page. Chapman's 'comodey of umors' in its only edition of 1599 was most likely printed from the writer's papers, on the evidence of its variant speech headings, descriptive stage directions, and the omission of major character entrances. Several stage directions appear in the margins, including '*Enter Lemot*' when

---

[32] Paul Menzer, 'The Tragedians of the City? Q1 *Hamlet* and the Settlements of the 1590s', *Shakespeare Quarterly* 57 (2006), 162–82, makes the point that there was a clear distinction between the zones designated by 'in the City' and 'about the City', the former referring to the inns used for playing inside the city walls, the latter to the suburbs where the Rose stood. Henslowe consistently used the term 'about the city' in the contracts his players signed to say where they would be allowed to play. None of the Admiral's plays said they had been played 'in the City', as the first quarto of *Hamlet* claimed in 1603.

his arrival is heralded in speech. The Clark Library copy of the quarto has six marginal corrections in a seventeenth-century hand, four to speech prefixes and two correcting text. The entire play was printed as prose, except for three couplets and two additional lines. Most of it obviously meant to be verse, it was first changed into verse lines by R. H. Shepherd in his 1873 edition, followed by T. M. Parrott in his edition of Chapman's *Comedies* in 1914. As with other play-texts, setting verse as prose was a consequence of the manuscript copy lacking clear line divisions.

Old Fortunatus appeared in 1600, the year the company moved to the Fortune, and *Sir John Oldcastle* shortly after, with its Prologue digging at the Rose's new neighbours. Both of these plays had their own reasons for getting the publicity of print. *Look About You* also appeared that year, probably a delayed printing since it announced itself as a play of the Lord Admiral's Men and makes no mention of Howard's elevation in 1597 to Nottingham. On the other hand *The Shoemaker's Holiday* was rushed into print less than a year after its first success on stage. Its 1600 quarto names Howard as Nottingham but still specifies no author. By this time both duopoly companies were getting their plays into print, each issuing more plays in these years than ever before or after. Munday's two *Huntingdon* plays were entered in the Register in December 1600 and printed in 1601. Robert Yarington copied *Two Lamentable Tragedies* for the press in 1601 and *Patient Grissill* was also entered on 18 March 1600, though its appearance in print was held back for another three years as we have seen. That gap went with the flow drying up. The next Admiral's play into print was *1 Honest Whore* in November 1604. It designated no company on its title-page although the first version of *Doctor Faustus* coming out in the same year did. The next play was Samuel Rowley's history of Henry VIII in 1605, *When you See me you Know Me*, 'playd by the high and mightie Prince of Wales his servants', and credited to Rowley as a Prince's man, only the second play to be credited to a company writer. Most of the subsequent publications seem to have been fairly casual, such as *Captain Thomas Stukeley*, entered in the Stationers' Register in August 1600 but not printed until 1605. In 1607 Dekker's *The Whore of Babylon* followed the pattern of printing the company's history plays, acknowledging 'the Princes Servants' as its actors, but this was clearly an author's publication, coming out with extensive marginal notes in Dekker's name.

In the succeeding years almost none of the new Fortune plays appeared in print. *The Roaring Girl* must have been a special case because of Moll Frith's notoriety. It was printed in 1612, a year after the play's fame on stage, its title-page declaring 'As it hath lately beene Acted on the Fortune-stage by the Prince his Players'. *The Duchess of Suffolk* was not printed till 1631, as was Haughton's *Hoffman*, both appearing two years before *The Jew of Malta* at last made its appearance under the fresh stimulus of Beeston and Heywood. Middleton's other play of 1611 for the company, *No Wit / No Help Like a Woman's*, did not come into print until 1657, and *The Blind Beggar of Bethnal Green* not until 1659. Haughton's *The Devil and his Dam* (*Grim the Collier*) was the last to come out, in 1662. Like the manuscript of *Jugurtha* all of these belated publications were most likely prompted by the respect that had accrued to early plays as part of the heavy royalist nostalgia for all the things people felt Protector Cromwell had taken from them. These very belated publications were all dubious texts, clearly subjected to substantial revision through the intervening years. Middleton's *No Wit / No Help Like a Woman's* for instance shows ample signs of revision. It has act breaks inserted, an indoor playhouse practice the Fortune never adopted. Between Acts 4 and 5 in the surviving text a stage direction, '*Manent Widow and Mrs Low-water*', shows that no real act break was needed. And at 3.1.279–82 (E7 of the 1657 octavo) Weatherwise says the year is not 1611 when Middleton sold it to the Fortune company but 1638: 'now in One thousand six hundred thirty and eight, the Dominical Letter being G, I stood for a Goose'.[33] That was the year when Shirley staged the play in Dublin. First performed not long after *The Roaring Girl*, it was enough of a highlight in the company's plays of that year to appear twice at court, the second time before the company's own patron, Prince Henry,[34] but not enough to be put into print then.

In her comprehensive survey of the early modern play-texts claimed at one time or another to be based on memorial transcription Laurie Maguire identified forty that at one time or another were thought to have contents entered from memory rather than from written copy.[35] Of those seven are plays from the Admiral's repertory: *Edward I* (Q 1593), *The Massacre at Paris* (Q 1594?), *A Knack to Know an Honest Man* (Q 1596),

---

[33] See John Jowett, 'Middleton's *No Wit* at the Fortune', *Renaissance Drama* n.s. 22 (1991), 191–208. The speaker is Weatherwise, who probably gave his name to the play for its court performance. In 1611 the dominical letter was F, but Jowett does not think Middleton set down F rather than G.

[34] The court's recorders called it *The Almanac*, remembering its chief gull and 'humours' character Weatherwise, who is obsessed with almanacs and sets up a masque featuring almaniac signs. Whereas the *No Wit* title picks out Mistress Low-water's disguising to help her brother Beveril and the coupling of *Wit* and *Help* accounts for the whole plot, the court's title picks up only the 'humour' of Weatherwise. Jowett suggests (pp. 194–97) that for the court to describe the play by its leading comic's name matched the use of the names Falstaff, Parolles and Benedict and Beatrice for other plays in the court lists.

[35] Laurie Maguire, *Shakespearean Suspect Texts: The 'Bad' Quartos and their Contexts*, Cambridge University Press, 1996, Tables 3, 5, 6, 7, 14, 19, 22 and 34.

The Blind Beggar of Alexandria (Q 1598), *The Death of Robert Earl of Huntingdon* (Q 1600), *Doctor Faustus* (Qq 1604, 1616) and the additions to the 1602 quarto of *The Spanish Tragedy*. While the theory of memorial transcription has been largely discarded, the texts so identified do show evidence of casualness or incompetence in the process of their transcription for the press. If to these cases we add the manifestly poor texts of *Look About You* (Q 1599), *Stukeley* (Q 1605), and *Hoffman* (Q 1631), along with some of the plays printed very late such as *The Blind Beggar of Bethnal Green* (Q 1659) and *Grim the Collier* (1662), the list of 'good' play-texts surviving from the Admiral's repertoire shrinks to a small number indeed. Some texts do seem to have been transcribed professionally and carefully for the press, notably Yarington's script of *The Double Tragedy*. For the most part, however, the Admiral's plays largely appear to have derived from minimal staged texts rather than the 'allowed book' maximal versions.

It can hardly be doubted that, for all the likelihood of intervention by Chapman and Dekker to secure the appearance in print of their own plays, a substantial majority of the surviving Admiral's plays read as if they were printed from theatre copies rather than authors'. Most of the play-texts show not just the usual signs of rapid and careless setting, but have stage directions, mislineations and evidence of cutting that reflect a manuscript not originally intended for the press, and certainly not edited for the reader. In the general picture of the printing of plays a number of surviving play manuscripts have verse lines written without line breaks, sometimes not even with marks to identify where the verse lines ended. That helps to explain the peculiar practices with verse lineation in many quartos, where verse was set as prose and sometimes prose as verse. The process of transcription behind most of the Admiral's plays suggests that they were not author's but company copies.[36]

---

[36] Variation in the length of the printed texts is also striking. In the order of their performance according to the *Diary*, the line-lengths are as follows: *The Jew of Malta* 2417; *The Massacre at Paris* 1586; *1 Tamburlaine* 2469; *Doctor Faustus* 1518 / 2122; *A Knack to Know an Honest Man* 1805; *The Wise Men of West Chester* (ms) 1705; *2 Tamburlaine* 2249; *Longshanks* (Peele's *Edward I*) 2686; *Disguises* (*Look About You?*) 3212; *Old Fortunatus* 2884; *The Blind Beggar of Alexandria* 1611; *Captain Thomas Stukeley* 2982; *The Spanish Tragedy* 2967; *An Humorous Day's Mirth* 1995; *Dido and Aeneas* [Marlowe's *Dido* 2017]; *The Downfall of Huntingdon* 2840; *Englishmen for my Money* 2685; *The Death of Huntingdon* 3053; *The Two Angry Women of Abingdon* 3037; *The Shoemaker's Holiday* 2295; *1 Sir John Oldcastle* 2719; *Patient Grissill* 2677; *Two Lamentable Tragedies* 2757; *Jugurtha* (ms) 2000 (unfinished); *The Battle of Alcazar* 1592; *Grim the Collier* (*The Devil and his Dam*) 2231; *The Blind Beggar of Bethnal Green* 2643; *Friar Bacon and Friar Bungay* 2155; *Hoffman* 2618; *1 The Honest Whore* 2686; *When You See Me, You Know Me* 3095; *The Whore of Babylon* 2874; *The Roaring Girl* 2893; *No Wit / No Help Like a Woman's* 3126; *The Duchess of Suffolk* 2244. These figures are mostly taken from the through-line numbering of the MSR editions.

At both extremes of the printing period, in 1597 and in 1662, in almost all cases the compositors seem to have set the text as they read it in their manuscripts, regardless of whether it was meant to be verse or prose. The quarto of *An Humorous Day's Mirth* runs for just under 2,000 lines, all set as prose, though much of it reads as if it had been designed as verse. Even the scene-closing rhyming couplets were set as prose, as appears at 1389–90, where the final lines of the scene in the quarto run like this:

I will in silent live a man forlorne, mad, and melancholy, as a cat, and never more weare hat band on my hat.

For all that the last nine words of this make a perfect pentameter any manuscript that has all its rhyme-endings set as prose and no verse lineation would give the compositors a bigger problem than it would give to the players who had to speak the lines.

There is only space here to look at the text of one Admiral's play in detail, but it does have a characteristic story to tell. Chettle wrote *The Tragedy of Hoffman* as a single-author play at the end of 1602. On 29 December Henslowe lent five shillings to Thomas Downton of the Admiral's 'to geve unto harey chettell in perte of paymente for A tragedie called Hawghman' (*Diary*, p. 207). Because there is no record of any further payments it was probably not completed till after Henslowe's entries stop in March 1603. That may also mean that it went instead to Worcester's, which would explain how it came later to Christopher Beeston's Queen Henrietta's Men, since the 1631 quarto title-page claimed: 'As it hath bin divers times acted with great applause, at the *Phenix* in *Druery-lane*'.[37] This implies that it moved companies on the same track as *The Jew of Malta*, published as a Cockpit play in 1633 and which we know had been an Admiral's play since 1594. Moreover *Hoffman* has two brothers who are named Mathias and Lodowick, the same as the rivals for Abigail in *The Jew of Malta*. One of Hoffman's rivals kills the other under Hoffman's plotting, as Barabbas makes his pair do in *The Jew*. Using the same names for the two sons who are tricked into killing each other in a duel suggests a closer affinity than simply the renown of Marlowe's play. It seems likely that Chettle in 1602 chose his names for *Hoffman* with a reference to the Admiral's company's most famous murdering farce in his mind.[38]

---

[37] See Harold Jenkins, *The Tragedy of Hoffman*, Malone Society Reprints, Oxford, 1950, p. v.

[38] T. S. Eliot admiringly called *The Jew of Malta* a 'farce, the terribly serious, even savage comic humour, the humour which spent its last breath in the decadent genius of Dickens' (*Selected Essays*, p. 123).

The one surviving quarto of *Hoffman* was poorly printed, with sloppy presswork and inadequate locking-up of the type in the formes, a multitude of press corrections and much of the text not very carefully set with an uncomfortably large number of reversed u/n letters. On the final page the verse ends abruptly, perhaps because, as commonly happened with ageing manuscripts, the last page of the original was damaged or lost. The truncated text gives the story no formal conclusion. Hoffman curses the love that has altered his impulse to comprehensive revenge, while the threat of being killed by the burning crown that he had used to murder his chief enemies is still hanging over him. This confirms the likelihood that the manuscript given to the press had already endured a long and decaying life in storage. Three gaps in the typesetting also suggest that there were unbridgeable breaks in the manuscript copy (at TLN 199, 1376 and 1697), and if we can judge from syntax and meaning other gaps seem likely. It was evidently a well-worn manuscript, possibly copied from an old allowed playbook since one stage direction at 4.2 for the entry of the Duchess Martha asks for '*as many as may be spar'd*' to line her procession. The text also shows signs of quite a few corrections and alterations. Like the first printing of *No Wit, No Help*, the 1631 text despite being composed at a time and for a playhouse using continuous staging was printed showing five act breaks, and at the end of the first act (TLN 411) Hoffman says 'So shut our stage up, there is one act done / Ended in *Othos* death.' As with the Middleton play this must indicate later revision to fit it for an indoor playhouse.

The assumption that it underwent changes during that long life is endorsed by two imperfect attempts made at least ten years after Chettle first wrote it to alter the name of the character killed in the first scene, Prince Otho. He is Hoffman's first victim, murdered with a burning crown after being shipwrecked at the opening. Once he has killed him, Hoffman takes his name and identity (another company disguise trick) to pursue his next revenges. On sig. F (Scenes 3.1 and 2), after a speech heading '*Hoff*' at sig. F1 while Hoffman is disguised as Prince Otho there are two references in stage directions to 'Hoffman' on F2, but then his speech headings become '*Sarl*', for '*Sarloys*', a Norwegian general previously named by Old Stilt in 3.1 (F1ᵛ). This speech heading continues in use on F2ᵛ and on to F4ᵛ. On sigs. G and H he enters as '*Sarlois*' in 4.1, and is '*Sarl*' in all the next speech headings. At sig. H2 he re-enters halfway through 4.2 as '*Hoffman*' again, and remains under that name until the end. He is still called 'Hoffman' through TLN 2103–32 where the script reaffirms his pretence of being Otho, so it was clearly not a change of speech prefix to mark his disguise. The way these changes fail to coincide with the quarto's printed formes indicates that they were already there in the revised manuscript and not a printer's misreading.

The reason for this renaming for Hoffman's alias was the death of the company's patron Prince Henry in late 1612, because Chettle's own original name for Otho was Prince Charles, Henry's brother who succeeded him as Prince of Wales. The metre makes it clear that at first Chettle had his name as the monosyllabic 'Charles'. The switch to Otho was not made very consistently through the manuscript, and nearly as many uses of 'Charles' survive in the printed text as 'Otho'. In 1602, when Chettle was composing the play, James's younger son was only two years old and nobody was yet prepared to speculate openly that he would become the English heir apparent. Abandoning the name 'Prince Charles' for the revenger's first victim, however, became essential after November 1612. Hoffman's Charles then had to become 'Otho', says Harold Jenkins, editor of the MSR edition, to remove the obvious association, but the change was made imperfectly. Several references in 3.2 and elsewhere survive to 'Prince Charles' (1226, 1229 and 1314, especially in Ferdinand Duke of Prussia's varying references to Hoffman as Otho or Charles).

Like the 'Sarloys' change these alterations were made in the manuscript well before it reached the compositor of the 1631 quarto. At first 'Otho' was inserted consistently after the opening scene's shipwreck, since the new name appears in a stage direction at 108, at 111 and after and in the speech headings, until he is killed with the burning crown. The same name is used of a shipwreck victim in the next scene, at 288 and 380, when Lorique furthers Hoffman's revenge plan by claiming misleadingly that it was Otho who killed Hoffman, not the other way round. In 1.3 Hoffman enters to proclaim his imposture using the name Otho, and in Act 2 at 490 a herald proclaims Hoffman as Otho to be Prussia's heir in place of Ferdinand's foolish son Jerome. In 2.2 this elevation is repeated (537). In 2.3 when Hoffman adopts the disguise of a hermit to develop his plots the speech headings start calling him '*Clo.*' for *Clois*, his first name. As the hermit Clois tells the lovers Lodowick and Lucibella that they are to be murdered by Ferdinand and must flee through Prince Otho's lodging, giving them the key. When they have fled he gives the hermit's gown back to Lorique and as Prince Otho he meets Mathias, telling him that Lucibella has run off with a Grecian, and sends Mathias off to kill them. In 3.1 Mathias finds the lovers and stabs them both, killing Lodowick. Hoffman keeps his pretence of being Otho for the new arrivals, the Dukes of Saxony and Austria, the second of whom Hoffman quietly stabs.

Up to here the post-1612 renaming seems largely well done, although the monosyllabic Clois might have done better than Otho as a replacement for Charles.

Confusion reigns thereafter. It is in 3.2 that the clowns first mention Sarloys. Hoffman is given that speech heading from 1209 till the end of 4.1 (1680), where the original name returns. 'Sarl' takes Otho back to being Charles at 1226 and 1229, but for the clown Stilt he is 'Otho' again at 1307. He is 'worthy nephew *Charles*' to Ferdinand at 1314, whereas at 1363 and 1396 Stilt again calls him 'Prince *Otho*'. Act 4.1 (Sig. G) opens with a stage direction for 'Sarlois' and his 'Princely uncle' Ferdinand, and at 1567 Lorique enters '*hastily*' shouting about Jerome's 'treason' against Ferdinand, naming 'My Princely Master! *Otho* of *Luningberg*', to which Jerome inconsistently replies that he did not aim at his father Ferdinand but at 'my cozen *Charles*.' Both Jerome and Ferdinand then die from Lorique's poison, but when Saxony asks 'yong *Otho* what art thou poyson'd too?' Hoffman answers that he is well. A few lines later (1649) Saxony again addresses him as 'Prince *Otho*'. Hoffman, still speaking here under the speech heading '*Sarl*', tells Lorique in private when the Duchess Martha, Otho's mother, is mentioned that 'they suppose me to be *Otho* her son' (1673). Through the rest of the play the name Otho replaces Charles seven more times, at 1795, 1796, 1879, 1895, 2135, 2262 and 2574, and then the hero becomes Hoffman again in all subsequent references and speech headings. But four times more he goes back to being Charles in exchanges between the conspirators Hoffman and Lorique (1852 *Hoffman*: 'Prince *Charles*'; 2009 *Lorique*: 'my Princely Master *Charles*', 2101 and 2223). Nonetheless, at 2132–35 Lorique confesses to the mother

> *Hoffman* forc't me to conceale
> The murder of my Lord, and threatned more
> Then death by many torments, till I swore
> To call him *Otho*, and say he was your son.

This spread of the two names through the text shows that 'Otho' was meant to be the replacement for 'Charles' but that it was not altered thoroughly enough in the manuscript. On stage the players would presumably have made their own corrections to the text.

The secondary issue, the use of 'Sarloys' for Hoffman, has its own puzzles. Harold Jenkins suggests that the compositor misread his first name '*Clois*', which had been used in some speech headings up to then, as '*Sarl*'. Hoffman has '*Clo.*' as his speech heading when he is dressed as the hermit in 2.3 at 683, 690, 707, 728, 747, 759, 775, 777, 781, 786, 791, 793,

799, 811, 817 and 830, although he is '*Hoff*' once at 742. At his re-entry in 3.1 he is '*Clo.*' and again at 902 and 936, but '*Hoff.*' at 921 and in his third speech at 961 and subsequently (sig. E2 – F1). It is later in Sig. F that he becomes '*Sarl.*' We might conjecture that '*Sarl*' was a second attempt at replacing '*Charles*', perhaps at some later time than when the prince's name first became an embarrassment. This all suggests that the manuscript behind the printer's text shows decades of various book-keeper's emendations. One wonders how distant what was sold to the printers in 1631 was from the 'allowed book' the company originally had licensed in 1603.

The relatively poor quality of so many of the Admiral's company texts has had the same malign effect on their reception as it has on the versions of the Shakespeare plays that exist in early and 'bad' quarto or octavo form. If they are read carefully, however, and especially when they are viewed as plays on stage they are not nearly so troubling as they seem when thought of as the carefully composed author's verse that critics used to think them. They lack the centuries of polish that have been applied to the longer Shakespeare versions from the First Folio that we now prefer to read. The few editions of the Admiral's company's plays so far in print give little sense of them as good theatre, and few of them have much of the footnoting that dominates the Shakespeare editions. If they were published as stage scripts, whether oratorical like the Marlowes or farcical like *The Blind Beggar of Alexandria* or *Look About You*, their stage quality would be unquestionable.

4

Staging at the Rose and the Fortune

For more than thirty years up to 1625 the Admiral's company seems to have sustained the practices that the *Diary* tells us they ran from 1594. The successor companies at the Fortune did the same under King Charles up to 1642. The company played all the year round at their open-air venues the Rose and subsequently the Fortune, giving no regard, unlike their opposites, to seasonal changes of weather or daylight hours. And they appear to have kept broadly the same sort of repertory throughout. This was drastically in contrast to the Chamberlain's Men, who in October 1594, within five months of being set up, tried to secure an indoor venue so that they could play at a city inn for the winter. When that move was thwarted their backer James Burbage started an amazingly bold plan, building his own indoor playhouse inside the city in the Blackfriars precinct near St Paul's where a previous playhouse had once housed a company of boy players. Local residents blocked Burbage's venture on the nimby principle, and in the event the Chamberlain's did not fulfil their ambition to run at different summer and winter venues for another fourteen years, until after the long plague closure of 1608–09. But separate venues, outdoors for summer and indoors for winter, were always their preference.

Even after the Chamberlain's seasonal changes began to prove such a triumph with the gentry in the second decade of the seventeenth century the company backed by Alleyn and Henslowe stayed loyal to their original policy. Alleyn did make attempts to imitate the Blackfriars by investing in an indoor venue of his own, the so-called Porter's Hall venture at Puddle Dock in 1615. But for all his good connections at court through running their bear-baitings and Henslowe's status as Groom of the Chamber they were never able to match the King's Men and the dominance they acquired over gentrified playgoing tastes with the Blackfriars. Whatever might have gone through Henslowe's and Alleyn's minds the Admiral's players themselves appear to have been quite content with their populist outdoor venues accommodating much greater numbers of playgoers than the indoor venues. For them to use only the Rose and the Fortune seems normative to us because our thinking is still ruled by knowing that Shakespeare spent his ten greatest years writing exclusively for the Globe. That the Globe was a superannuated extension of a venture dating back thirty-three years to 1576, and a second-best option from 1594 onwards, is a concept too easily lost behind the present-day glow of 'Shakespeare at the Globe'. From the outset the two companies of the duopoly followed strikingly alternative policies over their habitual playing-places. The Globe became half of the Chamberlain's policy of using outdoor and indoor venues seasonally, while the Rose and its successor the Fortune made the constant base for the Admiral's policy of running only outdoor performances throughout the year.

That is one fundamental feature of their practice that distinguishes the Admiral's from its opposite across the city. Both the Globe and the Fortune, built by the same carpenter in 1599 and 1600, were based on a plan that James Burbage first set up in 1576 with the Theatre's framing timbers, later used to shape the Globe. The innovatory Blackfriars, a model for all subsequent indoor theatres, was the real innovation. A second distinction is that the Admiral's two outdoor venues were radically different from one another. We will probably never know to what extent the Fortune's difference from the Rose was dictated by concerns about staging practices thrown up by the six years of performances at the Rose, practices that the Fortune must at least in part have been designed to alter, or how much the distinct shapes of the two playhouses were determined by simply physical considerations like the need to exploit the square shape of the Fortune's plot of land to the maximum. The archaeological excavations have told us quite precisely how the smaller Rose was elongated in 1592 from a fourteen-sided polygon into a cup-shape, still with fourteen sides but extended rather irregularly by lengthening the galleries on each flank to provide a bigger yard and more seating. The Fortune was built square by the carpenter who had just completed the round Globe, but in other respects it was meant to match the Globe, in its design, its capacity and its decoration. The Fortune's galleries had the same number of bays as the twenty-sided Globe and were of similar size, and the builder's contract keeps specifying the need to copy the Globe.[1] If there were any developments in playhouse design or thinking between the Theatre in 1576 and 1600 when the Fortune opened, they must have been incorporated in Alleyn's new

---

[1] See John Orrell, 'Building the Fortune', *Shakespeare Quarterly* 44 (1993), 127–44.

playhouse. When it burned down in 1621 John Chamberlain wrote that it had been 'the fayrest play-house in this towne'.[2] But then he used the identical term to describe the Globe when it was rebuilt in 1614 after its fire.

The chief difference between the 1592 Rose and the 1600 Fortune was the radical contrast between the shallow and elongated hexagon of the Rose's stage with posts upholding the stage cover at the very front edge, and the deep and rectilinear Fortune stage with its well-inset posts upholding the stage cover. That shape change must have been the principal development between the older, smaller venue on Bankside and the new one in Clerkenwell. For all the differences, though, the Admiral's Men developed at the Rose a set of standard staging practices that lasted at their second venue until Parliament closed all the playhouses in September 1642. So first we should look at the pair of huge benefits our good knowledge of the Admiral's two playhouses brings us, what the archaeologists have found about the shape of the Rose and what the 'cheefe carpenters' contract for building the Fortune tells us. That should help us to study what the surviving texts suggest about how the company might have staged the plays written for the two open-air venues.

The Rose playhouse occupied a former rose garden about a hundred yards south of the Thames. Its first structure in 1587, so far as archaeological analysis of its ground plan from what survives as its 'footprint' in the earth of modern Southwark can tell, was designed as a regular fourteen-sided polygon. Jon Greenfield has shown that the peculiar number of sides in this polygon can quite easily be set out with only a single surveyor's rod (16 feet 6 inches long), and some cord.[3] The outer walls had a diameter (using the old 'imperial' sizes of feet and inches) of about seventy-three feet across. Each of the fourteen outer sides of the foundations uncovered in 1989 measures the standard length of one rod.[4] Inside these outer walls the galleries were set out as fourteen bays averaging twelve feet six inches across and about eight feet from front to rear, their inner walls making the flanks of the central space or 'yard', which was forty-seven feet in diameter. The southernmost bay contained the main doorway. Originally thought to have been wider than the other thirteen sides, it has now been established as having a dimension identical to the others. The bay to admit the audience was positioned on the

[2] *Letters of John Chamberlain*, II. 415.
[3] See Jon Greenfield (with Andrew Gurr), 'Questions about the Rose', *Antiquity* 78 (2004), 330–40, p. 334.
[4] Julian Bowsher, in 'The Rose and its Stages', *Shakespeare Survey* 60 (2007), p. 37, states that the original idea that the entrance bay was wider than the others has proved to be an error.

polygon's southern flank that opened onto the north side of Maiden Lane, a road that (now renamed Park Street, though more apt for cars than grass) still runs parallel to the river a quarter-mile upstream from London Bridge. The stage, shaped roughly as a very broad and irregular hexagon jutting out in front of three bays of the polygon's flank, stood opposite this main doorway on the northern side of the polygon.

The building method and materials were standard for most Elizabethan structures built on a domestic or larger scale. Brick foundations were laid on top of a polygonal trench packed with local stones. On this foundation wall roughly eighteen inches high was set a prefabricated timber frame, its chief basal element a set of oak beams or 'bressumers', each a foot or so wide. Mortised and tenoned into those stood the whole interlocking timber frame, prefabricated and marked to fit piece by piece. The oak framing timbers were originally cut and shaped flat on the ground in a timber yard far upriver, then dismantled and re-erected interlocked on the site to make a self-supporting three-dimensional structure. Each of the fourteen vertical posts at the angles of the outer frame would have been perhaps thirty feet tall by at least one foot square, held by three sets of horizontal beams locked into the frame by mortice and tenon joints. Besides the horizontal cross-beams, others ran inwards to the inner wall's verticals, outlining the frame for the two or three levels of the galleries.[5] The fourteen vertical beams in the angles of the outer wall weighed over a ton each, a massive job for the erectors if they did not have the haulage skills with ropes they shared with the local shipbuilders along the Thames in nearby Bermondsey. The inner gallery walls were constructed parallel to this outer frame of timber posts, probably, if the contract for the Fortune is any guide, at floor-heights for the lowest level of twelve feet from the ground, with above them eleven and nine feet heights respectively. The upper levels each had an inward 'jetty', jutting nearly a foot forward from those below them, so that the gallery fronts jutted some distance into the yard. This helped people choosing to stand at the back of the yard by the inner walls to take some shelter from London's rain. In both sets of wall frames the panels between the framing timbers were

---

[5] We can be certain that the Fortune had three levels of gallery, but it has been suggested that the Rose may only have had two, since the erosion trench around the fringes of the yard left by the rain that dripped from the covering thatch is positioned rather too close to the inner walls of the galleries to admit an overhanging 'jetty' of two feet that three levels with two jutties would give. See Jon Greenfield, 'Reconstructing the Rose: Development of the Playhouse Building between 1587 and 1592', *Shakespeare Survey* 60 (2007), p. 31. Considering the effect of feet scuffing the erosion trench when it rained and thus extending the broken area, this question has to count as still unsettled.

in-filled with split oak laths; lime plaster was then poked between the laths and smoothed over to make an even surface. A similar finish with added wall plaster and paint was applied to the 'gentlemens roomes' next to the stage. The timber and plaster exterior was limewashed as a preservative for both plaster and timbers. Flooring and the benches inside the frame were constructed out of deal (pine) from the Baltic, a softer and cheaper wood than oak. The whole interior was painted, and grotesque carvings in oak were applied or pilastered onto the main posts as colourfully painted 'Satyrs' or gargoyles, conspicuous features of the interior decoration.

The stage was built to jut out from the northern gallery bays once the polygonal frame had been completed. These three bays served as the tiring house for the players. They had glazed windows at the rear to bring in light to the dressing room where the actors prepared themselves before making their entrances. Some years later a penthouse cover was fitted over the rear entranceway into the tiring house to shelter the players and perhaps any lords who wished to enter through the tiring house to sit on the stage balcony and watch the play. The stage's flanks stuck out from the bays outside the three that made the tiring house, pushing into the yard at an angle. That allowed one entranceway onto the stage from each of the three complete northernmost bays. The stage's main entry-point was the middle one of the three, sometimes now called the 'discovery space', a broad opening with most likely a pair of doors. The other two points of entry probably had single doors or curtained openings angled towards each other in the adjacent bays.

A central opening onto the stage was an essential feature of the staging, not least because it allowed access for the most commented-on event in *2 Tamburlaine*. In the second part (4.3) of the two most famous plays Alleyn brought to the Rose, Tamburlaine stands in a chariot hauled onto the stage by four kings he has conquered, exhorting his 'pampered Jades' in the famous speech that Ancient Pistol misquotes. Pulling the chariot out of the tiring house demanded a wider opening than either of the more normal doors in the flanking bays provided. The central bay in a fourteen-sided polygon with its wide opening at the back of the stage allowed it to stand almost directly opposite the bay where the audience entered into the yard from Maiden Lane.[6]

---

[6] The iconic significance of the central opening, or '*locus*', and its function as the entry-point for figures of authority in contrast to flanking doors and the '*platea*', or margins of the stage where the characters of lower class and clowns prowled, has been demonstrated by Robert Weimann. See *Author's Pen and Actor's Voice, Playing and Writing in Shakespeare's Theatre*, Cambridge, 2000, esp. pp. 183–92. The first deductions by the archaeologists about the Rose's foundations made the playhouse entrance bay wider than the others, an error reproduced in the Greenfield and Gurr article in *Antiquity* 78. The correction was noted by Julian Bowsher in 'The Rose and its Stages', p. 37.

From what was said about the Rose's neighbouring playhouses on Bankside, the Swan built in 1595 and the Globe four years later, it seems that the Rose was by some degree the smallest of the three. In 1602 Henslowe wrote of it as 'the littell Roosse' (*Diary* p. 213). It must have been chiefly as a result of its limited size that at the beginning of 1592 he set out to enlarge it in the only direction he could, to the north. The original structure had probably cost less than £300,[7] and the enlargement, for which we have precise figures and specifications,[8] cost him another £126. In effect it involved a substantial expansion of auditorium space. The builders elongated the most eastern and western bays of the originally symmetrical polygon by six and a half feet northwards to provide extra galleries on each side and more standing room in the yard. To do this they had to demolish the existing stage and tiring house and take the timber frame apart, a straightforward task given Elizabethan building techniques using interlocked timbers. An additional stretch of galleries was constructed on each side, east and west, and the bays to the north containing the stage and tiring house were then re-erected to an only slightly different design. This enlargement might have added something like another five hundred places to the original capacity of nearly two thousand people.

The work must have included some improvements both to the stage and to the tiring house, although sadly the archaeological remains give little tangible evidence about what the alterations above ground level might have created. It has been suggested that one of the 1592 improvements added a roof over the stage that was not there in the original 1587 construction. A cover or 'shadow' upheld by posts on the stage certainly existed subsequently, but the idea that the original Rose lacked any stage cover is itself tenuous. We know almost nothing of what plays might have been staged at Rose 1, so we lack evidence for descent machinery or even a minimal roof over the stage to protect the player's expensive costumes from the rain. That helps to make the question of Rose 2's stage posts important, as we shall see below.

The re-created Rose of 1592 had a similar shape for its stage to its predecessor. Still a hexagon, now elongated and even less regular than its predecessor, the three bays of the tiring house behind it still provided

[7] Jon Greenfield, 'Reconstructing the Rose', pp. 28–29, points out that Henslowe's £816 contract with Cholmley of January 1586 was for catering, not building, and proposes the construction cost was about £250.

[8] Henslowe listed his expenses in considerable detail, including the cost of a barge to convey the new timbers to the site, loads of 'syxpennynaylles', laths and lime, and wages for the thatcher, carpenters and painters (*Diary*, pp. 9–13).

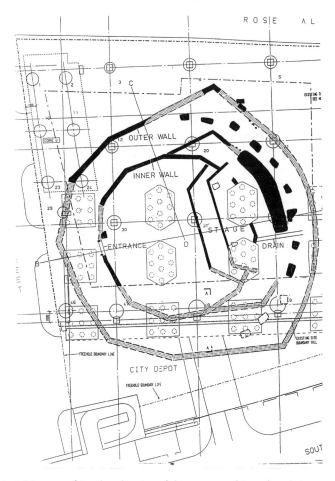

Figure 8. A Museum of London drawing of the two sets of Rose foundations uncovered in 1989. Its alignment is east–west, the western flank being at the top of the picture. Park Street, on the south side, is to the left. The shapes of the two stages, the later one further back to the right, are clearly evident. The section of galleries and stage at the bottom of the outline, in grey, has not yet been excavated. The hexagonal and square shapes with circles inside are the modern concrete foundations of Southbridge House, demolished in 1986.

shallow angles so that entrants from either flanking door could quickly face one another. That was good for confrontations on stage such as Oberon's with Titania ('Ill met by moonlight . . .') or John a Kent's with John a Cumber when the Englishman and the Scotsman were each disguised as the other. The stage's hexagon was irregular because the two flanking edges projected at a sharper angle into the yard than the angle each bay of the polygon had with its neighbour. The earlier stage's front edge, built on a brick foundation, was rather less than twenty-seven feet across on the yard side. The flanks angling into the galleries were roughly fifteen feet, while the width of the *frons scenae* at the rear with its three angles was thirty-seven feet six inches. From the tiring house's central bay with its wide opening to where the groundlings stood in the yard with their chins on the stage rim both stages were barely sixteen feet in depth. The later stage, six feet six inches further north, may have been slightly wider than the first and therefore had a slightly bigger floor space, though until its eastern flank is excavated we cannot be sure of its exact dimensions. Neither stage had much more than five hundred square feet of floor space, markedly smaller than any calculated for other stages of the time, including the Fortune's.

The Rose's yard was surfaced with what has been identified as a standard version of Elizabethan mortar, sand and river sediment mixed with cinders supplemented with cement and hazelnut shells. The hazelnut shells and cinders, advertised as good road-surfacing material in a pamphlet of 1592,[9] were a by-product of Southwark's local soap factories. The mortar surface both in Rose 1 and Rose 2 seems to have been raked at an angle of almost ten degrees, sloping downwards to the centre, although no evidence was found for a drain from the centre to the exterior of the building. However, the remains of what seems to have been a barrel-head were uncovered near the centre in front of the stage. The rake would have made it easier for the crowd at the rear to see the stage over the heads of those in front of them.[10] Mortar was also found on the under-stage area, sloping slightly down to the south, presumably helping mud-free access under the stage to the trapdoor.

The debris the archaeologists found in the yard included a lot of un-reuseable remains of the demolished theatre, chiefly thatch from the gallery roof and lath and plaster from the walls. Under that, among the yard's mortar remains and in the sections of the galleries below where the lowest level of benches would have been the archaeologists found plenty of human deposits, including genuine food residues, not only unburned hazelnut shells but walnut shells, plumstones, figs, cherrystones, grape pips, and remnants of apples, pears and elderberry seeds plus seeds of blackberry, raspberry and sloeberry, along with remnants of rye, oat

[9] See John Orrell, 'Nutshells at the Rose', *Theatre Research International* 17 (1992), 8–14.
[10] That is the view of Julian Bowsher, 'The Rose and its Stages', p. 43.

Figure 9. John Norden's picture of the Rose with six sides, engraved for *Civitas Londini*, 1592. He evidently did not bother to count the number of sides in the polygon he drew, found in 1989 to be fourteen in all.

and wheatbread and marine and freshwater oyster shells. In addition, fragments were found of pottery for both cooking and carrying food, and some slotted pottery moneyboxes.[11] Playgoing must have been more than a bit like a modern picnic. Human debris also included bits of shoes, a broken scabbard, part of a spur, a ring, and coins and a Nuremberg money token. Besides the food debris relics found underneath the gallery floors included lots of small items from men's and women's clothing, fragments of cloth of different kinds, a lot of variously coloured beads and pins, fragments of lace and broken hair combs.

Few other signs of use with obvious significance for the staging have been discovered so far by the archaeologists. Since everything besides the

[11] Studies of the archaeology and its lessons include Julian Bowsher, *The Rose Theatre: An Archaeological Discovery*, Museum of London, 1998; Christine Eccles, *The Rose Theatre*, London, 1990; Jon Greenfield and Andrew Gurr, 'The Rose Theatre, London: The State of Knowledge and What We Still Need to Know', *Antiquity* 78 (2004), 330–40; Andrew Gurr and John Orrell, 'What the Rose Can Tell Us', *Antiquity* 63 (1989), 421–29; and *Documents of the Rose Playhouse*, ed. Carol Chillington Rutter, Manchester, 1984, revised edition 2001. The most substantial account of the archaeological finds is Bowsher and Miller's, *The Rose and the Globe – Playhouses of Tudor Bankside, Southwark: Excavations 1988–91*, Museum of London, 2009.

Figure 10. Norden's supplementary engraving made in 1600 of the Rose (Norden called it The Stare, perhaps misinterpreting the Tudor Rose on its flag as being a star). He positioned it in between the old Bear Garden nearest the Thames, and the recently opened Globe on the other side of Maiden Lane. Cholmley's house selling food and drink is located on the south-western flank of the site.

footprint of what was left at ground level when the playhouse was demolished is debris from the building's demolition in 1604 or thereabouts what stood above the footprint on the upper levels is still matter for conjecture. We cannot even be sure that there were three levels of galleries and not just two. Nor is there any clear evidence of how the members of the audience who wanted a superior position would have climbed up to the upper gallery level or levels. Either of two options that were noted in other playhouses might have been used, internal stairways or an external stair turret.[12] A map of Paris Garden Manor showing the Swan in 1628 gives it a single stair turret on its north-eastern flank, just where the Rose might have a tower in the section not yet excavated. Until the eastern part of the Rose site can be excavated we can only speculate that the base for a turret might be found there. External access by a stair turret to the galleries had two advantages. First, it left more space free for seats that would otherwise

---

[12] The evidence about stair turrets is considered at length in Gurr, 'The Bare Stage', *Shakespeare Survey* 47 (1994), 29–43, esp. pp. 40–43.

Figure 11. A drawing by Jon Greenfield of the Rose Theatre Trust, showing a hypothetical and slightly off-centred view of the Rose and its stage in profile as seen from the yard entrance-way.

be needed for interior stairways, and secondly it brought the latecomers in at the back, not through the front press of the crowd as the *ingressi* from the yard do to the lowest galleries in De Witt's drawing of the Swan.

Having the last arrivals enter a crowd directly from the yard as De Witt shows at the Swan can be confrontational, to say the least. But until more digging can be done there is nothing to say that the Rose did have a similar space-saving fixture. Nothing of the Rose's remains uncovered in 1989 seems to show any *ingressi* like those in the Swan drawing. The Paris Garden map showing the Swan with a single stair turret on its north-eastern side actually conflicts with Henslowe's contract for the Hope in 1614, which orders the builder to create 'two stearecasses . . . of such largnes and height as the stearecasses of the saide playehouse called the Swan'.[13] Identifying the Swan as having two turrets where the map shows

---

[13] E. K. Chambers, *Elizabethan Stage*, II. 466.

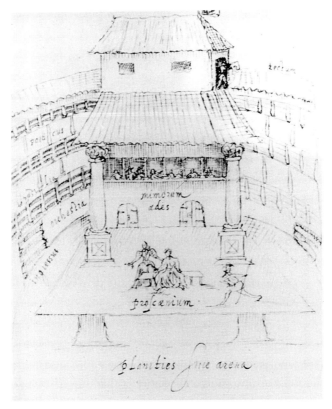

Figure 12. Van Buchell's copy of De Witt's drawing of the Swan made in 1596. The steps from the yard to the lowest gallery are marked '*ingressus*'.

only one does not encourage reliance on the Paris Garden map as evidence about the Swan, but it does curiously suit the Rose with its fourteen sides and so-far hidden eastern flank. The map of the Swan shows a stair turret positioned at one of the vertical posts exactly like the placing of the stair turret foundation uncovered at the Globe in October 1989. It is just conceivable that the artist mapping Paris Garden, instead of depicting the Swan, copied an old map showing the Rose.

The two most obvious anomalies in what we know of the Rose's stage structure may be interrelated. One is the lack of depth for its stage area compared with the two other stages we have evidence for, De Witt's Swan with its square stage and the Fortune contract's specification that its stage should be forty-three feet wide and should reach into the middle of the yard, that is, by more than twenty-seven feet in a square surround

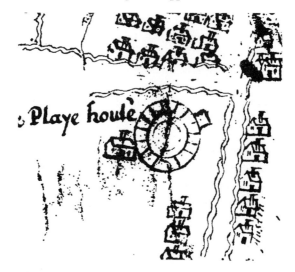

Figure 13. The fourteen-sided playhouse with stair tower depicted in the Paris Garden map of 1628, representing the Swan.

of galleries. The Rose's stage, a hexagon of less than thirty-five feet wide with a depth of less than half that, was anything but square. The second anomaly is its stage posts. De Witt depicted the Swan stage having two heavy and elaborately carved Romanesque posts set on each side of centre stage, while the Fortune contract specifies 'a shadowe or cover' over the stage, which would certainly have required substantial posts supporting it. On the other hand the Rose's archaeologists found no post base at all for the first stage of 1587, and while in the 1592 second stage they did find one complete base and a portion of the other, both of them were positioned at the stage's very front edge.

This peculiar location of the posts at the stage's front edge, utterly unlike the substantial supports at the Swan, would have made walking round them impossible and even pretending to hide behind them distinctly awkward. Several plays performed at the post-1592 Rose, however, do require the use of stage posts. William Haughton's *Englishmen for My Money* has the chief foreign gulls, strangers to London, led around the town in what one of them calls the 'groterly dark' (Scene 7, TLN 1408),[14] and made to blunder into the posts (TLN 1654) when Frisco (Frisk) guides two of them through what appear to be foggy streets to find his master's house in

---

[14] As elsewhere, I use the Malone Society Reprints edition, ed. W. W. Greg, Oxford, 1916, and its through-line numbers.

Crotched-Friars. Frisk says he is in Tower Street, while the Frenchman Delio says he is in Leadenhall and the Italian Alvaro in Fenchurch Street. Leading them, Frisk says 'now for a durtie Puddle, the pissing Condit, or a great Post, that might turn these two from Asses to Oxen by knocking their Hornes to their Fore-heads' (1641–43). They bump into one post which Frisk claims is 'the May-pole on *Ivie-bridge* going to *Westminster*' (1655–56), then they hit the other whereupon Frisk says 'Oh now I know in deede where I am; wee are now at the fardest end of *Shoredich*, for this is the May-pole.' (1659–61). The stage posts were used for one purpose or another in many plays. Orlando Furioso in Greene's play of that name, possibly staged at the first Rose, hangs verses on a 'tree' which must have been a stage post, as Shakespeare's rather different Orlando does later in the Globe's *As You Like It*. However, the most obvious role of the posts at playhouses like the Globe, for concealment – used by both Benedict and Beatrice in the orchard scenes of *Much Ado* – does not seem to have been tried in the Rose plays. So perhaps they were positioned too close to the stage's edge where the bulk of the yard's standers were. The archaeological evidence does put them too near the edge of the stage to allow any player to hide behind them.

Another possible use of stage posts, however, was to depict trees or similar vertical structures. Rose plays such as *John a Kent and John a Cumber* have references to players climbing trees, and special property trees are specified in the *Diary*'s inventories of 1598, including 'j baye tree', 'j tree of gowlden apelles', and 'Tantelouse tre'. Were they attached to the stage posts, or did they stand free, without any other support? A similar sort of added feature might have served for the arbour where Horatio is hanged in *The Spanish Tragedy*, which must have been substantial enough to carry a hanging man. Conceivably the trees and the arbour were made for particular plays at the Rose to stand in for the deficient stage posts, since the posts' forward position would have prevented them from being used in the way plays like *John a Kent* required. In that play Munday did insert directions for four antic clowns to appear, two from each 'end of the Stage', a third 'from under the Stage', and the fourth 'out of a tree, if possible it may be'. That was for a play staged in 1595 when the Rose had its posts on the front edge of the stage. One antic appearing from each side, one from below and one somewhere above up a tree would make the four appearances encompass the entire stage. They all exit into the tiring house, which would therefore not have been the best place for a tree unless it was asymmetrically positioned at one side of the stage, away from the central opening. Very likely Munday had it in mind to have the fourth figure emerge from some image of a tree offset from the stage balcony. The four distinct positions would suit the narrow reach of the Rose's stage much better than they would the square stage of the Swan and other playhouses.

Study of the Rose since 1989 has produced a remarkable number of tangible finds. We now know its basic shape, most of the 'footprint' it imposed on the marshy ground of Bankside, the materials used for its foundations and much of the structure that was set up on those remains, including the lath and lime plaster that filled the wall frames and the Norfolk reed used to thatch the roof of the galleries and the stage. We have a remarkably detailed record, both of the debris left from the building and of the Rose's playgoers. But a great deal still awaits further digging and analysis. The remains are wonderfully tangible, but a huge amount of the information we might try to deduce from them is still guesswork.

The most obvious question of all is why the Rose was enlarged only five years after it was first built. Deciding to enlarge it in 1592 by shifting the northern flank with the stage and tiring house six feet backwards could have had several motives behind it. One of them might have been a rethink about the stage and perhaps a desire to add a cover upheld by stage posts. We do know that some time after 1592 the Rose certainly did have a substantial stage cover or 'heavens', because in June 1595 Henslowe paid 7 pounds 2 shillings for 'carpenters worke & mackinge the throne in the hevenes'.[15] That means a roof structure must have been in place by then, substantial enough to hold a windlass with ropes that could let down a chair or 'throne' with a boy or small man sitting in it. But it may be that the 1592 stage retained its elongated hexagon shape and angled bays with their separate entrances from the first stage simply because the chief gain from the rebuild had to be an increase in audience capacity, not acting space. If that was the priority, conceivably the narrowness of the stage between front edge and *frons scenae* was what forced the builder to set the new stage posts right on the front edge. The archaeologists are sure that the one stage post base that has been uncovered so far was freshly constructed in 1592 and that nothing underlies it that might have been previously the base for an older stage cover, one possible reason why its location was positioned so far forward. Bowsher and others are convinced that Rose 1 had no stage cover, however inherently unlikely it is that the players would let their expensive costumes get wet under London's chronically bad weather.

[15] *Diary*, p. 7.

Another possibility is that the relative smallness of the Rose in its original form made it possible not to stand the cover on posts like at the Swan and the Globe but on supports located slantwise somewhere in the gallery frame. That was a feature of the Hope in 1614 since it was intended to double as a baiting arena. Its stage had to be removable, and any stage posts holding up the cover would have got in the way. The bases for the posts at Rose 2 were an innovation which would have been unnecessary for Rose 1 if it had a post-free stage cover. Such a design with braces rather than vertical pillars might, however, have called for canti-levered supports, which were not generally employed in 1587. Perhaps the wider spread of the new Rose 2 galleries alongside the stage made it impossible to renew any such bracing design to support a stage cover. The new post bases definitely were built at the front edge of the stage in 1592, and the inconvenience of such a location there does leave us thinking that they must have been a belated design feature set up to provide what had only slowly come to seem a necessity, shelter for the players from London's rain.

It does seem that the most substantial motive for the Rose's enlarge-ment in 1592 was to increase the auditorium capacity by four or five hundred bodies. Squeezing in the maximum numbers I think must have been the chief reason for the long slim stage shape at the original Rose, since it gave priority to the standers in the yard over the players. That priority was retained in 1592. If we can believe De Witt's drawing the Swan's stage was almost square with a flat *frons scenae*, as were those of the Globe and the Fortune. Rectilinear stages evidently were mostly preferred over the long and shallow Rose type. That would explain why the Fortune plan rejected the Rose's priorities in order to imitate the design of the other playhouse stages.

Alleyn located the Fortune on what was then the northern edge of the city, outside the city walls in the parish of St Giles Cripplegate, not far beyond London Wall. He had been raised there and had donated poor relief to the parish for some years before the building of the Fortune became an issue. Conceivably, as Susan Cerasano has conjectured, his 'retirement' from playing in 1597 was to give him time to work on his plan to build the new playhouse there.[16] He did not sign the contract for its construction until 8 January 1600 but it is unlikely to have been a sudden decision or its location a fortuitous accident. On the evidence of Charles

---

[16] S. P. Cerasano, 'Edward Alleyn's "Retirement"', *Medieval and Renaissance Drama in English* 10 (1998), 98–112.

Howard's letter quoted below he was apparently buying timber and other materials for it some time before he signed the contract.

To secure his expenditure and his contract Alleyn had to get the Lord Admiral's support against the local justices of Middlesex, and he got it. Only four days after it was signed Howard as the Earl of Nottingham wrote from Richmond Palace to the Middlesex justices as follows:

Weareas my Servant Edward Allen (in respect of the dangerous decaye of that Howse which he and his Companye have now, on the Banck, and for that the same standeth verie noysome for resorte of people in the wynter tyme) Hath thearfore nowe of late taken a plott of grounde neere Redcrossestreete London (verie fitt and convenient) for the buildinge of a new Howse theare, and hath provided Tymber and other necessaries for theffectinge thearof, to his great chardge: Forasmuche as the place standeth verie convenient for the ease of People, and that her Majestie (in respect of the acceptable Service, which my saide Servant and his Companie have doen and presented before her Highenes to her great likeinge and Contentment, aswell this last Christmas as att sondrie other tymes) ys gratiouslie moved towards them, with a speciall regarde of favor in their proceedinges: Theis shalbe thearefore to praie and requier youe, and everie of youe, To permitt and suffer my saide Servant to proceede in theffectinge and finishinge of the saide New howse, without anie your lett or molestation, towards him or any of his woorkmen. And soe not doubtinge of your observacion in this behalf, I bidd youe right hartelie farewell. Att the Courte, at Richmond, the xijth of Januarye, 1599.

                                                                    Notingham.[17]

On 9 March in Lent two months later, however, a Privy Council letter contradicting the first one went to the Middlesex justices to stop what was going on in 'White Crosstreete', ordering that 'no soche theatre or plaie-howse be built there'. Howard was evidently not present when the Council sent this letter. Then early the next month, probably at Alleyn's instigation, twenty-seven signatories from the parish petitioned the Council asking for the building to be allowed because it would augment their Poor Relief funds. Consequently on 8 April the Privy Council sent another letter to the Middlesex magistrates repeating the gist of Howard's letter of 12 January. This time Howard signed it along with George Carey and Cecil. Finally on 22 June a more general letter renewing the concept of the duopoly went to all three authorities, the Lord Mayor and the magistrates of both Middlesex and Surrey, ordering them to allow the Fortune and the Globe and to have the Curtain pulled down in order to keep only the two suburban play-houses licensed (in fact the Curtain survived for longer than any of the others, from its opening in 1577 till its final closure in 1625).

[17] Chambers, *The Elizabethan Stage*, IV. 326.

On 22 December 1599 Alleyn took out a lease on the land for his Fortune property, situated between Golding Lane and Whitecross Street, for £240. In 1610 he took out a reversionary lease for £100 and bought the freehold for another £340. This freehold gave him twelve additional tenements, probably built for Alleyn himself since he spent £120 'for other privat buildings of myn owne.' In 1600 the playhouse cost £520 to build, of which £440 went to Peter Street as the chief carpenter and the rest to painters and decorators, including the carvers of the 'satyrs', the gargoyle-like relief work capping the columns in the auditorium. Henslowe was named in the contract, but did not become a financial contributor till he took over a moiety (half) of the playhouse and its profits on 4 April 1601 for 24 years from the previous 25 March at a rent of £8 a year.[18] The Henslowe lease refers to two entrances to the playhouse, both accessible from Golding Lane via a passage thirty feet long by fourteen wide running eastwards from the south-west angle, 'from one doore of the said house to an other'.

One of the most tangible blessings among the many of its founder's papers preserved by Dulwich College is the contract agreed between Alleyn and Henslowe on the one side and Peter Street on the other to build the Fortune. Signed on 8 January 1600, it makes explicit and precise references to the other playhouse Street had recently completed near the Rose in Southwark. After specifying the foundations and an external measurement of eighty feet square outside with a fifty-five-foot square of yard space inside, it asks for: 'three Stories in height, the first or lower Storie to conteine Twelve foote of lawfull assize in height, the second Storie Eleaven foot of lawfull assize in height, and the third or upper Storie to conteine Nyne foote of lawfull assize in height; All which Stories shall conteine Twelve foote and a halfe of lawfull assize in breadth througheoute, besides a juttey forwardes in either of the saide twoe upper Stories of Tenne ynches of lawfull assize, with Fower convenient divisions for gentlemens roomes, and other sufficient and convenient divisions for Twoe pennie roomes with necessarie seates to be placed and sett, aswell in those roomes as througheoute all the rest of the galleries.'[19] The archaeologists found that the Rose and the Globe had bays of the same twelve-foot six-inch average breadth, a striking indication of standardisation in gallery space between the 1580s and 1600. The similarity was made specific for the

---

[18] Chambers, *The Elizabethan Stage*, II. 435–42 and 173–92, p. 435.
[19] The contract is reproduced in facsimile in several books. The most convenient transliteration is by Chambers, *The Elizabethan Stage*, II. 436–39.

rest of the galleries, too: 'with suchelike steares, conveyances, & divisions withoute & within, as are made & contryved in and to the late erected Plaiehowse on the Banck in the saide parishe of Ste Saviours called the Globe'. We will return to the Fortune's stairs and entrances shortly.

The stage was to be rectilinear: 'a Stadge and Tyreinge howse to be made, erected & settupp within the saide Frame, with a shadowe or cover over the saide Stadge, which Stadge shalbe placed & sett, as alsoe the stearecases of the saide Frame, in suche sorte as is prefigured in a plot thereof drawen, and which Stadge shall conteine in length Fortie and Three foote of lawfull assize and in breadth to extende to the middle of the yarde of the saide howse.' The stage with its square posts upholding the canopy was to be forty-three feet wide, and if it was indeed made to extend into the middle of the yard its depth from the *frons scenae* outwards was half of the yard's fifty-five feet, or twenty-seven feet six inches. The roofing was not to be the Globe's economical thatch (ultimately very costly, since it was what caught fire and burned it all down), but tiles. 'And the saide Frame, Stadge and Stearecases to be covered with Tyle, and to have a convenient gutter of lead to carrie & convey the water frome the covering of the saide Stadge to fall backwards." The decoration was to match the Globe's. 'And the saide howse and other thinges beforemencioned to be made & doen to be in all other contrivitions, conveyances, fashions, thinge and things effected, finished and doen according to the manner and fashion of the saide howse called the Globe, saveinge only that all the princypall and maine postes of the saide Frame and Stadge forwarde shalbe square and wroughte palasterwise, with carved proporcions called Satiers to be placed & sett on the top of every of the same postes.' It is a nice calculation whether or not the square shapes specified for the square Fortune's pillars were meant to counter the round shapes of the polygonal Globe's pillars. All this other than the paintwork was to be completed between January and 25 July 1600.

Unhappily the 'plot thereof drawen', the groundplan accompanying the contract, is lost, very likely from months of consultation in the builder's hands. Its absence leaves us asking where for instance the auditorium staircases were. First, were they internal, as they might have been at the Rose, or were they like the Globe external in the form of stair turrets outside the frame? As we have noted about the Rose, if they were internal they would have limited the amount of available seating space in the galleries. The contract's requirement to copy the Globe should have meant making stair turrets, foundations for which were uncovered when the original Globe was excavated in 1989. There they form an angled lobby attached to and bent round one of the great vertical posts of the outer frame. The 'two narrow doors' that John Chamberlain reported everyone using to escape from the Globe fire in 1613 must mean that the only exits from the Globe's yard and galleries were at the foot of the two stair turrets. Such an economical design should have featured at the new Fortune as well, perhaps at two of the structure's four corners. A reference from 1643 speaks of soldiers guarding 'both gates' at the Fortune.[20] Secondly, if external, on which side or corners would they have been positioned? If the entrances were one in Golding Lane, as the Henslowe lease indicates and as ease of access would dictate, and the other along an alley leading from the lane eastwards, they should have been on the south and the western sides or corners of the square. This would most likely mean that the stage was positioned opposite them on the northern flank, as it was at the Rose, facing the rear half of the auditorium where the stairs released their visitors into the galleries. This is nearly the opposite of the Globe stage's position on the south-western flank of its polygon, but it does reproduce the Rose's configuration with its entrance to the yard on the south side and its stage on the northern flank. Conceivably Alleyn was unusual for an Elizabethan in wanting the sun to shine down on him when he posed at the front edge of the stage. Either that or he and his fellow-players wore broad-brimmed hats for most of their parts.

When we turn to what the staging must have been like at the two playhouses we need first to consider why, in what must have been a deliberate contrast to the Rose, the Fortune's stage was made almost square. It was certainly far bigger than the Rose stage. Its width at forty-three feet was six feet more than the Rose's, and the extension into 'the middle of the yard', half of its fifty-five feet, should have made it more than a third deeper. That gave it a total floor space of 1,160 square feet, more than twice the second Rose's 500. The Fortune was larger in overall size than the second Rose, but the thrust of its rectilinear stage into the square yard space was very emphatic by comparison with the Rose's squeezed hexagon. Staging the scene with the four antics described above in Munday's *John a Kent* would have looked quite different on the new squared stage from its appearance at the elongated Rose. The fourth of the 'antiques' might have climbed down from the Fortune's stage balcony, although a stage post might equally have done the job if the climber could have got there inconspicuously enough. At the Fortune the Rose's symmetry with one figure appearing at each side of the stage, the third from below and

---

[20] Bentley, *Jacobean and Caroline Stage*, VI. 174.

the fourth above would have been lost. We do not know the exact
positioning of the Fortune's stage posts, but there were two, and using one
as a tree would have lost any symmetry except that of height. This is one of
the many puzzles raised by the difference between the two stages. How the
players might have switched from an almost linear two-dimensional blocking
and choreography at the Rose to square-based three-dimensional movements at the Fortune is a question for which we have no evidence at all,
only speculation. Without resorting to a Laban-like attempt at identifying the most likely choreography of the stage moves such a question is,
perhaps mercifully, beyond our capacity here.

Doubt about where the two stair turrets stood in the Fortune's 'plot
thereof drawen' is also a factor when we look at the one illustration of
the Fortune that might still exist. The Utrecht engraving of London from
the north, thought to have been made in 1600–01,[21] includes a square
building of at least two storeys with a 'hut' on top that closely resembles
the conventional over-stage structures depicted in Norden's and De Witt's
drawings of the Bankside playhouses. In 1959 Leslie Hotson published a
conjecture that the engraving might actually show the first Fortune while
it was being built.[22] Like other of Hotson's eccentric ideas this conjecture
received little support and was subjected to a thoroughgoing dismissal
from G. E. Bentley, chiefly on the grounds that it shows only two storeys
instead of three and no stair turrets.[23] If the stair turrets were on the
southern side his last argument is hardly a strong one, since the view is
from the north. Nor is the location, close to Austin Friars, very far from
where we would expect to find the Fortune. The square structure does,
unsurprisingly, fit the contract details, and the 'hut' on top is remarkably
like the engravings by Norden of other theatres. I remain unconvinced
but attracted by the possibility that the Utrecht engraving does give us a
rough image of the almost finished Fortune.

The Fortune's capacity must have been larger than the two thousand of
the second Rose, perhaps at its fullest not far behind the three thousand
that the Swan and the Globe were said to accommodate. *The Roaring
Girl*'s claim that 'Within one square a thousand heads are laid' was a 1611
assessment of its normal capacity, though unless the thousand heads were

---

[21] See *Tudor London: A Map and a View*, ed. Ann Saunders and John Schofield, London Topographical
Society, 2001.

[22] *Shakespeare's Wooden O*, London, 1959, pp. 304–13. For a detailed analysis of the whole Utrecht
engraving ignoring Hotson, see Herbert Berry, 'The View of London from the North and the
Playhouses in Holywell', *Shakespeare Survey* 53 (2000), 196–212.

[23] *Jacobean and Caroline Stage*, VI. 145.

Figure 14. A detail from the 'View of the City of London from the North', just possibly showing the newly built Fortune with a stage hut on top.

only those in the yard and an even larger number sat in the surrounding galleries it must have been distinctly an underestimate of its total holding.

The Fortune raised its flag, said to show an image of Dame Fortune, for its first performances in the autumn of 1600, staging either or both of Dekker's *1 Fortune's Tennis* and *Old Fortunatus* to herald the new venue's name. Alleyn was still the company's controlling force, and his old favourites prevailed throughout his years at the new playhouse. How far the staging of such old plays might have changed between the Rose and the Fortune is guesswork and the limits to what we can deduce about how the plays were staged impose similar constraints. As Evelyn Tribble has said, 'The very paucity of information about the use of stage space is a powerful indication of the tacit, invisible, and profound understanding of the stage that must have underpinned the work of the companies.'[24] Such automatic understanding is not easy to tease out of just a few explicit statements or even to find in stage directions. Some broad assumptions, however, must be taken as valid. It was in the nature of such a tight team-like company structure that most of the plays, certainly all those for which we have texts from the 1590s, went through a process that might be thought of as a kind of accelerated evolution. Features that helped and features that hindered the success of a play on stage might be introduced at any step in the long progress from the writer's or writers' original scripted invention to the first enactment on stage and its repetitions and emendations afterwards. The *Diary* shows that taking a play from inception to realisation on stage was a very rushed and collaborative process. A playbook of between fifteen hundred and three thousand lines of verse and prose could never have been thought of as a static and fixed entity. The writer's fair copy was subject to alteration by the Master of the Revels, so was inevitably cut and trimmed through the two or three weeks while it was being prepared for the stage, as the 'parts' were transcribed and learned and properties and special costumes made ready. Doubling, the allocation of bit parts and the blocking of moves for each scene were planned and rehearsed in the mornings, chiefly on the day of the first performance.[25] It was a high-speed process where nothing would ever be so fixed it could not be changed. The very speed of production meant that nothing was sacred.

Nonetheless, the enlarged Rose of 1592 was designed to accommodate quite a number of plays whose texts survive, and their stage directions and other features tell us something about what its stage was expected to let the players do. Most of the writers regularly contracted kept on writing for Henslowe so they knew the playhouse where their work would appear on stage and the players who would perform it very well. Moreover, since most of the plays written for the Admiral's Men after 1594 were taken on to the Fortune its structure must have been designed to accommodate them in basically similar ways. As a result we have a uniform group of plays all of which were written in the expectation that they would be staged at those two playhouses. Reconciling the two bodies of knowledge about the playhouses and their plays ought to advance what we know of

---

[24] 'Distributing Cognition at the Globe', *Shakespeare Quarterly* 56 (2005), 135–55, p. 144.
[25] For deductions about the rehearsal process, see Tiffany Stern, *Rehearsal from Shakespeare to Sheridan*, Oxford, 2000.

how the writers expected their products to appear in performance. That might also say something about what was done to the scripts in the process of preparing them to be staged.

First, the surviving play-texts. They fall into three categories. Some were written in the years before Henslowe paid for his second Rose. They, or their surviving texts, may or may not show alterations made to fit them to the Rose 2 stage. Next are the plays written for and staged at Rose 2, and third are the plays written for the Fortune from 1600 onwards. The first category is the least specific. We can be fairly sure, for instance, that *Faustus* was staged at the Theatre before it came to the Rose in 1594, and the two *Tamburlaines* may have travelled with it. These plays belong to the years before London playing was confined to the Rose and the Theatre and all playing at inns and innyards was stopped, so the writers must have known that they could not rely on their plays being staged at any particular London playhouse with specific features like windlasses for hoists and trapdoors. That confidence only came after 1594, particularly at the Rose when Henslowe enlisted his durable teams of collaborators to write for Alleyn and his fellows. So we should find the most reliable evidence about staging from the second category.

In the first category, plays which survive from stagings before 1594 include *The Battle of Alcazar* (a 1594 quarto with a 1601 'plot' for a Fortune revival), *Friar Bacon and Friar Bungay* (a 1591 quarto, with a revival at the Fortune in 1602), *Orlando Furioso* (a 1594 quarto, with the 'part' of Orlando annotated by Alleyn),[26] *The Spanish Tragedy* with additions in the 1602 quarto, the two *Tamburlaines*, *Faustus*, *The Jew of Malta*, *King Edward the First* (*Longshanks*) and perhaps *Alphonsus of Aragon*.[27]

The second category, plays listed in the *Diary* as 'ne' from 1592 onwards and hence probably written with the Rose's new stage specifically in mind, in the order of their appearances in the *Diary*, comprise *1 Henry VI*, *A Knack to Know a Knave*, *The Massacre at Paris*, and *Titus Andronicus*, then as Admiral's plays *A Knack to Know an Honest Man*, *John a Kent and John a Cumber* (if it is the *Westchester* manuscript), *Disguises* (most likely the play printed in 1600 under the name *Look About You*), *Old Fortunatus*,

---

[26] Nothing in the *Diary* says that the Admiral's ever restaged Greene's play.

[27] Scott McMillin includes *Alphonsus of Aragon* in his list (*The Elizabethan Theatre and The Book of Sir Thomas More*, Cornell, Ithaca, 1987, p. 116), on the grounds that the 'owld Mahemetes head' listed in a Henslowe inventory (*Diary*, p. 319) was for Greene's play, which he identifies as the otherwise unknown *Mahomet*. Other plays, *George a Greene*, *King Leir* and *The Taming of a Shrew* together with *Orlando Furioso*, which may have appeared at the Rose, are not generally considered to have become Admiral's plays.

The Blind Beggar of Alexandria, Captain Thomas Stukeley, An Humorous Day's Mirth, The Downfall of Robert Earl of Huntingdon, Englishmen for my Money, The Death of Robert Earl of Huntingdon, The Two Angry Women of Abingdon, The Shoemaker's Holiday, 1 Sir John Oldcastle, Patient Grissil, Two Tragedies in One, Jugurtha (in a late and incomplete transcript), *Grim the Collier of Croydon, The Blind Beggar of Bethnal Green,* and perhaps Peele's *David and Bethsabe*. This last case is doubtful because the only reference to it, probably an Alleyn purchase from the time he knew Peele in the late 1580s, is Henslowe's payment on 3 October 1602 for 'poleys & worckmanshipp for to hange absolome' (*Diary*, p. 217), which may have been for Worcester's, not the Admiral's. In the 1599 text of Peele's play that survives, Absalom hangs suspended by his hair for over 100 lines. Henslowe's date would put its staging in the years when Worcester's were using the Rose.[28]

For the third category, the Fortune plays, there is the smallest quantity of evidence. From this group we have only the 'plots' of *2 Fortune's Tennis* and *Alcazar*, along with printed texts for *Hoffman, 1 The Honest Whore, When You See Me You Know Me, The Whore of Babylon, The Roaring Girl,* Middleton's *No Wit / No Help Like a Woman's* and *The Duchess of Suffolk*.

Altogether the three categories give us at least ten plays staged at Rose 2 from 1592 onwards, another twenty-two written specifically for staging there, and seven plays written for the Fortune, with a substantial number of the Rose 2 plays transferring to the Fortune. Of these thirty-nine texts we can assume that almost all the Admiral's company plays, both those inherited from earlier companies such as the five Marlowes and the nineteen staged at the Rose from 1594 onwards, were found suitable for staging at the Fortune. We know of at least eight that were – *Friar Bacon and Friar Bungay, The Battle of Alcazar,* the two *Tamburlaines, Faustus, The Jew of Malta, Jugurtha* and *Grim the Collier*. We should of course take care to note that the printed texts of the plays and even the manuscripts for the two of them cannot signify what was staged without careful analysis of the character of each text and its likely proximity to the 'allowed book', the manuscript with the signature of the Master of the Revels at its end that licensed it for performance and made it the 'promptbook' used for staging. Since the version normally staged was likely to be trimmed in one way or another out of the complete licensed manuscript, none of which we have, the likelihood that the extant texts misrepresent

---

[28] There is no other reference to the play in Henslowe, but the reference to Absalom's rope in 1602 might posit a revival of the old play then, conceivably based on the printed text of 1599.

the plays as they were actually staged is substantial.[29] Some of the texts
seem to have come from the author end of the staging process, others
from the stage end, and it is regrettable guesswork just where in that long
business of making alterations they emerged from, let alone the case of
those plays noted in the previous chapter such as *No Wit* and *Hoffman*
that were altered for other stages before printing.

So far as the differences between the two stages are concerned the only
variation we have clear note of is use of the stage posts. While the Rose plays
such as *Englishmen for My Money* did use the Rose's posts to touch and
bump into, the Fortune's plays could use theirs additionally for concealment, as Will Summers does in Sam Rowley's history play *When You See
Me You Know Me*.[30] The likely choreography of stage movement in either
two (on the Rose's narrow stage) or three (on the Fortune's rectilinear stage)
dimensions is a question for future research and experimentation. Both
stages had physical features basically similar enough to help identify the
broad sweep of such movements and their likely variations. Perhaps most
valuably because most tangibly we have the luck to possess two versions of
one play, written in about 1588, probably first bought by Alleyn and staged
somewhere before the 1592 Rose was opened for him, then at the recon-
structed Rose and finally restaged at the Fortune in 1601. *The Battle of
Alcazar*'s 1594 quarto printed from a text prepared by Peele in about 1590
along with the 'plot' of 1601 made for its restaging at the Fortune have
something to say about how staging was done at the two playhouses.

The Rose stage differed from the Fortune's not just in its shape but in
its *frons scenae*. The Rose's two angles in its *frons* gave it three faces. If each
of these had its own door the flanking pair set at an angle would make
them incline symmetrically towards each other. That is a feature to keep
in mind when considering entrances and exits at Rose 2. All three doors
are called on for use in Scene 3 of *Sir John Oldcastle* and in several other
plays. The central opening must have been wider than those on each side
(in *Oldcastle* it is the lord's 'gate'), since it had to admit Tamburlaine in
his chariot hauled on stage by four kings. In that form it would have
supplied all the functions claimed for it by Robert Weimann's concept of
authoritative *locus* and pedestrian *platea*.[31] The flanking doors were most

---

[29] See Gurr, 'Maximal and Minimal Texts: Shakespeare v. the Globe', *Shakespeare Survey* 52 (1999),
68–87.

[30] Alexander Leggatt, *Jacobean Public Theatre*, London, 1992, pp. 103–5, has a good note on
Summers's clowning.

[31] See Weimann, *Author's Pen and Actor's Voice: Playing and Writing in Shakespeare's Theatre*,
Cambridge, 2000, Chapter 7.

likely ordinary planked wooden doors, not unlike the pair shown by De
Witt in his drawing of the Swan, though the Rose's were most likely
single. Planked single doors could easily be lifted off their hinges and left
as openings behind a hanging or arras concealing the interior of the tiring
house from the view of the crowd in the yard.[32] The rectangular Fortune's
frons was planar, a flat front with presumably a similar set of three
doorways, the widest in the centre, but without the angles that enabled
a player at the Rose entering by one flanking door to come face to face
with his antagonist entering from the other. At the Fortune, as at the
Globe, entering from the tiring house would have been a matter of
striding some yards directly forwards before turning to face whoever else
was on stage.

The staging of *The Battle of Alcazar* in its two states, the 1594 quarto
written by Peele in about 1588 for a substantial company and staged at the
Rose, and the 'plot' of 1601 prepared for the Fortune, gives us a means to
measure the traditional practices which dictated how the plays were
devised for the two stages. We know that this play was popular when
Alleyn played it with Strange's in 1592 (assuming it was the play Henslowe
usually named '*Muly Molocco*'),[33] so it is hardly surprising that Alleyn
chose to revive it along with his other ageing greats while he was pushing
the Fortune as his new venue. The 'plot' of 1601 tells us something about
his own understandably conservative role in restaging his older favourites
in the forms most familiar to him.

Peele when he first wrote it in 1588 had a good idea of how his play
would be staged. He took care to design its multitude of characters for a
company with resources of the right size. The 1601 'plot' seems to follow
his text as it appears in the 1594 quarto fairly faithfully, merely adding
some gory dumbshows to amplify what Peele's Presenter declares at the
outset to each act, while cutting one scene and trimming other parts to fit
the play for staging by sixteen adults and ten boys (the Fortune company
appears to have had more boys on hand than Peele expected). Only the
four senior roles, the Moor, King Sebastian, Abdelmelec and Stukeley, were
not doubled. Standard stage devices appear, including Tamburlaine's
chariot for Alleyn's villainous Moor with his treasure, and a versatile sick
chair which Abdelmelec, the virtuous Moroccan leader, is carried in on.
He stays seated in it dead through Act 5 as a witness to the battle, his body
then taken from it to be replaced by his living successor Hamet, who is

---

[32] See Gurr, 'Doors at the Globe: The Gulf between Page and Stage', *Theatre Notebook* 55 (2001), 59–71.
[33] Charles Edelman argues for this in his edition, p. 24. I am strongly inclined to accept his view.

crowned (with, as David Bradley says, 'the diadem that Moroccan kings did not wear')[34] at the finale in the same chair, differently draped, now serving as a throne.

Where Peele set up a 'presenter' who described what was to follow in each act, the 1601 maker of the 'plot' took care to have each of his descriptions illustrated on the spot by means of a dumbshow coloured by gruesome spectacles. Bradley thinks that these dumbshows were a means to bring Peele's old text up to date for Londoners. He says (p. 175) that:

> The style of the play itself was dated almost beyond recovery and the ambition of the Plotter to turn it into a bloody extravaganza, largely by elaborating the dumb-shows, forced him into solutions that can be perfectly well understood according to the rules of his theatre, but which must have seemed bizarre, even to his contemporaries.

Bradley here seems to assume that dumbshows were out of date by 1600, not a view that is very easy to sustain. The simplest enactment of the presenter's speeches is at the beginning of the second act. In the Quarto Peele specifies:

> Alarum. And then the presenter speaketh.
> Now warre begins his rage and ruthless raine,
> And Nemisis with bloudie whip in hand,
> Thunders for vengeance on this Negro moore.

After eight lines of this speech a stage direction calls for '*Three ghosts crying Vindicta*'. The presenter continues:

> Hearke Lords, as in a hollow place a farre,
> The dreadfull shrikes and clamors that resound,
> And sound revenge upon this traitors soule,
> Traitor to kinne and kinde, to Gods and men.
> Now Nemisis upon her doubling drum,
> Movde with this gastly mone, this sad complaint,
> Larumes aloud into Alectos eares,
> And with her thundering wakes whereas they lie,
> In cave as darke as hell, and beds of steele,
> The furies just impes of dire revenge,
> Revenge cries Abdilmelecs grieved ghost,
> And rouseth with the terror of this noise
> These nymphs of Erybus. Wreake and revenge

---

[34] David Bradley, *From Text to Performance in the Elizabethan Theatre*, Cambridge, 1992, p. 170. Bradley's book is in essence a study of the *Alcazar* 'plot', though it covers a lot of vital ground in the process.

Ring out the soules of his unhappie brethren,
And now start up these torments of the world,
Wakt with the thunder of Ramusians drum,
And fearefull ecchos of these grieved ghosts,
Alecto with her brand and bloudie torch,
Megaera with her whip and snakie haire,
Tysiphone with her fatall murthering yron,
These three conspire, these three complaine & mone,
Thus Muly Mahamet is a counsell held,
To wreake the wrongs and murthers thou hast done.

The 'plot' gives us the 1601 specifics for this. Nemesis with, as the Quarto says, 'her doubling drum' (not the usual whip) enters on the stage balcony. Below her the three ghosts, Kendall as Abdelmelec with the boys Harry and Dab as young brothers, enter and lie down behind the central hangings. The Furies enter each carrying their own weapon, Megaera her whip. As the 'plot' has it,

	Enter the Presenter: to him
Sound sennet	*2 domb shew*
	Enter above Nemesis, Tho: Drom to
	Them 3 ghosts wm kendall Dab. (& Harry:)
A whipp	*to them lying behind the Curtaines 3*
Brand &	*Furies: Parsons: George &Ro: Tailor*
Chopping	*one with a whipp: a nother with a blody*
knife:	*torch: & the 3ᵈ wth a Chopping knife: exeunt*[35]

Nemesis and the three Furies thus enact the presenter's foretelling of murderous revenge on the Alleyn villain. The third dumb-show preluding the deaths of King Sebastian and Stukeley is even more specific and more demanding.

Enter Nemesis above: Tho: Drom to her 3 Furies bringing in the Scales: Georg Somersett Tom Parsons and Robin Tailor: to them 3 divells mʳ Sam: H Jeffes & Antho: Jeffes to them 3 ghosts: w. kendall Dab & Harry the Furies First Fech in Sebastian & Carrie him out again, which done they Fech in Stukeley & Carrie him out, then bring in the Moore & Carrie him out: exeunt

Most of the presenter's twenty-two lines here ignore the gruesome deaths being foretold behind him while speaking only of Spain's duplicity to Sebastian about supplying soldiers for his invasion. This is the show that calls for '*3 violls of blood & a sheeps gather*', blood to mark the victims and organs to be weighed, one from each victim, in the Furies' scales. A sheep or calf's gather, also called the pluck, was the heart, liver and lungs held

---

[35] Reproduction of the manuscript text has been slightly edited here.

together in a bladder, a kind of raw proto-sausage. Each of the three pieces of gut could be drawn out and flourished on stage from a different victim. The three vials of blood, either ink, vinegar or animal blood, which did not congeal but created laundry problems, made an obviously splashy extra. A boy would have had to visit the local butcher every morning before an *Alcazar* performance to get the gather and the '*raw flesh*' of Muly's dead lion. As the presenter says, the stage shows a 'lake of bloud and gore' in which Sebastian has 'drencht himselfe'.

Bradley may be right to claim that the dumbshows were intended to add colour in 1601 to an out-of-date play. It looks to me, however, much more like a straightforward series of spectacles designed to amplify the play's blood and revenge motif that would have been part of the original staging that Peele himself had in mind. His presenter speeches, reflected with heavyweight precision in the 1601 dumbshows, provide the kind of details that envisage just what the 'plot' sets out. The man who Bradley calls the 'Plotter' knew his script well and summoned players and properties to fulfil its expectations. The Furies with their identifying weapons are present in all three central dumbshows, even bringing in dead men's heads for the bloody banquet of the fourth Act. They present on stage a literal-minded version of what the verse in each case describes. The deaths of the monarchs in Act 5, for instance, are illustrated by a tree with crowns hanging on it that fall one by one as it is shaken.

A comparison of the 1594 quarto with the plot suggests that the tastes Jonson mockingly said old-fashioned playgoers still yearned for in the Hieronimo and Andronicus revenge plays got strong support from the players. The only substantial change between the early staging of *Alcazar* and the version re-enacted at the Fortune in 1601 was cutting Act 3 Scene 2, and that was to ease the problems of doubling when several Moorish characters were in blackface. The Fortune would have made the Rose's central opening along with the balcony above it for the three dumbshows with Nemesis and the Furies seem less focal, since the Rose's understanders at the front stage edge were in much closer proximity to the gore, but the greater spread of the Fortune's stage could have made the fighting in particular more three-dimensional, and the ceremonial processions as the dead were carried offstage would have had more distance to parade over as they marched round the stage margins. Otherwise the evidence from *Alcazar* largely suggests the company kept its allegiance at the Fortune to the practices they had learned at the Rose.

The *Alcazar* plot is revealing because it shows how durable was Alleyn's own acceptance of the presentation on stage of the divide between bad and good, presented literally in black and white. In Peele's *Alcazar* text the non-black moors are called 'manly' and virtuous whereas the 'Negro moore' is cunningly villainous.[36] It may well be that what Bradley calls *Alcazar*'s 'bizarre' restaging by Alleyn in 1601 stimulated Shakespeare soon after to reverse this convention when he staged his simple soldier as a black man while his black-hearted machiavell posed as a simple soldier.[37] We might speculate how far Alleyn's fame as the player of that atheist Tamburlaine and the damnable Faustus raised alarming questions about his personal theology, an issue that calls attention to the number of biblical plays he got the company to introduce in 1600–02. Concern about the damnation of Faustus is apparent in his playing the part with a cross on his breast for insurance.[38] His own theological concern about Tamburlaine must have been intensified by the devilish roles that we know he played in blackface, most notably the great villain in *Alcazar*.[39] Muly was probably one of many early stage characters where black-faced Moors on the London stages were villains.

   Characters from Morocco and the Barbary coast were not always standardised in blackface. Different plays seem to have either blacked the players or given them a tawny colouring, or even kept their normal white complexions.[40] The company seems usually to have read the difference morally. A black face meant a black villain, like Aaron the Moor in *Titus Andronicus*. Alleyn played Muly Mahamet in blackface for *Alcazar* even though it made trouble for its restaging in 1601, a point that Bradley makes clear in his analysis. Being a ruler Muly needed an army of black supporters besides his queen Calipolis and his son. Muly's virtuous Moroccan enemies were mostly played in whiteface, but Peele's play demanded also a variety of Europeans on stage, Portuguese, Spanish, Italians, and an Englishman in Thomas Stukeley. Such a number of different races complicated the company's doubling. You could not put two groups of Moors on stage without either playing some of them in

[36] Reginald Scot in *The Discovery of Witchcraft* noted that Catholic writers thought Satan could appear to people either in the form of a goat or as a blackamoor (p. 51).

[37] Iago was a reversed stereotype, the apparently simple soldier who is actually a godless villain, confronting his opposite in the person of Othello. This point is made at greater length in an article by Gurr, 'A Black Reversal', in *Shakespeare* 4, special issue (2008) 148–59.

[38] Samuel Rowlands wrote of Alleyn's iconic self-defence with his cross in *The Knave of Clubs*, 1609, p. 29.

[39] See Charles Edelman (ed.), *The Stukeley Plays. The Battle of Alcazar* by George Peele, *The Famous History of the Life and Death of Captain Thomas Stukeley*. The Revels Plays, Manchester University Press, 2005, p. 18.

[40] An informative article about the use of cosmetics and chemistry to create tawny complexions is by Andrea R. Stevens, '"Assisted by a Barber": The Court Apothecary, Special Effects, and *The Gipsies Metamorphosed*', *Theatre Notebook* 61 (2007), 2–11.

whiteface or putting a major strain on the unavoidable business of doubling the minor parts. A single player might play a 'Negro Moor' only if he had to do no doubling. Aaron, Othello, and the Prince of Morocco in *The Merchant of Venice* stood alone on stage. On the other hand when Alleyn chose to play in blackface at the Rose and Fortune he gave his book-keeper a lot of trouble over doubling. Charles Massey, for instance, had to play not just the Moor Zareo but a Portuguese Duke and a Spanish ambassador in adjacent scenes, with a time for changing his appearance of no more than 25 lines of verse. Richard Jones played successively a Portuguese, a Spaniard and a Berber spy. Both had therefore to be white Moors, not what the text specifies as Alleyn's blackened appearance.

David Bradley's attempt to reconcile *Alcazar*'s 1594 text with the 'plot' raises a number of more general questions that challenge conventional views, especially about doubling. One is raised by the roles of Dick Juby, who seems to have played both the Moroccan Queen Abdel Rayes and the young Portuguese lord, Christophero de Tavera. He was used as a boy player in two other 'plots', one of mid-1597, *Frederick and Basilea*, and one of 1602, *1 Tamar Cham*.[41] But the same Dick Juby had a son baptised in 1602. That raises some physiological doubt whether the distinction between boys with unbroken voices playing pages and women as against adults who never played women was quite as rigid as is required by the idea that the boys worked as apprentice learners of their trade only so long as their voices stayed unbroken. Our principal concern here, though, is the mix of colours given to the play's numerous Moors. We have to assume that players of black Moors could not generally be involved in doubling unless they played other black-skinned creatures such as the dumbshow's devils. This explains why some Moors had to be white and others black.

Bradley's *From Text to Performance* examines this in fine detail. Essentially his aim is to disprove Greg's longstanding claim that the 1594 quarto text of *The Battle of Alcazar* was severely cut for touring, and that the subsequent 'plot' was taken from a much fuller text. Bradley shows that the text fits with the 'plot' if we make allowances for the difficulties the 1601 plot-maker found with the need for extensive doubling. When eight of the characters are Moors and the Europeans are Portuguese, Spanish, Irish and English, each in their distinct national costumes, you would expect trouble with the doubling. It could be quick and easy so long as the Moors were Arabs wearing large cloaks that encompassed all their bodies except their swords. Difficulties arose when they wore blackface. Bradley's

---

[41] The standard spelling of the time, 'Cham' is usually written nowadays as 'Khan'.

analysis of the relationship between the printed text of 1594 and the 'plot' of 1601 suggests that the stage manager or 'plotter' was determined to use the distinction of black from white to represent the bad against the good.

We could take this a little further. Alleyn's wish to play Muly Mahamet in blackface has some intriguing implications over, for instance, his playing of Tamburlaine. Would Marlowe himself have wanted his hero to be seen as a stereotyped devilish villain in blackface? For all his death in the sequel just after burning and cursing the Koran, Marlowe did set Tamburlaine out as a constant anomaly. He is unique, a tragic hero distinct even in not dying at the end of the initial play. To prejudice audience reception of his actions by using the familiar signals to stereotype him as a black and wicked monster like Aaron and Iago would have closed down on all the wonder that the play was meant to and did generate for its early audiences. How Alleyn chose to represent Tamburlaine on stage is a question of some seriousness, given how diversely the early audiences viewed his tragedy. The best evidence, I think, so far as the printed text can tell us how the play was first staged, is found in his use of clothing, always a key feature of the company's staging. We first see Tamburlaine in the shepherd's gown of his Scythian origins. Under it, though, he wears a complete suit of armour and carries a curtle-axe or cutlass. Was this armour thought to be European garb, or Moroccan, Turkish or Scythian? What Marlowe did with the royal headgear in the play seems to supply the best answer.

The text printed in 1590 makes use of crowns rather than the traditional Turkish turbans worn in other early plays. Cosroe is told:

> Behold, my Lord, *Ortygius* and the rest
> Bringing the Crowne to make you Emperour.
> *Enter* Ortigius *and* Ceneus *bearing a Crowne, with others.*   (1.1.134–35)[42]

Cosroe accepts 'th'Emperiall Diadem', not by 'divine right' of inheritance but because he is the strongest holder of the title, a pretence that Tamburlaine soon dismisses. When Zenocrate first meets Tamburlaine she calls him 'Shepheard', noting his humble gown, but he promptly throws it off to show her his hidden steel, saying that a warrior's features are 'adjuncts more beseeming *Tamburlaine*'. (1.2.43). Techelles says that Tamburlaine makes kings kneel, 'Spurning their crownes from off their captive heads'. (57). Tamburlaine tells Zenocrate that she herself is worth more than 'the Persian Crowne / Which gratious starres have promist at my birth'

---

[42] Quotations are from Bowers (ed.), *The Complete Works of Christopher Marlowe*, Cambridge, 1973.

(91–92). Subsequently Mycetes, defeated by Tamburlaine, plays his own game with his crown. He says, 'They cannot take away my crowne from me. / Here will I hide it in this simple hole' (2.4.14–15). Tamburlaine, entering and finding it, returns it to Mycetes. So far, and in the scene of victory with Cosroe when Tamburlaine gives him the crown of Persia to add to the one he is already wearing (2.5.1), he only holds the crowns. He does not wear one, though he listens to Theridamas speaking afterwards of the glory of a crown (2.5.55–64). To the dying Cosroe he proclaims that his own aim is 'The sweet fruition of an earthly crowne' (2.7.29), but only when Cosroe is dead does he put the Persian crown on his head, the stage direction specifying '*He takes the Crowne and puts it on.*' (2.7.52). This game is extended in 3.3, when Bajazeth gives the Turkish crown to Zabina his queen to wear, as Tamburlaine gives his Persian one to Zenocrate (113 and 124). After the battle Zenocrate offers the crown she is wearing to Tamburlaine, 'Now let me offer to my gracious Lord, / His royall Crowne againe, so highly won' (218–19). Waving at Zabina he replies 'Nay take the Turkish Crown from her, *Zenocrate*, / And crowne me Emperour of *Affrica*', whereupon she takes Zabina's Turkish crown from the hands of Theridamas (3.3.224) and sets it on Tamburlaine's head. During the feast after Damascus Tamburlaine gives 'a course of crowns' to his three generals, at the stage direction '*Enter a second course of Crownes*'. (4.4.107). So many crowned heads argue against the idea of any of the players wearing Turkish turbans, unless they were small enough to allow a crown to be perched overtopping them.

Marlowe seems to have wanted his hero to appear at first bare-headed. That is how Richard Knolles, writing fifteen years after Marlowe, described him in his *Generall Historie of the Turkes*, 1603. Drawing on extensive accounts of the Turkish dynasties that Marlowe had also read, he gave this account of Tamburlaine's appearance:

Hee was a man of the middle stature, somewhat narrow in the shoulders, otherwise well limed, and of great strength. In his eies sat such a rare majestie, as a man could hardly endure to behold them without closing his owne: and many in talking with him, and often beholding of him became dumbe; which caused him oftentimes with a comely modestie to abstain from looking too earnestly upon such as spake unto him, or discoursed with him. All the rest of his visage was amiable and well proportioned: he had but little haire on his chinne: and ware the haire of his head long and curled, contrarie to the manner of the Tartars, who shave their heads, having the same alwaies covered: whereas he contrariewise was for the most part bareheaded, commanding his sonne also to be so by his tutors brought up: his haire was of a dark colour, somewhat drawing toward a violet right beautifull to behold: which his mother comming of the race of *Sampson* (as he gave it out) willed him to nourish, in token of his discent: the cause that made him to be the more respected of his men of war; most part of them believing that in those haires was some rare vertue, or rather some fatall destinie: an old practise of many great commaunders of former ages, to fill the heads of their souldiours with some strange opinions conceived of them, to bee the more of them honoured; as if in them had ben some one thing or other more than in other men. His lively counterfeit, as I find it expressed by them that write the best of him, you may here behold, with the testimonie of his greatnesse following.

The title-page and engravings of the Turkish sultans in Knolles's book give all of them turbans. The book depicts all the leading rulers – Ottoman I, Amurath, Bajazeth, Mahomet I, and on p. 235 Tamburlaine. Knolles's verbal description of Tamburlaine, taken from a variety of accounts, was accompanied by a portrait of the hero bare-headed. Crowning Tamburlaine's head in the middle act of the play would be a proclamation of his military (and social) success, a cool supplanting of Cosroe's own earlier claim when he assumed the imperial crown. I think Marlowe chose to make his head bare at the outset, and that Alleyn adopted his iconic point. It certainly went with him starting dressed as a shepherd, and doffing his gown to show his armour beneath.

But that digresses from what the Admiral's 1601 'plot' tells us about the staging of *The Battle of Alcazar* in 1601. Peele laid it down that his villain Muly should first enter like Tamburlaine, though he did not specify four kings to pull him. His Act 1 Scene 2 opens with this stage direction:

Enter the Moore in his Chariot, attended with his sonne. Pisano his captaine with his guard and treasure.

The 'plot' is specific. It outlines the whole scene in an initial description, with a note in the margin at the beginning '*sound sennett*' and at the end: '*Alarum* : *Enter in a Charriott Muly Mahamett & Calipolis* : *on each side a page moores attendant Pisano m͏ʳ Hunt & w. Cartwright and young Mahamet Antony Jeffes* : *exit m͏ʳ Sam manet the rest* : *to them m͏ʳ Sam a gaine exeunt*'. Nothing in the plot says how the chariot is drawn on stage, unless it is pulled by the attendant pageboys and moors. The same husband and wife repeat their entry in a chariot in Scene 21 of *Stukeley*,[43] which tells the Engishman's story up to the same battle. In 1601 Muly's arrival was a deliberate reminder to the Fortune audiences of *Tamburlaine*'s device,

---

[43] Another Admiral's play, a prequel of sorts to *Alcazar*, it tells Stukeley's life story in Ireland, England and Rome to his death on the Barbary coast. It first appeared in the *Diary* on 8 December 1596, with ten performances up to 27 June 1597. It was entered in the Stationers' Register on 11 August 1600, and printed in 1605.

suggesting not just that the company kept its transporting chariot on hand but that they expected to use it in several plays. They could not, of course, supply real horses on stage, which explains the trick in *Tamburlaine* of having the four kings pull it. The more routine arrivals in the other plays, with Muly and his queen riding together and presumably carrying his 'treasure' in the chariot with them, required black-faced men or boys to haul it.

Otherwise the *Alcazar* quarto lays down surprisingly few demands for its staging besides the butcher's supplies. It has the usual specifications 'Enter', or 'Manet', with a few calls for trumpets or other routine demands, and one distinctive direction: '*Enter Muly Mahamet with lyons flesh upon his sworde*' (TLN 582), the famous entry when he tells his queen, echoed by Ancient Pistol, 'Hold thee Calypolis feed and faint no more.' The 'plot' records the graphic details introduced to supplement Peele's words. The manuscript is in columns, giving the scenario scene by scene including the names of the players and their main actions. Each column has a narrow margin to the left listing the properties needed for each scene. Two of the dumbshows have been noted above. The third revenge dumbshow is a bloody banquet for which the marginal note specifies '*Dead mens heads & bones banquett blood*'. In the plot it specifies '*Dead mens heads in dishes*'. That makes sense of the inventory of special clothes and properties in the *Diary* (p. 318) which include 'iiij Turckes hedes', presumably for this *Alcazar* banquet. Other plays used decapitated heads carried onstage swinging by the hair like Macbeth's. *Stukeley* in Scene 12 displays the head of O'Neill in this way. The *Diary*'s main property inventory (pp. 319–20) includes 'owld Mahemetes head' and 'Jerosses [Iris's?] head', plus one boar's and two lions' heads and Cerberus's trio.

If nothing else, comparison between Peele's quarto text and the plot of *Alcazar* shows how much the Fortune production embellished the words on Peele's pages. To these visual images we might add that Henslowe's list of properties offered resources for noise as well as spectacle. Besides seventeen swords of various kinds, it has nine iron 'targets' or shields, which would have resounded loudly when broadswords were clashed on them, plus one of copper and four of wood. Hammering a broadsword on a metal shield produced as much of the noise of war as anyone could want on stage. We might even wonder, since *Alcazar* brings in Muly's body at the finale, whether the mention of 'the Mores lymes' in the inventory of clown's and hermit's suits and other items (*Diary*, p. 318) does not mean that he was brought on stage dissected and stuffed with straw. That is certainly what Muly Mahamet Seth says at the end he will have done to the corpse and put on display. The plot's mutilated ending invites such guesswork.

All the inventories of properties and apparel (*Diary*, pp. 317–25) are revealing.[44] So far as stage clothing is concerned they list only the exceptional items that as signal features were a special cost to the company, such as 'vj grene cottes for Roben Hoode', 'ij Danes sewtes, and j payer of Danes hosse', 'Will. Sommers sewtte', and 'Tamberlynes cotte with coper lace'. The company also had to have specially tailored the women's gowns for the boys, such as 'iiij ferdingalles' and 'Eves bodeyes'. More routine clothing must have been owned and supplied for use by individual players. Besides the special costumes the lists of special properties include 'j chyme of belles', 'j rocke, j cage, j tombe, j Hell mought' (probably the cage was for Bajazeth and his wife in *Tamburlaine*, and the hell's mouth for *Faustus*),[45] a bedstead, coffins, 'ij mosse banckes', 'j poopes miter', also needed for *Faustus*, 'j lether hatchete', presumably for non-fatal beheadings, six different crowns, and 'j cauderm for the Jewe' for the finale of another Marlowe favourite, *The Jew of Malta*. Weapons include seventeen foils, the shields and metal targets already noted, and 'Cupedes bowe & quiver'. Lion skins and bear skins, a bull's head and two lion's heads, with 'j bores heade & Serberosse iij heades' are in the lists, plus 'j snake' and 'j great horse with his leages', presumably for use as the Trojan horse, the legs detachable for storage. Larger properties include 'j frame for the heading in Black Jone', 'j tree of gowlden apelles', 'Tantelouse tre', and 'j whell and frame in the Sege of London'. Enigmas include 'the clothe of the Sone and Mone', which may have been a painted cloth for pinning to the *frons scenae*, and 'j dragon in fostes', most likely a device to spout fireworks. The inventories show ample provision for things to catch the eye in supplement to the words. By far the heaviest expenditure and the highest value lay in the clothing.[46] Tudor tailors of course were always on

[44] A useful study of the signifiers that clothing represented is Randall Nakayama's '"I know she is a courtesan by her attire": Clothing and Identity in *The Jew of Malta*', in *Marlowe's Empery. Expanding his Critical Contexts*, ed. Sara Munson Deats and Robert A. Logan, Newark, 2002, pp. 150–63.

[45] David Bevington has some sensible comments on the staging of the play's two versions in 'Staging the A- and B-Texts of *Doctor Faustus*', in *Marlowe's Empery*, Nebraska, 2002, pp. 43–60. Fitting the first version to staging at the Rose and the later to the Fortune is tempting, but nothing in either text justifies doing so.

[46] Alan C. Dessen and Leslie Thomson's *Dictionary of Stage Directions in English Drama, 1580–1642*, Cambridge, 1999, quotes many stage directions from Admiral's plays. While most of them match the language and stage structure of other plays, some are distinctive for the forms of staging they imply. Entries worth noting, if only because they recur in several of the company's plays, include *alarum, alias, arbor, ascent, banquet, bed of state, behind curtains, bell, blazing star, chair* (either a

hand to remake clothes and to conceal worn patches with ornamental embellishments.

For music the list includes 'iij trumpettes' and a drum for ceremonial and military use, a treble viol, a basse viol, a bandore, a 'sytteren' (cittern, a lute-like string instrument), and a sackbut. Music at the Rose and the Fortune is not to be ignored, though it never played as big a part in staging as the Blackfriars consort eventually provided for the King's Men. Most of the instruments were there for solo or very small group perform-ances. The trumpets and drums were used for offstage military commands (drums for infantry, trumpets for cavalry) or ceremonial flourishes such as sennets, while the strings and woodwinds were used onstage to accom-pany songs. Neither the Rose nor the Fortune seem to have been aug-mented with a music room on the stage balcony, as the Globe was once it began to partner the Blackfriars as that company's summer venue, although the relatively few Fortune plays postdating 1608 leave it as little more than an assumption. Musical accompaniments to the songs needed musicians on stage with the players, as happened with the frustrated '*music*' brought on to accompany Prince Richard's intended serenade of Lady Faukenbridge in *Look About You*. Similarly the light and rapid syncopated drumming of the tabor ('tabber' may be an onomatopoeia for its sound, perhaps) and the shrill pipe that accompanied the dancing of jigs were all sounded onstage, not from behind a curtain on the stage balcony. The history plays and others made use of the noises of war with drums and trumpets, mostly for battle commands and to announce royal entries and ceremonials. Harmonious sounds were an integral feature of most spectacles, and given the skills with their instruments that many players had, even offstage sounds were not unknown for occasional mood-music.

A classic instance of how the Admiral's early staging practices developed has to be found not so much in the *Tamburlaines* as in *The Spanish Tragedy*. The archetypal revenge tragedy, imitated in *Hamlet*, *Antonio's Revenge*, *The Revenger's Tragedy*, and other plays that often supplied

throne or chair of state, or a sick chair to carry dying men), *chambers, chariot, chime, devils, discover, drop, dumbshow, ensign, execution, fall, fireworks, flourish, garland, ghost, gibbet, glass* (magical perspective), *globe, ground, habit, halter, hammer, hearse, horn, hunt, knocking, ladder, letter, light, litter, mad, make a lane, masque, meat, morris, mouth, music, open, painting, paper, patch, picture, post, prison, purse, rabble, rank, retreat, rich, rifle, ring, rock, sceptre, scutcheon, sennet, shift, shirt, shoot, shop, show, skirmish, sleeping, spaniel, staff, stag, stand, state, study, sword, table, tent, thunder and lightning, thunderclap, tire* (headtire), *tomb, torch, towel, train, treasure, tree, trumpet, walls, whip,* and *window.* Quite a few of the items named in this list also appear in the *Diary*'s inventories.

explicit visual reminders of the Admiral's original, its finale was the model catastrophe lodging in every London spectator's mind. Its ingenious staging of Hieronimo's revenge by means of the play within the play has attracted a lot of speculation about how the Rose might have handled it, but Kyd's play had other innovative features too. James Shapiro points out that 'we can search the canons of Marlowe, Shakespeare, Jonson, Webster, and others in vain for instances where characters are put to death the same way that convicted felons were in Elizabethan England',[47] yet, he notes, *The Spanish Tragedy* was a striking exception. Alexandro is bound to the stake for burning on stage in 3.1, and Pedringano is actually hanged on stage in 3.6. This was drastic stage realism. Shapiro also points out that five years after writing the play Kyd, like Alexandro, became a victim of torture (and, we might add, died of it less than a year later). Shows of gruesome realism that reflected London's street realities are a feature of the *Alcazar* plot and many other Admiral's plays.

Colourful displays of blood as in *Alcazar* were a distinctive feature of the company's staging throughout. We should not forget that *Titus Andronicus* was also staged at the Rose in January 1594, possibly with Alleyn in the company. But the Admiral's productions had many other graphic features too.[48] The lists of clothes and properties testify to the ample resources for visually exciting staging. To those items we can add the devices for disguise games described in Chapter 2. Some of those smaller features (sic) included items not listed in the inventories, such as Barabbas's distinctive nose in *The Jew of Malta*. William Rowley in *A Search for Money. Or The Lamentable complaint for the losse of the wandring Knight, Mounsieur l'Argent. Or Come with me, I know thou lovest Money. Dedicated to all those that lack Money*, 1609, tells of a visit to a usurer's house. The owner, when he opens his well-locked door, is described by Rowley with Dickensian colour as having:

as ill a head in forme (and worse in condition), then ever held a spout of lead in his mouth at the corner of a Church, an old moth-eaten cap buttoned under his chinne: his visage (or vizard) like the artificiall Jewe of Maltaes nose, the wormes fearing his bodie would have gonne along with his soule, came to take and indeed

---

[47] '"Tragedies naturally performed": Kyd's Representation of Violence', in *Staging the Renaissance: Reinterpretations of Elizabethan and Jacobean Drama*, ed. David Scott Kastan and Peter Stallybrass, London, 1991, pp. 99–113, p. 100.

[48] Alexander Leggatt's *Jacobean Public Theatre* has a sound introduction to the main features of open-air staging at the Fortune, Curtain, Red Bull and Globe from 1603. Chapters 3 and 4, on productions and acting, are particularly valuable. It studies four plays in detail, one of them *The Honest Whore*, a Fortune play (pp. 149–63 are about *1 The Honest Whore* and its sequel).

had taken possession, where they peept out still at certaine loopeholes to see who came neere their habitation: upon which nose, two casements were built, through which his eyes had a little ken of us, the forepart of his doublet was greasie Sattin, stil to put him in mind of his patron Satan. (C2v)

Another half-page elaborates this Fagin-like image, including the point that his nose was well preserved by sack (Elizabethan sherry, a fortified wine that did not double-ferment on the voyage from Portugal as other wines did). When he became enraged, 'the bloud ranne about his guiltie nose, with the very suddaine skrewing of his face.' (C3v). For us the key to this description, in spite of the spectacles perched on the reddening nose and the sherry that generated the bottle-shape, is the term 'artificiall'. This usurer's nose was presumably real, whereas the stage Jew of Malta's was similar but a fake. Alleyn's false nose as Barabbas was a memorably comic feature of his role, one renewed in Chapman's Leon. The saviour's cross he wore on his breast when he played Faustus was a different matter, a personal safeguard against his possible damnation.

Besides the comedies of disguise, which no doubt included the use of false voices as well as false noses, such as Redcap's stammer, the Admiral's at the Rose and Fortune used a wide range of standard staging devices. The war games with clashing swords and metal shields that Richard Fowler later made notorious have been noted above. They used fireworks for offstage cannon as well as for the imps from Hell in their devil plays. Besides the smoky devilry of *Faustus* that John Melton noted they ran clowns and devils in plays like *Grim the Collier* with boys as black devils, fireworks spouting from their various bodily orifices as they ran round the stage. The effect of such spectacles cannot readily be caught in words or stage directions. Alexander Leggatt notes how the texts of the many plays with clowns offer only a rough guide to the exploits they offered on stage. In several of the printed texts, as he sees it, 'what we have is scripted clowning'.[49]

Apart from *Alcazar* not much has been said here about one of the features of Rose and Fortune staging that is most often commented on or assumed, the use of spectacle. Given the rise of anti-Catholic iconoclasm in the wake of the Reformation ritualistic spectacles were not generally thought to be a praiseworthy activity, any more than they are now except as shows for tourists. In Shakespeare's time poets understandably held that their words were superior to the visual tricks of stage shows. In his addition to Stowe's *Annales* of 1615 Sir George Buc described Londoners'

---

[49] Ibid., p. 98.

skills at what he openly called 'the *scandal* of Images and Idolls'.[50] For all
Buc's concern, the stages did put on elaborately special shows appealing to
the eye and not just in the bloody and gruesome realism flaunted for
shock effect in *Alcazar*'s dumbshows. Dekker in particular enjoyed
scripting accounts of complicated dumb-shows. His overtly spectacular
moralising in the shows he wrote for *The Whore of Babylon* where Truth
counterbalances Falsehood had an earlier model in *Old Fortunatus* at the
Fortune. For that play he wrote this prescription for a symbolic dumbshow at the beginning of the third scene in Act 1:

> *Musick sounds: Enter* Vice *with a gilded face, and hornes on her head: her garments
> long, painted before with silver halfe moones, increasing by little and little, till they
> come to the full: in the midst of them in Capitall letters this written:* CRESCIT EUNDO:
> *her garment painted behind with fooles faces and divels heads: and underneath it in
> the midst this written,* Ha, Ha, He: *she and others wearing gilded visards, and attird
> like devils, bring out a faire tree of Gold with apples on it: after her comes* Vertue,
> *a coxcombe on her head, all in white before, and this written about the middle:* SIBI
> SAPIT: *her attire behind painted with Crownes, and Laurell garlands, stuck full of
> stares, held out by hands, thrust out of bright cloudes, and among them this written,*
> DOMINABITUR ASTRIS: *Shee and other Nimphes all in white with coxecombs on
> their heads, bring a tree with greene and withered leaves mingled together, and little
> fruit on it: after her* Fortune, *one bearing her Wheele, another her Globe; and last,
> the* Priest.

Dekker chose to mark the triumphant return of Vertue in Act 5 (5.2.261–62)
with the much simpler '*Enter* Vertue, *crownd: Nymphes and kings attending
on her, crownd with Olive branches and lawrels, musicke sounding.*'

Detailed and not always decipherable though such descriptions are, we
have to consider carefully just what the impact of such shows would have
been on the original viewers. They were generally popular, if Dekker's
persistence in putting them into his Fortune plays is any guide.[51] Dumbshows
and other stage spectacles appealed to a taste that had its own durability.
Even at the less intellectual levels appealing to the least literate, visual
shows could catch the attention and grip the imagination. We need only
to look at the many surviving monuments to the dead to see how strongly

---

[50] *Annales*, 1615, sig. Ooo2v. Buc's term was recently adopted for the title of a book by Marguerite
A. Tassi, *The Scandal of Images: Iconoclasm, Eroticism, and Painting in Early Modern English Drama*,
Susquehanna University Press, 2005.

[51] As late as 1639 the Fortune company got into trouble with the authorities for staging an old play,
The Cardinal's Conspiracy, 'in contempt of the ceremonies of the church', when they set up an altar
with basin and candlesticks as a mockery of the Catholic church. It brought a heavy fine down on
them. Such Protestant mockery of Catholic rituals became particularly dangerous in the last years
of King Charles's control over the 'citizen' repertories.

visual symbols stood up against the destructive rigours of early iconoclasm. Several of the Admiral's company writers, most notably Munday, Dekker and Middleton, turned in later years to writing the scenarios for London's annual parades and Lord Mayor's pageants. Making such shows was probably the most conspicuous mark of how every year the values of the city and citizens came to reconcile themselves with the daily business of playing. It would be quite wrong to see the use of spectacle on the open-air stages put out of countenance by Inigo Jones's masques at court, though it may be true that the gulf between the courtly playgoers of the Blackfriars and the expectations of a 'citizen' clientele at the Fortune was at least in part enhanced (as both cause and effect) by the difference between those two sorts of popular spectacle.

5

The company's repertory practices

Sir George Buc was Master of the Revels from 1610 until his mental collapse in the year up to October 1622, when he died.[1] Well before 1610 he was a keen play-reader and playgoer. By 1606 he was deputising for Tilney, the then Master, licensing play manuscripts for the press. He bought his own printed playbooks and took an active interest in them, as we know from his 1599 copy of *George a Greene* that survives in the Folger Shakespeare Library.[2] On its title-page Buc wrote out the answers he received to his question about who wrote the play from Edward Juby of the Admiral's and William Shakespeare of the Chamberlain's. It was Buc who seems to have decided after 1615 that he would choose no more plays for performance at court from the Fortune or the Red Bull. By 1622 he had lost control of his mind, and he died on 31 October.

Evidence for his decision to ignore the plays of the two open-air playhouses comes very largely from the Revels Office's own record of court performances.[3] Intriguingly, though, the Revels papers from Buc's last two years in office, around 1620, include some pieces of paper with remarkable scrawls on them. They look like discarded scraps but were kept along with the more important papers. One scrap has a list of play titles on it, including what was probably the age's most famous and certainly the most quoted play, *The Spanish Tragedy*.[4] Several other titles from the list, *Hamlet*, *Philaster* and *The Maid's Tragedy*, had been staged

---

[1] Buc's life has not been recorded in detail. The most scrupulous study of his work as Master of the Revels appears in Richard Dutton, *Licensing, Censorship and Authorship in Early Modern England. Buggeswordes*, Palgrave, London, 2000. In 1615 when he wrote of the 'scandal' of ritualistic shows and spectacle, he probably had court masques in mind.

[2] See Alan H. Nelson, 'George Buc, William Shakespeare, and the Folger *George a Greene*', *Shakespeare Quarterly* 49 (1998), 74–83.

[3] See John H. Astington, *English Court Theatre 1558–1642*, Cambridge, 1999, Appendix pp. 249–67.

[4] The scraps are reproduced by Frank Marcham in *The King's Office of the Revels 1610–1622. Fragments of Documents in the Department of Manuscripts, British Museum*, London, 1925. The one depicted in Illustration 13 appears on page 10.

at court through the previous few years. The most extraordinary pairing, though, is 'The Tradgedy of Ham . . .' immediately followed by 'The Tradgedy of Jeronimo', the Admiral's play. The conjunction prompts some thought.

As a whole the list on this scrap of paper may be no more than an idle jotting-down of play-titles, since the whole list was crossed out subsequently. Conceivably, though, it began as an *aide memoire* listing plays thought most feasible to be staged for the court in 1619 or 1620. The handwriting looks like Buc's own, as are other notes in this collection of scraps. Inserting the subtitles for two of the plays, one listed as *The Mayor of Quinborough or Hengist K. of Kent*, was the first time the two titles for Middleton's one play were put together, and the other *Phil . . . or Love lies a bleed . . .* [ing], the subtitle that appeared on *Philaster*'s first title-page in 1620, is just the sort of amplification Buc would have made. The paper is worn, with the right-hand side decayed so that the full play titles it recorded are missing.

If these jottings have any significance, they signal a remarkable idea, almost certainly a product of the tottering Buc's last thoughts about his annual obligation to provide the court with its long Christmas season of entertainments. They link Kyd's play about a maddened revenger to its equally famous successor, Shakespeare's *Hamlet*. It is as if Buc was inspired to offer the court the Palsgrave's company's old classic in sequence with the famous King's Men's play, long known to 'please all', as the author of *Daiphantus* put it in 1601.[5] By 1620 *Hamlet* was a classic in its own right, but to link it directly with Kyd's play of at least twelve years earlier demanded the long memory of an attentive and thoughtful play-goer like Buc. The older play may have warranted Jonson's derision in 1614 over such old-fashioned types as 'Hee that will sweare, *Jeronimo*, or *Andronicus* are the best playes yet' (*Bartholomew Fair*, Induction), but Buc's linkage of the two made the kind of connection that we recognise much more readily today than we might have expected anyone to do in 1620.

Given Buc's mental collapse soon after, he may well have taken both plays as having direct application to himself in his tortured function as the court's presenter of plays. That after all is the role both mad Hieronimo and mad Hamlet are given by their king when each stages his own murderous play within the play. The two revenger-heroes have the job both of presenter and censor of what they stage at court ('Have you heard

---

[5] See Gurr, '*Hamlet* and the auto da fé', *Around the Globe* 13 (2000), 15.

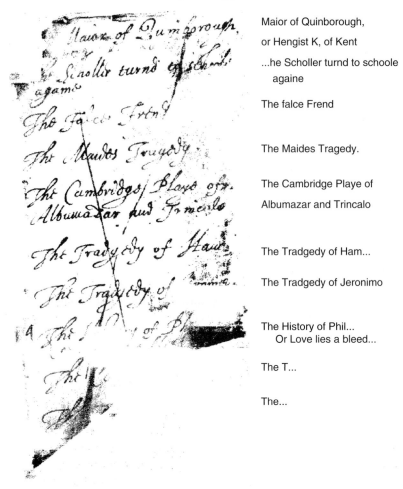

Maior of Quinborough,
or Hengist K, of Kent
...he Scholler turnd to schoole
    againe

The falce Frend

The Maides Tragedy.

The Cambridge Playe of
Albumazar and Trincalo

The Tradgedy of Ham...

The Tradgedy of Jeronimo

The History of Phil...
    Or Love lies a bleed...

The T...

The...

Figure 15. The Revels Office paper, with a transcript.

the argument? Is there no offence in't?' asks Claudius suspiciously). It is truly sad that Buc's inspiration for a double bill of the two plays seems, like so many lovely ideas, to have been crushed under the practical difficulties of organising that season's performances. Perhaps one or both of the companies owning them did not have their play available in their repertory that autumn. Certainly the Palsgrave's company did not appear at court in 1620. Their sole court performance after 1615 was of an unnamed play in the presence of the king on 3 January 1619.[6] It is just possible that this last appearance was prompted by Buc's interest in staging Kyd's play along with Shakespeare's, a final try-out for the company that owned Kyd's play in the king's presence. But we do not know which play it was that the company staged in January 1619, and Buc in any case crossed his list out.

For all the attractiveness to moderns of this putative link between *The Spanish Tragedy* and *Hamlet* (the Royal Shakespeare Company chose to play *The Spanish Tragedy* at their Swan alongside *Hamlet* at the main theatre in 1997) we need to give careful scrutiny to the question why the Fortune company fell so completely off the Revels lists for the court after 1615, along with its neighbour and fellow-occupant of an open-air playhouse the Red Bull company. For the Master to ignore the Palsgrave's so totally cannot have been simply because the company's royal patron was absent through these years and therefore not available to enjoy his company's work. It is true that in previous seasons a patron's company would routinely be summoned to entertain him or her over the Christmas season. But the Lord Palsgrave, the Elector Palatine who became for a startlingly brief time King Frederick V of Bohemia, was an absentee from court even before 1615. He was first granted patronage of the company because he married the princess Elizabeth a few months after Prince Henry died, on 14 February 1613,[7] when they were both aged seventeen. After the wedding the pair went straight into residence at his palace in Heidelberg while he pursued his role in central Europe as leader of the anti-Catholic cause. He was offered the kingship of Bohemia in 1619, a disastrous gift immediately setting against him the Catholic potency of the Hapsburgs of Spain and Austria. Beside the Protestant princes in Germany his only allies were Denmark, the Netherlands and his peace-loving British father-in-law. His forces were resoundingly defeated at the battle of the White Mountain near Prague in 1620. That cost him all his Palatinate lands including his capital at Heidelberg. For the next ten years he and his wife lived in exile in the Netherlands.

Such overseas distractions, while elevating his status as leader of the Protestants against the Hapsburgs, meant the Elector Palatine had no presence at the English court at all, which may have been one reason why

---

[6] *Malone Society Collections 6, Chamber Accounts 1558–1642*, Oxford, 1961, p. 70.
[7] He was nominated King of Bohemia in August 1619 and crowned on 4 November, but his rule lasted only four days. He died in 1632. Elizabeth his widow continued to call herself Queen of Bohemia until her death in 1662.

Buc decided to overlook his company. The same cannot be said, however, for Queen Anne's Men at the Red Bull who lost access to court performances at the same time. From 1615 up to her death in March 1619 Queen Anne was certainly on hand, although her alienation from her husband meant that for the most part she pursued her own theatrical entertainments at Somerset House, then called Denmark House. She attended a performance at court by her company on 17 December 1615, and another by the King's Men four days later. She saw plays by companies other than hers in November and December 1616 and through the following winter. The last performances at court she attended were three plays by her company which she saw along with Prince Charles in March 1617. That, however, was after Queen Anne's Men had shifted their location from the outdoor Red Bull to the indoor Cockpit.[8] Finally on 4 May 1617 she saw *Cupid's Banishment*, a special event performed by a group of young ladies. Through her last illness until her death in 1619 she never returned for a court performance. Nor did the Red Bull company. Apart from that single performance by the Lord Palsgrave's Men on 3 January 1619 neither of the outdoor playhouse companies ever performed at court again.

The different events that eclipsed the patrons of the two companies still using the outdoor playhouses through the Christmas season are one possible factor in the Master's decision from 1615 to ignore their plays. A much simpler and more obvious reason, though, was snobbery. Class distinctions dominated English society. The gulfs between artisan and merchant, citizen and gentry were signalled in the varieties of dress dictated (and frequently ignored) by the sumptuary laws as thoroughly as they were flaunted in other attitudes of the kind of which some instances are given below. The most striking counter-example in all of the last millennium where distinct social classes conjoined is the playgoing habits of London society from 1590 until the first decade of the new century,[9] simply because through the duopoly years there were just the two suburban amphitheatres available for every playgoer. Even then the playhouses themselves priced their distinct sections to keep the different classes apart, twopenny galleries from gentlemen's rooms, galleries from groundlings. The lowest gallery according to the Fortune contract was fenced with 'stronge yron pykes' to keep the standers in the yard from climbing into them. For all its divisions, the unity created by sharing events socially in large crowds, however separated they were around the

[8] See Gurr, *The Shakespearian Playing Companies*, Oxford, 1996, pp. 324–25.
[9] See Gurr, 'Traps and Discoveries at the Globe', *Proceedings of the British Academy* 94, 1997, 85–101.

auditorium, broke up when the King's Men finally secured the use of their indoor playhouse, the Blackfriars, after 1608.

The sixfold price differential between access to the open-air playhouses and the Blackfriars created a barrier of social difference that never disappeared subsequently. In part from 1609, and completely from 1660, theatre in London became a middle and upper-class preserve. The first Stuarts made plays respectable and gave a social cachet to being seen at the Blackfriars and Cockpit indoors that such displays could never have enjoyed before. This of course eventually guaranteed the closure of all playgoing, gentle and citizen, indoor and outdoor alike, when Parliament went to war with the king. Until then, from 1603 and especially after 1608 plays and playgoing became a major part of the courtly routine. Even during her long exile at The Hague King James's daughter Elizabeth, wife of the exiled King of Bohemia, had her courtiers stage Fletcher's *The Scornful Lady* on 15 March 1629.[10] In April 1638 she thanked Sir Thomas Roe for sending her a copy of Inigo Jones's masque *Britannia Triumphans*, one of Henrietta Maria's recent successes at Whitehall. Playing at the Fortune and Red Bull through these years was a quite different phenomenon from what was staged by the King's Men at Blackfriars. The only grandee known to visit the Fortune after 1615 was the Spanish ambassador Gondomar, who had his own political reason for making that visit. The emergence of 'unlicensed' theatre and music-hall stages in the eighteenth and nineteenth centuries shows that the working-class appetite for theatre did not disappear, but by then it had for centuries been priced out of most artisans' and apprentices' reach. In London popular theatre lasted at the outdoor playhouses until 1642, but it did not really make its mark again in London until the Dickensian theatre of Vincent Crummle in the nineteenth century.

The usual label given to the Fortune and Red Bull repertoires between about 1615 and 1642, that they were 'citizen' rather than 'gentry' playhouses, calls for complicated deconstruction and only very tentative acceptance. Ample evidence from contemporary declarations is there, although the gentry's contempt for old-fashioned and lower-class plays was never admitted as merely a matter of money and social class. That does nonetheless seem to have been its chief cause. When Christopher Beeston moved Queen Anne's Men's plays from the outdoor Red Bull to his new indoor playhouse in Drury Lane a gang of handicraft apprentices attacked the new venue because he had removed their favourite plays

---

[10] See *The Letters of Elizabeth Queen of Bohemia*, compiled by L. M. Baker, London, 1973, p. 78.

to somewhere much more expensive. Their grievance was over the impossible cost to them of the new playhouse. When later they gathered at the Fortune where their plays were still available at manageable prices in order to renew their assault on the new indoor venue they were declaring where their loyalties lay. Unfortunately we cannot identify any of the plays that Beeston took out of their reach from the Red Bull in 1616 to have performed at the Cockpit. The dearth of information about the repertories in these years is a major impediment. Too much of the story about how the Fortune and the Red Bull developed into 'citizen' play-houses is rooted in thin air. So the question of just what kind of play and just what kind of audience the company's repertory at the Fortune was aimed at needs scrupulously sceptical inspection.

The apparent growth of a 'citizen' identity after the duopoly disap-peared and a new repertory developed was witnessed by a lot besides Jonson's contempt for the old-fashioned tastes that preferred Kyd's play to his own more innovative writing. Derision at the old repertory itself became a new fashion among the gentry well before 1615. Much of the evidence for how quickly the more gentrified tastes shifted away from the heavy verse rhythms of Marlowe and Kyd is apparent in the boy company plays of the first decade in the century, particularly the satirical and 'railing' plays of the Blackfriars boy company which were very largely written as prose. Beaumont's *Knight of the Burning Pestle* mocked the naivety of a citizen husband and wife who cannot comprehend satire and ask why the boys will not stage 'the legend of *Whittington*, or the life and death of sir *Thomas Gresham*? with the building of the Royall Exchange? Or the story of Queene *Elenor*, with the rearing of London bridge upon wool-sacks?'[11] Not long after Beaumont's play had its brief launch on the Blackfriars stage in 1607 the idea of fools spouting quotable verse and using large but incomprehensible words became a mark of the unsophisti-cated playgoer. Beaumont's mock-apprentice Rafe offers a speech by huffing Hotspur from *1 Henry IV* as his party piece. In the Cambridge play *Albumazar* (1615), one of the plays noted on Buc's scrap of paper, Thomas Tomkis made his rustic clown declare about wooing his mistress 'then will I confound her with complements drawn from the Plaies I see at the Fortune and Red Bull, where I learne all the words I speake and understand not.'[12] This was mockery of the audiences rather than their plays, of course. For so long as only two companies had exclusive access

---

[11] Francis Beaumont, *The Knight of the Burning Pestle*, 1613, Induction.
[12] *Albumazar*, sig. C4^v.

to London playing places they could maintain a parity of quality and esteem. Once the duopoly broke down in 1600 tastes and the provision of plays catering for such tastes diverged markedly. Kyd and Marlowe's plays and Alleyn's other old favourites kept the Fortune repertory locked in what Buc and the more advanced tastes thought were an increasingly outdated style, as was the Queen Anne's repertory at the neighbouring Red Bull.

How this should have come about in playgoers' minds, and how far it was the plays and how much the ambience of the playhouse audiences is a question complicated first of all by the status and interests of the Fortune's impresarios, Henslowe and Alleyn. As a Groom of the Chamber from 1593 onwards Henslowe always had much better access to the court than did the Burbages. He was a lot defter too in his dealings with the Master of the Revels, since the *Diary* shows how regularly he paid his dues, whereas in 1604 Tilney had to take the Burbages to the other kind of court in order to secure arrears of fees due to him from the last ten years.[13] As Master of the Bears Alleyn regularly supervised entertainments for Elizabeth and James (I particularly relish the story of what happened when he had a pack of dogs set onto a pair of the Tower's lions: the lions sensibly ran away. No wonder bears were usually blinded before they were baited). Alleyn also joined in the attempts to imitate the Blackfriars with his Porter's Hall project to set up a new indoor playhouse in 1614. But the Revels Office and the government never gave Alleyn any help with social climbing, either for himself or for his acting company at the Fortune.

The underside or rather the social overside of the Red Bull and Fortune becoming known to dismissive gentlemen and writers as merely venues for citizens is their apparent loss of credibility with the gentry who now flocked to the Blackfriars. Such a shift in patronage got plenty of notice. In his epistle for the publication of the Fortune's hit *The Roaring Girl* in 1612, Middleton claimed that you could see the changes in theatre fashion by analogy with changes in the fashions of dress. 'The fashion of playmaking, I can properly compare to nothing, so naturally, as the alteration in apparell. For in the time of the Great-crop-doublet, your huge bombasted plaies, quilted with mighty words to leane purpose was onely then in fashion. And as the doublet fell, neater inventions beganne to set up. Now in the time of sprucenes, our plaies followe the nicenes of our Garments, single plots, quaint conceits, letcherous jests, drest up in hanging

[13] Mary Edmond, 'On Licensing Playhouses', *Review of English Studies* 46 (1995), 373–74.

sleeves, and those are fit for the Times and Tearmers.' For new spruceness to be proclaimed at the Fortune with its repertory of Marlowe, Peele and Kyd was not even mildly disarming. Middleton wrote his half-apparent dismissal of the change in fashion in the midst of its repertory of 'huge bombasted plaies' like *The Spanish Tragedy* and Marlowe's epics, in contrast with what we must assume he meant by the 'neater inventions' of more recent times such as, presumably, *The Roaring Girl*. Middleton was acknowledging how fashion had shifted away from the Fortune's core repertory while denying that such changes had any impact on the Fortune's playgoers who were reading his comment on them, an ambivalent view that must have been shared by the company staging the play.

One factor that does seem likely to have influenced Buc's decision to ignore the open-air playhouse repertories after 1615 was not only their ageing repertories but the age of their style of acting, still 'quilted with mighty words to leane purpose'. This is a factor that goes all the way back to Alleyn's own large-scale acting of Marlovian roles in contrast to what we take to be Richard Burbage's quieter art of 'personation'. Hearing lines from the manuscript 'part' that Alleyn spoke as Greene's Orlando in *Orlando Furioso*, we can hear what Middleton had in mind (I have capitalised the proper names).

> Extinguish proud Tesyphone those brandes
> fetch dark Alecto, from black Phlegeton
> or Lethe waters, to appease those flames
> that wrathfull Nemesis hath sett on fire.[14]

How openly the Fortune company continued to imitate Alleyn's celebrated action of 'stalking and roaring' on stage while he was away from them through the 1597–1600 period and after he finally retired in 1603 is not easy to show. Joseph Hall, later a bishop, wrote derisively in 1597 of seeing Tamburlaine on stage with 'The stalking steps of his great personage',[15] registering the extravagance of his body language even that early. The *Diary*'s evidence does imply that while Alleyn was away the company moved towards a new mode but that they returned to stage his huffing parts after he restarted at the Fortune in 1600. His favourite roles, Tamburlaine, Faustus, Barabbas, Hieronimo and Tamar Cham, all featured

---

[14] *Two Elizabethan Stage Abridgements: The Battle of Alcazar & Orlando Furioso*, Oxford, MSR, 1922, p. 188.
[15] *Virgidemiarum* II. Liber 1, Satire iii. The book was entered in the Stationers' Register on 31 March 1597, and published that year, so the verse was probably written in 1595 or 1596.

most strongly while he was in the company. Yet his most celebrated roles – certainly Hieronimo, Tamburlaine and Faustus – did stay on in the repertory performed in his style by players like Fowler until well after 1625. What we cannot calculate with any precision is how far such stalking and roaring might have come to characterise the company's style. If so, and for all Middleton's dismissive comparison in 1611 of changing plays to the transience of fashions in clothing, its distinctive appeal must have ensured those plays continuing as the beating heart of the company's repertory. We should not ignore the indications suggesting that the company developed a house style of acting to match Alleyn, and clung to it and what it brought to the repertory long after his final retirement. That as much as anything would have ensured the fixity of the label 'citizen' for their repertory.

How far the gradual separation in reputation between the outdoor playhouse companies and those who played indoors might have begun when Alleyn's style showed itself distinct from Burbage's is a matter for fairly idle speculation, however much of a temptation identifying such a difference may be. It is true that loud speech and violent movement was a feature of playing noted at the Fortune, but it is still a long stretch to say that Alleyn himself was ultimately responsible for the 'citizen' reputation that the Fortune and Red Bull developed in contrast with the Blackfriars repertory through the Jacobean and Caroline years. Alleyn's own self-parody as the 'fustian king' in 1593 does consort well with Middleton's comment on how out of date the bombasted plays were thought to be by 1611. Assuming the later players did reproduce it, Alleyn's physically robust style must have remained a feature whenever the company staged any of the older repertory at the Fortune.

If Buc's idea of staging a pair of revenge plays at court had any basis in the company repertories of 1620 the catalyst must have been Hieronimo. We cannot say with much confidence that whoever took these roles on after Alleyn retired in 1603 tried seriously to imitate his style in the part, but later commentators did continue to write derisively about what they called the loud-mouthed stalking that they thought had become characteristic of the Fortune and Red Bull style of acting. It does seem that Alleyn's style was popular enough to generate a whole new era of imitators. The noisiest and most ferociously physical of all the later players, Richard Fowler, began his career at the Fortune before 1618. He was a signatory for the Fortune lease on 31 October that year and was one of the nine Palsgrave's sharers listed by Herbert in 1622. His reputation as a physical player at the same playhouse is on record in a reminiscence in *Knavery in All Trades* (1664), where various gentry delivered their memories about the pre-Interregnum theatre. One says:

Fowler you know was appointed for the Conquering parts, and it being given out he was to play the Part of a great Captain and mighty Warriour, drew much Company; the Play began, and ended with his Valour; but at the end of the fourth Act he laid so heavily about him, that some Mutes who stood for Souldiers, fell down as they were dead e're he had toucht their trembling Targets; so he branisht his Sword and made his *Exit*; ne're minding to bring off his dead men; which they perceiving, crauld into the Tyreing house, at which, *Fowler* grew angry and told 'em, Dogs you should have laine there till you had been fetcht off; and so they crauld out again, which gave the People such an occasion of Laughter, they cry'd that again, that again, that again.[16]

This late anecdote suggests that Fowler's fame came from the way he kept up the Fortune's long-standing tradition of target fighting on stage, the metal shields or targets that resounded to his banging on them with his heavy broadsword, and that he stalked and roared like Alleyn in his militant roles.

The outdoor playhouses were convenient for such athletics, and were exploited for more than Fowler's theatrical sword-swinging. Mounting profitable sessions of formal combats by professional swordsmen on the open-air stages was an old tradition at the open-air playhouses. Through several winters in the 1620s the Fortune and Red Bull and in the 1630s the Globe were all licensed by the Master of the Revels, Henry Herbert, in Lent while the playhouses were officially closed, to run prize fights along with shows of acrobatic rope-dancing and tumbling. He licensed the Red Bull on 21 March 1622 and the Fortune on 15 and 19 March 1624 for that purpose.[17] Using the large stages of the outdoor playhouses for sporting events was a tradition going back to the 1570s. This carries with it the implication that the companies sustained a similarly vigorous kind of entertainment in their plays, with the consequent attraction of sportive audiences. Use of the Globe for that kind of sport in its off-season could be one reason why Shirley contrasted the tastes of Globe audiences against those at the Blackfriars in the prologue to his *Doubtful Heir*.[18] The presence of sports-minded and energised audiences must have helped to create the fracas at the Red Bull in 1620 where a feltmaker's apprentice sitting on the edge of the stage to view a play issued a challenge for a duel to the player

[16] Quoted by G. E. Bentley, *The Jacobean and Caroline Stage*, Oxford, 1940–68, II. 440.
[17] N. W. Bawcutt, *Herbert*, pp. 140, 161.
[18] See Gurr, *The Shakespeare Company 1594–1642*, Cambridge, 2004, p. 148.

who accidentally hit him with his sword. The fact that the player responded to the written challenge only by reporting it to the authorities presumably shows his desire along with his company not to lose his employment on stage to any injury or detention by the authorities. But it does show the energy of the audiences as well as the players.

A major but largely indeterminable reason for the two outdoor companies that started at the Rose as the Admiral's and then Worcester's and grew into citizen status at the Fortune and the Red Bull as the Prince's and Queen Anne's Men keeping their 'citizen' image was their readiness in both cases to sustain their old and famous repertories. The roles that Alleyn made famous in the 1590s including Marlowe's core plays *Faustus* and *Tamburlaine* were always integral to the Fortune's reputation. The few texts that survive from the company's Jacobean years support the idea that the choice of new plays remained conservative and kept to the same pattern. Their last known published play, *The Duchess of Suffolk* in 1624, about the heroic exploits of Henry VIII's sister against Marian persecution, was a late contribution to the Foxean history tradition that dated back to 1600. The London setting for *The Roaring Girl* in 1611 picked up the model of the famous *Long Meg of Westminster* recorded in the *Diary* as a hit in 1595, and of Dekker's *Shoemaker's Holiday*, celebrating the feats of the handicraft apprentices of 1599 where a gang of bold shoemakers armed with cudgels outface a wedding party of gentlemen armed with swords. That was matched by Moll Frith's antics in the later play. Nothing survives to suggest that either the Fortune or the Red Bull company ever tried to imitate the Fletcherian tragicomic mode that developed from 1609 onwards at the indoor Blackfriars and Cockpit. The conservatism of the repertory does seem to have been deliberate.

Some evidence suggests that the Fortune company went rather less down-market than the Red Bull. They rejected Dekker's *If This Be Not a Good Play, the Devil Is in It*, much to his annoyance, but the Red Bull took it. Alexander Leggatt thinks that the Red Bull must have been more ready than the Fortune to use the clownage and fireworks that feature in the extant text, though other Fortune plays like *Faustus* and *Grim the Collier* would call that in question. Other writers of this period did link the two playhouse repertories together as sharing the same kind of excessive verbiage. In Tomkis's play *Albumazar*, written for performance at Trinity College Cambridge in 1614, his rustic declares that he will confound his beloved with compliments from the Fortune and Red Bull, 'where I learne all the words I speake and understand not'. He goes on to parody *The Spanish Tragedy*, 'O lippes, no lippes, but leaves besmear'd with mel-dew!"[19] Tomkis wrote his play a couple of years before Jonson voiced his derision over tastes that held on to *Titus Andronicus* and Kyd's play. Both writers drew on and contributed to the wash of feeling that was beginning to differentiate between the two kinds of repertory and led Buc to reject the more artisan-related one as fare not suitable for the court.

A final factor, both cause and effect of the signs of age in the repertory, may have been the persistence of jigs at the Fortune and Red Bull. A concluding song and dance act was a notable way of ending every outdoor performance. Henslowe paid "ij yonge men" 6s 8d for two jigs on 12 December 1597 (*Diary*, p. 85). Eventually jigs became a mark of lower-class shows and disorderly audiences. In October 1612 the Middlesex magistrates ordered that jigs at the Fortune must be suppressed, and even tried to extend their ban to all playhouses in London.

Whereas Complaynte have beene made at this last Generall Sessions, that by reason of certayne lewde Jigges songes and daunces used and accustomed at the play-house called the Fortune in Gouldinglane, diverse cutt-purses and other lewde and ill disposed persons in great multitudes doe resort thither at th'end of every playe, many tymes causinge tumults and outrages wherebye His Majesties peace is often broke and much mischiefe like to ensue thereby, Itt was hereuppon expresselye commaunded and ordered by the Justices of the said benche, That all Actors of everye playhouse within this cittye and liberties thereof and in the Countye of Middlesex that they and everie of them utterlye abolishe all Jigges Rymes and Daunces after their playes.[20]

At about this time the clown John Shank left the Fortune company for the King's Men, and a balladeer lamented the loss of his repertory of jigs as a result, not just from the Fortune but from the Globe, which makes it fairly certain that the King's Men had abandoned jigs by this time. But the Fortune never did. As late as 1673 Henry Chapman wrote in a small booklet that that 'a Pamphlet now a dayes, finds as small acceptance as a Comedy did formerly, at the *Fortune* play-House, without a Jig of *Andrew Kein's* into the bargain' (epistle to *The City of Bath Described*). Andrew Cane was the celebrated clown of the Fortune's last twenty years. If the two companies did persist in closing their performances with a jig by the company clown the tradition could only have intensified the divergence between the deliberately old-fashioned 'citizen' playhouses and the upwardly mobile Globe and indoor repertories.

[19] sig. C4^v–D1.
[20] Chambers, *Elizabethan Stage*, IV. 340–41.

A final event adding to speculation about the citizen character of the Fortune is the famous visit by the Spanish Ambassador Gondomar on 16 July 1621, six months before the fire that destroyed the playhouse. The meticulous reporter John Chamberlain wrote to Dudley Carleton at the Hague that he 'is growne so affable and familiar, that on Monday with his whole traine he went to a common play at the Fortune in Golding-lane, and the players (not to be overcome with curtesie) made him a banket when the play was don in the garden adjoining'.[21] The adjacent garden belonged to Alleyn, and he must have had a hand in the visit and the feast that followed. But the choice of playhouse to visit was the adroitly self-publicising Gondomar's, and we might well wonder if his decision to take his party to what had become known as a 'citizen' playhouse largely peopled by the local artisans and apprentices was not a deliberate act of Spanish self-advertisement to the commoners. The players, well known for their history plays asserting the Foxean mythology of the anti-Catholic cause and soon to stage a new play about Catholic persecution, *The Duchess of Suffolk*, which anticipated Middleton's *Game at Chess* by enhancing anti-Spanish enthusiasm in London audiences, welcomed the visitation by entertaining the Spanish with a summer-time feast in their garden. That suggests the visit was indeed a diplomat's publicity stunt. It is certainly to the players' credit that in spite of the familiar bias in their repertory they responded to it so courteously. Gondomar probably could not have done the same with the King's Men at the Globe, in use then instead of the winter Blackfriars. His decision to choose the Fortune adds substantially to the image we have of their repertory by then as both heavy with Protestant loyalism and aimed at the citizenry rather than the gentry. The absence of the court and nobility and London's law students through the summer just made Gondomar's populist trick so much more blatant.

What this evidence of a social and cultural division between the two types of playhouse does affirm most clearly is the way each type gradually, through a probably uncalculating and certainly unselfconscious process, came to select its preferred audiences. Even the tradition of closing a play with a jig reflects the Fortune's and the Red Bull's openness to citizen preferences more than to the gentry of London. The crowds of salesfolk, artisans and apprentices who Alexander Gill in 1632 called dismissively 'Prentizes and Apell-wyfes'[22] were always seen as typical Fortune audiences.

---

[21] *Letters*, II. 391.
[22] Verses written against *The Magnetic Lady*, in Jonson, *Works*, ed. Herford and Simpson, 11 vols., 1925–52, XI. 347.

This is a distinctive factor in the history of the ex-Admiral's company. It marks an exact difference from the Shakespeare company, which moved upmarket both with and after its Shakespeare heyday. What needs to be done here is to identify, through the relatively small proportion of the repertory that survives, what evidence can be found in the plays that reflected and upheld this company focus.

Most historians of early theatre in London, at least for the period up to 1610 or so, assume that the need to engage the very large audiences that filled the open amphitheatres meant that each company saw the others as rivals. In *Playing Companies and Commerce in Shakespeare's Time* Roslyn Knutson issued a reproof for such an oversimplification. The licensed companies had a shared interest not unlike that of the merchants, members of the great livery companies, who protected their monopolies with their own 'companies' and a mass of statutes to regulate how each of them would work and trade. Government supported such monopoly control since it helped their own authority especially with such potentially troublesome activities as printing and the price of food and clothing. The monopoly companies and perhaps especially from 1594 to 1600 the duopoly of the two theatre companies licensed to perform on the flanks of London were always careful to protect the shared interests of the groups working within their sphere.

The two playing companies of 1594 of course had no overarching 'livery' company to protect them. They did have the Master of the Revels upholding their right to perform specific plays and keep their workplaces licensed under Privy Council control. But they had no authority to limit the start of new companies such as those at the Swan in 1596 and at the Boar's Head in 1600. That was for the Privy Council, a body which showed little concern for such day-by-day regulation of private enterprises. When Pembroke's Men opened at the Swan Henslowe and the Admiral's certainly saw them as dangerous rivals, and quickly swallowed up their leading players once the Privy Council was finally moved to suppress them when they staged the 'seditious' *Isle of Dogs* in 1597. Whether the Admiral's also saw their opposites in the Shakespeare company as rivals or as colleagues we have no direct way of knowing. They certainly interchanged frequent jokes about each other's repertories, but building the Globe within fifty yards of the Rose has been seen as a direct challenge and affront by the Chamberlain's to the Admiral's. Yet it has also been claimed that Alleyn was planning his move from the Rose to the north as early as 1597, so the switch that took place in 1599–1600, with the northern company moving to Bankside and the Bankside company taking their place in the north, could be viewed as an adroit renewal of the original plan of 1594 to locate one company on each side of the City.[23] We cannot doubt that both companies were fully aware of the terms of the original duopoly deal and its value to them both. It does make quite good sense to see the switch as one planned by both companies.

Sharing interests in a quasi-monopoly is one thing, but sharing interests when each product has to be a unique offering is quite another. Since the bulk of regular playgoers were familiar with both repertories, a point the writers could never ignore as the constant cross-references to each other's plays by both companies affirm, they both faced a two-sided challenge. They had to produce novelty, but a kind of novelty lodged firmly in the familiar traditions. And by 1599 the two established repertories were what London's playgoers certainly knew best. So with only the two companies regularly offering plays, what was written for each of them to stage had to take pretty exact notice of what the other was doing. Their reception included an automatic process of cross-reference by their audiences, whether overt or subterranean. We have already noted some of the more parodic allusions in the Admiral's plays to the other repertory. In its way that was a mark of the intimate closeness shared by the two repertories. I think the real difference between them only grew up later, as one company developed *Pericles, Cymbeline* and the Fletcher romances while the other continued to ride on its core of older plays.

The surviving play-texts do show some marks distinguishing the Admiral's from their opposites in the 1590s, differences that intensified later. *The Shoemaker's Holiday* was ostensibly written to celebrate the handicraft apprentices of London, and young men were a conspicuous feature among playgoers at the Rose. Manual workers, the groups of youngsters most troublesome to the Lord Mayor, were furthest socially from the gentry who by 1600 were flocking to the Blackfriars, separated as much by the plays they favoured as by their clothing and weaponry. Young men of seventeen and older who worked for a minimum of seven years as apprentices in the handicraft trades were at the bottom end of the artisan scale, seen by the authorities as the most likely to commit riots and disorders, and not without reason. Their woollen caps made them all too visibly distinct from the gentry in their silk and velvet with swords at their sides and feathers in their hats. William Fleetwood wrote to Lord Burghley about an afternoon disturbance 'very nere the Theatre or Curten at the

---

[23] See Susan Cerasano, 'Edward Alleyn's "Retirement"', *Medieval and Renaissance Drama in English* 10 (1998), 98–112.

tyme of the Playes there' on a hot day in June 1584, when 'there lay a
prentice sleping upon the Grasse, and one Challes *al.* Grostosk dyd turne
upon the Too [toe] upon the belly of the same prentice, whereupon the
apprentice start up and after wordes they fell to playne blowes; This
Challes exclaimed and said that he was a gentleman and that the appren-
tise was but a Rascall; and some there were litell better then rouges that
tooke upon theym the name of gentilmen and said the prentizes were
but the skomme of the worlde.' That shows a level of social hostility that
could easily rise, partly because the handicraft youths were known to
be easily provoked. A gang of apprentices rioted the next day, but were
suppressed. The day after, another troublemaker picked a quarrel at
the Theatre door with 'certen poore boyes, handicraft prentises', and
more violence ensued. No wonder Nashe in *Pierce Penilesse* (1592) should
write that 'some of them (I meane the ruder handicrafts servants) never
come abroade, but they are in danger of undoing'.[24] When Dekker picked
out Deloney's *The Gentle Craft* with its overtly paradoxical title as the basis
for his 'Pleasant Comedy of the Gentle Craft' he knew exactly what he was
doing. Nor was he supplying a simple compliment to London's shoemakers. The play sets up two opposite views of London citizen conduct,
upholding one as good and the other as despicable, grossly selfish capitalism
against benign and benevolent capitalism. The Mayor of the play's opening,
Sir Roger Oatley, represents the wrong values, his successor Simon Eyre
stands for the good. The play offers a broadly populist perspective,
essentially hostile to the ungenerous in London merchant society.

Dekker did not write his play in straightforward praise of London's
workers. David Scott Kastan finds social antagonisms framing the play,
but claims that 'the romantic logic of the plot overwhelms the social and
economic tensions that are revealed'.[25] He finds it non-realistic, 'a fantasy
of class fulfilment', where at the end 'middle-class desire for social
mobility and aristocratic insistence upon social stratification are both
accommodated'. I would argue that Dekker lays down a much sharper
critique than that of citizen values, embedded in two obvious and
opposed tendencies of citizen life. Its values are not simply the warm
and wild generosity of Simon Eyre, giver of great feasts to the artisan and
apprentice community of the city, nor the congenial fellowship and
loyalty of his workers. Dekker wrote with a firm political bias towards
the need for social generosity in the rich and against individual avarice.

---

[24] Thomas Nashe, *Pierce Penilesse*, 1592, F3v.
[25] *Staging the Renaissance*, ed. Kastan and Stallybrass, pp. 151–63, esp. p. 151.

That was the basis for the attack on Sir John Spencer that prompted the play. Dekker argued, as other plays in the company's repertory do, for class malleability, a social flexibility that both the Earl of Lincoln and the Lord Mayor Sir Roger Oatley agree in their opening discussion must be resisted. The citizen mayor's daughter is in love with the earl's noble nephew, and both dignitaries agree that such love is a bad thing since as Oatley declares 'Poor citizens must not with courtiers wed.' While they agree that citizens have money and gentlemen want to spend it, they also agree that such social interchange must be stopped.

The figure of Oatley was Dekker's thin disguise for the citizen who had been London's Lord Mayor in 1594–95, Sir John Spencer. Epitome of all that Dekker and the Admiral's players must have hated most among the city's great magnates, Spencer, a massively wealthy but notoriously spend-thrift member of the Clothworkers' Guild, for decades had led the anti-theatre protests from Guildhall. He wrote a multitude of the harshest letters to the Privy Council against its continuing tolerance of playgoing. In his year as Lord Mayor he faced the Southwark riots and a mob who erected an executioner's scaffold outside his house to show what they thought of him. His wealth had helped him to buy and develop a magnificent brick-built mansion in Bishopsgate, Crosby Place, the most opulent of all the great city houses.[26] Spencer's acquisitiveness made him the antithesis of the fortunate shoemaker Simon Eyre who as Lord Mayor gave London the great building of Leadenhall for public use.

In 1599 when Dekker wrote his play Spencer was in a well-publicised conflict over his only daughter Elizabeth about who she would marry. The argument matched the position of Oatley's daughter Rose at the outset of the play with remarkable precision. Like Oatley, Spencer hated the thought of his daughter and heir marrying a penniless aristocrat. Both men locked their daughters away from any contact with their lovers. Rose's first speech in the play voices her grief.

> Here as a theefe am I imprisoned
> (for my deere *Lacies* sake) within those walles,
> Which by my fathers cost were builded up
> For better purposes: here must I languish
> For him that doth as much lament (I know)
> Mine absence, as for him I pine in woe.[27]

---

[26] Crosby Hall survived the great fire of 1666 and was still notable enough to be transferred stone by stone in 1908 to a site on the Thames in Chelsea, where it is now being restored.

[27] *The Shoemaker's Holiday*, *Dramatic Works*, ed. Bowers, I. 30.

Spencer's Elizabeth was being courted by William, the second Lord Compton, who that March, just before Dekker started his play, had Spencer put in the Fleet for beating and bruising his daughter and refusing to pay the agreed dowry. On 15 March John Chamberlain reported the current gossip. 'Our Sir John Spenser of London was the last weeke committed to the Fleet for a contempt, and hiding away his daughter, who they say is contracted to the Lord Compton, but now he is out again and by all meanes seekes to hinder the match, alledging a precontract to Sir Arthur Henninghams sonne: but upon his beating and misusing her, she was sequestred to one Barkers a proctor and thence to Sir Henry Billingsleyes where she yet remaines till the matter be tried.'[28] The battered Elizabeth was locked up by Billingsley, who had succeeded Spencer as Lord Mayor in 1595 and repeated to the Council the wording of Spencer's letter about the troubles that came from playgoing. Elizabeth eventually managed to smuggle herself out of her second imprisonment in a baker's basket, much more effectively than Falstaff in his buck-basket. That July, four months after the scandals of March and April, the Admiral's bought and staged Dekker's play. Appealing strongly to the young in the Rose's audiences the central aspect of the play's propaganda was social mobility along with the more humane version of citizen values that Dekker upheld in his presentation of Simon Eyre's endless generosity.

Such an overt condemnation of mayoral attitudes is a feature of Dekker's play worth bearing in mind because it upholds in the Admiral's repertory a view that they shared with their opposites. In its time *Romeo and Juliet* was distinctive and even radical for the way it favoured young love over family authority, whose effects are now identified in British law as what are called 'forced marriages'. Shakespeare was radical for consistently favouring young love in his comedies as much as in *Romeo and Juliet*. In *The Merry Wives of Windsor* he gave the young citizen Anne Page a penniless gentleman for her husband by her own choice against the wishes of both her parents. The Admiral's plays show a similarly hostile view of paternal authority. William Haughton's *Englishmen for My Money* awards Pisaro's three daughters to their English lovers rather than the rich foreigners he had chosen for them. The author of *Stukeley* in 1596 upheld the idea too and other plays by different Henslowe collaborators did the

---

[28] Chamberlain, *Letters*, I. 67. After the marriage Spencer refused ever to see his daughter or his grandchildren, and kept his riches to himself until he died in 1610. It took Compton only three years to spend all he then inherited.

same. Dekker was soon to collaborate with Haughton on that archetypal story of the tests of interclass love, *Patient Grissill*. In all these plays virtue and independence of mind generally lay in young citizen women.

This was not a concept that sat easily in the minds of the many young and penniless playgoing gentry. Their social class forbade them to take paid employment and their best hope of fortune came from marriage to the daughters of rich merchants, as young Fenton does in *Merry Wives*. In social practice love and money were substantially divisive. When the Chamberlain's Men realised their early ambition to perform at the more costly indoor venue at Blackfriars through the winters, their tradition of dismissing parental authority drew many sympathetic ears. Such a view might well have become less a principle for the Fortune company to uphold as it catered more and more to citizen tastes. Yet the values set out in *The Shoemaker's Holiday* seem to have continued to reflect the Admiral's repertory in ways that were to become as much a hallmark of the 'citizen' playhouses as it was of the Blackfriars plays. Essentially celebratory of its own tradition (Dekker in his play manages to quote from both *The Spanish Tragedy* and *Tamburlaine*, long the favourites in the company's repertory),[29] it might be a little too much to claim that we can see him in 1599 heralding the company's future loyalty to the artisan and apprentice element in its audiences. But the number of times the quarto of 1600 was reprinted does show its continuing popularity. It reappeared in 1610, 1618, 1624, 1631, and 1657, a frequency making it as popular as *Romeo and Juliet* and even ahead of *The Merry Devil of Edmonton*. Judging by reprints, from the company's entire repertory only Kyd's and Marlowe's plays outstripped it.

Dekker's play shows that the company's loyalty to the mercantile interests of the city was a far more complex thing than its ostensible 'citizen playhouse' identity implies. Simply projecting the loyalties ostensibly set out in *The Shoemaker's Holiday* as uncritical support for citizen values is untenable, as the few extant company plays from the Jacobean period demonstrate. The second part of Heywood's *If You Know Not Me You Know Nobody*, written either for the Prince's company or for its Red Bull neighbour in 1605, is what Ceri Sullivan has called 'a pantomime of commercial disaster'.[30] Along with Dekker's flop *The Whore of Babylon* it

---

[29] It also names *Soliman and Perseda*, the story told as the play within the play of *The Spanish Tragedy*, which has not been identified here with the company. Possibly it should be, since if it was by Peele it might have been another of Alleyn's purchases from the author.

[30] Ceri Sullivan, *The Rhetoric of Credit. Merchants in Early Modern Writing*, Fairleigh Dickinson University Press, Madison, 2002, p. 87.

does celebrate the Armada victory but its basic story of how fragile mercantile venturism was does not show unmixed fortune or virtue. Heywood seems to have set up the building of Thomas Gresham's Royal Exchange as his main subject, the legend proposed by Beaumont's parodied Citizen in *The Knight of the Burning Pestle* a couple of years later as a good subject for a citizen play. But whether Heywood wrote the Gresham story to hail an achievement to be celebrated equally with the other Elizabethan glories and without any qualification is open to doubt. It could be viewed as a legend that fitted well with Dekker's glorification of merchant generosity in *The Shoemaker's Holiday*, but the conditions of mercantile London in 1605 that Sullivan describes demand a much more careful reading of the evidence and of Heywood's play than would be satisfied under the plain 'citizen' label.

Whatever the strength or directness of the company's aim at citizen values, its continuing fidelity to the traditional repertory established by 1599 is quite clear. It was a system that Henslowe's teams of collaborative writers had a vested interest in maintaining. One substantial feature of the old-fashioned plays that the *Diary* makes evident is how many proved popular enough to have sequels written from them. The players, taking up the same roles in the sequels, renewed the tradition as they affirmed the writing system itself. History plays would naturally run as a series when the whole story was too long for a single play, but others generated popular characters who got sequels to themselves, like Tom Stroud from *The Blind Beggar of Bethnal Green*. No easy generalisation about lost sequels and plays running in series is really possible because the evidence shows diverse patterns, and too many sequels are known only by their titles in the *Diary*. The most obvious precedent was Shakespeare's first *Henriad*, climaxing in *Richard III*. Since all four of his plays ended up in the Chamberlain's repertory, where they were certainly played together, that might be seen as a model for the other company's history plays. But the evidence that the first *Henriad* was written for different companies and that the companies first performing them disappeared indicates that Shakespeare's plays did not stay together, and indeed through the first years were not performed as a sequence at all. The emphasis on the Stanley family, particularly *Richard III* where Shakespeare adopted Hall's version of the Stanley family legend that the Earl of Derby ensured Richmond's victory at Bosworth by changing sides, and who Shakespeare makes crown Richmond at the end of the play, argues that he planned them all either for Derby's own company or for his younger brother's,

Lord Strange's Men.[31] Yet while *1 Henry VI* was introduced as 'ne' to the Strange's repertory at the Rose on 3 March 1592 the later two and probably also *Richard III* belonged to Pembroke's before they were all taken up for the Chamberlain's.[32] This argues that plays written as a sequence could still accrue independent identities with different playing companies. Richard III was of course already a favourite subject in theatre, one version having been staged in the 1580s by the Queen's Men.

In any case when Shakespeare wrote his first two histories there were already one and most likely two precedents for the *Henriad*, at least one of which was designed for performance as a pair. The Prologue to *2 Tamburlaine* claims that it was only the success of the first part that led to its sequel. That was true if we can believe that one of the many deliberate shocks Marlowe set up with his first play was to have a hero who does *not* die at the end of the tragedy. Other plays were more obviously designed from the start to have sequels. On the evidence of the 'plot' of *2 Seven Deadly Sins* Tarlton in 1588 or earlier meant his two Queen's Men plays to be a pair from the outset, with four of the seven sins portrayed in the first play and the other three (Envy, Sloth and Lechery) in the second. The recent theory that Kyd chose not only to write *The Spanish Tragedy* as the first revenge play but to accompany or anticipate it with a prequel, a version of the play now usually known as *1 Hieronimo*, the story of the original murder that must be revenged in the sequel, suggests that Kyd might have had a pair of sequential plays on stage even before the first *Tamburlaine* began to startle London in 1587.[33] Pre-programmed or not, plays with sequels took an early grip on London's audiences. They were a feature of the Admiral's run up to 1600, and for all we know were equally a feature of the Chamberlain's repertory.

From the 1580s there seem to have been two distinct types of conjoined play, the history, where the sequence of known events overruns the normal length for a single play, and the revenge play, where the first highlights a murder and its sequel carries out the act of revenge for the first murder. If Lukas Erne's reading of the two plays about Hieronimo is

---

[31] The Queen's Men's *True Tragedy of Richard III* made use of the same legend, with an even stronger emphasis on the family's contribution to the succession of Henry VII.

[32] Katherine Duncan Jones reckons that all three *Henry VI* plays were staged at the Rose before 1594 ('"Three partes are past": the earliest performances of Shakespeare's first tetralogy', *NQ* 248 (2003), 20–21), but the evidence is fairly tenuous.

[33] Lukas Erne, *Beyond* The Spanish Tragedy. *A Study of the Works of Thomas Kyd*, Manchester University Press, Manchester, 2001, Chapter 1.

correct Kyd's early model was copied by Marston in *Antonio and Mellida* and *Antonio's Revenge*, by Chapman in *Bussy D'Ambois* and *The Revenge of Bussy*, and possibly by Haughton and Chettle in the lost *Danish Tragedy* and *Hoffman*.[34] We might even wonder if there was once a prequel to *Hamlet*. In such speculative territory the detailed record we have for the Admiral's repertory through its first years is a vital asset.

Henslowe's day-by-day notation of playing for the Admiral's first three years tells us that the usual practice was to perform a sequel play on the day following the staging of the first part. This happened with the *Tamburlaines* and other paired plays such as *Caesar and Pompey*, although in the latter case Part 1 was first staged on 8 November 1594 and Part 2 not until 18 June 1595, seven months after Part 1's first appearance. The initial staging of Part 2 was followed by only one other performance, the day after Part 1 appeared for the eighth time. Neither play seems to have been restaged, although the loss of the daily records after 1597 leaves the possibility open. Sequels rarely had the same pulling power as their originals. The first *Tamburlaine* was much more popular than its sequel, appearing on stage twice as many times in 1594–95. For six of its seven presentations the sequel appeared the day after the first part. Kyd's *Spanish Tragedy* and its likely prequel *Don Horatio* appeared in sequence with Strange's Men in 1592, but only the second play, the famous revenge drama first published that year, was staged by the Admiral's in 1595. Why the Admiral's might have used only the second play will be considered below.

Some plays on popular topics, particularly the histories, were extended into as many as three in sequence, notably the three parts of *The Civil Wars of France*, written collaboratively between September and November 1598. Another was *The Blind Beggar of Bethnal Green* in May 1600, which produced one sequel in January 1601 and a further spin-off four months later. Henslowe named the third play *Tom Stroud* after its chief feature. Stroud appears in the first play as a comic bravo, and the two sequels (both lost) must have augmented his comedy. Writing history plays in a sequence seems to have proved markedly more attractive to the writers than other sorts of play. Munday's two *Huntingdon* plays, ostensibly from English history, made a sequence in 1597.[35] The lost *Earl Godwin* and *Cardinal Wolsey* similarly made pairs, as did *Sir John Oldcastle* and its

---

[34] Erne, *Beyond*, pp. 39–40.
[35] Munday's play and its sequel about Robin Hood were sent for licensing by the Master of the Revels as a pair (*Diary*, p. 88).

sequel and the Jacobean disguise play *When You See Me You Know Me*, all sequences taken from English history. The original sequence of the two *Tamburlaines*, and possibly their 1596 follower *Tamar Cham*, were written first as a single play complete in itself, followed by what was most likely an unpremeditated sequel. On the other hand most of the history sequences and others were written as a planned pair or trio. That must have been the case with *Hercules* in 1595, where the twelve labours were divided equally between the two plays. Others planned as pairs from the outset judging from the brief interval between the parts include *Earl Godwin and his Three Sons* (March and April 1598), *Black Bateman of the North* (May and June 1598), *The Two Angry Women of Abingdon* (both in January 1599), *Fair Constance of Rome* (both in June 1600, presumably based on Chaucer's 'Man of Law's Tale'), *Sir John Oldcastle* (both in October 1600), *Cardinal Wolsey* (June 1601), and *The Six Clothiers* (October and November 1601). The other kind, plays with sequels that were probably afterthoughts to exploit the success of the first play, include *The Seven Days of the Week* (1595 and 1596), *Fortune's Tennis* (September 1600 and December 1602), *The London Florentine* (December 1602 and March 1603), and *The Honest Whore* (1604), as well as *The Blind Beggar of Bethnal Green*. Other plays we assume were in two parts but of which only one is noted in the records are *Henry Richmond* (November 1599), and *Tom Dough* (July 1601). Many of the sequels had different collaborators, the unpremeditated ones using the success of the first while taking off in different directions, as did the second part of *The Honest Whore*.

An odd case of a sequel with no obvious precursor is Part 2 of *Godfrey of Boulogne*. In the record of the first run of Admiral's plays in 1594 it was the fourth play not to have been previously performed and like its three predecessors was listed as 'ne'. A play that must have been the first part was entered in the Stationers' Register for printing by John Danter on 19 June 1594, when the old companies had broken up, as 'an enterlude entituled Godfrey of Bulloigne wth the conquest of Jerusalem', but this apparently did not go on into print. Nothing in the Henslowe records for 1594 or earlier has anything about any previous *Godfrey* play, unless it was one listed for three performances without any indication that it was a second part. These entries lack any sign of the sequencing that put the second part directly after the first in performance. So they seem to have made this sequel stand on its own, not staging it as the second half of a pairing. Conceivably they did the same with *The Spanish Tragedy*. The first part of *Godfrey* may have accompanied *Tamburlaine* and *Faustus* in the old travelling Admiral's repertoire, though if so it seems not to have been transferred to the new company. In later years at the Fortune or the Red Bull Heywood seems to have conceived the two parts of *If You Know Not Me, You Know Nobody* as one play in two parts. That would go with performance on successive afternoons, and with what seems from the text to have been a revised division between the two parts made at a later time.

The Spanish Tragedy is a special case of two plays, but it is not clear whether one of them may have been a subsequent prequel rather than a sequel. The relationship between the two is a complex question largely because of the fashion it may have inspired, for presenting pairs of plays, the second a revenge play developing out of the death of the hero in the first. Was that sequence Kyd's own invention, or was it a later development? The play first printed in 1605 as 'THE FIRST PART of *Jeronimo*. With the Warres of Portugall, and the life and death of Don Andraea' seems on the face of it to be a later addition to the content of Kyd's original, although it, or more likely an earlier version of it, may have been paired with Kyd's play during its first recorded performances by Strange's Men in 1592. Strange's ran two 'Jeronimo' plays in sequence four times in 1592, on 13 and 14 March, on 30 and 31 March, on 22 (Saturday) and 24 (Monday) April, and on 21 and 22 May. The names Henslowe gave the prequel were 'the comodey of doneoracio' or 'doneoracio' (twice 'the comodey Jeronymo'), and for Kyd's play the plain 'Jeronymo'. That suggests the sort of sequencing of paired plays that Roslyn Knutson has identified.[36] *1 Jeronimo* better suits the term 'comodey', because while Don Andrea's death is shown, it ends rather with Horatio's triumph than with Andrea's tragic death.

None of the later performances of 'Jeronimo' by the Admiral's involved any pairing like the four occasions in 1592, so it seems that, for whatever reason, they never ran any version of the prequel *Jeronimo* printed in 1605. Alleyn may have retained its manuscript in his own possession, as he probably did Kyd's play, but he seems not to have given it to the Admiral's. Or, once the enormous popularity of Kyd's play was well established, the printed prequel might have been written and acquired by another company after 1592. While Kyd's play was well printed and most likely set from an authorial manuscript, the 1605 quarto of the prequel was clumsily or carelessly set in old-fashioned blackletter, with many obvious errata. It is only 1,200 lines long, whereas *The Spanish Tragedy* is 2,736. Moreover there are signs that the text as printed was

---

[36] *The Repertory of Shakespeare's Company, 1594–1613*, University of Arkansas Press, Fayetteville, 1991, pp. 50–53.

Figure 16. The 1615 title-page of *The Spanish Tragedy*. It is thought that the arbour may represent what was used on stage for Horatio to be hanged.

performed by and perhaps rewritten for a boy company, since its Jeronimo is said to have been of small stature.[37]

So far as the Admiral's is concerned the question which text was signified by the name '*The Spanish Tragedy*' and which by '*Jeronimo*' is mercifully one of the less teasing issues. In the *Diary* the first name does not appear, although in 1592 what Henslowe noted as the '*Spanish Comedy*', and also called *Don Horatio*, most likely signifies the prequel. The Admiral's staged a play Henslowe called *Jeronimo* as 'ne' on 7 January 1597 and thirteen more times after that. The play we know as *The Spanish Tragedy* was first printed in a lost quarto and reprinted as 'Newly corrected, and amended of such grosse faults as passed in the first impression' in 1592. A revised text, 'Newly corrected, amended, and enlarged with new additions of the Painters part, and others, as it hath of late been divers times acted', appeared in 1602.[38] Henslowe twice paid Ben Jonson for

---

[37] Arthur Freeman, *Thomas Kyd, Facts and Problems*, Clarendon Press, Oxford, 1967, argues that the prequel postdates *Hamlet* and *Julius Caesar*, and must have been written after 1602 for a boy company as a parody of the adult company play, while probably basing its plot on the Strange's Men's accompanying play of 1592. Lukas Erne, *Beyond The Spanish Tragedy*, Manchester, 2001, also believes it to be a parodic rewrite of the old text for a boy company. The point that its Jeronimo was noticeably small does imply that it was written in deliberate contrast to Alleyn's physically imposing figure in the Admiral's play.

[38] As a printed text it proved hugely popular. After the lost first quarto and its corrected version of 1592 more quartos appeared in 1594, 1599, 1602, 1603, 1611, 1615, 1618, 1623, and 1633.

making 'adicyons' to the play, in September 1601 and June 1602. I believe
the company's post-1594 *Jeronimo* was the Kyd text that came into print
in 1592. Kyd's play is probably the one first appearing in the *Diary*
performed by Strange's in 1592 as 'Jeronymo': '—Rd at Jeronymo the
14 of marche 1591 . . . iij li xj s.' It was not marked as 'ne', though its takings
were substantial. It reappeared another fifteen times up to 22 January 1593.
Its next appearance under that name was with the Admiral's in 1597.

The confusion of two plays under the one name takes us on to the
claim Webster made in his 1604 Induction for the third quarto of
Marston's *The Malcontent*. There Henry Condell was required on stage
to defend the King's Men's theft of Marston's play from the Blackfriars
boy company by saying 'Why not Malevole in folio with us, as well as
Jeronimo in decimo sexto with them?' That seems to indicate that the
former Chamberlain's company once used to stage a version of *The Spanish
Tragedy* or some other *Jeronimo* play that had since been stolen and restaged
by a boy company. This theory is lent some weight by the elegy for Richard
Burbage that lists among his famous parts 'ould Hieronymoe', and the less
reliable claim in the Cambridge Parnassus plays that Burbage had played
Hieronimo.[39] There is, however, little evidence besides Webster's Induction
and the elegy to suggest that a version of Kyd's play was ever in the hands
of the Chamberlain's Men. The play never appears in any later lists of
their repertory and *The Spanish Tragedy* continued to feature as a characteristic emblem of the Rose and the Fortune repertories until 1642.[40] The
most distinctive thing about Webster's Induction is its suggestion that a
boy company had been playing it. That might help to explain the boy
company features of the 1605 quarto.

---

[39] The elegy is quoted by Chambers, *The Elizabethan Stage*, II. 309. The *Parnassus* reference, from the
third of the St John's College Cambridge plays of 1601, gives Burbage and Kemp lines from *The
Spanish Tragedy* and *Richard III*.

[40] Different editors and commentators have offered widely divergent views about the two texts. Philip
Edwards (ed. *The Spanish Tragedy*, The Revels Plays, London 1959) dismissed the idea of Burbage
playing Hieronimo (Appendix F, pp. 146–47) and also the idea that *The First Parte of Jeronimo* was
a prequel (Appendix A, pp. 137–38). He affirmed the then popular line that *1 Jeronimo* was written
for the Admiral's late, in 1597, as a prequel designed to cash in on the popularity of Kyd's play.
More persuasively he also proposed that parts of Kyd's play contain echoes from *2 Tamburlaine*,
which would date it in or after late 1587 (Appendix C, pp. 141–42). On the other hand Andrew
S. Cairncross, in a double edition of *The First Part of Hieronimo* and *The Spanish Tragedy* (Regents
Renaissance Drama Series, Nebraska, 1967) took the two plays to be written as a pair by Kyd, the
generally inferior quality of the first play explained by its being, at 1,200 lines compared with the
other's 2,700, a 'bad' quarto. His analysis of some poorly rendered lines does turn them into
immaculately Kyd-like verse (pp. xv–xvii). On the other hand, he has no explanation for the
inconsistencies between the details in the stories told by the two plays. Erne's analysis in his book
I think supplants both of these theories.

Kyd's play itself was a regular success at the Rose and at the Fortune. Setting aside Jonson's derision which characterised it as a typical Fortune play *The Spanish Tragedy* became more quoted, whether in admiration or in mockery, than any other play of the whole period, including its most obvious successor *Hamlet*.[41] Its durability must in part at least have been a consequence of its fame in eleven printed quartos and the quotability of its most famous lines. Its antiquity must in some degree have guaranteed its continuing life while also emphasising the increasing age of the company repertory that contained it. In its way it was the first English 'classic', as Shakespeare's plays were to become in the eighteenth century. The Fortune had good reason to continue staging its 'huge bombasted plaies' like *The Spanish Tragedy* and Marlowe's epics alongside Middleton's 'neater inventions' of more recent times.

Every play must differ significantly from its peers. As a result, the typology of Elizabethan and Jacobean drama has always struggled when it attempts to identify distinctive play species or genres. When for instance does a play belong in the genre of 'humours' comedy and when is it a city satire? When is a history play also a tragedy and when is it heroic? More to the point, which plays influenced which in the historic sequence of playwriting that must have ruled the writers whenever they wanted to create a new play? The academic variant of this exercise, intertextuality, as it has evolved away from source-hunting may relieve us of the obligation to prove historical precedents but it does nothing to explain why each play should be so distinct from its peers. In this study, possibly for the wrong reasons, we have to give more emphasis to continuity than to innovations in staging and play design. Partly that is because we have more of the earlier play-texts than we have of later plays from the company's repertory. Partly, too, it signals the reputation the Fortune acquired of running an old-fashioned repertory with fireworks and jigs as a 'citizen' playhouse. The continuity of staging at the Fortune has more evidence to back it than there is for the introduction of innovative playwriting. We need to remember that the only play to survive from the thirteen written after the 1621 fire at the Fortune destroyed the company's stock of manuscript playbooks is the decidedly conservative *Duchess of Suffolk*, which shows so much of the traditional nostalgia for Tudor religious and political struggles that it even put on stage Henry Carey and Charles Howard, the two nobles who started the 1594 duopoly whence came the Admiral's

---

[41] See Claude Dudrap, 'La "Tragédie espagnole" face à la critique élizabethaine et jacobéenne', in *Dramaturgie et société*, ed. Jean Jacquot, 2 vols., Paris, 1968, II. 607–31.

Men. One of its scenes is located in Holland on the land of their current
patron, the Lord Palsgrave. The player Thomas Drue who wrote it was
obviously loyal to his company's long-established playing record.

The history plays are the most consistent surviving feature from the
Fortune years. In 1604 Samuel Rowley, always a loyal company player
and clown, wrote *When You See Me You Know Me* as a renewal of the
company's populist histories about the reign of Henry VIII. Composed
during the long break from playing in the plague of 1603–04, it made use
of the company's popular game of disguise with its title and some scenes,
but it was essentially a play using Henry VIII's need of a male heir as the
basis for praise of Prince Henry, the company's new patron.[42] It includes a
rich part for two clowns, one of them Will Summers, perhaps designed by
Rowley for himself. Part of its plot includes the meeting and love of
Henry's sister Mary for the Duke of Suffolk, a story renewed in full much
later in Drue's *Duchess of Suffolk*. Perhaps inevitably, Rowley's history
play does not stand up well to comparison with Shakespeare. Richard
Helgerson is patronising about his and Heywood's intellectual qualities.[43]
Starting from Judith Doolin Spikes's concept of the 'Elect Nation' plays
at the Rose and Fortune, Helgerson surveys the growth of what he calls a
'popular' concept of nationhood through the 1590s in both of the duopoly
repertories. His fifth chapter contrasts the upmarket Shakespearean
view of history with that of (his label) the 'Henslowe' writers. Without
differentiating the Admiral's from Worcester's or Fortune from Red Bull
plays (Heywood's two-part *If You Know Not Me, You Know Nobody* is
included in his coverage of the 'Henslowe' corpus) he registers between
the Shakespeare and non-Shakespeare histories 'how deep and pervasive
their differences are' (p. 235), starting with *1 Oldcastle*. He sees the
Henslowe origins in popular ballads rather than in Holinshed, and above
all in Foxe's militant Protestantism. He notes that Munday's Robin Hood
is a nobleman version of the folk hero, and that the heroes in his two
plays are all enemies of rebellion. He concludes: 'The situation of the
citizen and the Protestant – both figures who identify strongly with the
nation and its ruler but both of whom are intent on keeping some part of
themselves and their community free from the encroachment of national

---

[42] For a delicate analysis of the play's references to the current political situation, see Teresa Grant,
'History in the Making: the Case of Samuel Rowley's *When You See Me You Know Me*', *English
Historical Drama, 1500–1660*, ed. Teresa Grant and Barbara Ravelhofer, Palgrave, Basingstoke,
2008, pp. 125–57.
[43] Richard Helgerson, *Forms of Nationhood. The Elizabethan Writing of England*, University of
Chicago Press, 1994.

power – is central to the Henslowe version of English history. Neither of these figures is of much interest to Shakespeare, at least not in the strongly favorable way characteristic of the Henslowe plays' (p. 240). Other critics such as Jeffrey Knapp and Marsha S. Robinson use a more wide-angled and generous perspective but still cannot find the complexity or generate the variety of scholarly response that the Shakespeare plays receive. It is a pity that *The Duchess of Suffolk*, written in haste to supply the need for a wholly new repertory, about which Knapp is thoroughly dismissive, should survive as one of the company's few history plays with a readable text, though ironically it is almost the only ex-Admiral's play never to have been issued in a modern edition.

We might note that while the Chamberlain's Men generally specialised in plays about the royal lineage, a fraught but crucial political issue for the Tudor regime, the Admiral's Men, while using some of the same materials (Richard III, Henry V), also showed a liking for militant plays about great English warrior-conquerors such as John of Gaunt in Portugal, Thomas Stukeley's adventures in Ireland and the Mediterranean, and the mythical heroes Conan and Chinon. The liking for plays calling for onstage battles seems to have led to the longest-lasting feature of Fortune staging recorded in the company's repertory, sword and target fights.

From the Jacobean period an overview of the Fortune's history plays should not omit Dekker's *The Whore of Babylon*, which is well worth an aside. Dekker admitted that its reception on stage was a disappointment, though that did not stop him publishing it – the failure may even have prompted him to do so. The epitome of triumphalist nostalgia for a lost age and its victories, it shows a lot more than just the nostalgia for Tudor days common to the plays about Henry VIII and his second daughter. It is based on a heavily symbolic contrast between two women depicted as graphic opposites.[44] The English queen is the antithesis to the female Pope who Dekker feminised as the Babylonian whore, in what boils down to a celebration of England's much-acclaimed victory over the Spanish Armada. In his Preface for the reader of his dramatic poem (it was published complete with marginalia explaining the allegories and the only slightly adjusted historical names such as 'Campeius' for Edmund Campion) Dekker says 'I write as a poet, not as a historian.' Jean E. Howard even claims it is so exhibitionistic in its use of stage spectacles

---

[44] For an incisive comment on Elizabethan iconography of the female, which, however, regrettably does not look into *The Whore of Babylon*, see Stephen Orgel, 'Gendering the Crown', in *The Authentic Shakespeare*, London, 2002, pp. 107–28.

depicting the Catholic monsters that it can be said to use antitheatricality for its propaganda.[45] She considers the deliberately anachronistic and showy stagecraft is counterproductive (p. 53). Dekker's essential vision of honest truth confronting the deceptions of shape-shifting and Catholic disguise, written in the year after the Gunpowder Plot, is epitomised in 4.1.'s dumbshow.

Dumb shew. A cave suddenly breakes open, and out of it comes Falshood, (*attir'd as* Truth *is*) *her face spotted, shee stickes up her banner on the top of the Cave; then with her foot in severall places strikes the earth, and up riseth* Campeius; *a Frier with a boxe: a gentleman with a drawn sword, another with rich gloves in a boxe, another with a bridle.* Time, Truth *with her banner, and* Plain-dealing *enter and stand aloofe beholding all.*[46]

Dekker makes even the King of Spain call himself a fox for his skill at disguising the truth. By their contrasting tricks the many shape-shifters (virtuosi of disguise) implicitly uphold the value of Truth undisguised. It is indeed a poet's vision of history, using the tricks of disguise to characterise Catholic dishonesty.

Other features of spectacle were simpler. When we consider the company's use of magic on stage with the fireworks, lightning flashes, smoke and squibs spurting fire from the stage devils' various orifices that John Melton described, its continuity calls for little extra comment here. In fact, though, from 1600 onwards the company used magic and devils on stage much more in their comedies than in tragedies like *Faustus*. Chapter 2 identified William Haughton as the writer who launched the comedies set in London with *Englishmen for My Money*. The same writer seems to have started comedies about the Devil in 1600 with the precursor of the play now known as *Grim the Collier of Croydon*. Haughton's play, originally called *The Devil and His Dam*, stimulated a widespread fashion for plays mocking the Devil, usually in order to satirise contemporary society. The Chamberlain's Men picked this fashion up with *The Merry Devil of Edmonton* soon after, and a decade later bought *The Devil is an Ass* from Jonson, a satire based on the same device.[47] The existence of devil comedies in the company's repertory along with *Doctor Faustus* is yet another instance of their ability to stage burlesques of their own most

[45] *The Stage and Social Struggle in Early Modern England*, p. 50.
[46] *Dramatic Works*, ed. Bowers, II. 551.
[47] For a broad assessment of devilry on these stages, see John D. Cox, *The Devil and the Sacred in English Drama, 1350–1642*, Cambridge, 2000, especially Chapter 8. Chapter 7 is about the influence of *Doctor Faustus* on the subsequent repertories.

Figure 17. The 1616 title-page of *Doctor Faustus,* with a devil on stage.
It is unlikely to have been an accurate representation of what
the Fortune staged.

famous productions. Dekker picked up the idea in 1611 with a renewal of
the company's old story of the devil posing as Friar Rush in *If It Be not
Good, The Devil Is in It.* It was written for the Fortune but rejected and
staged instead by Queen Anne's at the Red Bull. In July 1601 Henslowe
had paid for an earlier play by Haughton and Day about the devil in the
same disguise called *Friar Rush and the Proud Woman of Antwerp* for the
Fortune. He paid for it in full in November 1601, and it was amended by
Chettle presumably for an improved production in January 1602.

In their own complex forms plays about the devil renewed the old game
of disguise as a device for stage illusion. As was noted in Chapter 2,
anything on stage involving overt illusion could be perilous because it
typified what the pulpits regarded as the devil's work. That is a basic
reason why disguise had always to be transparent to the audiences.
As John D. Cox has said, 'the impact of metadrama on stage devils was
more likely to be expressive than reductive, repeatedly calling attention
to the permeable boundaries between reality and illusion because no one

knew precisely where they were'.[48] Alleyn wearing a cross on his breast
while playing Faustus and the legend of the players finding one devil too
many on stage shows how permeable this boundary was thought to be.
The schizophrenic thinking that could set *Grim the Collier* alongside
Faustus in the Admiral's repertory shows how a similar kind of story
could become both horrifying and a joke, much as did using the same
false bottle nose for Barabbas and Leon the disguised usurer.

The company's continuity, with the writers conscientiously keeping
to the established company staging practices of the kind identified in
Chapter 4, does appear most obviously in the use of tricks exploiting
disguise. From Munday's *Wise Men of West Chester* at the end of 1595,
which made all its magic tricks matters of disguise, through its immediate
development in the parodies of *The Blind Beggar of Alexandria* and *Look
About You* and other plays from 1596 onwards, the repertory was packed
with disguise tricks, even in the histories. Munday's *Huntingdon* plays
picked up *Look About You*'s idea of disguising Robin Hood as a woman
and boy players dressed as ladies disguising themselves as women of a
different class. Chapman's hero disguised as a blind beggar was repeated
in *The Blind Beggar of Bethnal Green*, and similar disguise tricks appear in
plays such as *1 Sir John Oldcastle*, *When You See Me You Know Me*, *The
Whore of Babylon*, the devil comedies and Middleton's *No Wit / No Help
Like a Woman's*. It was one of the company's most constant games, both
in serious mode and as a comic device. It was simple, quick to stage and
easy to take on tour with the company's costumes. It shows a striking
degree of self-confidence given the current concerns about the dangers
of illusion and the eye's readiness to be deceived.

Middleton and Dekker's *The Roaring Girl* followed company fashion
by merging two distinct features of its repertory. One was registered first
in the lost *Long Meg of Westminster*, a popular play that ran through
eighteen performances between early 1595 and when the daily records stop
at the end of 1597. Long Meg was a familiar subject in extant ballads
indicating the sort of story that the Rose writers made their play from.
Anticipating the 'citizen' identity of the Rose and Fortune repertory,
Frederick Waage picks out these two plays as 'bearers of nostalgic nation-
alism', celebrations at different times of what he identifies as London's
'assertive women'.[49] He links both of them with the dream of Long Meg's

[48] *The Devil and the Sacred in English Drama, 1350–1642*, p. 165.
[49] Frederick O. Waage links them in 'Meg and Moll: Two Renaissance Heroines', *Journal of Popular Culture* 20 (1986), 105–117.

idealised Tudor society, 'a benevolent and harmonious society, hierarchically ordered, but without *serious* noble-bourgeois or court-city rivalries'. Meg and Moll, he says, 'figure in all literary genres – jestbooks, plays, fiction' (p. 106). Both were of course figures belonging in contemporary London, the other fashion that *The Roaring Girl* picked up. Nostalgia for the Moll Frith archetype of citizen London is not far from *The Shoemaker's Holiday* that Dekker wrote twelve years earlier with its celebration of the myth of Simon Eyre's benevolence. The 1590s was when the Dick Whittington myth of the poor apprentice rising to become Lord Mayor came back to life. We might reasonably link his renewed fame with the 'gentle' craftsmen of Dekker's play.

The Roaring Girl had one special feature that we know the company chose to make the most of at the Fortune, the absolutely current and notorious presence of Moll from the London streets of the time on stage in the play. The story told in the *Consistory of London Correction Book* in 1612 that she flaunted her cross-dressing on stage at a performance must be true, and must have had the company's full backing. Her exhibition not only showed that Middleton and Dekker's use of her in the play had her personal support but gave emphasis to the implication that the play was holding a mirror up to the London of its day. In that, if nothing else, the company was upholding its own tradition of celebrating the London citizenry that it expected to form the majority of its audiences at the Fortune.[50]

While the company's plays continued to support the primacy of love against forced marriage a more conservative morality was usually lurking as a fall-back position. Heywood wrote the conventionally moralistic *A Woman Killed with Kindness* for the later Rose company, Worcester's, at roughly the time when Chettle and others launched the equally uxorious and excessively conventional story of *Patient Grissill* at the Fortune. The double standard of the time between men and women over marital fidelity destroys the errant wife in *A Woman Killed with Kindness* but lets the male lover go free. A version of the same morality upholds the patience of Grissill against her husband's sixteen years of maltreatment. For all the celebrations of 'assertive' women in *Long Meg* and *The Roaring Girl* the weight of such moralism was always laid on the woman. In *1 Edward IV* Heywood rewrote the story of the king's mistress Jane Shore by introducing her as a good housewife before Edward seduced her, and then as a dying penitent, whereas the historical Shore outlived Edward by

[50] Mark Hutchings and A. A. Bromham, *Middleton and his Collaborators*, Tavistock, 2008, pp. 50–53, provide a careful analysis of the use of Moll Frith herself in the play.

42 years, becoming mistress of Hastings, Dorset and perhaps other nobles. The double standard for men and women was in part based on, and was used to justify, the need for purity of descent by blood. Citizen London accepted that cuckoldry and female lechery endangered the class-based social structure that relied on inheritance by blood lines, which roving males did not.[51] Heywood's most lenient or permissive play in this regard was *The Wise Woman of Hogsden* at the Red Bull, a different sort of celebration of assertive women. Plays by both of the 'citizen' companies show a thoroughgoing awareness of the social tensions of their day, and it would be wrong to read their prejudices too comfortably. What the Fortune plays seem to uphold with only one exception is the Simon Eyre version of generous citizen values as the basic need for a good society.

The exception was a play by Middleton. It was Dekker who launched the paradox inherent in *The Honest Whore*'s title at the Fortune only a couple of years after *Patient Grissill* in his two collaborations with Middleton. Shortly after *The Roaring Girl*, their third joint play for the company, Middleton gave the Fortune a solo play dealing in far more complex ways than Heywood's with the issues of a good marriage. *No Wit / No Help Like a Woman's* is a social comedy that utilises disguise in a distinct and specifically Middletonian variety of assertive womanhood. Opening with a prologue that acknowledges the social divide of the Fortune's galleries from its yard ('I doubt not, if attention / Seize you above, and apprehension / You below, to take things quickly, / We shall both make you sad and tickle ye'),[52] its heroine gives a new twist to the usual girl disguised as page game. She is a married woman who commands the plot with her wit and who triumphantly outwits everyone by disguising herself as a young gallant. All the play's male figures are helpless and useless, her own husband a version of the incredibly patient spouse Candido in 1 *The Honest Whore*, loyally seconding her by dressing down to pose as the young gallant's servant.

From the beginning of Middleton's play power is shown to lie not in men but in women. The young hero, Philip, protests in the very first line that 'I'm at my wit's ends', a statement that invokes the play's title directly. It is a woman's wit that will save the day. The witty hero is

---

[51] Because of their political weight royal marriages were an exception to this moralism. For a broad survey, including comments on *The Spanish Tragedy*, see Michael A. Winkelman, *Marriage Relationships in Tudor Political Drama*, Aldershot, 2005.

[52] The implication of this separation of the folk sitting in the Fortune galleries from those standing in the yard really depends on its negations. Those sitting in the galleries are inattentive, while those standing in the yard feel and 'apprehend' the play without necessarily understanding all that goes on.

Mistress Low-water, who in order to revenge herself and her husband on Lady Goldenfleece, a widow who refuses to return the lands her dead husband had stolen from them, disguises herself as what a stage direction calls '*a gallant Gentleman*', and pretends to woo and then marry her enemy. The subsequent revelation of her sex (as in Shakespeare the audience's information is always well ahead of the characters in the play) not only nullifies the marriage, like Jonson's trick in *Epicene*, but helps to resolve the many confusions that build up for the finale. Mistress Low-water gains total victory both for herself and her loyal husband and for the witless Philip. Besides its display of gulls and 'humours' characters characteristic of the company's older repertory (its biggest gull gave it the 'Almanac' title used for the play by the court scribes), Middleton's plot has many twists and turns, not least a device that makes Philip think his beloved is actually his own sister. For the first time in Middleton's proto-feminist opus the play's true hero is a married woman. As John Jowett says: 'There is a comic tension between her apologies to her husband for supplanting his role and her husband's inability to do anything other than fall into line with her stratagems.'[53]

We cannot conclude this survey of the few extant texts from the company's huge repertory without giving a little more consideration to the Marlowe plays and their influence. There can be no doubt that the Marlowe and the Kyd plays were always features of the Fortune repertory, and that the Fortune's audiences always enjoyed repeats of their old favourites. Whoever chose to give one of the duopoly companies in 1594 all of Shakespeare and the other all of Marlowe laid down a pair of durable traditions. *Tamburlaine* and *Faustus* continued to appear at the Fortune until 1642.[54] For a company that at the outset chose to base itself so firmly on such radically sceptical and challenging plays as Marlowe's, the subsequent 'citizen' repertory developing in the years when Sam Rowley and the other writers of history plays based their work on Elizabethan nostalgia must have seemed awkwardly conservative when performed alongside those classics.[55] We know that the mockery of orthodox authority in *Tamburlaine*, *Faustus* and *The Jew of Malta* was

[53] 'Middleton's *No Wit* at the Fortune', *Renaissance Drama* n.s. 22 (1991), 191–208, p. 198.
[54] The impact of *Tamburlaine* in 1620 at Ludlow in Shropshire was noted in Chapter 2.
[55] Marlowe's *Edward II* is the chief anomaly in his corpus. We do not know whether it came to the Admiral's but was not staged by them. After its original publication as an ex-Pembroke's play in 1594, it was republished in 1598 and 1612. Its last publication in 1622 had two title-pages, one continuing to ascribe it to Pembroke's, the other giving it to 'the late Queenes Majesties Servants at the Red Bull'. How it got to them we do not know.

informed by the republicanism of Lucan's *Pharsalia*, the first book of which Marlowe translated before he wrote *Tamburlaine*.[56] Similarly, the stimulus Marlowe found in the Babington Plot trials for treason in 1586 and the subsequent execution of Scotland's queen has been well laid out by Karen Cunningham.[57] This questioning of the standard and often-voiced orthodoxies of political and religious authority was somehow basic to the popular success of Marlowe's plays. Tamburlaine's chariot dragged onstage by four conquered kings and the humiliation of the Turkish emperor Bajazeth were regularly picked out as the play's most celebrated events on stage. They lodged durably in playgoers' memories. *Old Fortunatus* repeated Bajazeth as one of Fortune's four captive kings to make a visual reminder with Tamburlaine's much-used chariot of his conquest of traditional authority.

One feature of the Marlowe canon that has frequently misled the more traditional critics is his use of the parodic comic games that pervade plays like *The Jew of Malta* and *Faustus*. The dismissal by the Prologue to the first *Tamburlaine* of the conceits that clownage keeps in pay may have been written by Marlowe, but in a corpus of work where each play differs so radically from the others it is hardly surprising that after *Tamburlaine* and *Faustus* he should write such a black anti-Christian farce as *The Jew of Malta* before plunging into two most painful and politically loaded historical stories, one from recent French history and then one about English kingship. The plays were acquired by a variety of companies who first staged them. The two *Tamburlaines* and probably *Faustus* were sold to the old Admiral's company while *The Jew of Malta* and the *Massacre at Paris* went to Alleyn and Strange's Men, and finally *Edward II* went to the new and short-lived Pembroke's. That may be seen to suggest that Marlowe's diversity of subjects shines with the same diverse reflections of his own brief and varying career as his shifting between companies. But it seems equally clearly to signal Marlowe's constantly shifting exploration of new forms in his theatre games as much as in his writing.[58] The fact that the Admiral's company acquired such a remarkable diversity of

---

[56] Andrew Hadfield attempts to offer a cool summary of Marlowe's radicalism in *Shakespeare and Republicanism*, Cambridge University Press, 2005, pp. 59–66. He also claims, rather loosely, that Shakespeare's *Henry VI* plays and *Richard III* were versions of Lucan's concept of history.

[57] '"Forsake thy king and do but join with me": Marlowe and Treason', in *Marlowe's Empery*, Nebraska, 2002, pp. 133–49.

[58] In a recent article Kirk Melnikoff argues for Marlowe's use of wit and traditional comedians' games in several plays. See Kirk Melnikoff. '"[J]ygging vaines" and "riming mother wits": Marlowe, Clowns and the Early Frameworks of Dramatic Authorship', *Early Modern Literary Studies* Special Issue 16 (October, 2007) 8.1–37, http://purl.oclc.org/emls/si-16/melnjygg.htm.

radical plays at the outset of their own career was massively to their benefit. It can hardly be wrong to identify Marlowe with the Admiral's long career as much as we do Shakespeare with their opposites.

Much of the attractiveness of Marlowe's plays must have been the elements in them that triggered thoughts of social climbing among members of its 'citizen' audiences, whatever their endings seem to suggest. The Scythian shepherd who conquered kingdoms, Faustus born 'of parents base of stock', the outsider Barabbas who comes to govern Malta, all stand out in their alterity as strong individuals defying their humble origins, the type Harry Levin called 'the overreacher', and Emily Bartels more recently 'spectacles of strangeness'.[59] The plays echo and define issues that preoccupied most Elizabethans, all of them still struggling with the consequences of Henry VIII's overthrow of the longstanding Catholic hegemony. Jonathan Crewe[60] and Huston Diehl both argue that Marlowe's plays need to be located inside a cultural dialogue between the anti-theatrical ecclesiasts and the playwrights. In *Faustus*, says Diehl,[61] Marlowe

explores his culture's deeply conflicted attitudes toward the imagination, creating a protagonist whose imaginative powers are simultaneously marvellous and danger-ous, godlike and presumptuous, immortal and deadly . . . Marlowe associates the magical arts with the dramatic arts, the man who speculates in images with the playwright, magical and demonic spectacle with dramatic spectacle. His theater interrogates its own theatricality, creating spectacles that dazzle and seduce his audiences while dramatizing the fall of a protagonist who is bedazzled by demonic shows and seduced by his own power to manipulate images.

Tamburlaine, the tragic hero who defies even his theatrical genre by winning and not dying at the end of his first tragedy, was the charismatic figure of power who for once did not fall. No wonder so many Christian viewers saw him as an embodiment of God's whip and scourge. He was the ultimate challenge to orthodox quietism. In a quite basic sense the Admiral's and its successor Fortune company were always identifiable by their heritage of defiant Marlowe plays given them by the percipient figures who first set up the duopoly.

Why in the Prologue to *Faustus* did Marlowe specify not just low-born parents but make his hero the 'studious artisan'? Was he envisaged as a

[59] Harry Levin, *Christopher Marlowe: The Overreacher*, London, 1954; Emily Bartels, *Spectacles of Strangeness: Imperialism, Alienation, and Marlowe*, Philadelphia, 1993.
[60] Crewe, 'The Theatre of the Idols: Marlowe, Rankins, and Theatrical Images', *Theatre Journal* 36 (1984), 321–33.
[61] Diehl, *Staging Reform, Reforming the Stage: Protestantism and Popular Theater in Early Modern England*, Ithaca, 1997, pp. 76–77.

figure from Stowe's London, a self-taught learner like the ambitious apprentices who viewed the plays at the Rose?[62] The 'mechanick preachers' like Bunyan whose voices made themselves heard in and after the Interregnum were figures of that self-making kind, much like those playgoers such as Richard Norwood, surveyor and cartographer of Bermuda, who haunted the Fortune in 1612 writing plays.[63] Norwood had substantial talents and substantial ambitions. In 1632 he wrote a book about trigonometry and in 1637 *The Seaman's Practice* along with other books. It was for people like Norwood that Heywood claimed to have written *The Four Prentices of London*, 'the honest and hie-spirited Prentises the Readers'.[64] The handicraft workers celebrated in *The Shoemaker's Holiday* were the chief source of Guildhall's regular complaints about riots and disorder in London. Perhaps in its curious way it was Marlowe's influence that made the Admiral's so explicitly affirm their continuing alliance with those elements in their audiences at the Rose and the Fortune, and that in turn made the Fortune into a 'citizen' playhouse in the gentry's eyes, a reputation which led to what too many readers have dismissed as work much less inventive than their opposites the Shakespeare company.

Far back in 1934, William York Tindall, a US scholar who later went on to produce work on Samuel Beckett and English modernism, published a book called *John Bunyan, Mechanick Preacher*. Tindall wrote that he was qualified to write the book because he had read over 2,000 pamphlets from Bunyan's time, all composed by similar working-class lay preachers. This enabled him to claim that *Pilgrim's Progress* was only one of a flood of similar books from the time. The final sentence of his book stated with perfect truth that Bunyan died in 1688 and was buried in Bunhill Fields, also known as Tindall's Burying Ground. This book is in no way designed as a cemetery for the Admiral's plays, though its gross materiality, like that of Henslowe's *Diary*, may in places leave it seeming so. It tries to operate at ground level to make a possible foundation for re-enacting some of the plays. With luck it will not have quite the same durability as a cemetery, since the remains of the Rose, while still buried, might one day be re-excavated and produce some remarkable new discoveries about its main user company.

---

[62] Ruth Lunney, *Marlowe and the Popular Tradition*, Manchester, 2002, does a careful tracking of Marlowe's innovative role between 1585 and 1595.

[63] The effect of *Faustus* and Agrippa on the artisan John Norwood is clearly registered by Charles Whitney, *Early Responses to Renaissance Drama*, pp. 178–85.

[64] See Mark Thornton Burnett, *Masters and Servants*, p. 14. See also pp. 8–19 on apprentices.

APPENDIX I

The plays

The plays known from Henslowe's *Diary* and other sources to have been performed by the Admiral's are listed here in the order in which they were most likely first performed, or, in some cases, written. Of the total of 229 plays in the list regrettably 195 of them exist only as titles. The familiar name is given first, underlined and in italics, followed by the names of its writers where known and the year of first performance. From 1594 to 1597 all the company's performances at the Rose are recorded. Thereafter the records chiefly comprise payments to the writers and for costumes and properties, as registered in the *Diary*. Where a printed text survives, it is noted first by its entry in the Stationers' Register (SR), followed by what appears on the title-page, with notes of subsequent reprints up to 1660. The *Diary* notes are cited verbatim from the Foakes and Rickert edition. It gives most but not all of the performance dates up to the end of 1596 in the old style, when the new year began at Lady Day, 25 March. Most of the later listings from 1597 onwards are in the new style (*Diary*, p. 55). The takings are given in roman numerals in the old fashion, where l or li = one pound (libra), s = one shilling, and d = one penny (denarius), with 20 shillings or 240 pence to the pound. The 'l' of the Roman 50 should not be confused with the 'li' of an English pound. Henslowe's figures were his daily rent for the Rose, amounting to half the takings from the galleries. The company's share of the full take was an equal amount to Henslowe's plus the income from the yard, which would generally have brought them somewhere between the three pounds paid by 720 groundlings and the four from 960 sitters.

The initial repertory in May 1594 and after included a number of already famous plays like the two *Tamburlaines, Faustus, The Jew of Malta*, and *The Spanish Tragedy*. All the plays known to have preceded the company's creation in 1594 are marked at the end of the entry as 'old'. For their likely origins, including the character of the manuscripts that lie behind these and later printed texts, see Chapter 3 and the footnotes here.

The old plays, plus those written specifically for the Admiral's company at
the Rose from 1594 onwards and subsequently for performing at the
Fortune, are listed here so far as possible in the order of their first
performances where they can be identified from Henslowe's and other
records. The notes on the plays' first appearances in print, including their
title-pages, are chiefly based on the entries in W. W. Greg, *A Bibliography
of the Printed Drama to the Restoration*, 4 vols., London, 1939, Vol. I,
Stationers' Records. Plays to 1616. London (for the Bibliographical Society
at the University Press, Oxford), 1939, and Vol. 2, *Plays 1617–1689*. Roslyn
L. Knutson has a similar but shorter Appendix about the plays that were
entered in the *Diary* between July 1599 and June 1600, grouped by genre.[1]

1. *The Jew of Malta* (Marlowe, 1589, quarto). SR 17 May 1594, to
   N. Linge and T. Millington, *the famouse tragedie of The Riche Jewe
   of Malta*, and 20 November 1632 to N. Vavasour, *a tragedy called The
   Jew of Malta*. Q 1633; 'The Famous | TRAGEDY | OF | THE RICH IEVV | OF
   MALTA. | AS IT WAS PLAYD | BEFORE THE KING AND | QUEENE, IN HIS
   MAJESTIES | Theatre at *White-Hall*, by her Majesties | Servants at the
   Cock-pit. ‖ *Written by* CHRISTOPHER MARL. | LONDON; | Printed by *I. B.*
   for *Nicholas Vavasour*, and are to be sold | at his Shop in the Inner-
   Temple, neere the | Church. 1633.'[2] 'Rd at the Jewe of malta 14 of
   maye 1594 . . . xxxxviiij s; 4 of June 1594 Rd at the Jewe of malta . . . x s;
   13 of June 1594 Rd at the Jewe . . . iiij s; 23 of June 1594 Rd at
   the Jewe . . . xxiij s; 30 of June 1594 Rd at the Jewe of malta . . . xxxxj
   s; 10 of Julye 1594 Rd at the Jewe . . . xxvij s; 22 of Julye 1594 Rd at the
   Jewe of malta . . . xxxj[s]; 5 of aguste 1594 Rd at the Jewe of malta . . .
   xxvij s;[3] 7 of aguste 1594 Rd at the Jewe of malta . . . xvij s vj d; 2 of
   septembre 1594 —Rd at the Jewe of malta . . . xxiij s vj d; 20 of
   octobre 1594 —Rd at the Jewe of malta 1594 . . . xiij s; 9 of desembre
   1594 —Rd at the Jew . . . iij s;[4] 9 of Jeneuerye 1595 [1596] Rd at
   the Jew of malta . . . lvj s; 18 of Jeneway 1595 Rd at the Jewe of

---

[1] 'Toe to Toe across Maid Lane: Repertorial Competition at the Rose and Globe, 1599–1600', in *Acts
of Criticism. Performance Matters in Shakespeare and His Contemporaries*, ed. Paul Nelsen and June
Schlueter, Madison, 2006.

[2] The *Diary* records it as played 13 times by Strange's from February 1592 until 1 February 1593, once
by Sussex's on 4 February 1594, and twice more by Sussex's with the Queen's Men on 3 and 7 April
1594. It was the first Admiral's play to be staged at the Rose.

[3] There was some confusion over this dating. The columns appear to have fallen out of alignment by
this point, and two plays, *Galiaso* and *The Jew of Malta* were entered on the same date. The entries
for 7 and 8 August were duplicated for different plays. See *Diary*, p. 23.

[4] The small take at this performance may have led the company to drop the play for the next twelve
months. The other Marlowe plays continued to figure strongly.

malta . . . xxxviij s; 29 of Jenewary 1595 Rd at the Jewe of malta . . . xxv
s; 2 of febereary 1595 —Rd at the Jew of malta . . . lvij s; 17 of febreary
1595 Rd at the Jew of malta . . . xx s; 20 of aprell 1596 Rd at the
Jewe . . . xx^s; 14 of maye 1596 Rd at the Jew of malta . . . xxiiij s; 21 of
June 1596 Rd at Jew of malta . . . xiij s. Lent unto Robart shawe & m^r
Jube the 19 of maye 1601 to bye divers thinges for the Jewe of malta
the some of . . . vli; lent mor to the littell tayller the same daye for
more thinges for the Jewe of malta some of . . . x s; (property
inventory 10 March 1598) j cauderm for the Jewe' [old].[5]

2. *The Ranger's Comedy* (1593? lost). 'Rd at the Rangers comodey
the 15 of maye 1594 . . . xxxiij s; 18 of June 1594 Rd at the Rangers
comodey . . . xxij s; 22 of June 1594 – Rd at the Rangers comodey . . .
lviiij s; 5 of Julye 1594 Rd at the Rangers comodey . . . xviij s; 17 of Julye
Rd at the Rangers comodey . . . xv^s; 1 of aguste 1594 Rd at the Rangers
comodey . . . xiij s vj^d; 20 of aguste 1594 Rd at the Rangers comodey . . .
xiiij s vj d; 16 of Septembre 1594 Rd at the Rangers comodey . . . xv^s; 2 of
octobre 1594 Rd at the Rangers comodey . . . x s; 19 of Jeneway 1594
[1595] Rd at the Rangers comodey . . . xv^s' [old].[6]

3. *Cutlack* (1594? lost). 'Rd at Cutlacke the 16 of maye 1594 . . . xxxxij s;
6 of June 1594 Rd at cutlacke . . . xj s; 17 of June 1594 Rd at cutlacke . . .
xxxv s; 24 of June 1594 Rd at cutlacke . . . xxv^s; 27 of June 1594 Rd at
cuttlacke . . . xxxvj s; 4 of Julye 1594 Rd at cutlacke . . . xxiiij s; 15 of Julye
1594 –Rd at cutlacke . . . xxxv s; 29 of Julye 1594 Rd at cutlacke . . . xxix^s;
8 of aguste 1594 Rd at cuttlacke . . . xiij s vj^d; 22 of aguste 1594 Rd at
cuttlacke . . . xxiij s vj d; 6 of septembre 1594 Rd at cutlacke . . . xj s;
26 of septembre 1594 Rd at cuttlacke . . . xiij s' [old].[7]

4. *Belin Dun* (*Bellendon*) (1594, lost). SR 17 May 1594, '*Ent. T. Gosson :
a booke intituled the famous cronicle of Henrye the First, with the life
and death of Bellin Dun, the firste thief that ever was hanged in*

---

[5] The initiation of the Admiral's performances on 14 May 1594 with a Marlowe text that had been played
by the Queen's and Sussex's Men barely five weeks before, on 7 April, suggests either that the powers
who set up the new company seized it from the older companies as a major asset for the new one, or that
the play was distinctive in being owned by Henslowe himself, and given to whatever company was
using the Rose, including Strange's in 1592–93 and Sussex's in 1594. This question has been heavily
debated. See Scott McMillin, 'Sussex's Men in 1594: The Evidence of *Titus Andronicus* and *The Jew of
Malta*', *Theatre Survey* 32 (1991), 214–23, Gurr, *The Shakespearian Playing Companies*, Oxford, 1996,
p. 75 n.42. If Alleyn played for Sussex's between Strange's and the Admiral's, he may have owned it.
[6] Henslowe records it as played on 2 April 1594 by the Queen's and Sussex's, and by the Admiral's
thereafter.
[7] Alleyn played the eponymous hero of this play, to judge by a reference to a poseur using 'Dunstons
browes, and *Allens* Cutlacks gate', that is, the frown of St Dunstan and Cutlack's stride (Everard
Guilpin, *Skialetheia*, 1598, B2v).

England.[8] '8 of June 1594 ne— Rd at Bellendon . . . xvij s; 15 of June 1594 Rd at belldendon . . . iij^li iiij s; 20 of June 1594 Rd at bellendon . . . xxx^s; 2 of Julye Rd at bellendon . . . xxxxij s vj d; 6 of Julye 1594 Rd at bellendon . . . xxxiiij s; 11 of Julye 1594 Rd at bellendon . . . xxvij s; 20 of Julye 1594 —Rd at bellendon . . . xxvij s; 25 of Julye 1594 —Rd at bellendon . . . xlviij s; 31 of Julye 1594 —Rd at bellendon the . . . xxvij s; 10 of aguste 1594 —Rd at bellendon . . . xxxiij s; 19 of aguste 1594 — Rd at bellendon . . . xxj s; 29 of aguste 1594 —Rd at belendon . . . xx^s vj d; 11 of septembre 1594 Rd at bellendon . . . xxiiij^s vj d; 23 of septembre 1594 Rd at bellendon . . . xvj s vj d; 13 of octobre 1594 —Rd at bellendon . . . xxij s; 11 of July 1596 Rd at bellendon . . . xxxv^s; (March 1597) 31 tt at belendon . . . 01 15 00–04 – 00; Aprell 1597 11 — tt at belendon . . . 01 00 00 – 14 – 00; (April 1597) 19 tt at belendon . . . 00 09 02 – 00 – 00; (April 1597) 28 m^r pd Rd at belendon . . . 01 00 –00 – 13 – 00; (May 1597) 20 tt at bellendon . . . 00 10 00 – 00 – 00; (June 1597) 15 tt at bellendon . . . 00 13 00 – 00 – 00; (June 1597) 25 tt at bellendon . . . 00 07 00 – 00 – 00; (property inventory 10 March 1598) Belendon stable.'[9]

5. *The Massacre at Paris* (*The Guise*) (Marlowe, 1592, octavo 1594?[10]). Oct. n.d. 'THE | MASSACRE | AT PARIS: | With the Death of the Duke | of Guise. | As it was plaide by the right honourable the | Lord high *Admirall* his Servants. | Written by *Christopher Marlow.* | AT LONDON | Printed by *E. A.* for *Edward White*, dwelling neere | the little North doore of S. Paules | Church, at the signe of | the GUN.' '19 of June 1594 Rd at the Gwies . . . liiij s; 25 of June 1594 Rd at the masacer . . . xxxvj s; 3 of Julye 1594 Rd at the masacer . . . xxxj s; 16 of Julye 1594 Rd at masacare . . . xxxj^s; 27 of Julye 1594 Rd at the masacar . . . xxij s; 8 of aguste 1594 Rd at the masacare . . . xxiij s vj d; 17 of aguste 1594 —Rd at the masacar . . . xx s; 7 of septembre 1594 Rd at masacar . . . xvij s vj d; 25 of septembre 1594 Rd at masacar . . . xiiij s; Lent unto w^m Borne the 19 of novembre 1598 upon a longe taney clocke of clothe the some of xij^s wch he sayd yt was to Imbrader his hatte for the gwisse . . . xij^s; lent w^m birde ales borne the 27 of novembre [1598] to bye a payer of sylke stockens to playe the gwisse in . . . xx^s; lent

---

[8] A similar entry, but with 'Rufus' instead of 'Henry', appeared in the Stationers' Register for 24 Nov. 1595. No printed text survives. Both entries may have been for a chapbook rather than a play. The proximity of their dates to the Admiral's new play can be read either way, making the printing either an effect or a source.

[9] Recorded as the first 'ne' play by the new company, it can hardly have been written after the company's formation in May, but may not have been performed by any other company previously.

[10] A fragmentary manuscript also exists (Folger Shakespeare Library ms J.b.8) in an unknown hand.

w^m borne to bye his stockens for the gwisse . . . xx^s; Lent unto w^m
Jube the 3 of novmbre 1601 to bye stamell cllath for A clocke for the
gwisse the some of . . . iij^{li}; Lent unto the company to lend the littell
tayller to bye fuschen and lynynge for the clockes for the masaker
of france the some of . . . xxx^s; Lent unto the companye the 8 of
novmbre 1601 to paye unto the littell tayller upon his bell for
mackeynge of sewtes for the gwesse the some of xx^s; Lent unto
the companie the 13 of novembre 1601 to paye the littell tayller
Radford upon his bill for the gwisse the some of . . . xx s; pd at the
apoyntmente of the company unto the littell tayller in fulle payment
of his Bille for the gwisse the 26 of novmbre 1601 some xxiiij^s 6^d; pd
at the Apoyntment of the companye the 10 of Janeway 1601 [1602]
unto EAlleyn for iij boockes wch wer played called the french docter
the massaker of france & the nutte the some of . . . vj li; (apparel
inventory c.1602, under 'frenchose') the guises.' [old].^{11}

6. *Galiaso* (1594, lost). '26 of June 1594 ne—Rd at galiaso . . . iiij^{li} iiij s;
   12 of Julye 1594 Rd at galiaso . . . xxxxvj s; 23 of Julye 1594 Rd at
   galiaso . . . xxxj^s; 5 of aguste 1594 – Rd at galiaso . . . xxiij s vj d; 12 of
   aguste 1594 Rd at galliaso . . . xviij s; 21 of aguste 1594 Rd at galiaso . . .
   xxj^s vj^d; 10 of septembre 1594 Rd at galiaso . . . xxv^s; 29 of septembre
   1594 Rd at galiaso . . . xvij^s; 25 of octobre 1594 Rd at galleaso . . . xj s.'^{12}
7. *Philipo and Hippolito* (1594, lost). '9 of Julye 1594 Rd at the phillipo
   & hewpolyto . . . iij^{li} ij s; 13 of Julye 1594 Rd at phillipo & hewpolyto . . .
   xxxx s; 18 of Julye 1594 Rd at phillipo & hewpolyto . . . xxxiij^s; 24 of
   Julye 1594 Rd at phillipo & hewpolyto . . . xxx^s; 3 of aguste 1594 Rd at
   phillipo & hewpolyto . . . xxx s; 7 of aguste 1594 Rd at phillipo &
   hewpolito . . . xxix s; 15 of aguste 1594 Rd at phillipo & hewpolyto . . .
   xxj s; 24 of aguste 1594 Rd at phillipo & hewpolyto . . . xxviij s; 4 of
   septmbre 1594 Rd at phillipo & hewpolyto . . . xxij s; 13 of septmbre
   1594 Rd at phillipo & hewpolito . . . xx s; 19 of septmbre 1594 Rd at
   phillipo & hewpolyto . . . xiiij s vj d; 7 of octobre 1594 Rd at phillipo
   & hewpolito . . . xij s.'^{13}
8. *2 Godfrey of Boulogne* (Heywood, 1594? lost).^{14} '19 of Julye 1594 ne—
   Rd at 2 pte of godfrey of bullen . . . iij^{li} xj s; 26 of Julye 1594 —Rd

---

^{11} Performed once by Strange's Men 'ne—Rd at the tragedey of the gvyes 30 [January 1593] . . . iij li
xiiij s', and then by the Admiral's from June 1594.
^{12} *Galiaso* was recorded as 'ne', the second newly written play after *Belin Dun*, on the 17th day of the
company's performances.
^{13} This was the third play not previously performed and listed as 'ne'.
^{14} The fourth play not previously performed and listed as 'ne'. Nothing is in the Henslowe records for
the Admiral's in 1594 about any previous *Godfrey* play. It may have been written as a sequel to the

at godfrey . . . xlvij s; 6 of aguste 1594 —Rd at the seconde parte
of godfrey . . . xxxvij s; 13 of aguste 1594 Rd at godfrey of bullen . . .
xxix s; 26 of aguste 1594 Rd at godfrey . . . xxvij s vj d; 8 of septmbre
1594 —Rd at godfrey . . . xxxx^s; 20 of Septmbre 1594 Rd at godfrey . . .
xxx^s; 6 of octobre 1594 Rd at godfrey of bullen . . . xx^s; 30 of octobre
1594 Rd at bullen . . . xv s; 27 of aprell 1595 —Rd at godfrey of
bullen . . . xxix s; 17 of maye 1595 Rd at godfey of bullen . . . xxij s;
16 of septmbre 1595 Rd at godfrey of bullen . . . xx^s.'

9. *The Merchant of Emden* (1594, lost). '30 of Julye 1594 ne—Rd at the
   marchant of eamden . . . iij^{li} viij s.'[15]

10. *Tasso's Melancholy* (1594, lost). '11 of aguste 1594 ne—Rd at tassoes
    mellencoley . . . iij li iiij s; 18 of aguste 1594 —Rd at tassoes mallencoley
    . . . xxxxvij s; 3 of septmbre 1594 Rd at Tasso . . . xxxxvj s; 18 of septmbre
    1594 Rd at tasso . . . xxvij s vj d; 8 of octobre 1594 Rd at tasso . . . xxvij s;
    23 of octobre 1594 Rd at tasso . . . xxiij s; 12 of novembre 1594 Rd
    at tasso . . . xxv^s; 3 of desembre 1594 Rd at tasso . . . vj s; 11 of Jenewary
    1594/5 Rd at tasso . . . xx^s; 21 of Jeneway 1594 —Rd at tasso . . . xxxvj s;
    15 of febreary 1594 Rd at tasso . . . xix s; 14 of maye 1595 Rd at tasso . . .
    xx^s; Lent unto Thomas deckers at the A poyntment of the company
    the 16 of Janeway 1601 toward the alterynge of tasso the some of . . .
    xx s; Lent unto my sone EAlleyn the 3 of novmbre 1602 to geve unto
    thomas deckers for mendinge of the playe of tasso the some of . . . xxxx
    s; lent unto wm birde the 4 of desembre 1602 to paye unto thomas
    deckers in part of pay ment for tasso the some of . . . xxs; (property
    inventory 10 March 1598) Tasso picter; (apparel inventory 13 March
    1598) Tasoes robe.'

11. *Mahomet* (1593? lost; *The Battle of Alcazar*?).[16] '14 of aguste 1594 Rd
    at mahomett . . . iij li v s; 27 of aguste 1594 Rd at mahemet . . . xxxx s;

Strange's *Jerusalem*, performed twice in 1592. Conceivably the 'godfrey' staged on 26 July, 13 and
26 Aug., 20 Sept., 16 and 30 Oct., and 27 April, 17 May and 16 Sept. 1595 was the old original. It
was highly unusual, though, to start a run by introducing the 'ne' Part 2 and never to stage the play
and its sequel in succession. I think that 'godfrey' was always Part 2. An entry in the Stationers'
Register on 19 June 1594 is for *an enterlude entituled Godfrey of Bulloigne, wth the conquest of
Jerusalem*', and printed as a translation by R. Carew of Tasso's Italian in 1594. For all its being
called an 'enterlude' in the SR, this seems not to have been a play. Its publication might have
spurred the writing of the plays, but there is nothing to say where or when Part 1 appeared. Unlike
other sequels in the Henslowe records, it seems to have been performed as a solo play without any
first part.

[15] This was the first of five plays in the *Diary* to record only a single performance.

[16] The first entry in the *Diary* under this name has no 'ne', so it must have been an old play.
Conceivably *Mahomet* was another name for *The Battle of Alcazar* with its Moorish subject,
although Charles Edelman only identifies that play's other name as *Muly Mollocco* (see note to
Alcazar, 153). Here, rather reluctantly, it is treated as a separate play.

9 of septmbre 1594 Rd at mahemett . . . xxxv^s; 21 of septmbre 1594 —
Rd at mahemett . . . xxviij s; 14 of octobre 1594 Rd at mahemett . . .
xxvj s; 6 of novembre 1594 Rd at mahemette . . . xv s; 4 of desembre
1594 Rd at mahemet . . . xj s; 5 of febreary 1594 Rd at mahemett . . .
xxvj s; Layd owt at the A poyntment of the company the 2 of agust
1601 for A parell for mahewmet the some of . . . x s iiij d; pd at the
A poyntment of the company for mackynge of divers thinges
for mahewmett unto dover the tayller . . . xij^s; pd at the apoyntment
of the company unto w^m whitte for mackynge of crownes & other
thinges for mahewmet the 4 of agust 1601 the some of . . . l s; pd
unto edward alleyn at the a poyntment of the company the
22 of aguste 1601 for the Boocke of mahemett the some of . . . xxxx^s;
(property inventory 10 March 1598) owlde Mahemetes head.' [old].

12. *The Venetian Comedy* (1594, lost). '25 of aguste 1594 ne—Rd at
the venesyon comedy . . . l s vj d; 5 of septembre 1594 Rd at the
venesyon comedy . . . xxxvj s vj d; 15 of septmbre 1594 —Rd at the venesyon comodey . . . xxxvj s vj d; 22 of septmbre 1594 Rd at the venesyon
comedy . . . xxv s; 3 of octobre 1594 Rd at the venesyon comodey . . . xvij
s; 11 of octobre 1594 Rd at venesyon comodey . . . xvj s; 11 of
novembre 1594—Rd at the venesyon comodey . . . xxj s; 26 of
novembre 1594 Rd at the venecyon comodey . . . xiij s; 10 of febreary
1594 —Rd at the venesyan . . . xx s; 25 of febreary 1594 Rd at the
venesyan comodey . . . xx s; 8 of maye 1595 —Rd at the venesyon
comody . . . xxx s.'[17]

13. *1 Tamburlaine* (Marlowe, 1586–7, octavo). SR 14 August 1590,
'*R. Jones: the twoo commicall discourses of Tomberlein the Cithian
Shepparde.*' Octavo 1590 'Tamburlaine | the Great. | *Who, from a
Scythian Shephearde,* | by his rare and woonderfull Conquests, |
became a most puissant and migh-|tye Monarque. | And (for his
tyranny, and terrour in | Warre) was tearmed, | The Scourge of
God. | *Deuided into two Tragicall Dis-*|courses, as they were sundrie

---

[17] Roslyn Lander Knutson, *The Repertory of Shakespeare's Company 1594–1613*, pp. 21–22, maintains
that five titles of Henslowe's at this time, *The Venetian Comedy*, *The Love of an English Lady*, *The
Love of a Grecian Lady*, *The Grecian Lady*, and *The Grecian Comedy*, actually signify only two plays,
which she designates *The Venetian Comedy* and *The Grecian Comedy*. Grouping the entries as two
plays makes them fairly equal in takings. However, the 'ne' performance of one of the 'Venetian'
titles (15), which Henslowe noted as 'venesyon & the love of & Ingleshelady', came only two days
after the fourth performance of 'the venesyon comedy' (12), and it would have been unusual to
repeat a play so quickly. I think that although it only had two performances, *The Love of an English
Lady* was a new play. When making his entry Henslowe started to write the name of the earlier
play, then corrected it but omitted to delete his false start. I find three plays, one less successful than
the others, where Knutson finds two.

times | shewed vpon Stages in the Citie | of London. | By the right
honorable the Lord Admyrall, his seruantes. | Now first, and newlie
published. | LONDON. | Printed by Richard Ihones: at the signe | of the
Rose and Crowne neere Hol-| borne Bridge. 1590.' 'Part 1. The
Conquests of Tamburlaine, | the Scythian Shepheard.' Reprinted
1593, 1597, 1606 (Part 1 alone).[18] '28 of aguste 1594 j Rd at tamberlen . . .
iij[li] xj s; 12 of septembre 1594 Rd at tamberlen . . . xxxxv[s]; 28 of
septembre 1594 —Rd at tamberlen . . . xxxj[s]; 15 of October 1594 Rd at
tamberlen . . . xxviij s; 17 of octobre 1594 Rd at tamberlen . . . xxxx[s]; 4 of
novebre 1594 —Rd at tamberlen . . . xxxix[s]; 27 of novembre 1594 Rd at
tamberlen . . . xxij s; 17 of desembre 1594 Rd at tamberlen . . . xxxj s;
30 of desembre 1594 Rd at tamberlen . . . xxij s; 27 of Jeneway 1594 —
Rd at tamberlen . . . xxx[s]; 17 of febreye 1594 Rd at tamberlen . . . xxx[s]; 11
of marche 1594 Rd at fyrste part of tamberlen . . . xxx[s]; 21 of maye 1595
Rd at j part of tamberlen . . . xxij s; 15 of septmbre 1595 Rd at j parte of
tamberlen . . . xxj s; 12 of novmbre 1595 Rd at j parte of tamberlen . . .
xviij s; (property inventory 10 March 1598) Tamburlyne brydell;
(apparel inventory 13 March 1598) Tamburlynes cotte with coper lace;
Tamburlanes breches of crymson vellvet.' (See also 25, *2 Tamburlaine*,
below) [old].

14. *Palamon and Arcite* (1594, lost).[19] '17 of septmbre 1594 ne—Rd at
palamon & a[r]sett . . . lj s; 16 of octobre 1594 Rd at palamon & arset . . .
xxvij s; 27 of octobre 1594 —Rd at pallaman & harset . . . xxxxvij s; 9
of novembre 1594 Rd at palamon . . . xij s.'

15. *Love of an English Lady* (1594, lost). '24 septmbre 1594 ne—Rd at
venesyon & the love of & Ingleshelady . . . xxxxvij s; 24 of octobre
1594 Rd at love of & Ingleshe ladey . . . xxiij s.'[20]

16. *Doctor Faustus* (Marlowe, 1588? quarto). SR 7 January 1601,
T. Busshell, *'a booke called the plaie of Doctor Faustus'*. Q1 1604 'THE |
TRAGICALL | History of D. Faustus. | *As it hath bene Acted by the
Right* | *Honorable the Earle of Nottingham his servants.* | Written by | Ch.

---

[18] In the *Diary* Part 1 was never entered as 'ne', which must indicate performances at the Rose or
elsewhere before the *Diary* starts in 1592. The first entry coming in August 1594 suggests it took the
new company some time to acquire its most famous plays.

[19] As a 'ne' play, this dramatisation of Chaucer's tale is unlikely to have been Richard Edwards's play
of that name, which was acted by students at Oxford for the queen in 1566. A play with the same
name as another Edwards text, *Damon and Pithias*, was staged at the Fortune in 1600 (Item 147). It
was quite usual for more than one writer to dramatise a famous story.

[20] Conceivably a sequel to *The Venetian Comedy*, since its first entry in September 1594 calls it
'venesyon & the love of & Ingleshelady'. Alternatively, Henslowe may have started to write the title
of the older play, corrected it, and then forgot to delete the first words.

Marl. | LONDON | Printed by V. S. for Thomas Bushell. 1604.'
Q2 1609, Q3 1611, Q4 1616 'The Tragicall History | of the Life and
Death | of *Doctor Faustus*. | Written by *Ch. Mar.* | *LONDON*, |
Printed for *Iohn Wright*, and are to be sold at his shop | without
Newgate, at the signe of the | Bible. 1616.' '30 of septmbre 1594 Rd at
docter Fostose . . . iij^{li} xij^s; 9 of octobre 1594 Rd at docter Fostus . . .
xxxxiiij s; 21 of octobre 1594 Rd at docter Fostus 1594 . . . xxxiij s; 5 of
novembre 1594 Rd at docterfostes . . . xxxiij s; 20 of novembre 1594 Rd
at docter fostes . . . xviij s; 8 of desembre 1594 – Rd at docterfostus . . .
xv^s; 20 of desembre 1594 Rd at docter fostes . . . xviij s; 27 of desembre
1594 Rd at Docter fostes . . . lij s; 9 of Jenewary 1594 Rd at docter
fostes . . . xxij s; 24 of Jeneway 1594 Rd at docter fostes . . . xxiiij s; 8 of
febreary 1594 Rd at docter fostes . . . xviij s; 31 of aprell 1595 Rd at
fastes . . . xxij s; 5 of June 1595 Rd at doctor Fostus . . . xvij s; 11 of
septmbre 1595 Rd at docter fostes . . . xxx s ij; 26 of septmbre 1595 Rd at
docter fostes . . . xiij s; 13 of febreary 1595 Rd at fosstes . . . xxv^s; 19 of
aprell 1596 Rd at Doctor fostes . . . xij s; 5 of maye 1596 Rd at Doctor
Fostes . . . xx s; 12 of June 1596 Rd at Docter fostes . . . xvij^s; 3 of July 1596
Rd at fostes . . . xiiij^s; 4 of novembre 1596 Rd at doctor fostes . . . xvij s;
17 of desembre 1596 Rd at docterfostes . . . ix s; 5 of Jenewary 1597 Rd at
docter fostes . . . v s; the xj of octobe be gane my lord admerals & my
lord of penbrockes men to playe at my howse 1597 . . . tt at docter
fostes . . . o;[21] Lent unto the companye the 22 of novmbre 1602 to paye
unto w^m Burde & Samwell Rowle for ther adicyones in docter fostes
the some of . . . iiij^{li}; (clothing inventory possibly 1602, under "Jerkings
and dublets") faustus Jerkin his clok; (property inventory 10 March
1598) the sittie of Rome[22] . . . j dragon in fostes.' [old].[23]

17. *The Grecian Comedy* (1593? lost). '4 of octobre 1594 Rd at the love of a
gresyan lady . . . xxvj s; 13 of novmbre 1594 Rd at the gresyan ladye . . .
xv^s; 23 of novmbre 1594 Rd at the greasyon comody . . . x s; 1 of
desembre 1594 —Rd at the gresyan comody . . . iiij s; 25 of desembre
1594 S steven—Rd at the greasyane comodey . . . xxxvj s; 10 of
Jeneway 1594/5 Rd at the greasyon comodey . . . xxviij s; 25 of
Jeneway 1594 Rd at the greasyan . . . xv s; 31 of Jeneway 1594 Rd

---

[21] The records for playing (*Diary* p. 60) began a new five-column system of entries in January 1597.
The meaning of the five columns has not been clearly identified. This first entry for *Faustus* seems
to have been aborted after beginning with the first of the five columns.

[22] F. G. Fleay conjectured that this was a backdrop painted for Faustus's appearance at the Vatican. It
may have been depicted on a special set of hangings for the play.

[23] The *Diary*'s first note of Marlowe's play, like the two *Tamburlaines*, lacks a 'ne', confirming that it
was an old play.

at the gresyan comody . . . xxviij s; 22 of febreary 1594 Rd at the
gresyan comodey . . . xx s; 24 of aprell Rd at the grecian comody . . . lj
s; 16 of maye 1595 Rd at the greasyan comodey . . . xxxiij s; 9 of
octobre 1595 Rd at the gresyan comody . . . x s' [old].[24]

18. *The French Doctor* (1593? lost). '18 of octobre 1594 Rd at the frenshe
docter . . . xxij s; 28 of octobre 1594 Rd at the frenshe docter . . . xv^s; 18 of
novmbre 1594 —Rd at the frenshe docter [189–08–00][25] . . . xxvij s; 3
of Jeneway 1594 Rd at the frenshe docter . . . xxj s; 30 of Jeneway
1594 Rd at the frenshe docter . . . xviij s; 7 of febreary 1594 Rd at
the frenshe docter . . . xxj s; 24 of febreary 1594 —Rd at the frensh
docter . . . xxxxxiiij^s; easter mondaye 1595 easter Rd at the Frenshe
doctor . . . liij s; 3 of maye 1595 Rd at frenshe docte^r . . . xj s; 24 of maye
1595 Rd at frenshe docter . . . xxij s; 19 of septmbre 1595 Rd at the frenshe
doctor . . . xvj s; 4 of July 1596 Rd at frenshe dacter . . . xiiij s; 29
of octobre 1596 Rd at the frenshe docter . . . xv^s; 9 of novmbre 1596 Rd
at the frenshe docter . . . xiiij s; pd at the Apoyntment of the companye
the 10 of Janeway 1601 unto EAlleyn for iij boockes wch wer played
called the french docter the massaker of france & the nutte the some
of . . . vj li' [old].[26]

19. *A Knack to Know an Honest Man* (1594, quarto).[27] SR 26 Nov. 1595,
'a booke intituled *The most rare and pleasaunt historie of A knack to knowe
an honest man*'. Q1 1596. 'A PLEASANT | CONCEITED COME | die, called
A knacke to know | an honest Man. | as it hath beene sundrie times
plaied about the | Citie of London. | LONDON, | Printed for Cuthbert
Burby, and are | to be solde at his shop by the | Royall exchange. 1596.'
'22 of octobre 1594 ne—Rd at a Knacke to Know a noneste . . . xxxx^s;
29 of octobre 1594 Rd at the Knacke to Knowe & oneste man . . .
xxxxvij s; 1 of novembre 1594 Rd at the Knacke to Knowe & onest
man . . . iij^{li} iiij s; 7 of novmbre 1594 Rd at the Knacke . . . xxxxiiij^s;
21 of novmbre 1594 Rd at the Knacke . . . xx^s; 29 of novmbre 1594 Rd
at the Knacke . . . xx s; 13 of desembre 1594 Rd at the Knacke . . . xij s;
7 of Jenewary 1594 —Rd at the knacke . . . xxij s; 13 of Jenewary 1594 —Rd

[24] Probably one play, variously noted as 'the love of a gresyan lady' and 'the gresyan lady'. Its first
staging in October 1594 was not marked 'ne', so it may have been old.

[25] This figure, presumably a total in pounds, shillings and pence, was interlined here, and may
constitute a running total of some sort, although it is difficult to identify where the totting up starts.

[26] Not marked as 'ne' on its first appearance, this may be another old play revived by the new
company. Its relatively small initial takings also suggest that it was not new.

[27] No sort of sequel to *A Knack to Know a Knave*, which hailed both Alleyn and Will Kemp as its stars
on its title-page and was acted by Strange's in 1592–93, the parallelism of titles was probably used as
a plug for the new play.

at the Knacke . . . xxxiij s; 6 of febreary 1594 Rd at the Knacke . . . xxiiij s;
26 of febreary 1594 Rd at the Knacke . . . xxiiij s; 10 of marche 1594
17 p—Rd at the Knacke from hence licensed[28] . . . xxiiij s; 23 of aprell
1595 Rd at the knacke . . . lv^s; 5 of maye 1595 —Rd at the Knacke . . . xxiij
s; 9 of June 1595—whittson daye —Rd at the Knacke . . . lv^s; 25 of aguste
1595 Rd at the Knacke to Know a nonest man . . . xvij s; 18 of septembre
1595 Rd at the Knacke . . . xiij s; 7 of Jeneway 1595 Rd at a Knack to
Know & onest man . . . xx s; 16 of aprell 1596 Rd at the Knacke . . . xj s;
3 of novembre 1596 Rd at the cnacke to knowe . . . xv s.'

20. *1 Caesar and Pompey* Part 1 (1594, lost). '8 of novembre 1594 ne—Rd
at seser & pompie . . . iij^{li} ij s; 14 of novembre 1594 Rd at sesor &
pompie . . . xxxv^s; 25 of novembre 1594—Rd at seser & pompey . . .
xxxij^s; 10 of desembre 1594—Rd at seser . . . xij^s; 18 of Jenewary 1594 Rd
at seaser . . . xxv^s; 1 of febreary 1594 Rd at seaser . . . xxiiij s; 6 of marche
1594 Rd at seaser . . . xx^s; 25 of June 1595 Rd at the j parte of seaser . . .
xxij s.'

21. *Diocletian* (1594, lost). '16 of novmbre 1594 ne—Rd at deoclesyan . . .
liiij s; 22 of novmbre 1594 Rd at deoclesyan . . . xxxxiij^s.'

22. *Warlamchester* (1594? lost). '28 of novmbre 1594 Rd at worlamchester
. . . xxiij^s; 30 of novmbre 1594 Rd at warlamchester . . . xxxviij s; 12 of
desembre 1594 Rd at warlamchester . . . xv^s; 29 of aprell 1595 —Rd at
warlamchester . . . xxix s; 10 of maye 1595 Rd at warlam chester . . .
xxix s; 30 of maye 1595 Rd at warlamchester . . . ix s; 16 of June 1595 —
Rd at warlamchester . . . xxv s' [old?].[29]

23. *The Wise Men of West Chester* (Munday, *John a Kent and John a
Cumber*? 1594, ms 1595). '2 of desembre 1594 ne—Rd at the wise man
of chester . . . xxxiij s; 6 of desembre 1594 Rd at wiseman of weschester
. . . xxxiiij s; 29 of desembre 1594 —Rd at the wissman of weschester . . .
iij^{li} ij s; 15 of Jenewarye 1594 Rd at the wiseman of weaschester . . . iij
li; 23 of Jenewary 1594 Rd at the wiseman of weascheaster . . . iij^{li} vj s;
4 of febreary 1594 Rd at wysman of weschester . . . iij li iiij s; 12 of
febreary 1594 Rd at wisman of weschester . . . liij s; 19 of febreary 1594
Rd at wisman of weschester . . . xxxxvj s; 28 of febreary 1594 Rd at the
wisman of weschester . . . xxxix s; 25 of aprell 1595 Rd at the wissman . . .
lviij s; 26 of aprell 1595 Rd at the wisseman of weschester . . . iij^{li}; 6 of

---

[28] This extra note is interlined; it is not clear what it refers to, nor the '17 p' added to the date.
[29] The absence of a 'ne' for the first performance of this play suggests it was an old text, but despite its seven appearances in 1594–95, nothing besides the name is known of it.

maye 1595 Rd at the wiseman . . . xxxx^s; 15 of maye 1595 Rd at the wisse
man of weschester . . . xxxvij s; 26 of maye 1595 —Rd at weschester . . .
xxxj s; 4 of June 1595 Rd at the wisman of weschester . . . xxij s;
11 of June 1595 Rd at wissman of weschester . . . xxxxvij s; 26 of aguste 1595
Rd at the wisman of wescheaster . . . xxxix s; 9 of septmbre 1595 —Rd
at the wise man . . . xxxxiiij s; 29 of septmbre 1595 Rd at the wiseman
. . . xv s; 6 of octobre 1595 —Rd at the wisman . . . xvij s; 19 of octobre
1595 —Rd at the wisman . . . xvij s; 7 (?) of novmbre 1595 Rd at
weschester . . . xx^s; 30 of desembre 1595 Rd at the wisman of weschester
. . . xxij s; 17 (?) of Jeneway 1595 Rd at wissman of weschester . . . xviij s;
4 of febreary 1595 Rd at wissman of weschester . . . xij s; 17 of aprell
1596 Rd at the wisman of weschester . . . xxx s; 30 of aprell 1596 Rd at
wisman . . . x s; 8 of June 1596 Rd at wisman of weschester . . . xxs; 7 of
July 1596 Rd at wisman of weschester . . . xvj^s; 8 July 1597 tt at the
wismane of weschester 00 01 – 00 – 03; 12 July 1597 tt at wismane of
weschester 00 18 00 – 01 – 00; 18 July 1597 tt at wisman 01 10 00 – 00 –
00; pd at the Apoyntment of the 19 of septmbre 1601 for the playe of the
wysman of weschester unto my sonne EAlleyn the some of . . . xxxx^s;
(property inventory 10 March 1598) Kentes woden leage.'[30]
24. *The Set at Maw* (*The Mawe*) (1594, lost). '14 of desembre 1594 ne—Rd
at the mawe . . . xxxxiiij s; 2 of Jenewary 1594 Rd at the seat at mawe
. . . xxiiij s; 17 of Jenewary 594 Rd at the mawe . . . xxv^s; 28 of
Jenewary 1594 Rd at the mawe . . . xxvij s.'[31]
25. *2 Tamburlaine* (Marlowe, 1586–7, octavo). SR 14 August 1590,
R. Jones. Octavo 1590, in the same edition with Part 1. 'Part 2. THE
SECOND PART OF | The bloody Conquests | of mighty Tamburlaine.
| With his impassionate fury, for the death of | his Lady and loue, faire
Zenocrate; his fourme | of exhortation and discipline to his three
| sons, and the maner of his owne death.' Reprinted 1593, 1597, 1605
(Part 2 alone). '19 of desembre 1594 Rd at the 2 parte of tamberlen . . .
xxxxvj s / 1 of Jenewary 1594 Rd at the 2 parte of tamberlen . . . iij^{li}

[30] A manuscript survives with the title 'The booke of John a Kent and John a Cumber', set in West
Chester, and signed at the end 'Anthony Mundy', with another hand supplying a mutilated date
'— Decembris 1596', which seems have been altered from 1595. The identity between the
manuscript with the altered date 1595 performed 'ne' in Dec. 1594 and the '*Wise Men*' title is still
a matter of some doubt, although Munday was certainly working for the company well before
Henslowe started registering payments to him in December 1597. I think the two titles must describe
the same play, so include it here as a very popular text in the company's series using magical games
with disguising. For a discussion of the play and the manuscript, see Chapter 2, pp. 58–59.
[31] The word 'mawe' inexplicably recurs as 'j mawe gowne of calleco for the queen' in the inventory of
10 March 1598 for '*Clownes Sewtes and Hermetes Sewtes, with divers other sewtes*'. The inventory note
may, of course, simply be Henslowe's spelling of 'more'. I owe this thought to John Astington.

ij s / 29 of Jenewary 1594 Rd at the 2 part of tamberlen . . . xxxxvij
s / 18 of febreary 1594 Rd at 2 parte of tamberlen . . . xxxvj s / 12 of
marche 1594 Rd at 2 parte of tamberlen . . . xxij s / 22 of maye 1595 Rd
at 2 p of tamberlen . . . xxv^s / 13 of novmbre 1595 Rd at 2 part of
tambrlen . . . xxxij s' [old].[32]

26. *The Siege of London* (1593? lost). '26 of desembre 1594 Rd at the
sege of london . . . iij^{li} iij s; 14 of Jeneway 1594 Rd at the seage of
london . . . xxviij s; 22 of Jeneway 1594 Rd at the seage of london . . .
xxxij s; 3 of febreary 1594 —Rd at the sege of london . . . xxxxv^s; 13 of
febreary 1594 Rd at the sege of london . . . xxix s; 3 of marche 1594 —Rd
at the sege of london . . . xxvj s; 14 of marche 1594 Rd at sege of london
. . . xiiij s; 30 of aguste 1595 Rd at the seage of london . . . xviij s; 20 of
septmbre 1595 Rd at the sege of london . . . xvij s; 13 of Jeneway 1595 Rd
at the sege of london . . . xv^s; 14 of June 1596 —Rd at sege of london . . .
xxx^s; 6 of July 1596 Rd at sege of london . . . xv^s; (property inventory
10 March 1598) j whell and frame in the Sege of London' [old].[33]

27. *Vallia and Antony* (1593? lost). '4 of Jeneway 1594 Rd at valy a for . . .
xj s; 20 of June 1595 Rd at antony & vallea . . . xx s; 6 of septmbre 1595
Rd at valia & antony . . . xiij s; 26 of octobre 1595 Rd at valia &
antony . . . xxvij s.'[34]

28. *The French Comedy* (1595, lost). '11 of febreary 1594 ne—Rd at
the frenshe Comodey . . . l s; 27 of febreary 1594 Rd at the frenshe
Comodey . . . xxxx^s; 12 of maye 1595 —Rd at the frenshe comodey . . .
xxviij s; 31 of maye Rd at frenshe comodye . . . xv s; 17 of June 1595 Rd
at the frenshe comodey . . . xxj s; 24 of June mydsomerdaye Rd at
the frenshecomodey . . . xxx^s; 18 Aprell 1597 —ne— tt at a frenshe
comodey . . . 02 00 01 – 01 – 00; 22 Aprell 1597 tt at frenshe comodey . . .
01 02 00 – 17 – 01; 26 Aprell 1597 —tt at frenshe comodey . . . 01 02 00 –
17 – 00; 2 Maye 1597 —tt at frenshe comodey . . . 01 00 00 – 09 – 03;
5 Maye 1597 tt at frenshe comodey . . . 01 07 01 – 00 – 00; 21 May 1597 tt
at frenshe comodey . . . 00 14 00 – 13 – 06; 1 June 1597 tt at frenshe

---

[32] As with the first play, Henslowe failed to record Part 2 as 'ne', which signifies that it was not new when
performed here. That can hardly be seen as confirmation that Philip Gawdy's account of the old
Admiral's company's accident when staging Part 2 late in 1587 was at the Rose (see Chapter 1, pp. 7–10).

[33] Lacking a 'ne' marking, and not appearing before December 1594, it may have come from the older
Admiral's. Its performance at the prime time for the Christmas season, St Stephen's Day, seems to
give it a prominence that is confirmed by its title, although the high takings, comparable to those at
'ne' performances, may simply reflect the fact that the day was an official holiday.

[34] This variously named play, for conventional reasons retitled *Antony and Vallia* by the editors of the
Diary, pp. 338, 344, has no 'ne' mark for its first performance, so it may resemble *The Siege of
London* in its origins.

comedy . . . 00 13 00 – 04 – 06; 16 June 1597 tt at frenshe comodey . . .
00 07 00 – 13 – 06; 23 June 1597 tt at frenshe comodey . . . 00 08 00 – 00 –
00; 2 July 1597 tt at frenshe comodey . . . 00 04 02 – 00 – 13; 16 July 1597
tt at frenshe comodey . . . 00 09 00 – 14 – 00.'[35]

29. *Long Meg of Westminster* (1595? lost). '14 of febreary 1594 j Rd at longe
mege of westmester . . . iij.^li ix s; 20 of febreary 1594 Rd at longe mege
. . . xxxxviij s; 29 of febreary 1594 Rd at longe mege . . . xxxviiij s; 4 of
marche 1594 Rd at longe mege on sraftusdaye[36] . . . iij.^li; 13 of marche
1594 Rd at longe mege . . . xxviij s; 30 of aprell 1595 —Rd at longe
mege . . . xxvij s; 1 of maye 1595[37] —Rd at longe mege . . . l s; 13 of
maye 1595 Rd at longe mege . . . xxviij s; 19 of June 1595 Rd at longe
mege . . . xxij s; 28 of aguste 1595 Rd at longe mege . . . xvij s; 14 (?) of
septmbre 1595 Rd at longe mege . . . xvj s; 4 of octobre 1595
Rd at longe mege . . . xj s; 1 of novmbre 1596 Rd at longe meage . . .
al holanday[38] . . . xxxxvij s; 5 of novmbre 1596 Rd at longe meage . . .
v s; 25 of novmbre 1596 Rd at long meage . . . xj s; 28 Janeway 1597 tt
at long mege . . . 0 07 01 30 – 11.'[39]

30. *The Mack* (1595, lost). '21 of febreary 1594 ne—Rd at the macke . . . iij.^li.'

31. *Seleo and Olympio* (1595, lost). '5 of marche 1594 ne—Rd at seleo &
olempo . . . iii.^li; 2 of maye 1595 —Rd at seleo & olempa . . . l s; 9 of maye
1595 Rd at selyo & olympo . . . xxvj s; 19 of maye 1595 Rd at olimpo
. . . xxiij s; 29 of maye 1595 Rd at olimpo . . . xxix s; 7 of June 1595 Rd
at olimpio . . . xv s; 4 of septmbre 1595 —Rd at olempeo & heugenyo
. . . xviij s; 3 of octobre 1595 Rd at olempeo . . . xv s; 22 of novmbre
1595 Rd at olempo . . . iiij s vj d; 18 of febreary 1595 Rd at olempeo . . .
x s.'[40]

32. *1 Hercules* (1595, lost).[41] '7 of maye 1595 —ne— Rd at the firste parte
of herculous . . . iij.^li xiij s; 20 of maye 1595 Rd at hercolas . . . iij.^li

[35] The six performances starting 'ne' on 11 February 1595 were followed by another 'ne' performance of 'a frenshe comedy' a little more than two years later, on 18 April 1597. The editors of the *Diary* believe that only one play was involved.
[36] Written within a rectangle, 'sraftusdaye' with its large takings designated Shrove Tuesday.
[37] Another traditional holiday.
[38] Presumably All Hallows, another holiday.
[39] The takings for the first performance Henslowe noted are quite as high as for any of the 'ne' plays, so the odd 'j' in the first entry may have been used, perhaps fortuitously, in place of a 'ne'. It stayed in the repertory up to at least 1610. Field's *Amends for Ladies* (1611) in 2.1. has a reference to 'Long Meg and the ship', and later someone speaks of gentlewomen going to a play at the Fortune.
[40] Probably the play also named *Olympio and Eugenio*.
[41] The first part of a play in two parts, probably designed to cover the twelve labours between them. Both parts were first staged in May 1595. The stories may have been taken from Jasper Heywood's translation of Seneca's *Hercules Furens*. A note in the *Diary* (p. 89) for 16 May 1598 records a payment for the two parts and three other plays to Martin Slater, who left the company in July

ix^s; 27 of maye 1595 Rd at j parte of herculos . . . iij li; 12 of June 1595
Rd at the j parte of herculos . . . iij^{li} j s; 1 of septmbre 1595 —Rd at the
j parte of herculos . . . iij^{li} iiij s; 22 of septmbre 1595 Rd at j parte of
herculos . . . xxxj s; 12 of octobre 1595 —Rd at j parte of herculos . . .
xxix s; 25 of octobre 1595 —Rd at j part of herculos . . . xxxij s; 24 of
novmbre 1595 —Rd at j herculos . . . xx s; 18 of desembre 1595 —Rd at
j part of herculos . . . xiij s; 6 of Jenewary 1595 Rd at hurculos the
j parte . . . iij li; Lent unto the company the 16 of maye 1598 to bye
v boockes of martine slather called ij partes of hercolus & focas &
pethagores & elyxander & lodicke wch laste boocke he hath not
delyverd the some of . . . vij^{li}; lent unto Thomas dowton the 16 of
July 1598 for to bye A Robe to playe hercolas in the some of . . . xxxx^s;
dd unto the littell tayller to bye . . . for the play of hercollas the 14 of
desembre 1601 the some of . . . xx s; pd unto the littell tayller
18 of desembre 1601 for divers thinges for the playe of hercolas the
some of . . . v^s; (inventory of 10 March 1598 for '*Clownes Sewtes and
Hermetes Sewtes, with divers other sewtes*') Hercolles lymes; ('*Note of all
suche bookes as belong to the Stocke, and such as I have bought since the
3d of March 1598*') 1 p^t of Hercules, 2 p^t of Hercules.'

33. *2 Hercules* (1595, lost). '23 maye 1595 ne—Rd at 2 part of hercolas . . . iij^{li}
x s; 28 of maye 1595 Rd at 2 parte of herculas . . . iij^{li} ij s; 13 of June
1595 Rd at the 2 part of herculos . . . iij^{li} ij s; 2 of septmbre 1595 —Rd
at 2 parte of herculos . . . iij li; 23 of septmbre 1595 Rd at 2 part of
herculos . . . xxiij s; 13 of octobre 1595 Rd at 2 parte of herculus . . .
xxv^s; 2 of novmbre 1595 —Rd at 2 part of herculas . . . xxviij s; 25 of
novmbre 1595 Rd of 2 part of herculos . . . xvj s; Lent unto the
company the 16 of maye 1598 to bye v boockes of martine slather
called ij partes of hercolus & focas & pethagores & elyxander &
lodicke wch laste boocke he hath not delyverd the some of . . . vij^{li}; lent
unto Thomas dowton the 16 of July 1598 for to bye A Robe to playe
hercolas in the some of . . . xxx^s; dd unto the littell tayller to bye . . .
for the play of hercollas the 14 of desembre 1601 the some of . . . xx s;
pd unto the littell tayller 18 of desembre 1601 for divers thinges for the
playe of hercolas the some of . . . v^s; (inventory of 10 March 1598 for
'*Clownes Sewtes and Hermetes Sewtes, with divers other sewtes*')
Hercolles lymes; ('*Note of all suche bookes as belong to the Stocke, and*

1597. Knowing his long record as leader of travelling companies, this payment probably means that
they were old manuscripts in Slater's possession. The payment kept them for the company.

such as I have bought since the 3d of March 1598') 1 p^t of Hercules, 2 p^t of Hercules.'

34. *1 The Seven Days of the Week* (1595, lost). '3 of June 1595 ne—Rd at the vij Dayes of the weacke . . . iij$^{.li}$ x s; 6 of June 1595 Rd at the vij dayes of the weack . . . xxxxiiij s; 10 of June 1595 Rd at the vij dayes of the wecke . . . iij$^{.li}$ vj s; 14 of June 1595 Rd at the vij dayes of the wecke . . . iij$^{.li}$ ix s; 23 of June 1595 Rd at the vij dayes of the wecke . . . iij$^{.li}$ v^s; 27 of aguste 1595 Rd at the weacke . . . liij s; 3 of sepmbre 1595 Rd at the vij dayes of the weacke . . . lij s; 13 of septmbre 1595 —Rd at the vij dayes . . . xxxviij s; 22 of septmbre 1595 —Rd at the vij dayes . . . xxxxiiij s; 6 of octobre 1595 —Rd at the vij dayes . . . xxxx^s; 14 of octobre 1595 Rd at the vij dayes . . . xvij s; 17 of octobre 1595 Rd at the vij dayes . . . xxviij s; 29 of octobre 1595 Rd at the vij Dayes . . . xiij s; 15 of novmbre 1595 Rd at vij Dayes . . . xviij s; 14 of desembre 1595 —Rd at the vij dayes . . . xxiiij s; 1 of Jenewary 1595 Rd at the wecke . . . xxxxij s; 25 of febreary 1595 Rd at wecke . . . xx s; 11 of novmbre 1596 Rd at the vij dayes . . . xxxv^s; 15 of novmbre 1596 —Rd at the vij dayes . . . xij s; 26 of novmbre 1596 Rd at weake . . . xvij s; 12 of desembre 1596 Rd at the vij dayes . . . ix s; 31 of desembre 1596 Rd at vij dayes . . . vj s.'

35. *2 Caesar and Pompey*, Part 2 (1595, lost). '18 of June 1595 ne—Rd at the 2 parte of sesore . . . lv^s; 26 of June 1595 Rd at the 2 parte of seaser . . . xx^s.'[42]

36. *Longshanks (King Edward the First)* (Peele, 1592, quarto).[43] SR 8 Oct. 1593, '*Entred for his Copie under thandes of bothe the wardens an enterlude entituled the Chronicle of Kinge Edward the firste surnamed Longeshank with his Retourne out of the Holye Lande, with the lyfe of*

---

[42] On this one occasion the two parts were performed on successive days, the last time either play appeared.

[43] On the grounds that the play of this name was staged as 'ne' in 1595, Chambers (*Elizabethan Stage* III. 460) dismisses the idea that it might have been a revival of Peele's 'Famous Chronicle of king Edwarde the first, sirnamed Edwarde Longshankes, with his returne from the holy land'. However, given that a quarto survived, that Alleyn bought at least one other play of Peele's, and that Peele and the company who first performed it no longer existed, I think this may mark the company staging a version of Peele's play. Alleyn, who knew Peele, also bought *Alcazar* (153) and *David and Bethsabe* from him, performed later by the Admiral's and Worcester's. On the other hand *Longshanks* may be related to the 'Harry of Cornwall' staged by Strange's with Alleyn at the Rose early in 1592. This play also deals with King Edward's life and the Barons' Revolt, but did not reappear in the Admiral's. The 'ne' *Longshanks* of 1595 may have been a new play written out of the popular line of English history plays that Peele initiated, while Peele's printed play was a discard. But Alleyn was paid £4 by the Admiral's for the book of *Longshanks* and another play on 8 Aug. 1602, suggesting a close relation to Peele's quarto. *Edward I* was among the group of so-called 'large' texts written before 1594 for an exceptionally large number of players. As such, it certainly pre-dates the Admiral's of 1594, who may have cut it down in size (perhaps thus making it 'ne') for their own use.

Leublen Rebell in Wales with the sinkinge of Quene Elinour.' Q1 'THE |
Famous Chronicle of king Edward | the first, sirnamed Edward
Longshankes, | with his returne from the holy land. | ALSO THE LIFE
OF LLEVELLEN | *rebell in Wales.* | Lastly, the sinking of Queene *Elinor,*
who sunck | *at Charingcrosse, and rose againe at Potters-* | hith, now
named Queenehith. | LONDON | Printed by Abell Ieffes, and are to | be
solde by William Barley, at his shop | in Gratious streete. 1593.' Q2
1599; 14 Aug. SR 1600, '*Ent. As a thing formerly printed and set over to
T. Pavier: an interlude called Edward Longe shankes.'*[44] '29 of aguste
1595 ne—Rd at longe shancke . . . xxxx s; 10 of septmbre 1595 —Rd at
longshancke . . . iij li; 30 of septmbre 1595 Rd at long shancke . . .
xxxij s; 21 of octobre 1595 Rd at longe shancke . . . xxx s; 9 of novmbre
1595 Rd at longshancke . . . xxxiij s; 26 of novembre 1595 Rd at
longshancke . . . xviij s; 10 of desembre 1595 Rd at prynce longshanke
. . . xxx s; 29 of desembre 1595 Rd at longshanckes . . . xxxij s; 5 of
febreary 1595 Rd at longshancke . . . xiiij s; 27 of febreary 1595 Rd at
longshancke . . . xxx^s; 21 of aprell 1596 Rd at longshancke . . . xiiij s; 28 of
aprell 1596 Rd at longshancke . . . xx s; 2 of June 1596 Rd at longshancke
. . . iiij^{li}; 9 of July 1596 Rd at longshancke . . . xv s; pd unto my sone
EA for ij bocke called phillipe of spayne & Longshanckes the 8 of agust
1602 the some of . . . iiij^{li}; (apparel inventory 10 March 1598 under
"*Gone and loste*") j longe-shanckes sewte; (apparel inventory 13 March
1598) j Longeshankes seute.'[45] [old?].

37. *Crack Me this Nut* (1595, lost). '5 of septmbre 1595 ne—Rd at cracke
me this nutte . . . iij li j s; 12 of septmbre 1595 —Rd at cracke me this
nutte . . . iij li; 24 of septmbre 1595 Rd at cracke me this nutte . . .
xxxxij s; 28 of septmbre 1595 —Rd at crack me this nutte . . . iij^{li} vj^{s};
8 of octobre 1595 Rd at cracke me this nutt . . . xxvj s; 20 of octobre
1595 Rd at cracke me this nutte . . . xxj s; 24 of octobre 1595 Rd at
cracke me this nutte . . . xxiij s; 5 of novmbre 1595 Rd at cracke me this
nutt . . . xxiiij s; 18 of novmbre 1595 —Rd at cracke me this nutte . . .
xxiiij s; 6 of desembre 1595 Rd at Crack me this nutt . . . xv^s; 2 of
Jeneware 1595 Rd at cracke me this nutt . . . ix s; 14 of Jeneware 1595
Rd at cracke me this nutte . . . xxiij s; 7 of febreary 1595 Rd at crackme
this nutt . . . xix s; 7 of maye 1596 Rd at cracke me this nutte . . . xviij s;
7 of June 1596 Rd at cracke me this nutte . . . xxviiij s; 23 of June 1596

---

[44] Both quartos have Peele's name at the end.
[45] The anomaly of the same item appearing both in a list of 'lost' clothing and as present in a different
list made three days later suggests that different chests or repositories were being checked.

Rd at cracke me this nutt . . . xij s; layd owt for the company to bye
buckerom for A sewt for the playe of the nutte to the littell tayller the
4 of desembre 1601 the some of . . . v s; pd at the Apoyntment of the
companye the 18 of Janewary 1601 unto EAlleyn for iij boockes w^ch
wer played called the frensh docter the massaker of france & the nutte
the some of . . . vj li.'

38. *The New World's Tragedy* (1595, lost). '17 of septmbre 1595 ne—Rd at
the worldes tragedy . . . iij^li v^s; 25 of septmbre 1595 Rd at the worldes
tragedy . . . xxxviij s; 7 of octobre 1595 Rd at the worldes tragedy . . .
xxxij s; 22 of octobre 1595 Rd at the worldes tragedy . . . xxxiij s; 3 of
novmbre 1595 Rd at the new worldes tragedy . . . xxix s; 27 of novmbre
1595 Rd at the newes wordles tragedy . . . xviij s; 12 of desembre 1595
Rd at the new worldes tragedy . . . xxxj s vj d; 22 of desembre 1595 —Rd
at the newe worldes tragedie . . . xx s; 8 of Jeneway 1595 Rd at new
worldes tragedie . . . xviij^s; 25 of Jeneway 1595 —Rd at the new worldes
tragedy . . . xiiij s; 27 of aprell 1596 Rd at new worldes tragedy . . . xxix s.'

39. *The Disguises* (Wadeson?[46] 1595, *Look About You*?). Q1 'A | PLEASANT |
COMMODIE, | CALLED | Looke about you. | As it was lately played by
the right honoura- | ble the Lord High Admirall his servants | LONDON,
| Printed for William Ferbrand, and are to be | solde at his shop at the
signe of the Crowne | neere Guild-hall gate. | 1600.' '2 of October 1595
ne—Rd at the Desgysses . . . xxxxiij s; 10 of octobre 1595 Rd at
the desgyses . . . xxix s; 16 of octobre 1595 Rd at desgysses . . . xs;
27 of octobre 1595 Rd at the desgyses . . . xix s; 30 of octobre 1595 Rd at
the desgysses . . . xxix s; 10 of novmbre 1595 Rd at Desgysses . . . xv^s.'[47]

---

[46] See the footnote to Item 172.

[47] This striking comedy set in English history is not listed under its published name by Henslowe,
despite its title-page's ascription to the Admiral's, so the date and its location here are tentative.
I suggested in Chapter 2 that it must be the play Henslowe called '*Disguises*', staged in October
1595. On the other hand he does note payments on 13 June and 23 July 1601, a year after the quarto
appeared, to Antony Wadeson (who may also be the writer known as 'antony the poyete', *Diary*
pp. 203–05) for 'A Boocke called the life of the humeros earlle of Gloster with his conquest of
portingalle'. This may be a sequel to *Look About You*, since Gloster, the chief hero of the six
disguisers in *Look About You*, declares at the end that he is off to Portugal. *Look About You*'s
printing in 1600 along with several other popular Admiral's plays suggests that it belongs to the
period 1595–98. It names the company patron simply as Lord Admiral rather than Earl of
Nottingham, whereas the title-pages of three plays printed earlier, Chapman's *An Humorous
Day's Mirth*, Dekker's *Shoemaker's Holiday*, and Porter's *Two Angry Women of Abingdon*, all of
1599, give both of his titles. Henslowe was calling the company 'm^r lord of notingame men' by 26
May 1599 (*Diary*, p. 121). Howard was promoted Earl of Nottingham in 1597, which might indicate
a date for this play and its preparation for the press before 1597. An entry in the Stationers' Register
would have helped to identify when the publisher first got hold of the manuscript, but there is
none. It seems unlikely that a publisher like Ferbrand, or Allde the printer, would have omitted
Howard's new title in 1600 if they thought it important, so it does seem likely that the text was

40. *The Wonder of a Woman* (1595, lost). '15 of octobre 1595 ne—Rd at the
wonder of a womon . . . liij s; 23 of octobre 1595 Rd at the wonder of a
woman . . . xxiij s; 4 of novembre 1595 Rd at the wonder of a womon
. . . xxvij s; 20 of novmbre 1595 Rd at a wonder of A womon . . . xx s;
4 of desembre 1595 Rd at wonder of A womon . . . xiiij s; 25 of desembre
1595 S stevens day Rd at the wonder of A womon . . . iij^{li} ij s; 15 of
Jeneway 1595 Rd at the wonder of A womon . . . xxvij s; 30 of Jeneway
1595 —Rd at the wonder of a womon . . . xj s; maye Daye 1596 Rd at the
wonder of a womon . . . xxij s.'

41. *Barnardo and Fiammetta* (1595, lost). '28 of octobre 1595 ne—Rd at
barnardo & philameta . . . xxxxij s; 6 of novmbre 1595 Rd at barnardo
. . . xvij s; 19 of novmbre 1595 Rd at barnardo . . . vj s; 3 of desmbre
1595 Rd at barnardo . . . vij s; 26 of desembre 1595 Rd at barnardo . . .
lviij s; 20 of Jeneway 1595 Rd at barnardo & phiameta . . . xj s; 12 of
aprelle ester munday Rd at barnardo & fiameta . . . xxx s.'

42. *A Toy to Please Chaste Ladies* (1595, lost). '14 of novembre 1595 ne—Rd
at a toye to please my ladey . . . lj s; 21 of novmbre 1595 Rd at a toye
to please chaste ladeyes . . . xxj s; 31 of novmbre 1595 —Rd at the toye to
please chaste ladeyes . . . xij s; 10 of Jeneway 1595 Rd at a toye to please
chaste ladeys . . . xviij s; 13 of aprell 1596 Rd at a toye to please chaste
ladeys . . . xxxix s; 9 of June 1596 Rd at the chaste ladye . . . xviij s; 12 of
July 1596 Rd at the toye . . . x s; 8 of novmbre 1596 —Rd at the toye . . .
xiij s; 27 of novmbre 1596 Rd at the toye . . . xj s.'

43. *Henry V* (1595, lost).[48] '28 of novembre 1595 ne—Rd at harey the v . . .
iij^{li} vj s; 2 of desembre 1595 Rd at hary the v . . . xxxv^{s}; 8 of desembre
1595 —Rd at hary the v . . . xxxxiij s; 16 of desembre 15695 Rd at hary
the v . . . xxix s; 28 of desembre 1595 —Rd at harye the v . . . lvj s; 5 of
Jeneway 1595 Rd at harey the v . . . xxvj s; 19 of Jeneway 1595 Rd at
harye the v . . . xx s; 6 of febreary 1595 Rd at hary the 5 . . . xviij s; 24 of
aprell 1596 Rd at hary the v . . . xv^{s}; 26 of maye 1596 Rd at hary
the v . . . xxiij s; 17 of June 1596 Rd at hary the v . . . xxvij s; 10 of

ready for the press before 1597 though not actually printed for another three years. That would
strengthen its assocation with the *Diary*'s '*Disguises*' of 1595.
[48] The spelling of the name is characteristic of Henslowe. His 'harey the vj' (*Diary* p. 16) was his note
of what is now taken to be Shakespeare's *Henry VI* Part 1. It is unlikely that this *Henry V* is *The
Famous Victories of Henry V*, as assumed by the *Diary* editors. The *Famous Victories* was published
in 1598, its title-page ascribing it exclusively to the Queen's Men. Moreover its publisher entered it
in the Stationers' Register in 1594, which does not fit a play first staged by the Admiral's as 'ne' at
the end of 1595. The *Famous Victories*' publication in 1598, four years after the text was registered,
may suggest a publisher trying to cash in on the popularity of the Admiral's more recent play.
Knutson conjectures that *The Famous Victories* might have been staged by the Queen's Men at the
Swan in 1595 and then acquired by the Admiral's, but the 'ne' date of 25 Nov. 1595 is too soon for that.

July 1596 Rd at hary the v . . . xiiij s; 15 of July 1596 Rd at hary the
v . . . xxij s; (apparel inventory 10 March 1598) j payer of hosse for thye
Dowlfen; (inventory of lost items, 10 March 1598), Harey the fyftes
dublet. Harey the fyftes vellet gowne; Harey the v. velvet gowne;
(apparel inventory 13 March 1598) Harye the v. satten dublet, layd
with gowld lace.'

44. *The Welshman* (1594, lost). '29 of novembre 1595 Rd at the welche
man . . . vijs.' [old?].[49]

45. *Chinon of England* (1595, lost). '3 of Jeneway 1595 ne—Rd at chinone
of Ingland . . . l s; 12 of Jeneway 1595 —Rd at chynon of Ingland . . .
l s; 21 of Jeneway 1595 Rd at chinon of Ingland . . . xxxiij s; 27 of
Jeneway 1595 Rd at chinon . . . xxj s; 11 of febreary 1595 Rd at chinon of
Ingland . . . xx^s; 23 of febreary 1595 Rd at chinone . . . lvj s; 22 of aprell
1596 Rd at chinon . . . xx s; 2 of maye 1596 —Rd at chinon . . . xx s; 16 of
maye 1596 —Rd at chynone . . . xxxiij s; 27 of maye 1596 Rd at chinone
. . . ix s; 1 of June 1596 Rd at Chinone of Ingland . . . iij^s; 27 of octobre
1596 Rd at chynon . . . lij s; 2 of novmbre 1596 Rd at chinone of Ingland
. . . xvij s; 10 of novmbre 1596 Rd at chinon . . . x s.'[50]

46. *Pythagoras* (1595, lost). '16 of Jeneway 1595 ne—Rd at pethageros . . .
iiij li j s; 23 of Jeneway 1595 Rd at pethagorus . . . xxxvj; 28 of
Jeneway 1595 Rd at pethagoros . . . xxx^s; 9 of febreary 1595 —Rd at
pethagores . . . xx^s; 15 of febreary 1595 —Rd at pethagores . . . xxxv^s; 23
of febreary 1595 shroft tewsday Rd at pethagores . . . xxxiiij s; 21 of
aprell 1596 Rd at pethagorus . . . xviij s; 4 of maye 1596 Rd at
pethagorus . . . xx s; 22 of maye 1596 —Rd at pethagoros . . . xxvij s;
31 of maye whittsenmunday Rd at pethagores . . . iij^{li}; 15 of June 1596
Rd at pethagores . . . xxiij^s; 14 of July 1596 Rd at pethagores . . . xxij s;
Lent unto the company the 16 of maye 1598 to bye v boockes of
martine slather called ij partes of hercolus & focas & pethagores &
elyxander & lodicke wch laste boocke he hath not yet delyverd the
some of . . . vij^{li}; (*Note of all suche bookes as belong to the Stocke, and
such as I have bought since the 3d of March 1598*) Pethagores.'

[49] This seems unlikely to be the same as *The Famous Wars of Henry I and the Prince of Wales, or The
Welshman's Prize*, for which Chettle, Drayton and Dekker were paid in full in March 1598. But its
one entry was not as a 'ne' play, and it never reappeared in Henslowe's day-by-day records.
[50] An entry in the SR on 20 Jan. 1596 to Gosson and Danter, is for '*a booke intituled the firste parte of
the famous historye of Chinan of England*', but no copy survives unless the SR entry was actually for
Richard Middleton's 'Famous Historie of Chinon of England', not a play, printed by Danter in
1597. Greg, *Bibliography* II. 968, dismisses the idea that it might be Part I of the play, partly because
it would have to have been rushed into print with quite exceptional speed.

47. <u>2 *The Seven Days of the Week*</u> (1595, lost). '22 of Jenewary 1595 ne—Rd
at the 2 wecke . . . iij li; 26 of Jenewary 1595 Rd at the 2 weake . . .
xxiiij s.'

48. <u>*Old Fortunatus*</u> (Dekker, 1595? quarto). SR 20 Feb. 1600, "*a commedie
called Old Fortunatus in his newe lyverie*, Q1 'THE | Pleasant Comedie
of | Old Fortunatus. | As it was plaied before the Queenes | *Majestie
this Christmas, by the Right* | Honourable the Earle of Notting- |
ham, Lord high Admirall of Eng- | land his Servants. | *LONDON* |
Printed by S. S. for William Aspley, dwelling in | Paules Church-
yard at the signe of the | Tygers head. 1600.'[51] '3 of febreary 1595 Rd
at the j per of fortewnatus . . . iij li; 10 of febreary 1595 Rd at
fortunatus . . . xxxx^s; 20 of febreary 1595 Rd at Fortunatus . . . xxij^s;
14 of aprell 1596 Rd at fortunatus . . . xviij s; 11 of maye 1596 Rd at
fortunatus . . . xviij s; 24 of maye 1596 Rd at Fortunatus . . . xiiij s;
the ixth of November [1599] Receved of phillipp Hinchlow to pay
Thomas Deckker in earnest of abooke cald the hole hystory of
Fortunatus xxxx^s by me Thomas downton . . . xxxx^s; Lent unto
Thomas dickers the 24 of novmbre 1599 in earneste of his Boocke
called the wholle history of fortewnatus the some of . . . iij^{li} wittnes
John: Shaa; Receaved of Mr Henshlowe this xxxth of novembre 1599
to pay M^r deckers in full payment of his booke of fortunatues . . . xx^s
By me Robt Shaa; Lent unto Thomas dickers at the A poynt ment of
Robart shawe the 31 of novmbre 1599 wch I borrowed of m^r greffen
for the altrenge of the boocke of the wholl history of fortewnatus
the some of . . . xx^s; Received of Mr Hinchlow for the use of the
Company x^{li} For to by thinges for Fortunatus . . . x^{li} By me Thomas
downton; pd unto m^r deckers the 12 of desembre 1599 for the eande
of fortewnatus for the corte at the a poyntment of Robart shawe the
some of . . . xxxx^s;[52] (property inventory 10 March 1598) j tree of
gowlden apelles' [old?].

49. <u>*The Blind Beggar of Alexandria*</u> (Chapman, 1595, quarto). SR 15 August
1598, '*Ent. W. Jones (provided it belong to no other man)*: The Blynde
Begger of Alexandrya'. Q1 'THE BLINDE | begger of Alexan- |dria, most
pleasantly discour- | *sing his variable humours* | in disguised shapes full

---

[51] The speedy printing and the Register's note '*in his newe lyverie*' indicate that the text was that of
Dekker's revision, completed at the end of Nov. 1599. The original play may have been old, since it
was not recorded as 'ne' at its first performance by the company in 1596, though it did take a lot of
money.

[52] This rewrite for a court performance heralding their new playhouse's name anticipates by twelve
days Henslowe and Alleyn signing the lease for the Fortune on 24 December.

of | *conceite and pleasure.* | As it hath beene sundry times | *publickly acted in London.* | by the right honorable the *Earle* | *of Nottingham, Lord high Ad-* | mirall his servants. | By George Chapman: Gentleman. | *Imprinted at London for William* | Iones, dwelling at the signe of the | *Gun, neere Holburne Conduict.* | *1598.*' '12 of february 1595 ne—Rd at the blind beger of elexandrea iiij^{li}; 16 of febreary 1595 Rd at the blind beager . . . iiij^{li} vj^{s}; 19 of febreary 1595 Rd at the blind beager . . . liij s; 22 of Febreary 1595 Shrove monday —Rd at the blind beager xxxvj s; 26 of febreary 1595 Rd at the blind beager . . . iiij^{li}; 15 of aprell 1596 Rd at the blynd beger . . . xxxx s; 26 of aprell 1596 Rd at the blind beger . . . xxxx s; 3 of maye 1596 Rd at the blinde beger . . . xxxv^{s}; 13 of maye 1596 Rd at blind beger . . . xxxx s; 18 of maye 1596 Rd at beger . . . xxxxix s; 3 of June 1596 Rd at the blinde beager . . . xxxxj s; 25 of June 1596 —Rd at the beager . . . xix s; 5 of July 1596 Rd at the beager . . . xvij s; 6 of novmbre 1596 Rd at the beager . . . xxx^{s}; 12 of novmbre 1596 Rd at the beager . . . xvj s; 2 of desembre 1596 Rd at the beager . . . xx s; 10 of desembre 1596 Rd at the beager . . . x s; 23 of desembre 1596 Rd at the beager . . . iij s; dd unto the littell tayller at the apoyntment of the companye the 2 of maye 1601 to bye divers thinges for the playe of – the blind begger of elexsandrea . . . iij^{li}; dd unto Radford the littell tayller the 5 of maye 1601 at the apoyntment of the companye to bye divers thinges for the playe of the blind begger of elexsandrea the some of . . . xxxx^{s}; Lent unto the littell tayller the 8 of maye 1601 at the apoyntment of the company to bye thinges for the blind begger of elexsandrea some x s; pd unto the cope lace man for iiij score ownce of cope lace at x d & ownce for the manes gowne & A sewte for the blind begger of elexsandria the some of . . . iij^{li} xiij^{s} 4^{d}.'

50. *Julian the Apostate* (1596, lost). '29 of aprell 1596 ne—Rd at Julian the apostata . . . xxxxvij s; 10 of maye 1596 —Rd at Julian apostata . . . xxvj s; 20 of maye 1596 Rd at Julyan apostata . . . xiiij s.'

51. *1 Tamar Cham* (1592? lost). '6 of maye 1596 ne—Rd at tambercame . . . xxxxvij s; 12 of maye 1596 Rd at tambercame . . . xxxxv s; 17 of maye 1596 Rd at tambercame . . . xxxxvj s; 25 of maye 1596 Rd at tambercame . . . xx s; 5 of June 1596 Rd at tambercame . . . xxviij s; 10 of June 1596 Rd at tambercame . . . xxviij s; 19 of June 1596 Rd at j parte of tambercame . . . xxxvj s; 26 of June 1596 Rd at j parte of tambercame . . . xxx s; 8 of July 1596 Rd at j parte of tambercame . . . xiiij s; 13 of novmbre 1596 Rd at tambercame . . . xvij s; pd unto my

sonne EAlleyn at the A poynt ment of the company for his Boocke of tambercam the 2 of octobre 1602 the some of . . . xxxx s.'[53]

52. *Phocas* (1596, lost). '19 of maye 1596 ne—Rd at tragedie of Focasse . . . xxxxv^s; 23 of maye 1596 Rd at tragedies of Focasse . . . xxxix s; 4 of June 1596 Rd at the tragedie of focas . . . xxxj s; 16 of June 1596 Rd at Focase . . . xx^s; 22 of June 1596 Rd at focas . . . l s; 5 of July 1596 —Rd at focasse . . . xxij^s; 17 of July 1596 Rd at focas . . . xxix s; Lent unto the company the 16 of maye 1598 to bye v boockes of martine slather called ij partes of hercolus & focas & pethagores & elyxander & lodicke wch laste boocke he hath not delyverd the some of . . . vij^{li}; (*Note of all suche bookes as belong to the Stocke, and such as I have bought since the 3d of March 1598*) Focasse.'

53. *2 Tamar Cham* (1592, lost).[54] '11 of June 1596 ne—Rd at 2 parte of tambercame . . . iij^{li}; 20 of June 1596 Rd at 2 parte of tmbercame . . . xxxv s; 27 of June 1596 Rd at 2 parte of tambercame . . . xx s; 8 of July 1596 Rd at 2 par of tambercame . . . xxiij^s.'

54. *Troy* (1596, lost). '22 of June 1596 ne—Rd at troye . . . iij^{li} ix s; 2 of Julyye 1596 Rd at troye . . . xxiiij^s; 7 of July 1596 —Rd at troye . . . xxix s; 16 of July 1596 Rd at troye . . . xxj s.'

55. *Paradox* (1596, lost). '1 of July 1596 ne—Rd at paradox . . . xxxxv^s.'

56. *The Tinker of Totnes* (1596, lost). '18 of July 1596 ne—Rd at the tynker of totnes . . . iij li.'

57. *Vortigern* (1596, lost).[55] 'lent unto Jeames donstall for to bye thinges for the playe of valteger . . . v^{li}; lent unto marten slater to by coper lace & frenge for the playe of valteger the 28 of novmbre 1596 . . . xxxx s; lent unto marten slater the 29 of novmbre 1596 to by for the play of valteger lace & other thinges . . . xxv^s; 4 of desembre 1596 ne—Rd at valteger . . . l s; 8 of desembre 1596 —Rd at valteger xxxv^s; 16 of desembre 1596 Rd at valteger . . . xxxv^s; 21 of desembre 1596 —Rd at valteger . . . xxv^s; 24 of

---

[53] This final payment must have been made when the playbook was transferred to Worcester's at the Rose, since it appears in Henslowe's list of that company's outgoings. Forty shillings was the usual payment for an old licensed playbook. A 'plot of The First parte of Tamar Cham', written for the Admiral's revival in 1602 judging by the cast list, was printed by George Steevens in his *Variorum* edition of Shakespeare, 1803. The original is now lost, but Steevens's transcript seems reliable.

[54] Despite its 'ne' marking here for the Admiral's, Part 2 had already been staged as 'ne' on 28 April 1592 by Strange's, with six performances in all, some of them probably of Part 1.

[55] Once confused with Middleton's *Hengist*, a name Alleyn gave to this play, it must have covered the same events in early English history. The entry for 22 June 1597 called it 'henges'. But unless Middleton chose to rewrite this older play in about 1615 for the King's Men, it is unlikely that the two were related.

desembre 1596 Rd at valteger . . . xij s; 39[56] of desembre 1596 Rd at valteger . . . xxij s; 1 of Jenewary 1596 Rd at valteger . . . xxxxv^s; 8 of Jeneway 1597 Rd at valteger xij s; 21 of Jeneway 1597 Rd at valteger xij s; 5 ffebreary 1597 tt at valteger . . . 01 09 05–13 – 09; 12 marche 1597 tt at valteger . . . 00 18 09 01 – 04; 2 Aprelle 1597 tt at valteger . . . 00 04 01–01 – 00; 22 June 1597 tt at henges . . . 00 06 00 – 11 – 06; pd at the Apoyntment of the company unto my sonne EAlleyn for A Boocke called vortiger the 20 of November 1601 the some of . . . xxxx^s; (apparel inventory 10 March 1598) a gercken for Valteger; (apparel inventory 13 March 1598) Vartemar sewtte.'

58. *Captain Thomas Stukeley* (1596, quarto). SR 11 August 1600. Q 1605: 'THE | Famous Historye of | the life and death of Captaine | *Thomas Stukeley*. | With his marriage to Alderman | Curteis Daughter, and valiant ending | of his life at the Battaile of | ALCAZAR. | *As it hath beene Acted.* | Printed for Thomas Pavyer, and are to be sold at | his shop at the entrance into the | Exchange, 1605.' 'Lent more the 8 of desembre 1596 for stewtleyes hosse . . . iij^{li}; 11 of desembre 1596 ne—Rd at stewtley . . . xxxx s; 14 of desembre 1596 —Rd at stewtley . . . xxxx^s; 28 of desembre 1596 Rd at stewtley . . . iij^{li} iiij s; 10 of Janeary 1597 —Rd at stewtley . . . xxviij s; 20 of Janeary 1597 Rd at stewtley . . . xj s; 10 Febreary 1597 tt at stewtley . . . 00 18 01.01 – 00; 15 marche 1597 tt at stewtley . . . 01 05 00–00 – 00; 14 Aprell 1597 tt at stewtley . . . 00 17 00 – 12 – 00; 18 Maye 1597 tt at stewtley . . . 01 12 01 – 17 – 00; 27 June 1597 —tt at stewtley . . . 00 14 00 – 01 – 06.'

59. *Nebuchadnezzar* (1596, lost). '19 of desembre 1596 ne—Rd at nabucadonizer . . . xxx^s; 22 of desembre 1596 Rd at nabucadonizer . . . xxvj s; 27 of desembre 1596 crismas day —Rd at nabucadonizer iij^{li} viij s; 4 of Jeneway 1597 Rd at nabucadonizer . . . xvj s; 12 of Janeary 1597 Rd at nabycadnazer . . . xiij s; 19 of Janeary 1597 Rd at nabucadonyzer . . . x s; 26 Janeary 1597 tt at Nabucadonizer . . . 0 09 02 00 – 03; 21 marche 1597 tt at nabucadnazer . . . 00 05 00–00 – 03.'

60. *That Will Be Shall Be* (1596, lost). '30 of desembre 1596 ne— Rd at that wilbe shalbe . . . l s; 3 of Jeneway 1597 —Rd at that wilbe shalbe . . . xxxxij s; Rd at the second time of playinge that wilbe shalbe the 4 of Janeary 1597 the some of . . . xxxx s;[57] 6 of Jeneway 1597 Rd at that wilbe shalbe . . . xxxxij s; 13 of Janeway 1597 Rd at that wilbe

---

[56] Three plays dated 28, 29 and 30 December had their dates corrected to 27, 28 and 29, but the '3' for the last entry was left unaltered.

[57] This entry appears in a separate listing along with three other performances, the first of *Jeronimo, Alexander and Lodowick*, and *A Woman Hard to Please*. All these other three were 'ne'

shalbe . . . xxij s; 18 of Janeway 1597 Rd at that wilbe shalbe . . . xv^s; 24 Janeway 1597 Rd at that wilbe shalbe . . . o 17 00.19 – 07; 2 Febreary 1597 tt at what wilbe shalbe . . . 01 18 01 03 – 00; 3 marche 1597 tt at what wilbe shalbe . . . 00 09 00 16 – 00; 6 Aprelle 1597 tt at what wilbe & shalbe . . . 00 07 03–00 – 08; 30 Aprelle 1597 tt at what wilbe shalbe . . . 00 14 00 – 17 – 08; 6 June 1597 —tt at what wilbe shalbe . . . 00 10 00 – 16 – 00; 5 July 1597 tt at what wilbe shalbe . . . 00 10 02 – 00 – 00.'

61. *The Spanish Tragedy (Jeronimo*, Thomas Kyd, 1587, quarto).^{58} SR 6 Oct. 1592; Q1592? (lost); Q1 'THE | SPANISH TRAGE- | die, Containing the lamentable | end of *Don Horatio*, and *Bel-imperia* : | with the pittifull death of | old *Hieronimo*. | Newly corrected and amended of such grosse faults as | passed in the first impression. | AT LONDON | Printed by *Edward Allde*, for | Edward White.' SR 18 Dec. 1592, '*Ordered in full Court that, whereas E. White has printed The Spanish Tragedy belonging to A. Jeffes, and Jeffes has printed the tragedy of Arden of Kent belonging to White, all copies be confiscated to the use of the poor of the Company, that each pay a fine of 10s., and that the question of their imprisonment be referred to the Master, Warden, and Assistants.*" Q2 'THE | SPANISH TRAGE- | die, Containing the lamentable | END OF DON HORATIO, AND | *Bel-imperia :* with the pittifull death | of old *Hieronimo*. | NEWLY CORRECTED AND | amended of such grosse faults as passed in | the first impression. | LONDON, | Printed by Abell Ieffes, and are | to be sold by Edward White. | 1594.'; Q3 1599; Q4 'THE | Spanish Tragedie : | Containing the lamen- | table end of *Don Horatio*, and *Bel-imperia :* | with the pittifull death of olde | *Hieronimo*. | Newly corrected, amended, and enlarged with | new additions of the Painters part, and | others, as it hath of late been | divers times acted. | Imprinted at London by W. W. for | *T. Pavier*, and are to be solde at the | signe of the Catte and Parrats | neare the Exchange. | 1602.' Q5 1603; Q6 1611; Q7 1615; Q8 1618; Q9 1623; Q10 1633. '7 of Jeneway 1597 ne^{59} Rd at Joronymo . . . iij^{li}; Rd at Joronymo the 7 of Janeway 1597 in perte of payment . . . vij^{li}; 11 of Janeway 1597 —Rd at

---

performances. That must be why the entry specified the second performance for *That Will Be Shall Be*, even though it gives the date as 4 rather than 3 January.

^{58} For the complicated story of the different texts the name *'Jeronimo'* might have been applied to, see Chapter 5, p. 186. The play printed in 1605 as 'The First Part of Jeronimo', a prequel to Kyd's work, has been excluded from this list of the Admiral's repertory for the reasons given there.

^{59} This mark has been erased at some point by an unknown hand. It is retained here because the exceptional amount of three pounds that Henslowe notes fits well with the high takings at most of the other 'ne' performances.

Joronymo . . . xxxx s; 17 of Janewary 1597 —Rd at Joronymo . . . xx s;
22 of Janewarye 1597 Rd at Joronymo . . . xix s; —tt at Joronymo . . .
01 04 01.15 – 06; 9 Febreary 1597 tt at Joronymo . . . 00 17 04 15 – 02;
8 marche 1597 tt at JoRonymo . . . 01 01 00.03 – 04; 21 Aprell 1597 tt
at Jeronymo . . . 00 17 00 – 03 – 04; 4 maye 1597 tt at Jorenymo 00 11
03 – 14 – 00; 25 maye 1597 tt at Joronymo . . . 00 19 00 – 14 – 06; 20
June 1597 —tt at Joronemo . . . 00 14 00 – 00 – 00; 19 July 1597 tt at
Jeronemo . . . 00 01 00 –13 – 01; 11 octobre 1597[60] tt at Joroneymo . . .
[illegible] 01 – 13 – 00;[61] Lent unto m^r alleyn the 25 of septembre 1601
to lend unto Bengemen Johnson upon hn writting of his adicians in
geronymo the some of . . . xxxx^s; Lent unto bengemy Johnsone at the
A poyntment of EAlleyn & w^m birde the 22 of June 1602 in earneste
of A Boocke called Richard crockbacke & for new adicyons for
Jeronymo the some of . . . x^{li,} [old].

62. *Alexander and Lodowick* (1596, lost). '14 of Janewary 1597 ne—Rd at
elexsander & lodwicke . . . lv^s; Rd at elexsander & ladwicke the
14 of Janewarye the fyrste time yt wasse played 1597 in perte . . . v^{li};
11 febreary 1597 ne —tt at elexsander & lodwecke . . . 03 05 00 17 – 00;[62]
12 Febreary 1597 tt at elesander & lodwicke . . . 01 14 09 13 – 00;
5 marche 1597 tt at elexsander & lodwicke . . . 01 15 00 13 – 00;
9 marche 1597 tt at lodwicke . . . 01 16 07.04 – 00; 20 marche 1597 tt
at elexsander & lodwicke 00 17 00–04 – 02; 29 marche 1597 Easter
tewsday tt at elexsander & lodwicke . . . 02 01 00–04 – 03; 5 Aprelle
1597 tt at elexsander & lodwicke . . . 01 02 00–03 – 05; 12 Aprell 1597 tt
at elexsander & lodwicke . . . 00 14 03 – 00 – 01; 27 Aprell 1597 Rd at
elexsander & lodwick . . . 01 02 00 – 00 – 00; 9 Maye 1597 —tt
at lodwicke & elexsand . . . 00 14 00 – 00 – 00; 17 Maye 1597 whittsone
T tt at elexsander & lodwicke . . . 03 00 00 – 03 – 04; 28 Maye 1597 tt
at elexsander & lodwicke . . . 00 13 01 – 10 – 00; 29 June 1597 S petters
daye tt at elexsander & lodwick . . . 01 02 00 – 14 – 00; 15 July 1597 tt
at elexsander & lodwicke . . . 00 08 00 – 13 – 00; Lent unto the
company the 16 of maye 1598 to bye v boockes of martine slather
called ij pertes of hercolus & focas & pethagores & elyxander &
lodicke wch laste boocke he hath not yet delyverd the some of . . . vij^{li};

[60] Henslowe here adds a marginal note 'the xj of octobe be gane my lord admirals & my lord of
penbrockes men to playe at my howse 1597' (*Diary*, p. 60).

[61] Everard Guilpin, *Skialethaia* (1598) Satire I line 92, offers confirmation that *The Spanish Tragedy*
was on stage in London just before 1597. In the same poem a few lines previously he alludes to
Shakespeare's *Richard II* (1595).

[62] This is the only case where a play was entered with two successive marks of 'ne'. See Chapter 3, p. 94.

pd unto marteyne slawghter the 18 of July for a boocke called elexsander & lodwicke the some of . . . xx^s; Lent unto Jewbe the 31 of marche 1598 to bye divers thinges for elexander & lode wicke the some of . . . v^{li}; (*Note of all suche bookes as belong to the Stocke, and such as I have bought since the 3d of March 1598*) Elexsander and Lodwicke.'

63. *A Woman Hard to Please* (1596, lost). '27 Janewary 1597 ne —tt at womane hard to please . . . 2 11 06 07 – 08; Rd at a womon hard to please the 27 of Janewary 97 . . . iiij^{li}; 29 Janeware 1597 tt at womon hard to please . . . 02 03 04–14 – 00; 1 febreary 1597 tt at womones hard to pleasse . . . 01 05 02 11 – 02; 4 febreary 1597 tt at womon hard to pleasse . . . 01 08 04–03 – 00; 8 febreary 1597 tt at womon hard to please . . . 01 09 01 02 – 01; 7 marche 1597 —tt at A womon hard to pleasse . . . 01 05 06.02 – 01; 28 marche 1597 Easter munday —tt at a womon hard to pleasse . . . 01 11 00–00 – 00; 8 Aprelle 1597 tt at womon hard to pleasse . . . 00 05 03–00 – 00; 16 Aprell 1597 tt at womon hard to please . . . 00 05 03 – 00 – 00; 10 Maye 1597 tt at womon hard to plesse . . . 00 17 03 – 10 – 00; 27 Maye 1597 tt at womon hard to pleasse . . . 00 05 00 – 00 – 00.'

64. *Osric* (1597? lost). '3 febreary 1597 Shrove munday —tt at oserycke . . . 01 09 03 02 – 01; 7 February 1597 —tt at oserycke . . . 00 14 07 16 – 00; [Worcester's] Lent unto the companye the 20 of septmbre 1602 to paye unto m^r smythe in perte of payment of of A Boocke called marshalle oserecke some of . . . iiij^{li}; pd unto Thomas hewode the 30 of septmbre 1602 in fulle payment for his Boocke of oserecke the some of . . . iiij^{li}; pd at the apoynttment of the companye the 3 of novmbre 1602 unto the tayller for the mackynge of the sewte of oserocke the some . . . xxvj s.'^{63}

65. *Guido* (1597, lost). 'lent unto my sonne for to by sylckes & other things for guido the 14 of marche . . iiij^{li} ix s; 19 marche 1597—ne—tt at guido . . . 02 00 00–03 – 01; 22 marche 1597 tt at guido . . . 01 04 00–03 – 00; 30 marche 1597 tt at guido . . . 02 17 00–00 – 00; 4 Aprelle 1597 —tt at guido . . . 01 08 00–04 – 03; 23 Aprell 1597 tt at guido . . . 00 16 01 – 11 – 00; (property inventory 10 March 1598) j tome of Guido; (apparel inventory 13 March 1598) j cloth clocke of russete with coper lace, called Guydoes clocke.'^{64}

---

^{63} This first recorded performance was not marked 'ne', and the play seems to have been abandoned after only two performances in 1597. The Heywood version that Worcester's paid for in 1602 may have been a rewrite.

^{64} Webster claimed to have written a play of this name, but he seems too young to have written this version, since he was born in 1580 and entered the Middle Temple in August 1598. Conceivably he revised it once he became a member of the Henslowe writing teams. The Melbourne manuscript contains a page in Webster's hand which may either be from *Guido* or from Marlowe's *The Guise*

66. *Five Plays in One* (possibly Heywood, 1597, lost). '7 Aprelle 1597 ne—tt
at v playes in one . . . 02 01 00–18 – 01; 15 Aprell 1597 tt at v playes
in one . . . 01 08 02 – 00 – 00; 20 Aprell 1597 tt at v playes in one
. . . 00 19 00 – 07 – 01; 25 Aprell 1597 —tt at v playes in one . . . 01 13
01 – 00 – 00; 6 Maye 1597 tt at v playes in one pd at the apoynttment
of the companye the 3 of novmbre . . . 00 16 00 – 03 – 00; 14 Maye
1597 tt at v playes in one . . . 00 07 00 – 00 – 00; 23 Maye 1597 —tt at
v playes in one . . . 01 00 03 – 00 – 01; 10 June 1597 tt at v playes in
one . . . 00 11 03 – 01 – 00; 28 June 1597 tt at v playes in one . . . 01 00
00 – 13 – 11; 27 July 1597 tt at v playes in one . . . 00 14 03 – 14 – 00;
(property inventory 10 March 1598) Argosse head; Cupedes bowe.'[65]
67. *Time's Triumph and Fortune's* (1593? lost). '13 Aprell 1597 tt at times
triumpe & fortus . . . 01 05 01 – 00 – 03' [old].[66]
68. *Uther Pendragon* (1597, lost). '29 Aprell 1597 ne—tt at vterpendragon
. . . 02 14 01 – 01 – 03; 3 Maye 1597 tt at vterpendagon . . . 01 05 00 –
01 – 00; 7 Maye 1597 tt at pendragon . . . 00 14 00 – 04 – 00; 12 Maye
1597 tt at pendragon . . . 0 17 00 – 00 – 00; 16 Maye 1597 whittsone
munday —tt at pendragon . . . 02 19 00 – 14 – 00; 2 June 1597 tt at
pendragon . . . 00 16 00 – 04 – 06; 13 June 1597 —tt at pendragon . . .
01 00 00 – 00 – 00; (*inventory of 10 March 1598 for Clownes Sewtes and
Hermetes Sewtes, with dievers other sewtes*) merlen gowne and cape.'[67]
69. *An Humorous Day's Mirth* (*Comedy of Humours*). (Chapman, 1597,
quarto). Q1 'A pleasant Comedy | entituled: *An Humerous dayes* |
Myrth. | As it hath beene sundrie times publikely acted by | the right
honourable the Earle of Not- | tingham Lord high Admirall | his
servants. | By G. C. | AT LONDON | *Printed by Valentine Syms* : | 1599.'
'11 Maye 1597 ne—tt at the comodey of umers . . . 02 03 00 – 13 – 00;
19 Maye 1597 tt at the comody of umers . . . 02 15 00 – 00 – 00;
24 Maye 1597 tt at comody of umers . . . 02 18 00 – 03 – 02; 31 Maye 1597
tt at the umers . . . 03 04 01 – 03 – 00; 4 June 1597 tt at the comodey
of umers . . . 03 06 02 – 14 – 06; 7 June 1597 tt at the comodey of
umers . . . 03 10 00 – 00 – 00; 11 June 1597 tt at the umers . . . 02 18 00
– 00 – 00; 17 June 1597 tt at comodey of umers . . . 02 10 01 – 04 – 01; 21
June 1597 midsomer daye tt at the comodey of umers . . . 03 00 00 –

(*Massacre at Paris*). See *The Works of John Webster*, ed. David Gunby, David Carnegie and Antony
Hammond, 3 vols., Cambridge, I. 126–28.
[65] The *Diary* editors conjecture that these items may belong to this play.
[66] Various attempts have been made to link this title to known plays, without any clear success.
Lacking a 'ne' entry, it may have been revived from an older repertory just this once.
[67] Merlin's gown is assumed by the *Diary* editors to belong to this play.

00 – 00; 7 July 1597 tt at Comodey of umers . . . 01 18 02 – 17 – 01; 13 July 1597 tt at comodey of umers . . . 01 10 01 – 11 – 01; 12 (?) octobe 1597 tt at the comodey of umers . . . 2 00 00 – 19 – 0; 4 novembre 1597 tt at umers . . . 00 16 03 – 00 – 14; (*Enventary of the 1598 the 10 of march Clownes Sewtes and Hermetes Sewtes, with dievers other sewtes* Verones sonnes hosse; (apparel inventory 13 March 1598) Labesyas clocke, with gowld buttenes; (*Note of all suche bookes as belong to the Stocke, and such as I have bought since the 3d of March 1598*) . . . The Umers.'

70. *Henry I* (*The Life and Death of Henry I*, 1597, lost).[68] '26 Maye 1597 ne —tt at harey the firste life & deth 02 10 01 – 03 – 09; 30 Maye 1597 tt harey the fyrste life & dethe . . . 00 19 06 – 00 – 00; 8 June 1597 tt at harey the firste liffe & death . . . 00 12 06 – 00 – 00; 14 June 1597 tt at harey the fyrste life & death . . . 00 14 00 – 00 – 00; 24 June 1597 tt at harey the firste . . . 00 14 00 – 00 – 00; 1 July 1597 tt at harey the firste . . . 00 06 01 – 12 – 11.'

71. *Frederick and Basilea* (1597, 'plot').[69] '3 June 1597 ne tt at frederycke & basellia . . . 02 02 01 – 13 – 04; 9 June 1597 tt at fredericke & baselia . . . 01 00 00 – 00 – 00; 18 June 1597 tt at fredericke & basilia . . . 00 11 00 – 14 – 06; 4 July 1597 —tt at fredericke & baselia . . . 01 00 01 – 14 – 06.'

72. *Martin Swart* (1597, lost). '30 June 1597 ne tt at liffe & death of marten swarte . . . 02 08 01 – 11 – 06; 6 July 1597 tt at life & deth of marten swarte . . . 02 10 01 – 13 – 09; 9 July 1597 tt at life & death of marten swarte 01 13 02 – 13 – 01.'

73. *The Witch of Islington* (1596? lost). '14 July 1597 tt at the wiche of Islyngton . . . 01 07 02 – 00 – 00; 28 July 1597 tt at the wiche of Iselyngton . . . 01 08 00 – 13 – 00.'

74. *Sturgeflattery* (1597, lost). '*Note of all such bookes as belong to the Stocke, and such as I have bought since the 3d of March 1598* . . . Sturgflaterey.'

---

[68] An entry for a play called 'the welche man' appears in the *Diary* for 29 November 1595, a day after the 'ne' performance of 'harey the v' (the *Diary* Index omits this entry). The reference compounds the question of the already puzzling dates for 'The famos wares of henry the fyrste & the prynce of walles' as 'ne' on 26 May 1597, and the payment on 13 March 1598 for 'a boocke wher in is a perte of a weallche man written wch they have promised to delyver by the xx day next folowinge' (*Diary*, p. 88). An entry in Alleyn's list of '*all suche bookes as belong to the Stocke, and such as I have bought since the 3d of March 1598*' is for 'Welchmans price' or *Prize*, which the editors of the *Diary* think may be *Henry I*. I suspect there were at least two plays about Henry I, one in 1597 and another in 1598. See *The Famous Wars* below (90).

[69] The 'plot' for *Frederick and Basilea* almost certainly dates from the time of its first staging in June 1597, since Martin Slater, who left the company in July of that year, is named in it, and Richard Jones and Thomas Downton, who were with Pembroke's until August and October of that year, are absent.

75. *Hardicanute* (1597, lost). '19 Octobre 1597 tt at hardicute . . . 00 16 00
– 00 – 1–; 3 novembre 1597 tt at knewtus 00 10– 00 – 14 00; (*Note all
suche bookes as belong to the Stocke, and such as I have bought since the
3d of March 1598*) Hardicanewtes.'[70]

76. *Friar Spendleton* (1597, lost). '31 octobre 1597 ne—tt at fryer spendelton . . . 02 00 01 – 014 – 00; 5 novembre 1597 tt at fryer spendelton
. . . 00 14 01 – 14 – 00; (*Note all suche bookes as belong to the Stocke,
and such as I have bought since the 3d of March 1598*) Frier Pendelton.'

77. *Bourbon* (1597, lost). '2 novembre 1597 tt at burbon . . . 00 16 30 – 12 –
00; (*Note of all such bookes as belong to the Stocke, and such as I have
bought since the 3d of March 1598*) Borbonne.'

78. *The Cobbler of Queenhithe* (1597, lost). 'Lent unto Robarte shawe the
23 of octobre 1597 to by a boocke for the company of my lord
admeralls men & my lord of penbrockes the some of . . . called the
cobler wittnes EAlleyn . . . xxxx^s; layd owt unto Robarte shawe to by a
boocke for the companey the 21 of octobre 1597 the some of . . . called
the cobler wittnes EAlleyn . . . xxxxs; (*Note of all such bookes as belong
to the Stocke, and such as I have bought since the 3d of March 1598*)
Cobler quen hive.'[71]

79. *Branholt* (Haughton, lost). 'lent unto Robarte shaw to by a boocke of
yonge harton the 5 of novembre 1597 the some of . . . x s.'[72]

80. *Alice Pearce* (1597, lost). 'layd owt for the companye to by tafetie &
tynssell for the bodeyes of a womones gowne to playe allce perce of
wch I dd unto the littell tayller the 8 of desembre 1597 . . . xx^s; lent unto
Robart shawe to by cop^r lace of sylver for a payer hosse in alls perce the
10 of desembre 1597 . . . xvjs; layd owt for mackynge allce perces bodeyes
& a payer of yeare sleaves the some of . . . vj s viij d;[73] (*The Enventary of
all the apparell for my* Lord Admiralles men, *tacken the* 10 *of marche*
1598.—*Leaft above in the tier-house in the cheast*) j payer of bodeyes for
Alles Pearce; (*Note of all such bookes as belong to the Stocke, and such as
I have bought since the 3d of March 1598*) Alls Perce.'

---

[70] Unmarked with any 'ne' like its immediate predecessor, this play may have entered the company's
repertory from the dissolved Pembroke's. After this there is only one more notation of a 'ne'
performance (*Friar Spendleton*). This was roughly the time when Pembroke's at the nearby Swan
were closed down. Some of their 'old' plays may have entered the Admiral's repertory along with
some of the players after July 1597.

[71] The payment was the right price for an old playbook. Who it was bought from is not stated. Since
Alleyn witnessed the purchase it clearly was not one of his. Most likely it came from Pembroke's.

[72] Entered immediately after *The Cobbler*, and witnessed by Alleyn, it is not possible to identify what
play Haughton was being paid for unless it was *Branholt*, for which 'viij y^{r}des of clothe of gowlde
for the womones gowne in bran howlte' was lent on the 26th of the same month.

[73] The first of these two entries for tailoring appears twice, in varying forms, *Diary* pp. 73, 74 and 85.

81. *Black Joan* (1597, lost). (*The Enventary taken of all the properties for my* Lord Admiralles men, *the* 10 *of Marche* 1598.) *Item,* j frame for the heading in Black Jone; (*Note of all such bookes as belong to the Stocke, and such as I have bought since the 3d of March 1598*) Blacke Jonne.'

82. *Mother Redcap* (Drayton and Munday, 1597, lost). 'layde owt the 22 of desembre 1597 for A boocke called mother Readcape to antony munday & m^r drayton . . . iij^{li}; layd owt the 28 of desembre 1597 for the boocke called mother Read cape to antony mundaye . . . v^s; pd unto antony munday & drayton for the laste payment of the Boocke of mother Readcape the 5 of Jeneway 1597 the some of . . . lv^s; (property inventory 10 March 1598) j syne for Mother Readcap; (*Note of all such bookes as belong to the Stocke, and such as I have bought since the 3d of March 1598*) Read Cappe.'

83. *Dido and Aeneas* (1597? lost). 'Layde owte for cop^r lace for the littell boye & for a valle for the boye A geanste the playe of dido & eneus the 3 of Jeneway 1597 . . . xxxix s; lent unto the company when they fyrst played dido at nyght the some of thirtishillynges wch wasse the 8 of Jeneway 1597 I saye . . . xxx s; (*The Enventory taken of all the properties for my* Lord Admiralles men, *the* 10 *of Marche* 1598.) j tome of Dido; (*The Enventorey of all the apparel of the* Lord Admeralles men, *taken the* 13th *of Marche* 1598, *as followeth*:) Dides robe'[74] [old?]

84. *Phaethon* (Dekker, 1598, lost). 'lent unto the company the 15 of Jeneway 1597 to bye a boocke of m^r dicker called fayeton fower pownde I saye lent . . . iiij^{li}; lent unto Thomas dowton for the company to bye a sewte for phayeton & ij Rebates & j fardengalle the 26 of Jeneway 1598 the some of three pownde I saye lent . . . iij^{li}; lent unto Thomas downton the 28 of Janeway 1598 to bye a white satten dublette for phayeton forty shyllenges I saye lent . . . xxxx^s; Lent unto Samwell Rowley the 14 of desembre 1600 to geve unto Thomas dickers for his paynes in fay^{e}ton some of x s / for the corte; Lent unto Samwell Rowley the 22 of desembre 1600 to geve unto Thomas deckers for alterynge of fayton for the corte . . . xxx s; Lent unto w^m Bird the 2 of Jeneway 1600 for divers thinges A bowt A bowt the playe of fayeton for the corte some of . . . xx^s; (*The Enventary of all the apparell for my* Lord Admiralles men, *tacken the* 10 *of marche* 1598) ij leather anteckes cottes with basses, for Fayeton;

---

[74] Most likely Marlowe and Nashe's play, printed in 1594, if the theory that almost all of Marlowe's plays went to the company in 1594 has any value. Greg thought that 'cupedes bowe', also in a 1598 inventory, belongs with this play too. The performance 'at nyght' was presumably for a private event, not at the Rose.

(property inventory 10 March 1598) Fayetones lymes, & Faeton charete; j crown with a sone[75]; (inventory of apparel 10 March 1598) j Faeytone sewte; (*Note of all such bookes as belong to the Stocke, and such as I have bought since the 3d of March 1598*) Phayeton.'

85. *The Downfall of Robert Earl of Huntingdon* (Munday and Chettle, 1598, quarto). SR 1 Dec. 1600. Q1 'THE | DOWNFALL | OF ROBERT, | Earle of Huntington, | AFTERWARD CALLED | Robin Hood of merrie Sherwodde : | *with his love to chaste Matilda, the* | Lord *Fitzwaters* daughter, afterwards | *his faire Maide Marian.* | *Acted by the Right Honourable, the Earle of* | Notingham, Lord high Admirall of | *England, his servants.* | Imprinted at London, for *William Leake,* 1601.' 'layd owt unto antony monday the 15 of febreary 1598 for a playe boocke called the firste perte of Robyne Hoode . . . v^li; Layd owt the 28 of marche 1598 for the licencynge of ij boocke to the m^r of the Revelles called the ij pertes of Robart hoode . . . xiiij s; Lent unto Robart shawe the 18 of novmbre 1598 to lend unto m^r Cheatell upon the mendynge of the firste pert of Robart hoode the some of . . . x^s; Lent unto harey Chettell at the Requeste of Robart shawe the 25 of novmbre 1598 in earneste of his comodey called tys no deseayt to deseve the desever for mendinge of Roben hood.for the corte . . . x^s;[76] (inventory of 10 March 1598 for *Clownes Sewtes and Hermetes Sewtes, with dievers other sewtes*) iiij Herwodes cottes, and iij sogers cottes, and j green gown for Maryan. vj grene cottes for Roben Hoode, and iiij knaves sewtes . . . j hatte for Robin Hoode;[77] (property inventory, 10 March 1598) j shelde, with iij lyones; (apparel inventory, 13 March 1598) Roben Hoodes sewtte . . . the fryers trusse in Roben Hoode; (*Note of all suche bookes as belong to the Stocke, and such as I have bought since the 3d of March 1598*) Roben Hode, 1.'

86. *Englishmen for My Money or A Woman Will Have Her Will* (Haughton, 1598, quarto). SR 3 Aug. 1601' '*a comedy of A woman Will have her Will*'. Q1 'ENGLISH-MEN | For my Money: | OR, | A pleasant Comedy, | called, | A Woman will have her Will. | Imprinted at London by W. White, | dwelling in Cow-Lane. 1616.' Q2 1626, Q3 1631. 'lent

---

[75] A crown adorned by a sun would be apt for a play about Phaeton, who drove the sun-chariot, also noted in this list.

[76] Not enough of the title is given in this entry to tell which of the two parts of the Robin Hood plays the court saw. It is only an assumption that the reference is to Part 1, *The Downfall.*

[77] The green garments for Marian and the six men are clearly for the *Downfall* and *Death* plays; conceivably 'Herwode' was written for 'Sherwode', a name on the title-page of both plays. The shield showing three lions in the list of properties of similar date was probably for Richard I in the same plays (*Diary*, p. 320n). Given the inventory's dating, it is unlikely to have been made for *The Funeral of Richard Coeur de Lion*, since that play was not bought until June.

unto Robarte shawe the 18 of febreary 1598 to paye unto harton for
a comodey called A womon will have her wille the some of . . . xx^s;
Lente unto dowton to paye unto horton in perte of paymente of his
boocke called a woman will have her wille . . . xx s; (*Note of all suche
bookes as belong to the Stocke, and such as I have bought since the 3d of
March 1598*) Woman will have her will.'

87. *The Death of Robert Earl of Huntingdon* (Munday and Chettle, 1598,
quarto). SR 1 Dec. 1600: Q1 'THE | DEATH OF | ROBERT, EARLE | OF
HUNTINGTON. | OTHERWISE CALLED | Robin Hood of merrie Sherwodde:
| *with the lamentable Tragedie of chaste* | MATILDA, his fair maid
MARIAN, | *poysoned at Dunmowe by King* | JOHN. | *Acted by the
Right Honourable, the Earle of* | Notingham, Lord high Admirall of |
England, his servants. | Imprinted at London, for *William* | *Leake*,
1601.' 'lent unto thomas dowton the 20 of febreary 1598 to lende unto
antony mondaye upon his seconde perte of the downefall of earlle
huntyngton surnamed Roben Hoode I saye lent the some of . . . x s;
lent unto Thomas dowton the 25 of febreary 1598 to geve unto chettell
in pert of paymente of the second perte of Robart hoode I saye lent
. . . xx^s; Lent unto Antony mondaye the 28 of febreary 1598 in perte of
paymente of the second perte of Roben Hoode . . . v^s; Lent unto
Robart shawe the 8 of marche 1598 in full paymente of the seconde
perte of the booke called the downfall of Roben hoode the some of
iij^{li} v^s; Layd owt the 28 of marche 1598 for the licencynge of ij boocke
to the m^r of the Revelles called the ij pertes of Robart hoode . . . xiiij s;
(inventory of 10 March 1598 for the *Clownes Sewtes and Hermetes
Sewtes, with dievers other sewtes*) *Item*, iiij Herwodes cottes, and iij
sogers cottes, and j green gown for Maryan. *Item*, vj grene cottes for
Roben Hoode, and iiij knaves sewtes . . . j hatte for Robin Hoode;
(apparel inventory, 13 March 1598) Roben Hoodes sewtte . . . the fryers
trusse in Roben Hoode; (*Note of all suche bookes as belong to the Stocke,
and such as I have bought since the 3d of March 1598*) Roben Hode, 2.'

88. <u>*The Miller*</u> (Robert Lee? >1597, lost). 'Layd owt unto Robarte lee the
22 of febreary 1598 for a boocke called the myller some of . . . xx^s.'[78]

89. <u>*Triplicity of Cuckolds*</u> (Dekker, 1598, lost). 'lent unto Thomas dowten
& Robart [Jube] shaw & Jewebey the j of marche 1598 to bye a
boocke of m^r dickers called the treplesetie of cockowlles the some of

---

[78] Robert Lee, or Leigh, is named in the plot of *The Dead Man's Fortune* of 1590–91 with Richard
Burbage, a 'Darlowe' and a 'b same' who may have been Samuel Rowley. The one pound in
payment must have been for an old playbook in Leigh's possession that Henslowe wanted for
himself. It does not seem to have been a company purchase. Nothing in the records indicates that
the company performed it.

five powndes I say lent . . . v^{li}; (*Note of all suche bookes as belong to the Stocke, and such as I have bought since the 3d of March 1598*) Treangell cockowlls.'

90. *The Famous Wars of Henry I and the Prince of Wales* (Drayton, Dekker, Chettle, 1598, lost).[79] 'a boocke wher in is a perte of a weallche man written wch they have promised to delyver by the xx day next folowinge I saye lent R money . . . xxxx s; lent unto the company to paye drayton & dyckers & chetell ther full payment for the boocke called the famos wares of henry the fyrste & the prynce of walles the some of . . . iiij^{li}; lent at that tyme unto the company for to spend at the Readynge of that boocke at the sonne in new fyshstreate . . . v^{s}; (*Note of all suche bookes as belong to the Stocke, and such as I have bought since the 3d of March 1598*) Welchmans price.'

91. *1 Earl Godwin and his Three Sons* (Drayton, Dekker, Chettle, Wilson, 1598, lost). 'layd owt for the company to bye a boocke of m^{r} drayton & m^{r} dickers m^{r} chettell & m^{r} willsone wch is called goodwine & iij sones fower powndes in perte of paymet the 25 of marche 1598 in Redy mony I saye . . . iiij li; layd owt the same tyme at the tavarne in fyshstreate for good cheare the some of . . . v^{s}; lent unto the company the 30 of marche 1598 in full payment for the boocke of goodwine & his iiij sonnes I saye lent . . . xxxx^{s}; Lent unto thomas dowton the 11 of aprell 1598 to bye tafitie to macke a Rochet for the beshoppe in earlle goodwine . . . xxiiij s.'[80]

92. *2 Earl Godwin and his Three Sons* (Drayton, Chettle, Dekker, Wilson, 1598, lost). 'lent unto m^{r} cheatell & m^{r} dickers the 6 of aprell 1598 upon the boocke of goodwine the 2 pert the some of . . . xx s; lent unto Thomas downton the 6 of June 1598 to leand unto drayton I saye leante . . . x s for the 2 pert of goodwine; lent unto the companey the 10 of June 1598 to paye unto m^{r} drayton willson dickers & cheatell

[79] Drayton and Chettle's play I suspect is different from the previous year's *Henry I*, if only because this play was paid for while it was being written. The reference to 'a weallche man' possibly indicates the growth of a liking for Welsh accents. An entry for 29 Nov. 1595 noting a play called 'the welche man' (*Diary*, p. 33) is probably not about this play.

[80] Immediately following the entry of 30 March noting full payment to Wilson, Dekker, Drayton and Chettle for the first *Goodwin* play is a note of the same four writers getting 40 shillings for 'a boocke called perce of exstone'. The lost 'perce of winschester' (102) does not appear as their 'next boock' until the end of July. Piers of Exton was the killer of Richard II in Shakespeare's play of 1595. Chambers (*Elizabethan Stage* II. 167) pointed out that the amount of the advance would cover a shortage in payments for *2 Goodwin*, and concluded that the name was a mistake for that play. I think it more likely that Shakespeare's play prompted one of the writers to think of Exton as a new subject, but when it never grew into a play Henslowe's advance was silently incorporated into the *2 Goodwin* payments.

in full paymente of the second perte of goodwine l s as foloweth drayton 30ˢ & willson xˢ & cheatell x s some is . . . l s; lent unto Thomas dowton the 26 of June 1598 to by satten to macke ij dubleattes for the 2 perte of goodwine the some of . . . vˡⁱ; (*Note of all suche bookes as belong to the Stocke, and such as I have bought since the 3d of March 1598*) 2 pᵗ of Goodwine.'

93. <u>King Arthur</u> (Hathway, 1598, lost). 'Lent unto the company the 12 of aprell 1598 to paye mʳ hathwaye in fulle payment for his boocke of kynge arthore the some of fower pownde I saye . . . iiijˡⁱ; lent unto Thomas Dowton 2 of maye 1598 to bye a Robe for the playe of the lyfe of arthure in money the some of . . . iijˡⁱ pd; the xiᵗʰ of Aprill Rd of Phillipp Hinchlow twenty shillings in earnesst of abooke cald the Lyfe of Artur king of England to be delivered one thursday next following after the datte herof I saye Rd xx s by me Ri: Hathwaye; (*Note of all suche bookes as belong to the Stocke, and such as I have bought since the 3d of March 1598*) King Arthur, life and death.'

94. <u>1 Black Bateman of the North</u> (Wilson, Drayton, Dekker, Chettle, 1598, lost).[81] 'lent unto cheattell upon the playe called blacke batmone of the northe the some of xx s wittnes Thomas dowton; Bowght of mʳ willsones drayton & dickers & cheatell for the companey a boocke called blacke battmane of the northe the 22 of maye 1598 wᶜʰ cost sixe powndes I saye layd owt for them . . . vjˡⁱ; lent unto Thomas dowton the 13 of June 1598 to bye divers thinges for black batmane of the northe the some of five pownd I saye lent . . . vˡⁱ; lent unto Thomas dowton the 14 of June 1598 to bye divers thinges for black batmane of the northe the some . . . iijˡⁱ; (*Note of all suche bookes as belong to the Stocke, and such as I have bought since the 3d of March 1598*) Blacke Battman.'

95. <u>Love Prevented</u> (Porter, 1598, lost). 'lent unto the company the 30 of maye 1598 to by A boocke called love prevented the some of fower powndes dd to Thomas dowton iiijˡⁱ mʳ porter.'

96. <u>The Funeral of Richard Coeur De Lion</u> (Wilson, Chettle, Munday, Drayton, 1598, lost). 'lent unto mr willsone the 13 of June 1598 upon A bocke called Richard cordelion funeralle . . . vˢ; lent unto cheattell the 14 of June 1598 in earneste of A boock called Richard cordeliones funeralle . . . vˢ; lent unto Cheattell the 15 of June 1598 in earneste of ther boocke called the funeral of Richard curdelion . . . vˢ; Lent unto mʳ

---

[81] I spell this with a middle 'e' from its chapbook source, rather than follow Henslowe's version of the name, which makes him seem too nearly the comic-book and Hollywood hero.

cheattell the 21 of June 1598 in earneste of a boocke called the fenerall of Richard curdelion the some of xxv^s I saye xxv^s wittnes w^m birde; lent unto antony munday the 23 of June 1598 in earneste of a boocke called the fenerall of Richard curdelion the some of . . . xx s; lent unto m^r drayton the 24 of June 1598 in earneste of a boocke called the funerall of Richard cordelion the some of . . . xxx s; Lent unto m^r willson the 26 of June 1598 the some of xx s wch is in full paymente of his perte of the boocke called Richard cordelion funeral . . . xx s.'

97. *Ill of a Woman* (*The Fount of New Fashions*)[82] (Chapman, 1598, lost). 'Lent unto m^r Chapmane the 16 of maye 1598 in earneste of a boocke for the companye wittnes w^m Birde . . . xxxx s; lent unto w^m birde the 23 of maye 1598 wch he lent unto m^r chappman upon his boock wch he promised us . . . xx s; lent unto the company the 10 of June 1598 to lend unto m^r chapman . . . x s; Lent unto Robart shawe & edward Jube the 15 of June 1598 to geve m^r Chapman in earneste of his boocke called the ylle of A womon . . . xx^s; Lent unto the company the 31 of septmbre 1598 to by A Boocke of m^r chapman called the Founte of new faciones pd in perte . . . iij^li; Lent unto the companey the 12 of octobre 1598 to paye unto m^r chapmane in fulle payment for his playe called the fowntayne of new faciones . . . xx^s; Lent unto Jube & Thomas dowton the 8 of novmbre 1598 to bye dyvers thinges for the playe called the fownte of new faciones some . . . v^li; Lent unto Robart shawe the 13 of novembre 1598 to bye wemenes gownd & other thinges for the fowntayne of newe faciones the some of . . . vij^li; lent unto Thomas dowton the 14 of novmbre 1598 to bye dyvers thinges for the playe called the fowntayne of newe faciones the some of v^li.'

98. *2 Black Bateman of the North* (Chettle, Drayton, Dekker, Wilson, 1598, lost). 'Lent unto Cheattell the 26 of June 1598 in earneste of A boocke called the 2 perte of blacke battman of the north & m^r harey porter hath geven me his worde for the performance of the same & all so for my money . . . xx^s; Lent unto m^r Cheattell the 8 of July 1598 upon A Boocke called the 2 perte of blacke battman the some of . . . iij^li; Lent unto m^r willsones the 13 of July 1598 in pert of payment of a boocke called the 2 pert of blacke battman the some of . . . x s; lent unto m^r wilsone the 14 of July 1598 in fulle paymet of a boock called the 2 pert of black battmane the some of . . . xv^s;

---

[82] The identity of this play of Chapman's has been disputed. In June 1598 he was paid for one called by Henslowe 'the ylle of A womon', and three months later for 'the Founte of new faciones'. Little besides male prejudice and the proximity of the timing connects the two, but Chapman's usual rate of production suggests that the two names must refer to the same play.

(*Note of all suche bookes as belong to the Stocke, and such as I have bought since the 3d of March 1598*) 2 p. black Battman.'[83]

99. *The Madman's Morris* (Wilson, Drayton, Dekker, 1598, lost). 'lent unto m^r willson m^r drayton & m^r dickers the 31 of June 1598 in earneste of A boocke called the made manes mores the some of . . . iij^li; Lent unto m^r drayton the 9 of July 1598 upon a Boocke of called the mad manes mores the some of . . . xx^s; pd unto m^r willsone & m^r deckers in fulle payment of A boocke called the mad manes moris the 10 of July 1598 the some of . . . xxxx^s. Lent unto w^m borne the 25 of July 1598 to by A sewte of satten for the playe of the made manes moris the some of . . . iiij^li xiij^s 4^d; (*Note of all suche bookes as belong to the Stocke, and such as I have bought since the 3d of March 1598*) Mad mans morris.'

100. *Hannibal and Hermes* (*Worse Feared than Hurt?*) (Wilson, Drayton, Dekker, 1598, lost). 'lent unto m^r willsone the 17 of July 1598 in earneste of a comodye called haneballe & hearmes the some of . . . x s; lent unto m^r willson m^r drayton & m^r dickers the 17 of July 1598 for A Boocke called Hanneballe & hermes the some of . . . iij^li; lent unto m^r willsone the 26 of July 1598 upon A Boocke called Haneballe & hermes the some of . . . xx s; Lent unto m^r ~~willso~~ drayton & m^r dickers the 27 of July 1598 in pert of a Boocke called Haneballe & Hermes the some of . . . xxx^s; pd unto m^r drayton & m^r deckers the 28 of July 1598 in full payment of a boocke called haneballe & hermes other wisse called worse feared then hurte . . . x^s.'

101. *Valentine and Orson* (Hathway, Munday, 1598, lost). 'lent unto Robart shawe & Jewbey the 19 of July 1598 for A Boocke called Vallentyne & orsen in fulle paymente the some of v^li to paye hathe waye & mondaye . . . v^li.'[84]

102. *Pierce of Winchester* (Dekker, Drayton, Wilson, 1598, lost). 'lent unto m^r deckers the same time [i.e., 28 July 1598] upon the next boock called perce of Winchester . . . x^s; Lent unto the company the 8 of aguste 1598 to paye mr drayton willsone & dickers in perte of payment of A boocke called perce of winschester the some of . . . l s; Lent unto the company the 10 of aguste 1598 to paye m^r drayton

---

[83] On the same day, 14 July, Henslowe entered a note 'Lent unto Harey Cheattell . . . upon a boocke called the playe of A womon Tragedye the some of v^li wch Robart shawe willed me to delyver hime . . . eather to dd the play or else to paye the mony wth in one forthnyght.' I have not included this title since it seems unlikely that Chettle delivered the playbook.

[84] A play was entered in the SR 23 May 1595 as '*an enterlude of Valentyne and Orsson, plaid by hir Majesties players*', and again as '*a famous history*' on 31 March 1600, but seemingly not printed. Perhaps Hathway and Munday rewrote it, as Shakespeare did several of the Queen's Men's plays.

willsone & dickers in fulle payment for a boocke called perce of winschester the some of . . . l s; Lent unto the company the the 23 of septmbre 1598 to bye divers thinges for perce of winchester the some of x^{li} dd unto thomas dowton I saye . . . x^{li}; Lent unto Thomas dowton the 28 of septmbre 1598 to bye divers thinges for pearce of winchester the some of . . . xxxx^s; payd for the company the 12 of octobre 1598 unto the lace man for the playe of perce of winchester the some of . . . v^{li} ij s; (*Note of all suche bookes as belong to the Stocke, and such as I have bought since the 3d of March 1598*) Perce of Winchester.'

103. *The Conquest of Brute* (Day, Chettle, 1598, lost). 'Lent unto the company the 30 of July 1598 to bye A Boocke of John daye called the con queste of brute wth the firste fyndinge of the bathe the some of . . . xxxx^s; Lent unto Hary cheattell the 8 of ~~aguste~~ in earneste of A Boocke called Brute the some of . . . ix^s; Lent unto hary cheattell the 9 of ~~aguste~~ septmbre 1598 in earneste of A Boocke called Brute at the A poyntement of Johne synger the some of . . . xx^s; Lent unto hary cheattell the 16 of septmbre 1598 in earneste of A Boocke called Brute . . . Hary cheattell untell this place owes us viij^{li} ix^s dew al his boockes & Recknynges payd; Lent unto the company the 12 of octobre 1598 to geve harey cheattell in perte of payment for for his playe called Brutte some of x^s; Layde owt for the company the 18 of octobre 1598 for A boocke called Brutte the some of . . . to harey chettell . . iij^{li}; Lent unto the company the 22 of octobre 1598 to paye harey cheattell for his boocke called Brute in fulle payment the some of . . . l s; Dd unto same Rowley the 12 of desembre 1598 to bye divers thinges for to macke cottes for gyantes in brutte the some of . . . xxiiij^s.'[85]

104. *Hot Anger Soon Cold* (Porter, Chettle, Jonson, 1598, lost). 'lent unto the company the 18 of aguste 1598 to bye a Boocke called hoote anger sone cowld of m^r porter m^r cheatell & bengemen Johnson in full payment the some of . . . vj^{li}.'

105. *Chance Medley or Worse Feared than Hurt* (Wilson, Munday, Dekker, Drayton, 1598, lost). 'Lent unto the company the 19 of aguste 1598 to paye unto m^r willson monday & deckers in perte of payment of

---

[85] The first payment of forty shillings to Day was the price for an old playbook. The subsequent payments to Chettle in 'earnest' suggest a comprehensive rewrite. Conceivably there were two plays, but the proximity of the payments makes it more likely that Chettle rewrote Day's old play. In March 1599 Henslowe paid the licensing fee for 'A boocke called brute grenshillde', which was probably this play.

A boock called chance medley the some of iiij^{li} v^s in this maner
willson xxx^s cheattell xxx s mondy xxv^s I saye . . . iiij^{li} v^s; pd unto m^r
drayton the 24 of aguste 1598 in fulle payment of A Boocke called
chance medley or worse a feared then hurte[86] the some of . . . xxxv^s.''
Lent unto the company the 30 of aguste 1598 to geve in earneste of a
boocke called worse a feard then hurte unto m^r drayton & dickers
the some of . . . l s; Lent unto the company the 4 of aguste [Sept.]
1598 to paye in fulle payment for A Boocke called worse A feared
then hurte unto m^r drayton & m^r dickers the some of . . . l s.'[87]

106. *Vayvode* (Chettle, 1598, lost). 'Lent unto Thomas dowton the 21 of
aguste 1598 to by A sewte & a gowne for vayvode the some of ten
pownde I saye lent . . . x^{li}; Lent unto Thomas dowton the 22 of
aguste 1598 to by divers thinges for vayvode the some of . . . xxxxvj^s;
Lent unto Thomas dowton the 24 of aguste 1598 to bye divers
thinges for vayvode the some of . . . xiiij s; lent unto Robart shaw
the 25 of aguste 1598 to paye the lace manes byll ij^{li} xvj^s vj d & the
tayllers bylle xxviij s vj d some is . . . iiij^{li} v^s . . . for vayvode; Lent
unto harey cheattell the 29 of aguste 1598 at the apoyntment of
thomas dowton For his playe of vayvode the some of . . . xx^s; pd
unto my sonne Edward alleyn the 21 of Janeway for the playe of
vayvod for the company the some of xxxx^s I saye pd . . . 1598 . . . xxxx^s;
(*Note of all suche bookes as belong to the Stocke, and such as I have
bought since the 3d of March 1598*) Vayvode.'[88]

107. *Catiline's Conspiracy* (Wilson, Chettle, 1598, lost). 'Lent m^r willsone
the 21 of aguste 1598 in earnest of A Boocke called cattelyn some
of . . . x^s; Lent unto hearey cheattell the 26 of aguste in earneste of
A Boock called cattelanes consperesey the some of . . . v^s; Lent unto
m^r willsone the 29 of aguste 1598 at the Request of hary cheattell in
earneste of cattelyne the some of . . . x^s.'

108. *1 Civil Wars of France* (Dekker, Drayton, 1598, lost). 'Lent unto the
companey the 29 of septmbre 1598 to by A boocke of m^r drayton &
m^r dickers called the firste syvell wares in france . . . vj^{li}; Lent unto

---

[86] Drayton and Dekker had full payment for a play, *Hannibal and Hermes*, given the same alternative
title 'worse A feared then hurte' on 28 July.

[87] The same subtitle was applied to both *Hannibal and Hermes* (100 above) and to this play, which
seems more apt for a comedy. It is unlikely that Henslowe confused the two, since the plays were
by different writers.

[88] Judging by the payment of £2 to Alleyn this was an old playbook of Chettle's that Alleyn sold to
the company. Chettle's receipt of one pound may mean that he revised it for the new production.
Alleyn was not playing as a sharer through these years.

Thomas dowton the 8 of octobre 1598 to bye divers thinges for the playe called the firste sevelle warres of france the some of . . . vj^{li}; Lent unto Thomas dowton the 11 of octobre to bye divers thinges for the play called the first syvell wares of france the some of . . . iiij^{li}; Lent unto w^m Jube the 20 of Janewary 1598 to lend m^r dickers in earneste of his playe called the firste Intreducyon of the syvell wares of france the some of . . . iij^{li}.[89]

109. *Mulmutius Dunwallow* (Rankins, 1598, lost). 'Lent unto the company the 3 of octobre 1598 to by A boocke of m^r Ranckenes called mul mutius donwallow the some of . . . xx^s.'

110. *Connan, Prince of Cornwall* (Drayton, Dekker, 1598, lost). 'payd unto m^r drayton and m^r dickers the 16 of octobre 1598 in pert of payment for A boocke called connan prince of cornwell the some of Bradeshaw . . . xxx^s; pd unto Bradshaw at the Requeste of m^r drayton & m^r dickers in perte of payment of ther Boocke called the connan prince of cornwellsome of . . . x^s; Layd owt for the companey the 20 of octobre 1598 unto m^r drayton & m^r dickers for A Boocke called connan prince of Cornwell the some of . . . iiij^{li}.'

111. *2 Civil Wars of France* (Drayton, Dekker, 1598, lost).[90] 'Layd owt for the company the 3 of novmbre 1598 to m^r drayton & m^r dickers for A Boocke called the second perte of the syvell wares of france the some of . . . vj^{li}; Lent unto Robart shaw & Jewbey the 19 of novmbre 1598 to bye divers thinges for the playe called the 2 pert of the syvelle wares of france . . . x^{li}; Lent unto Jewby the 24 of novembre 1598 to bye divers thinges for the playe called the 2 perte of the syvell wares of france the some of . . . x^{li}.'

112. *3 Civil Wars of France* (Drayton, Dekker, 1598, lost). 'Lent unto Robart shawe the 18 of novmbre 1598 to lend unto m^r dickers in earneste of A boocke called the 3 perte of the syvell wares of france some . . . xx^s; Pd unto m^r drayton & m^r dickers the 30 of desembre 1598 for A Boocke called the 3 perte of the syvell wares of france the some of . . . v^{li}.'

113. *'Tis no Deceit to Deceive the Deceiver* (Chettle, 1598, lost). 'Lent unto harey Chettell at the Requeste of Robart shawe the 25 of novembre

[89] This last payment may either be for a prequel to add to the three parts of the *Civil Wars*, or more likely a payment for changes to the first part.

[90] Immediately before the first entry about this sequel is a note of a loan to Shaa and Juby 'to lend unto m^r Chapmane one his playe boocke & ij ectes of A tragedie of bengemens plotte the some of . . . iij^{li}.' Neither has survived, and there is nothing to say which plays the entry refers to.

1598 in earneste of his comodey called tys no deseayt to deseve the
desever for mendinge of Roben hood.for the corte . . . x^s; lent unto
the company the 28 of novembre 1598 to geve harey cheattell in
earneste of hes boocke called tis no desayt to deseave the desever
the some of . . . xx^s.'

114. *War without Blows and Love without Suit* (Heywood, 1598, lost).
'Lent unto Robart shawe the 6 of desembre 1598 to bye A Boocke
called ware wth owt blowes & love wth owt sewte of Thomas hawodes
some of . . . iij^{li}; Lent unto Robart shawe the 26 of Janewary 1598 to
paye Thomas hawode in full payment for his boocke called ware wth
owt blowes & love wth owt stryfe the some of . . . xxxx^s.'

115. *The Four Kings* (Chapman, 1599, lost). 'Lent unto m^r chapman the
4 of Jenewary 1598 upon iij ackes of A tragedie wch Thomas dowton
bad me dd hime the some of . . . iij^{li} / called . . . ; Lent unto Robart
Shawe the 8 of Janewary 1598 to paye mr chapman in fulle payment
for his tragedie the some of . . . iij^{li} / called . . . ; pd unto the m^r of
the Reveulles man for the lysansynge of A boocke called the 4 kynges
. . . vij s.'[91]

116. *1 The Two Angry Women of Abingdon* (Porter, 1597, quarto). Q1
'THE | PLEASANT HISTORIE OF | the two angrie women | of
Abington. | With the humerous mirthe of *Dick Coomes* | and *Nicholas
Proverbes,* two | Servingmen. | *As it was lately playde by the right
Honorable* | the Earle of Nottingham, Lord high | Admirall, his
servants. | *By Henry Porter* Gent. | Imprinted at London for Joseph
Hunt, and | *William Ferbrand,* and are to be solde at the Corner of |
Colman-streete, neere Loathburie. | 1599.' 'lent unto Thomas dowton
the 31 of Janewary 1598 to bye tafetie for ij womones gownes for the ij
angrey wemen of abengton the some of . . . ix^{li}.'[92]

---

[91] Chapman was paid a total of £6 in two instalments for a tragedy, of which he supplied three acts on
4 Jan. 1599 and was paid in full on 8 Jan. The title was not specified, but on 22 Jan. he got a loan of
£3 for *The World Runs on Wheels* (*Diary,* p. 268), a title that indicates a comedy. So it seems likely
the book called 'the 4 kynges' for which the Revels was paid on 18 March 1599 was Chapman's
tragedy.

[92] As many as three plays might be noted in the entries for Henry Porter. It is possible that the first
'*Angry Women*' play, the only one with a surviving text, should be placed earlier in the historical
sequence, perhaps late in 1597, after *The Merry Wives of Windsor* appeared with the other duopoly
company. Plays were not generally given to the press so soon as a year after first being staged (the
Shakespeare company's *Henry V*, printed less than a year after its first appearance, was uniquely fast
getting to the press). The evidence about Porter's sequel or sequels at the end of 1598 does not mean
the first play could not have appeared at least a year before. Its title-page citation of 'humorous'
characters suggests it post-dates 1597. The second part of *The Angry Women* (120) and the possible
third, '*Two Merry Women*', have not survived. The third may never have been completed.

117. *William Longsword* (Drayton, 1598, lost). 'Lent unto thyomas downton the 20 of Janewary 1598 to lend unto m^r drayton in earneste of his playe called w^m longserd the some of . . . xxxx^s; I receved forty shillinges of m^r Phillip Hinslowe in part of vj^{li} for the playe of William longsword to be deliv^{r}d p^{r}sent wth 2 or three dayes the xxj th of January / 1598 / Mih Drayton.'

118. *Joan As Good As My Lady* (Heywood, 1599, lost). 'Lent unto Thomas dowton the 10 of febreary 1598 to bye A boocke of m^r hewode called Jonne as good as my ladey . . . iij^{li}; Lent unto Thomas downton the 12 of febreary 1598 to paye m^r hawode in full payment for his boock called Jonne as good as my Ladey the some of . . . ij^{li}.'

119. *Friar Fox and Gillian of Brentford* (1599, lost). 'Lent unto Thomas dowton & samwell Redly the 10 of febreary 1598 to bye A boocke called fryer fox & gyllen of branforde the some of . . . v^{li} x^s.'

120. *2 The Two Angry Women of Abingdon* (Porter, 1598, lost). 'Lent unto Thomas dowton the 22 of desembre 1598 to bye A Boocke of harey poorter called the 2 perte of the 2 angrey wemen of abengton . . . v^{li}; Lent unto Thomas downton the 12 of febreary 1598 to by divers things for the playe called the 2 perte of the angrey wemen of Abington . . . ij^{li}; Lent unto Thomas downton the 12 of feberye 1598 to pay m^r poorter in fulle payment for his boock called the 2 perte of the angrey wemen of Abington the some of . . . ij^{li}; (28 Feb. 1599) Lent unto harey porter at the Requeste of the company in earneste of his boocke called ij mery wemen of abenton the some of forty-shellengs & for the Resayte of that money he gave me his faythfulle promysse that I shold have alle the boockes wch he writte ether him sellfe or wth any other wch some was dd the 28 of february 1598 I saye thomas downton Robart shawe.'

121. *The World Runs on Wheels, or All Fools but the Fool* (Chapman, 1599, lost). 'Lent unto Thomas downton the 22 of Janewary 1598 to Leand unto m^r Chapman in earneste of A Boocke called the world Rones A whelles the some of . . . iij^{li}; Lent unto m^r Chapman the 13 of febreary 1598 in pert of payment of his boocke called the world Ronnes A whelles . . . xx^s; Lent unto Robarte shawe the 2 of June 1599 to paye unto m^r chapman for his Boocke called the world Runes a whelles some of . . . xx^s; Lent unto w^m Borne & Jewbey the 21 of June 1599 to lend unto m^r chapman upon his Boock called the world Ronnes a whelles the some of . . . xxxx^s; Lent unto Thomas dowton the 2 of July 1599 to paye m^r chapman in full payment for his Boocke

called the world Rones a whelles & now all foolles but the foolle some of . . . xxx s.'[93]

122. <u>*Troy's Revenge, or The Tragedy of Polyphemus*</u> (Chettle, 1599, lost). 'Lent unto samvell Rowley the 16 of febreary 1598 to lend in perte of payment unto harye chettell upon his boocke of polofemos . . . xx^s; Lent unto Thomas downton the 27 of febreary 1598 to paye unto harey cheattell in fulle payment for a playe called Troyes Revenge wth the tragedy of polefeme the some of fyftye shellenges & strocken of his deatte wch he owes unto the company fyftye shelenges more . . . l s; Hary cheattell hath strocken of his deate as foloweth 1598 unto the companye / pd of his deate in his boocke of polefeme . . . l s; Lent unto the littell tayller the 4 of octobre 1599 to bye divers for the play of polefeme the some of . . . viij^s.'

123. <u>*The Spencers*</u> (Chettle, Porter, 1599, lost). 'Lent unto harey cheattell the 4 of marche 1598 in earneste of his boocke wch harey porter & he is writtinge the some of . . . x^s . . . called the spencers; Lent unto Robarte Shawe the 22 of marche 1598 to paye unto m^r porter in full paymente of his play called the spencers the some of . . . v^{li} x s; Lent unto Thomas downton the 9 of Aprell 1599 to bye dyvers thinges as 4 clathe clockes & macke up a womones gowne the some of . . . x^{li} / for the spencers; Lent unto Thomas downton the 14 of Aprell 1599 to macke divers thinges for the playe of the spencers the some of . . . xv^{li}; Delyvered unto Thomas downton boye Thomas parsones to bye dyvers thinges for the playe of the spencers the 16 of Aprell 1599 the some of . . . v^{li}; Hary cheattell hath stricken of his deate as foloweth 1598 unto the companye . . . pd of his deate in his boocke of the spencers . . . x s.'

124. <u>*Troilus and Cressida*</u> (Dekker, Chettle, 1599, 'plot'). 'aprell 7 daye 1599 Lent unto Thomas downton to lende unto mr dickers & harey cheattell in earneste of ther boocke called Troyeles & creasse daye the some of . . . iiij^{li}; Lent unto harey cheattell & m^r dickers in perte of payment of ther boocke called Troyelles & cresseda the 16 of Aprell 1599 . . . xx^s.'[94]

---

[93] Henslowe (*Diary* p. 268) also had Chapman's receipt for £3 for this play dated 22 Jan. 1599. I agree with Chambers (*Elizabethan Stage* III. 252) that this play is unlikely to be the same as the *All Fools* that Chapman sold to the Blackfriars Boys in 1604, and published in 1605 as 'Presented at the Black Fryers, And lately before his Majestie. Written by George Chapman'. From Henslowe's final entry it looks as if Chapman thought of the new title for this play at the last minute, and could have re-activated it for the Blackfriars in 1604. The printed version does read more like a boy company play than an Admiral's.

[94] The absence of any completed payments for this play may result from a gap in the *Diary*'s records between April and May 1599. The survival of a partial 'plot' certainly indicates that it was staged.

125. *Orestes Furens* or *The Tragedy of Agamemnon* (Dekker, 1599, lost). '2 of maye 1599 . . . Lent more the same time unto m^r dickers in earnest of A Boocke called orestes fures . . . v^s; pd unto the mr of Revelles man for lycensynge of A Boocke called the tragedie of agamemnon the 3 of June 1599 . . . vij s; Lent unto m^r dickers & m^r chettell the 26 of maye 1599 in earneste of A Boocke called [~~troylles & creseda~~] the tragede of Agamemnon^{95} the some of . . . xxx^s.'

126. *The Shoemaker's Holiday* (Dekker, 1599, quarto). Q1 'THE | SHO-MAKERS | Holiday. | OR | *The Gentle Craft.* | With the humorous life of Simon | Eyre, shoomaker, and Lord Maior | of London. | As it was acted before the Queenes most excellent Ma- | jestie on New-yeares day at night last, by the right | honourable the Earle of Notingham, Lord high Ad- | mirall of England, his servants. | Printed by Valentine Sims dwelling at the foote of Adling | hill, neere Bainards Castle, at the signe of the White | Swanne, and are there to be sold. | 1600.' Q2 1610, Q3 1618, Q4 1624, Q5 1631, Q6 1657. 'Lent unto Samewell Rowley & Thomas downton the 15 of July 1599 to bye A Boocke of Thomas dickers Called the gentle Craft the som of . . . iij^{li}.'

127. *A Pastoral Tragedy* (Chapman, 1599, lost). 'Lent unto Thomas downton the 17 of July 1599 to lend unto m^r chapman in earneste of A pastrall tragedie the some of . . . xxxx^s.'^{96}

128. *The Stepmother's Tragedy* (Dekker, Chettle, 1599, lost). 'Lent unto Thomas deckyers the 24 of July 1599 at the Requeste of Samwell Rowly & Thomas downton in earneste of A Boocke called step-mothers tragedy . . . x^s; Lent unto harey Chettell & Th^d the 23 of aguste 1599 in earneste of his playe Called the stepmothers tragedie the some of . . . xx^s; Lent unto w^m birde Thomas downton & Jewbey the 25 of aguste 1599 to paye harye Chettell for his Boocke called the stepmothers tragedie the some of . . . xvij s; this 14th of October 1599 Receaved by me Robt Shaa of phillip Henslowe to pay H. Chettle in full paiment of a booke Called the stepmothers tragedy for the use of the Company iiij li I say Receaved . . . 4^{li}.'

129. *Bear a Brain* (Dekker, 1599, lost). 'Lent unto Robarte shawe the 1 of aguste 1599 to paye m^r deckers for a boocke called [better latte than

---

^{95} The second title was interlined above the name *Troilus and Cressida*. It looks like a replacement, but since the first name was not struck through it may have been a sub-title. Greg and Chambers thought Dekker's 'orestes fvres' more suitable to a play about Agamemnon than the famous title.
^{96} The *Diary* also records a receipt from Chapman dated 17 July for forty shillings 'for a Pastorall ending in a Tragedye in part of payment'.

never] beare a braine⁹⁷ the some of xxxxˢ in fulle payment lent unto mʳ deckers at that time xxs so all is . . . iijˡⁱ.'

130. *Page of Plymouth* (Jonson, Dekker, 1599, lost). 'Lent unto wᵐ Borne alles birde the 10 of aguste 1599 to Lend unto bengemyne Johnsone & thomas deckers in earneste of ther boocke wᶜʰ they be awrittenge called page of plemoth the some . . . xxxxˢ; Lent unto wᵐ Birde Thomas downton wᵐ Jube the 2 of Septmbre 1599 to paye in fulle payment for A Boocke called the lamentable tragedie of page of plemoth the some of . . . vj li; Lent unto Jewbey & Thomas towne the 12 of Septmbre 1599 to bye wemen gownes for page of plemoth the some of . . . xˡⁱ.'

131. *The Poor Man's Paradise* (Haughton, 1599, lost). 'Lent unto Thomas downton the 20 of aguste 1599 to lend unto hawghton in earneste of A Boocke called the poore manes paradice the some of xiijˢ; Lent unto Thomas downton the 25 of aguste 1599 to paye [harey chettell] Thomas hawton for his Boocke called the poore manes paradice the some of . . . xvij s.'

132. *The Scots Tragedy* or *Robert II* (Chettle, Dekker, Jonson, Marston, 1599, lost). 'Lent unto Thomas downton the 3 of Sepᵗᵐᵇʳᵉ 1599 to lend unto Thomas deckers Bengemen Johnson hary Chettell & other Jentellman in earneste of A playe called Robart the second Kinge of scottes tragedie the some of . . . xxxxˢ; Lent unto Samwell Rowly & Robart shawe the 15 of septmbre 1599 to lend in earneste of A Boocke called the scottes tragedi unto Thomas dickers & harey chettell the some of . . . xxˢ; Lent unto hary chettell the 16 of septmbre 1599 in earneste of A Boocke called the scottes tragedie the some of . . . x s; Lent unto wᵐ Borne the 27 of Setmbre 1599 to lend unto Bengemen Johnsone in earneste of A Boocke called the scottes tragedie the some of . . . xxˢ.'⁹⁸

133. *Tristram de Lyons* (1599, lost). 'the 13 of October 1599 Lent unto Thomas Downton for the Booke of Trystram de lyons . . . 3 ˡⁱ.'

134. *1 Sir John Oldcastle* (Drayton, Hathway, Munday, Wilson, 1599, quarto). SR 11 Aug. 1600, '*Ent. T. Pavier : the first parte of the history of the life of Sir John Oldcastell, Lord Cobham : Item the second and last parte of the history of Sir John Oldcastell, Lord Cobham, with his*

---

⁹⁷ 'beare a braine' is interlined above the original title. Greg thought 'bear a brain' must be an alternative title for *The Shoemaker's Holiday*, but the name's interlining in the entry suggests not. Roslyn Knutson, 'Commercial Significance', thinks the payment of only forty shillings meant it was an old playbook.

⁹⁸ The day after his last payment to Jonson for *The Scots Tragedy* Henslowe wrote 'Lent unto wᵐ Borne the 28 of septmbre 1599 to Lent unto mʳ maxon the new poete mʳ mastone in earneste of A Boocke called - - - the some of . . . viijˢ', but did not insert any name. This was Marston's only appearance in the *Diary*.

martydom.' Qi 1600 'The first part | Of the true and hono- | rable historie, of the life of Sir | *John Oldcastle, the good* | Lord Cobham. | *As it hath been lately acted by the right honorable the Earle of Notingham Lord high Admirall of England his servants.* | LONDON | Printed by V. S. for Thomas Pavier, and are to be solde at | his shop at the signe of the Catte and Parrots | neere the Exchange. | 1600.' 'this 16th of October 99 Receved by me Thomas downton of phillipp Henchlow to pay m^r monday m^r drayton & m^r wilsson & haythway for the first perte of the lyfe of Sr Jhon Ouldcasstell & in earnest of the Second perte for the use of the company ten pownd I say receved . . . 10^{li}; as A gefte Received of M^r hincheloe for Mr Mundaye & the Reste of the poets at the playnge of Sr John oldcastell the ferste tyme . . . . x^s.'[99]

135. *2 Sir John Oldcastle* (Drayton, Wilson, Hathway, 1599, lost).[100] 'this 16th of October 1599 Received by me Thomas downton of phillipp Henchlow to pay m^r monday m^r drayton & m^r wilsson & haythway for the first perte of the lyfe of Sr Jhon Ouldcasstell & in earnest of the Second perte for the use of the company ten pownd I say receved . . . 10^{li}; Received of m^r Henchlow for the use of the Company to pay m^r drayton for the second perte of Sr Jhon ould Casell foure pownd I say recevd . . . iiij^{jli} per me Thomas Downton; Dd unto the littell tayller at the apoyntment of Robart shawe the 12 of marche 1599 to macke thinges for the 2 perte of owld castell some of . . . xxx^s.'

136. *Patient Grissill* (Chettle, 1599, quarto). 'Lent unto Robarte shawe the 18 of march 1599 to geve unto the printer to staye the printinge of patient gresell the some of . . . xxxx^s.'[101] SR 28 March 1600, 'Ent. C. Burby: the plaie of Patient Grissell." Qi 'THE | PLEASANT | *COMODIE OF* | Patient Grissill. | As it hath beene sundrie times lately plaid | by the right honorable the Earle of Not- | tingham (Lord high Admirall) his | servants. | LONDON. | Imprinted for Henry Rocket, and are to | be solde at the long Shop under S. Mildreds | Church in the Poultrey. | 1603.' 'Lent unto thomas dickkers harey chettell w^m harton in earneste of A Boocke called patient grissell at the a poyntment of Robart shawe by his letter the some of three powndes the 19 of desembre 1599 . . . iij^{li}; Received in

[99] The receipt is in Rowley's hand, the words 'as A gefte' added in the margin by Henslowe. Subsequent entries, starting 17 Aug. 1602, are for Dekker to make additions for the play's performances by Worcester's company when they came to the Rose.

[100] The SR entry is for two *Oldcastle* plays, but the second part seems never to have reached the press. Like the first, it was given to Worcester's to play at the Rose, presumably because it was closer to the Globe with its misrepresentation of Oldcastle as Falstaff than was the Fortune.

[101] For a comment on the usual lapse of time between staging and printing, see above Chapter 3, p. 110.

earnest of patient Grissell by us Tho: dekker, Hen: Chettle and willm Hawton the sume of 3.li.of good & lawfull money, by a note sent from m^r Robt Shaa: the 19th of December.1599 . . . 3^{li} By me henry chettle. / W. Haughton / Thomas Dekker; Receved by me Samuell Rowlye of phyllyp henchloe for harrye chettell in Earneste of the playe of patient Gryssell for the Use of the Comepanye . . . xx s; Receaved of m^r Henshlowe the 26th of decemb^r 1599 to pay Tho: Deckers: H. Chettle: & Will: Hawton for pacient Grissill vj^{li} I say Receaved . . . vj^{li} by me RobtShaa; Lent unto Thomas deckers the 28 of desembre 1599 in earneste of a playe called pacyent gresell the some of . . . v^s; Lent unto w^m harton the 29 of desembre 1599 in earnest of patient gresell some of . . . v^s; Receaved of Mr Henshlowe this 26th of January 1599 xx^s to geve unto the tayler to buy a grey gowne for gryssell I say Receaved . . . xx^s by me RobtShaa; Lent unto Robarte shawe the 18 of march 1599 to geve unto the printer to staye the printinge of patient gresell the some of . . . xxxx^s.'

137. *Cox of Collumpton* (Day, Haughton, 1599, lost). 'Lent unto Robart shaw the 1 of novmbre 1599 to Lend unto wm harton in earneste of A Boocke called the tragedie of John cox some of . . . xx^s; the 1 of novmbre 1599 W. Haughton received of m^r. Hunselowe in parte of payement.of the the tragedie John Cox the some of . . . 20^s; Willyam Haughtonn receyved of m^r Hinchloe in part of payment of the Tragedy of Cox of Collunption the som of . . . 20^s. pd & quite. John Daye; Lent unto w^m harton & John daye at the Apoyntment of Thomas dowton in earnest of A Boocke called the tragedie of cox of collinste^r the some of . . . xx^s; the xiiijth of November 1599 Received of M^r phillipp Hinchlow to pay to william hauton & Jhon day for the tragedy of Cox of Collomton the som of three pownd receved in full . . . iij^{li}.'[102]

138. *2 Henry Richmond* (Wilson, 1599, lost). 'Receaved of m^r Ph: Hinchlow by a note under the hand of m^r Rob: Shaw in full payment for the second pert of Henrye Richmond sold to him & his Companye the

---

[102] Simon Forman saw this play at the Rose on 9 March 1600: 'Item the plai of Cox of Cullinton & his 3 sonns henry peter and Jhon on St Markes dai Cox him selfe shot an Arrowe thorow His unkells head to have his Land & had it and the same dai 7 yers on Mr Jarvis shot cox throughe the hed & slue him. and on saint markes dai a year after his older sonn henry was drowned by peter ^ jhon in his Xan fate. and on St. Markes dai a year after peter & Jhon both slue them selves for peter being fronted wth the sight of a bear viz a sprite apering to Jhon & him when they sate upon devision of the landes in likenes of a bere & ther wth peter fell out of his wites and way lyed in a darke house & beat out his braines against a post & Jhon stabed him self & all on St Markes dai & remember how m^r hammons sonn slue him & where he way sleying of his father his father entreating for mercy to his sonn could find no mercy whereupon he promised that his sonn should betray him selfe by laughing & so he did was executed for yt.'

somme of eight powndes Current moneye the viij^t daye of November 1599 . . . viij^{li} By me R Wilson; (letter from Shaw to Henslowe, 8 Nov. 1599, *Diary*, p. 288) Mr Henshlowe we have heard their booke and lyke yt their pryce is eight poundes, wch I pray pay now to m^r wilson, according to our promysse, I would have Come my selfe, but that I ame troubled wth a scytation. yo^{rs} Robt Shaa.'^{103}

139. *Two Lamentable Tragedies* (Haughton, Day, 1599, quarto).^{104} 'Two Lamentable | Tragedies. | The one, of the murther of Mai- | ster Beech *a Chaundler in* | Thames-streete, and his boye, | done by *Thomas Merry.* | *The other of a young childe mur-* | thered in a Wood by two Ruffins, | *with the consent of his Uncle.* | By ROB. YARINGTON. | LONDON | Printed for *Mathew Lawe,* | and are to be solde at | *his shop in Paules Church-yard neere unto* | *S. Austines gate, at the signe* | *of the Foxe.* 1601.' 'Received of m^r Henseslowe in earnest of the tragedie of merie the some of xxs. The 27th of noveb. W Haughton. J. D.; Rec^d of m^r Hinchloe more in ernest of The Tragedy of Thomas Merrye 20^s Joh. Day. W. Haughton; Recd more of m^r Hinchloe upon the same booke 10^s By John Day; Lent unto w^m Harton the 21 of novmbre in earneste of her boocke called merie the some of . . . x^s; Lent unto w^m harton & John daye the 27 novmbre 1599 in earneste of A tragedie called mereie the some of . . . as may a pere . . . xx^s; Lent unto w^m hawton & John day the the 5 of desembre 1599 in earneste of ther boocke called mereye at the a poyntment of Robart shawe the some of . . . as may a pere . . . xx^s; Lent unto John daye the 6 of desembre 1599 in earneste of A Boocke called merye as maye a pere . . . x^s; pd unto w^m hawgton & John daye the 6 of desembre 1599 in full payment of ther boocke called the tragedie of merie the some of . . . xxxx^s; pd unto the m^r of the Revelles man for lycensynge of A Boocke called Beches tragedie the some of . . . vij s.'

140. *The Tragedy of Orphenes* (Chettle, 1599, lost). 'Received of m^r Henselow in earnest of the orphanes T . . . d. the somme of x.^{s} the 27th of novembre; lent unto harey chettell the 27 of novmbre 1599 in

^{103} The verso of the letter has what looks like Wilson's draft 'plot' of the first scenes, *Diary*, p. 288.
^{104} The *Two Lamentable Tragedies* printed in 1601, which the *Diary* calls *The Tragedy of Thomas Merry*, is chiefly about Merry's act of murder. This explains the change of name to 'Beches tragedie' in the licence application. It was one plot in a complex story, the other being of a 'young childe murthered in a wood'. Henslowe paid Haughton and Day for writing it. The name 'Rob. Yarington' is appended at the end of the 1601 quarto, and has led to the assumption that he was the author. Robert Yarington was a scrivener enrolled in 1601 (Bernard M. Wagner, 'Robert Yarrington', *Modern Language Notes* 45, 1930, 147–48). He was presumably employed to copy the play for the printer, and may have continued as a company scribe. In 1612 the company's Antony Jeffes paid bail for a 'Yerrington' and two other men.

earneste of A Boocke called the orphenes tragedie the some of x s as maye A peare a bowe by his hand crossed some of . . . x s; Lent unto harey chettell the 27 of novmbre 1599 in earnest of A Boocke called the tragedie of orphenes the some of . . . x^s as maye a pere; Lent unto Samwell Rowley the 24 of septmbre 1601 to paye unto harey chettell in pert of payment for A Boocke called the orfenes tragedy some of . . . x s.'[105]

141. *The Arcadian Virgin* (Chettle, Haughton, 1599, lost). 'Lent unto harey chettell & w^m harton the 13 of desembre 1599 in earneste of his Boocke called arkeadian virgen the some of . . . x^s; Lent unto harey chettell & w^m harton the 17 of desembre 1599 in earneste of ther boocke called arkedian virgen the some . . . v^s.'

142. *The Italian Tragedy* (Day, 1600, lost). 'Lent unto John daye the 10 of Jeneway 1599 in earnest of his Boocke called the etalyan tragedie of - - - the some of . . . xxxx^s at the apoyntment of Robart shawe.'[106]

143. *Owen Tudor* (Drayton, Munday, Hathway, Wilson, 1600 lost). 'Lent unto mihell drayton antony monday m^r hathwaye & m^r willsone at the apoyntment of Thomas downton in earneste of A playe called owen teder the some of . . . iiij^{li}; ye 10 of Jeneway 1599 Receyved in pert of payment & in ernest of a playe called Owen Tewder the some of foure poundes wittnes o^r hands . . . iiij^{li} Ri: Hathwaye RWilson An: Mundy.'[107]

144. *Truth's Supplication to Candlelight* (Dekker, 1600, lost). 'Lent unto Thomas towne the 18 of Janewary 1599 to lend thomas dickers in earneste of A playe Boocke called trewghtes suplication to cande-lighte some of . . . xx^s as may a pere; 18° die Januarij. 1599 Receaved by mee Thomas Dekker at the handes of Mr Phillip Hynchlow the Some of twenty Shillinges in ernest of a play Called Truethes supplication to Candle-light By mee Thomas Dekker wittnes thomas towne;[108] Lent unto Thomas dickers at the apoyntment of

---

[105] The *Diary* editors read this title as '*The Orphan's Tragedy*'. The name Orphenes is classical, perhaps the story of Orphe, to whom Apollo gave the gift of prophecy but who Bacchus changed to stone. The first two notes about it appear amongst some seemingly random entries with various dates (*Diary*, p. 62). The first four entries are in fact receipts all dated 27 Nov. 1599, including the one noted above, which is probably Chettle's. Some inches below is the second entry recorded here. This is almost identical to another that fits more obviously into the historical sequence (*Diary*, p. 127). The later payment made on 24 Sept. 1601 suggests that the completed play was not delivered to the company for nearly two years.

[106] Worcester's paid 'm^r smythe' on 7 March 1602 an 'earneste' for a play called '& etallyon tragedie' which may have been a rewrite of Day's play.

[107] The receipt was cut out of the original, and is now in the Belvoir Castle collection. See *Diary*, p. 267.

[108] This receipt too was cut out of the original, and is now in the Belvoir Castle collection. See *Diary*, p. 267.

the company the 30 of Janeway 1599 in erneste of A Boocke called trewth suplication to candelithe . . . xx^s Rd by w^m harton for hime; Received by me william Haughton for the use of Thomas dickers on the 30th of Januarie the some of . . . 20^s In parte of payement for the booke of truths supplycation to candle light.'

145. *Jugurtha* (Boyle, 1600, ms).[109] 'lent unto me Wbirde the 9 of februarye to paye for a new booke to will: Boyle.cald Jugurth xxx^s w^c if you dislike Ile repaye it back . . . xxxs.'

146. *The Spanish Moor's Tragedy* (Dekker, Haughton, Day, 1600, lost). 'sence we left playing Layd owt for the company the 13 of febrearye 1599 for a boocke called the spaneshe mores tragedie unto Thomas deckers w^m harton John daye in perte of payment the some of . . . iij^{li}.'[110]

147. *Damon and Pythias* (Chettle, 1600, lost). 'Received in pert of payment of damon and Pytheas this 16 of February 1599 . . . xx^s. By me henry chettle; Layd owt for the company the 16 of febreary 1599 in earnest of A Boocke called damon & pethyas as maye a peare some is . . . xx s to hary chettell; Lent unto w^m Birde the 10 of marche 1599 to geve harey chettell in earneste of his Boocke called damon & pethias the some of . . . xxvj s; Lent unto harey chettell the 26 of aprell 1600 in perte of payment of A Boocke called damon & pethias at the a poyntment of Robart shawe the some of . . . xxx^s henry Chettle; payd to Harry Chettle in full payment of vj^{li} for his booke of Damon & Pithias xxxxiiij s; pd unto the m^r of the Revelles man for licensynge of A Boocke called damon & pethias the 16 of maye 1600 some of . . . vij s.'

148. *The Seven Wise Masters* (Chettle, Dekker, Haughton, Day, 1600, lost). 'Receaved of mr hinchlow the 1 of march to paye to harry

---

[109] A manuscript survives in a folio with five other plays (Bodleian MS. Rawl. Poet. 195) headed by the name 'JUGURTHA or THE FAITLESS COSEN GERMAN A TRAGEDY' (Bentley, *JCS* III.36). Henry Herbert when Master of the Revels in 1624 re-licensed an old play, '*Jugurth*, an old play, allowed by Sir George Buc, and *burnt, with his other books*' (Bawcutt, *Herbert*, p. 151). The original "allowed book" may have been lost in the Fortune fire of 1621, and the company acquired a new copy from somewhere for re-licensing by Herbert. The continued staging of the play at the Fortune is confirmed by Edmund Gayton, who wrote in 1654 that the players at the 'citizen' playhouses could be ordered by their audiences to play 'sometimes *Tamerlane*, sometimes *Jugurth*, some times the *Jew* of *Malta*, and some times parts of all these'. Heywood published a translation of Sallust's history of the Catiline conspiracy and the life of Jugurtha of Numidia in 1608. The incomplete Bodleian manuscript of the play was written in a mid-century hand.

[110] A play called *Lust's Dominion* was printed in 1657 with a cancel title-page attributing it to Marlowe. It has sometimes been identified with this play, although Chambers noted (*Elizabethan Stage* II. 427) that Dekker, Haughton and Day were not recorded as receiving 'full payment' to mark its completion.

chettell Thomas decker William hawton & Jhon daye for a boocke called the 7 wise m^{rs} the some of . . . xl^s Wbirde; Lent unto hary chettell the 2 of marche 1599 in earnest of A Boocke called the 7 wisse masters the some of . . . xxx s; Lent unto Samwell Rowly the 8 of marche 1599 to paye unto harey chettell & John daye in fulle payment for A boocke called the vij wisse masters the some of . . . l s; Receaved of Mr Henslowe to lay out for the play of the 7 wise M^{r}s in taffataes & sattyns the some of . . . xx^{li} in behalfe of the Company by me Robt Shaa; Receaved more of Mr Henshlowe to lay out for the play of the 7 wyse maisters in behalfe of the Company . . . x^{li}; Receaved more of Mr Henshlowe to lay out for the play of the 7 wyse maisters in behalf of the Company . . . viij^{li} by me Robt Shaa.'

149. *Ferrex and Porrex* (Haughton, 1600, lost). "Lent w^m harton at the apoyntment of Robart shawe the 3 of march 1600 in earneste of a Boocke called ferex & porex the some of . . . vij^s; Lent unto w^m harton the 18 of marche 1599 in earneste of A Boocke called ferex & porex the some of . . . xx^s; Lent unto w^m harton the 25 of march 1599 in earneste of his Boocke called ferex & porexe the some of . . . v^s; Receaved of Mr Henshlowe in behalfe of the Company to pay Will: Haulton in full payment of his play of ferrex & Porrex iij li iij s . . . iij^{li} iij s by me RobtShaa; pd for licencynge of A Boocke to the m^r of the Revelles called ferex & porex . . . vij s.'

150. *The English Fugitives* (Haughton, 1600, lost). 'Lent unto w^m harton the 16 of aprell 1600 in earneste of A Boocke called the Ingleshe fegetives the some of . . . x s | w^t Haughton; Item received more of m^r Henchelowe in earnest of ye englishe fugitives on the 24th of Aprill. by me received . . . 20s | w^t Haughton.'

151. *The Golden Ass or, Cupid and Psyche* (Dekker, Day, 1600, lost). 'Receaved of m^r Henshlowe in behalfe of the Company to geve Tho: Deckers & Jhon Day in earnest of a booke Called The golden Ass & Cupid & Psiches . . . xxx^s by me RobtShaa; Lent at the apoyntment of Robart shawe to Thomas deckers & John daye & harye chetell the 10 of maye 1600 in perte of payment of A Bocke called the gowlden asse cuped & siches some of . . . iij^{li} by John day to the use of Th Dekker Harry Chettle and himselfe; pd at the apoyntment of Robert shawe the 14 daye of maye 1600 in fulle payment of a Boocke called the gowlden asse cuped & siches to thomas deckers & hary chettell John daye some of . . . xxx^s; Lent unto Thomas dowton the 5 of June 1600 to bye a sewt for his boye in the playe of cuped & siches the some of . . . xxxx^s.'

152. *The Wooing of Death* (Chettle, 1600, lost). 'Receaved by me Henry Chettle of Mr Henshlowe in earnest of a booke Called the wooinge of deathe . . . xxˢ By me henry chettle.'

153. *The Battle of Alcazar* (Peele, 1588, quarto and 'plot', 1601). Q 1594 'THE | BATTELL | OF ALCAZAR, FOUGHT | in Barbarie, betweene Sebastian king | of Portugall, and Abdelmelec king | of Marocco. With the | death of Captaine | *Stukeley.* | As it was sundrie times plaid by the Lord high Admir- | rall his servants. | Imprinted at London by Edward Allde for Richard | Bankworth, and are to be solde at his shoppe in | Pouls Churchyard at the signe of the | Sunne. 1594' [old].[III]

154. *The Devil and his Dam or Grim the Collier of Croydon* (Haughton, 1600, Q *Grim the Collier of Croydon*). 'Lent unto wm harton the 6 of maye 1600 in earneste of a Boocke wᶜʰ he wold calle the devell & his dame . . . vˢ.'[112]

155. *Strange News out of Poland* (Haughton, Pett, 1600, lost). 'Received of Mʳ Henshlowe the 17ᵗʰ of May 1600 in behalfe of the Company to pay Will: Haulton & mʳ pett in full payment of a play Called straunge newes out of Poland . . . vjˡⁱ; Dd unto the littell tayller at the apoyntment of Robart shaw the 25 of maye 1600 for to macke sewtes for the playe called strange newes owt of powland . . . iijˡⁱ.'

156. *1 The Blind Beggar of Bethnal Green* (Chettle, Day, 1600, quarto). SR 14 Sept. 1657 '*a booke called the pleasant history of the Blind Begger of Bednall Greene, declaring his life and death &c.*'[113] Q1 'THE | BLIND-BEGGAR | OF | BEDNAL-GREEN, | WITH | The merry humor of *Tom Strowd* the | *Norfolk* Yeoman, as it was divers | times publickly

---

[III] Very likely the play performed 14 times by Strange's in 1592–93 as *Muly Mollocco,* the 'plot' indicates that the Admiral's revived it for Alleyn in mid-1601. Just possibly it is the same play as the one revived in August 1594 under the name *Mahomet* (see 11). Roslyn L. Knutson, 'Marlowe Reruns: Repertorial Commerce and Marlowe's plays in Revival', in *Marlowe's Empery,* ed. Sara Munson Deats and Robert A. Logan, Newark, 2002, p. 29, considers it likely that 'Mahomet' was 'Muly Mollocco' or *Alcazar.*

[112] In 1662 a 12ᵐᵒ volume of three plays was issued, including one with the title 'GRIM The *Collier* of *Croyden;* OR, The *Devil* and His *Dame*: WITH The *Devil* and Saint *Dunston.* By I. T.' Greg and others identified it with Haughton's play of May 1600, but since no note of full payment was made in 1600, they assumed the play for the Admiral's was never finished. Knutson agreed. However, the printed play does have an epilogue by St Dunstan saying 'we deserve to name / This play of ours, The Devil and his Dame', and *Twelfth Night* (1601) has an allusion to the play's devil, 'Castiliano' (1.3.34). Moreover *Wily Beguiled* (1602) was based on *Grim the Collier.* So Haughton's play must have been finished and performed by the Admiral's in 1600 in the text printed in 1662. See *A Choice Ternary of English Plays, Gratiae Theatrales* (1662), ed. William M. Baillie, Binghamton, NY, 1984. The *Diary* editors link Haughton's play with the 'like unto licke' played by the short-lived Pembroke's in October 1600.

[113] Since the blind beggar dies in neither part of the play, this entry may not be for the play but for a ballad or chapbook telling a version of the stage story. The issue of the quarto two years later, however, argues that it was for the play.

acted by the Princes | Servants. | *Written by* JOHN DAY. | LONDON, | Printed for *R. Pollard,* and *Tho. Dring,* and are to | be sold at the *Ben Johnsons* Head, behind the | *Exchange,* and the *George* in *Fleetstreet,* near Saint | *Dunstans* Church. 1659.' 'Receaved of Mr Henshlowe the 26th of May 1600 in behalfe of the Company to pay H. Chettle & Jhon Day in full payment of a booke Called the blynd begger of bedall greene the some of . . . v^{li} x^s.'[114]

157. *1 Fair Constance of Rome* (Munday, Drayton, Hathway, Dekker, Wilson, 1600, lost). 'Receaved of Mr Henshlowe thys 3th of June 1600 in behalfe of the Company to An: Munday & the rest in perte of payment for a booke Called the fayre Constance of Roome the some of . . . iij^{li} v^s; pd unto drayton hathway monday & deckers at the a poyntment of Robart shawe in full payment of A Boocke called the fayer constance of Rome the 14 of June 1600 some of . . . xxxxiiij^s; (letter from Shaa to Henslowe, *Diary* p. 294) I praye you Mr Henshlowe deliver unto the bringer hereof the some of fyve & fifty shillinges to make the 3^{li} –fyve shillinges wch they received before, full six poundes in full payment of their booke Called the fayre Constance of Roome. whereof I pray you reserve for me Mr Willsons whole share wch is xj s. wch I to supply his neede delivered hime yesternight. yor Lovinge Frend Robt Shaa.'

158. *2 Fair Constance of Rome* (Munday, Drayton, Hathway, 1600, lost). 'Lent unto Robart shawe the 20 of June 1600 to lend them hathway in earneste of ther second perte of constance of Rome the some of . . . xx^s.'

159. *1 Fortune's Tennis* (Dekker, 1600, lost). 'Lent unto Robart shawe the 6 of septmbre 1600 to paye unto Thomas deckers for his boocke called the fortewn tenes some of . . . xx^s.'[115]

160. *Robin Hood's Pennyworths* (Haughton, 1600, lost). 'Lent unto Samwell Rowley the 20 of desembre 1600 to lend unto w^m harton

---

[114] Which of the two parts appears in the 1659 quarto or whether it is a merged text is not at all clear. The 'Prince's Servants' who played it are unlikely to be Prince Henry's. It may have survived as a part of the Fortune repertory until the Prince Charles (II) company performed it there in the late 1630s. Since Tom Stroud plays a major part in the surviving quarto, and lacking identification of which part it might be, I have attached its description both to this and to the 'Tom Strowd' sequel of 1601, although the quarto reads like a first play rather than a sequel. Since the 26 May payment was a 'full' one, the ten shillings paid 'in earnest' three weeks after the May payment, with no play's name supplied, may have been for the sequel, which in the event did not appear for another six months.

[115] The absence of any further note about this play would suggest it died along with other aborted Dekker texts, if it were not for the survival of the 'plot' of a play marked as the second part from late 1602. The company moved from the Rose to the Fortune not long before this, so a play with such a name would have been appropriate now.

in earneste of A Boocke called Roben hoodes penerthes . . . xx s; Lent unto william hawghton the 27 of desembre 1600 in earneste of his Boocke called Roben hoodes penerthes . . . x s; Lent unto wm Hawghton the 4 of Jenewary 1600 in pert of payment of A Boocke called Roben hoodes penerth some of . . . x s; pd at the A poyntment of w^m Birde unto w^m harton for his playe of Roben hoodes penerthe the 13 of Janewary 1600 . . . xxxx^s.'

161. *Hannibal and Scipio* (Rankins, Hathway, 1601, lost). 'Receaved by us Richard Hathway & willm Rankins in pert of payment for the play of Hanniball & Scipio the summe of forty shillinges we say receaved the 3 day of Januarye 1600 . . . xxxx^s By us Wi: Rankins Ri: Hathwaye; Lent unto m^r Ranckens & hathway in earnest of A Boocke called hanyball & sepius the 3 of Janewary 1600 some of . . . xxxx^s; Lent unto m^r hathway & Ranckens the 11 of Janewary 1600 in perte of payment of A play called haneball & sepius . . . v^s; pd unto m^r Ranckene & m^r hathwaye the 12 daye of Janewary in fulle payment of A Bocke called haneball & sepies some of . . . iij^{li} xv^s.'

162. *Wherin is Scogan and Skelton* (Hathway, Rankins, 1601, lost). 'Lent unto mr hathwaye & mr Rancken the 23 of Janewary 1600 in earneste of A Boocke wherin is skogen & scellton some of . . . x s wittnes EAlleyn; Lent at the Apoyntment of samwell Rowley & thomas towne unto m^r Ranckens & m^r hathwaye the 26 of Janewary 1600 in earneste of A Boocke called wherin is skogen & skelton the some of . . . xxx s; Lent unto m^r hathwaye & m^r Ranckens ypon A boocke wherin is skogen & skelton at the a poyntment of samwell Rowley the 5 of febreary 1600 some of . . . xx^s; Lent unto mr Ranckens the 8 of febreary 1600 in eareste . . . ij s; Lent unto m^r hathwaye the 25 of febreary 1600 for A Boocke wherin is skelton & skogen at the A poyntment of Samwell Rowleye in perte of payment the some of . . . xxxx^s Samuell Rowlye; pd unto m^r Ranckens & m^r hathwaye at the apoyntment of the company the 8 of m^{r}ch 1600 in full payment of A Boocke wherin is skogen & skelton the some of . . . xviij s; dd unto the littell tayller at the apoyntment of the companye the 2 of maye 1601 to bye divers things for the playe of [skelton & skogen]^{116} the blind begger of elexsandrea . . . iij^{li}.'

163. *2 The Blind Beggar of Bethnal Green* (Haughton, Day, 1600, quarto?). 'Received of m^r Henchlowe in ernest of the second parte of the blind

---

116 Chapman's *Blind Beggar of Alexandria* is inserted above *Skelton and Skogen*, which is not deleted. Other evidence for a revival of Alleyn's 1596 play with its parodic Marlowe roles in 1601 is minimal, but its interlining here can hardly be accidental. Clothing was bought for it in May 1601.

begger of Bednall Greene the Sum of . . . 40^s 29 of January 1600. W^t Haughton J Day; Lent unto w^m Harton & J daye at the apoyntment of Samwell Rowly the 29 of Janewary 1600 in earnest of A Boocke called the second perte of the blinde beager of bednowle grene wth thomme strowde some of . . . xxxx s; Lent unto w^m harton & John daye in earnest of A Boocke called the 2 pert of tthome strowde the 10 day of febreary 1600 some of . . . xxx^s; pd at the apoyntment of Samell Rowley unto John daye & w^m harton for A Boock called the second perte of thome strowd the 10 of m^{r}ch 1600 the some of . . . xxx s; dd unto the littell tayler the 27 of aprell 1601 for the yousse of the companye to bye A sutte & lace for the 2 perte of strowde the some of . . . xxx s; pd unto John daye at the apoyntment of the company 1601 after the playnge of the 2 perte of strowde the some of . . . x s; pd unto John daye & w^m hawghton in fulle payment of A playe called the 2 perte of strowde the 5 of maye 1601 some at the apoyntment of Samwell Rollye . . . x s.'

164. *The Conquest of Spain* (Hathway, Rankins, 1601, lost). 'Lent unto m^r hathwaye & m^r Ranckens the 24 of m^{r}ch 1600 in earnest of A Boocke called conqueste of spayne some of . . . x s at the A poyntment of Samewell Rowly; Lent unto m^r hathwaye & m^r Ranckens the 4 of Aprell 1601 in earneste of A playe called the conqueste of spayne the some of . . . v^s; Lent unto m^r hathway & m^r Ranckens the xj of Aprell in earneste of A Boocke called the conquest of spayne by John a gant some of . . . xx^s; Lent unto m^r hathwaye & m^r Ranckens the 16 of aprell 1601 in perte of payment for A Boocke called the conqueste of spayne some of . . . iiij s; (letter to Henslowe from Rowley, undated) M^r hynchlo I praye ye let M^r hathwaye have his papars agayne of the playe of John a gante & for the Repayemente of the money backagayne he Is contente to gyve ye a byll of his hande to be payde at some cartayne tyme as In yor dyscressyon yow shall thinke good, wch done ye maye crose it oute of yor boouke & keepe the byll, or else wele stande so muche indetted to yow & kepe the byll o^r selves. Samuell Rowlye.'

165. *All Is Not Gold that Glisters* (Chettle, 1601, lost). 'Layd owte at the A poyntment of Samwell Rowly unto harey chettell in perte of paymente for A Boocke called al is not gowld y^t glesters the laste of m^{r}che 1601 some of . . . xxxx^s; pd unto harey chettell the 6 of aprell 1601 in full payment of A Boocke called al is not gowld that glysters at the A poyntment of Samwell Rowley some of . . . iiij^{li}.'

166. *The Conquest of the West Indies* (Day, Haughton, 1601, lost). 'Lent unto John daye & w^m hawghton the 4 of aprell 1601 in earnest of

playe called the conqueste of the weste enges at the apoyntment of
Samwell Rowlye the some of . . . xxxx s; (letter from Rowley to
Henslowe 4 April 1601) Mr Hinchloe I have hard five shetes of a
playe of the Conqueste of the Indes & I dow not doute but It wyll be
a verye good playe tharefore I praye ye delyver them forty shyllynges
In earneste of yt & take the papers Into yor one hands & on easter
eve thaye promyse to make an ende of all the Reste Samuell Rowlye
lent the 4 of aprell 1601 — xxxx s; Lent unto m^r smyth & w^m
hawghton the xj of Aprell 1601 in earnest of A Boocke called the
conquest of the weste enges at the apoyntment of samwell Rowly the
some of . . . xx s; Lent wm haughton in earneste of the playe called
the conquest of the west enges the 2 of maye 1601 the some of . . . v^s;
Lent unto John daye the 21 of maye 1601 in earnest of A Boocke
called the [vj yemen] of the weste [enges] enges the some of . . . xx s
at the a poyntment of Samwell Rowley; (note by Day to Henslowe
6 June 1601) about the plot of the Indyes I have occasion to be absent
therefore pray delyver it to will hauton fidler by me John Daye; Lent
unto Samwell Rowley the 5 of agust 1601 to lend in perte of payment
unto John daye & w^m hawghton of A Boocke called the weaste enges
some of x s; Lent unto wm hawghton & John daye the 11 of aguste
1601 in pert of payment of ther playe called the west enges some
of . . . xx s; Lent unto John daye the 26 of aguste 1601 in pert of
payment of A Boocke called the weast enges the some of . . . x s; Lent
unto the company the 1 of septmbre to Lend John daye in pert of
payment of A Boocke called the weaste enges some of . . . x s; Lent
unto my sonne & w^m Jube the 31 of Septmbre 1601 to bye divers
thinges & sewttes & stockenes for the playe of the weaste enges the
some of . . . x^{li} x s; pd the tayllers bille Radford & w^m whites bell at
the apoyntment of Robart shawe & Jube the 10 of octobre 1601 for
the playe of the weaste enges the some of . . . lvij s; pd the 21 of
Janeway for xij oz of lace . . . for Indies—x s.'

167. *King Sebastian of Portugal* (Dekker, Chettle, 1601, lost).[117] 'Lent unto
Jubey the 18 of Aprell 1601 to lend unto Thomas deckers & hary
chettell in earneste of A Boocke called kinge sebastiane of portingalle

---

[117] Some years after the battle of Alcazar where most of the Portuguese court were slaughtered, leaving
Spain to take over the country, a man claiming to be King Sebastian and a survivor of the battle
received a lot of credibility, though Spain understandably disagreed. English enmity to Spain made
many in London uphold his claim. The title of this play suggests it was written in support of the
pretender's case. In 1628 Massinger, under pressure from the Master of the Revels, had to adapt his
play for the King's Men on the same subject, *Believe As You List*, and set it in ancient Carthage.

the some of . . . xx s; Lent unto the company the 16 of maye 1601 to paye unto Thomas deckers & harye chettell in perte of payment of A playe called kynge sebastion of portingall the some of . . . xxxx^s; pd at the apoyntment of EAlleyn the 22 of may 1601 unto Thomas deckers in fulle payment of a boocke called kynge Sebastian of portyngall the some of . . . iij^{li}.'

168. *The Six Yeomen of the West* (Haughton, Day, 1601, lost). 'Lent unto wm hawghton the 20 of maye 1601 in earnest of the vj yemon of the weaste the some of . . . x s Lent more unto wm hawghton . . . v^s; Lent unto John daye the 21 of maye 1601 in earnest of A Boocke called the [vj yemen] of the weste enges the some of . . . xx s at the apoyntment of Samwell Rowley; Lent at the a poyntment of Samwell Rowlye the 4 day of June 1601 unto John daye in pert of payment of A Boocke called the vj yemon of the weaste the some of . . . xxx^s; pd at the A poyntment of Samell Rowlye unto w^m hawghton in perte of payment of A Boocke called the vj yemon of the weste the 6 of June 1601 the some of . . . xv^s; [letter from Rowley, undated] Mr Henchloe I praye ye delyver the Reste of the Monye to John daye & wyll hawton dew to them of the syx yemen of the weste; Lent unto Samwell Rowleye the 8 of June 1601 to paye unto w^m howghton in fulle paymente of A Boocke called the vj yemon of the weste the some of . . . xxx^s; Lent unto the company the j of July 1601 to bye divers thinges for the vj yemen of the weaste the some of fortye shellenges . . . xxxx^s; Lent unto the littell tayller at the A poynt ment of the 2 of July 1601 to bye divers thinges of the vj yemen of the weste some of . . . xx s; pd unto the cope lace man the 2 of July 1601 at the A poyntment of the company for copre lace for the vj yemen of the weaste some of . . . ix s; pd at the A poyntment of the company the 3 of Julye 1601 to the copre lace man for owld deates the some of . . . iiij^{li}; pd at the A poyntment of the company the 3 of Julye 1601 unto the coper lace man for lace for the vj yemon of the weaste some of . . . vj^s; pd unto the coper lace man for coper lace for the vj yemen of the west the 4 of July 1601 the some of . . . 10 A ownc 36 onces . . . vj s; pd at the A poyntment of Robart shawe the 6 of Julye 1601 unto the littell tayller for mackynge of sewtes for the vj yemen the some of . . . xxij s.'

169. *3 Tom Strowd* (Day, Haughton, 1601, lost).[118] 'Lent unto John daye at the apoyntment of Samwell Rowley the 21 of maye 1601 in earnest

---

[118] An extension of the first two parts, both called *The Blind Beggar of Bethnal Green* above.

of A Bocke called the 3 pert of thome strowde the some of . . . x s; lent unto wm hawghton the 18 of July 1601 in perte of payment of the 3 pert of Thome strowde . . . x s; lent mor the same time unto John daye in earnest of A Boocke called the 3 pert of Thome strowde some of . . . v^s; (undated note from Rowley to Henslowe) M^r hincheloe I praye ye delyver to John Daye Thurtye shyllyngs whych Is upon the thurd parte of Tom Strowde Samuell Rowlye; Lent unto Samwell Rowley 1601 the 25 of July to lend unto John daye & w^m hawghton in pert of payment of A Boocke called the third pert of Thome strowde the some of . . . 40^s; Lent unto Samwell Rowley the 30 of July 1601 to paye unto John daye & w^m hawghton in fulle payment of A Boocke called the third perte of thome strowde the some of . . . iij^{li} v^s; Lent at the a poyntment of the company the 27 of aguste 1601 unto dover the tayller to bye dyvers thinges for the 3 perte of thome strowd the some of . . . xxx^s; Lent unto the company the 1 of septmbre 1601 to bye blacke buckrome to macke a sewte for a fyer drack in the 3 pert of thome strowde the some of . . . iij s vj d; Lent unto the company the 3 of septmbre 1601 to paye the tayller dover for mackenge of divers thinges for the third perte of tome strowde the some of . . . l s; Lent unto the company the 3 of septmbre 1601 to paye unto the m^r of the Revelles for licensynge of the 3 perte of thome strowde & the Remaynder of carnowlle wollsey . . . 10 s; Lent unto the company the 10 of septmbre 1601 wch them sellfes must paye for to paye unto dover the tayller upon his bill for the 3 pert of thome strowde the some of . . . xiij^s 4^d; pd at the apoyntment of the company the 23 of septmbre unto m^r bramfelld for v y^{r}des of Roset brode cloth the some of . . . xxx^s for the 3 pert of thome strowd.'

170. *1 Cardinal Wolsey* (Chettle, 1601, lost). 'Lent unto Samwell Rowlye 1601 to paye unto harye chettell for writtinge the Boocke of carnalle wolseye lyfe the 5 of June some of . . . xx s; Layd owt at the A poyntment of my sonne & the company unto harey cheattell for the altrynge of the boocke of carnowlle wollsey the 28 of June 1601 the some of . . . xx s; Lent unto Robart shawe the 4 of Julye 1601 to paye unto harey cheattell for the Boocke of carnowlle wollsey in fulle pay ment the some of . . . xxxx^s; Lent unto the companye the 17 of July 1601 to geve unto hary chettell for the Boocke of the carnawlle wollsey to paye unto m^r Bromffelld the some of . . . xx^s; Lent unto Robart shawe the 7 of aguste 1601 to bye divers thinges tanye cottes for the playe of carnowle wollsey the some of . . . xxx^s; Lent the same tymes unto the littell tayller for the same playe of carnowlle wollsey

some of . . . vij s; Bowght of mr stonne merser the 10 of aguste 1601 ij pylle velvet of carnadyn at xx^s y^{r}d & sattenes at xij s & tafeties at xij s & vj d wch I layd owt for the company some is for the playe of carnawll wollsey . . . xxj^{li}; Layd owt more for the playe of carnowlle wollsey for tynsell & tyffeney & lynynge & other thinges the same tyme dd unto Jewby the some of . . . iij^{li} x s; Lent unto Robart shawe the 11 of aguste to bye cottes for the playe of carnowlle wollsey the some of . . . xx s; Lent unto Robart shawe the 12 of aguste 1601 to bye divers thinges for the playe of carnowlle wollsey the some of . . . xx^s; Lent unto the littell tayller the 12 of agust to bye divers thinges for the playe of carnowlle wollsey at the apoyntment of my sonne the some of . . . x s; Layd owt at the A poyntment of the company the 13 of agust 1601 for ij tayllers billes & w^m whittes bille after the playe of carnowells wollsey the some of . . . viij^{li} 4^s; pd unto the tyer man the 14 of aguste 1601 for mony wch he layd owt to bye teffeny for the playe of carnowlle wollsey some of . . . xiiij d.'

171. 2 *Cardinall Wolsey* (Chettle, Munday, Drayton, Smyth, 1601, lost).[119]
'Lent unto Robart shawe the 18 of aguste 1601 to paye unto harey chettell for his Boocke of carnowlle wollsey the some of . . . xx^s; Lent unto the companye the 20 of agust 1601 to bye A docters gowne for the play of carnowlle wollsey the some of . . . x s dd to Radford; Lent unto Robart shawe the 21 of aguste 1601 for velvet & mackynge of the docters gowne in carnowlle wollsey the some of . . . xx^s; Lent unto Robart shaw the 24 of aguste 1601 to lend unto harey chettell in earenest of A play called j pert of carnall wollsey the som of . . . xx^s; Lent unto the company the 3 of septmbre 1601 to paye unto the m^r of the Revelles for licensynge of the 3 pert of thome strowde & the Remaynder of carnowlle wollsey . . . x s; Lent unto Robarte shawe to lend unto hary chettell & antony mundaye & mihell drayton in earneste of A Boocke called the Rissenge of carnowlle wolsey the 10 of octobre 1601 . . . xxxx^s; Lent unto harey chettell by the company at the eagell & the chillde in pert of payment of A Boocke called the

---

[119] Confusion rules the entries for the two plays about Cardinal Wolsey. Chettle wrote one play for which he began to receive payments in June 1601, and wrote another with Munday and Drayton, payments for which started in October. F. P. Wilson (ed. *When You See Me, You Know Me*, Malone Society Reprints, 1952, p. ix) considers that the second part, or 'the rising', then became the first part in the entries. The separate entries for the two plays here have been allowed to overlap, and which payments were made for which play left in doubt. The full payment on 12 Nov. 1601 for 'the firste pert' may actually mark its switch from being the second part. Conceivably the payment to Chettle on 28 June was to divide the original play into two. We assume that the second play about the 'Rissenge' of Wolsey was about his younger days, and hence became Part 1.

Rissynge of carnoll wollsey the some of . . . x s 6 of novmbre 1601; Lent unto the company the 9 of novmbre 1601 to paye unto m^r monday & hary chettell in pert of payment of A Boocke called the Rissynge of carnowlle wollsey the some of . . . x s; Lent unto the company the 12 of novmbre 1601 to paye unto antony monday & harye chettell mihell drayton & smythe in fulle payment of the firste pert of carnowll wollsey the some of . . . iij^{li}; Lent unto thomas downton the 15 of maye 1602 to paye harey chettell for the mendynge of the fyrste perte of carnowlle wollsey the some of . . . xx^s. Lent unto Thomas downton the 18 of maij to bye maskyngsewtes antycke for the 2 perte of carnowlle wollsey the some of . . . iij^{li} v^s; Lent unto Thomas downton the 20 of maij to by a grene sewt & wovon sleves the some of for wollseye . . . l s; Lent unto Thomas downton the 27 of maij 1602 to bye w^m someres cotte & other thinges for the 2 pert of wollsey the some of . . . iij^{li}; Lent unto Thomas downton the 27 of maye 1602 to by Rebatous & other thinges for the 2 pert of carnowlle wollsey the some of . . . xxv^s; Lent unto thomas downton the 2 of June 1602 to to paye unto the coper lace mane in fulle payment for lace for the 2 pert of wollsey . . . xxvj s; (paper from William Playstow for payments to the Master of the Revels) bookes owinge for / 5 / per mei Willplaystowe / baxters tragedy / Tobias Comedy / Jepha Judg of Israel & the cardinall / love parts frendshipp.'

172. *The Earl of Gloster* (Wadeson, 1601, lost). 'June 13th 1601 Borrowed of m^r Phillip Hinsloe by me Anthonie wadeson the sum of xx^s in earnest of a booke cald the honorable lyfe of the Humorous Earle of Gloster wth his conquest of Portugall . . . xx^s wittnes Thomas Downton Ant Wadeson; Lent at the A poyntment of Thomas downton the 13 of June 1601 unto Antony wadeson in earneste of A Boocke called the life of the humeros earlle of gloster wth his conquest of portingalle some of . . . xx s; Lent unto antony wadsone at the apoynt ment of A boocke called the onarable lyfe of the hewmerus earlle of gloster some of x^s.'[120]

173. *Friar Rush and the Proud Woman of Antwerp* (Day, Haughton, 1601, lost). 'Lent unto John Daye & w^m hawghton at the A poyntmente of Robart shawe in earneste of A Boocke called fryer Rushe & the

---

[120] The 'humorous' Gloucester featured strongly in *Look About You*, staged some time before its publication in 1600. At its close the earl announces that he is off to fight in Portugal, suggesting that the unknown writer of *Look About You* may have been Wadeson, since most sequels were undertaken at least in part by the same writers.

prowde womon the some of . . . xx^s the 4 daye of Julye; Lent unto Robart shawe the 14 of July 1601 to geve unto w^m hawgton & John daye in earneste of A Boocke called the prowde womon of anwarpe frier Rushe the some of . . . xxx^s; dd unto w^m hawghton at the Apoyntment of Samwell Rowlley the 31 of septmbre 1601 in pert of payment of A Boocke called the prowde womon of anwarpe the some of . . . x s; Lent unto Samwell Rowley by the apoyntment of the companye the 9 of novmbre 1601 to paye unto w^m hawghton for his boocke of the prowd womon of Anwarppe the some of . . . xx^s; Lent unto Samwell Rowlley the 29 of novmbre 1601 to paye w^m hawghton in fulle paye for his play called the prowd womon of anwarpe the some of . . . xx^s; Lent unto Robart shawe the 21 of Janewarye 1601 to geve unto harey cheattell for mendinge of the Boocke called the prowde womon the some of . . . x s.'

174. *2 Tom Dough* (Day, Haughton, 1601, lost).[121] 'lent unto John daye the same time [30 July 1601] in earnest of A Boocke called the 2 pert of thome dowghe the some of . . . x s; Lente unto the company the 3 of septmbre 1601 to paye unto John daye & wm hawghton in pert of payment of A Boocke called the 2 perte of thome dowghe . . . iij^{li}; Lent at the Apoyntment of Robart shawe the 11 of septmbre 1601 to lend unto w^m hawghton in pert of payment of the 2 pert of thome dowghe some of . . . x^s.'

175. *1 The Six Clothiers* (Hathway, Smith, Haughton, 1601, lost). 'Lent at the apoyntment of Samwell Rowley the 12 of octobre 1601 to m^r hathwaye & wenworte smyth & w^m hawghton in earneste of A playe called the vj clothers the some of . . . xxxx^s; Lent at the apoyntment of samwell Rowlley the 22 of octobre 1601 unto m^r hathwaye & wentworthe smyth & w^m hawghton in pert of paymente of A Boocke called the vj clothers some . . . iij^{li}.'

176. *2 The Six Clothiers* (Hathway, Smith, Haughton, 1601, lost). '(4–7 Nov. 1601) Lent unto Samelle Rowley & Robert shawe to paye unto m^r hathwaye & m^r smyth & w^m hawghton for A Boocke called the 2 perte of the vj clothers . . . xxxx^s; Receaved by us Ri. Hathway; wenworth Smyth & william Haughton of Mr Hinslye the summe of forty shillinges in earneste of the play called the second perte of the sixe clothyers. Ri: Hathwaye W: Smyth.'

---

[121] Nothing exists in the *Diary* to suggest that Day or anyone else wrote a first part of this play. Henslowe was too precise to confuse it with *2 Tom Strowd*, the alternative name for *2 The Blind Beggar of Bethnal Green*, which he had fully paid for on 5 May. Moreover, the second entry for *2 Tom Dough* is on the same day as an entry for *3 Tom Strowd*.

177. *Too Good to be True* (Chettle, Hathway, Smith, 1601–2, lost). 'Lent
    at the apoyntment of the company & my sonne unto hary chettell in
    earnest of a playe called to good to be trewe the some of v^s the 14 of
    novmbre 1601; pd at the apoyntment of Robart shawe & thomas
    towne unto m^r Hathwaye & m^r smythe in perte of payment of
    A Boocke called to good to be trewe the 6 of Janewary 1601 the
    some of . . . l s; pd at the apoyntment of Robart shawe the 7 of
    Janewary 1601 unto hary cheattell & m^r Hathwaye & m^r smyth in
    fulle payment for A Boocke called to good to be trewe the some
    of . . . iij^{li} x s; [letter from Shaa to Henslowe, 7 Jan. 1602] I pray you
    Mr Henslowe deliver in behalfe of the Company, unto the fifty
    shillinges wch they receavd the other day, three poundes & tenn
    shillinges more, in full payment of six poundes the pryce of their
    play Called to good to be true. yo^{rs} Robt Shaa.'

178. *Judas* (Haughton, Bird, Rowley, 1601, lost). 'Lent unto w^m harton
    the 27 of maye 1600 in earneste of A Boocke called Judas the some of
    . . . x s;[122] pd unto w^m Borne at the apoyntment of company the 20 of
    desembre 1601 in earnest of A Boocke called Judas wch samewell
    Rowly & he is a writtinge some of xx s; pd at the apoyntment of
    the company in fulle payment for A Boocke called Judas unto w^m
    Borne & Samvvelle Rowley the 24 of desembre 1601 the some of v^{li};
    Lent unto antony Jaffes the 3 of Janewary 1601 to bye cloth for the
    playe of Judas the some of . . . xxx^s.'[123]

179. *The Spanish Fig* (1601, lost). 'pd at the apoyntment of EAlleyn the
    6 of Janewary 1601 in perte of payment of A Boocke called the
    spaneshe fygge the some of . . . iij^{li}.'[124]

180. *Pontius Pilate* (1601? lost). 'pd unto Thomas deckers at the apoynt-
    mente of the company for A prologe & a epiloge for the playe of

[122] See Chapter 1, p. 41.

[123] The single entry on 27 May 1600 was made of an 'earnest' to William Haughton. Although for this
    year the records are not complete, the lack of any further entries suggests that he abandoned the
    idea. Nineteen months later, in Dec. 1601, the players Rowley and Bird appear to have taken his
    idea on again, and were paid in full for their writing on 24 Dec. As Knutson, 'Commercial
    Significance', p. 126, suggests, they may have worked from Haughton's original papers. This
    would confirm the idea that Haughton's version never reached the stage.

[124] Judging by the concision of the entry, the failure to name a writer, and the payment being
    authorised by Alleyn, this was most likely another old play that he was reviving, if it was not Bird
    and Rowley's *Judas* of the month before. The same may be true of *Pontius Pilate*, since that
    payment was only for a prologue and epilogue. The second entry after *Pontius Pilate*, on 18 Jan.
    1602, was a payment of £6 to Alleyn for three old plays, *The French Doctor*, *The Massacre at Paris*
    and *Crack me this Nut*. The last two were revived in Nov. 1601.

ponescioues pillet the 12 of Janewary 1601 the some of . . . x s; (inventory of apparel 10 March 1598) My Lord Caffes gercken.'[125]

181. *Malcolm King of Scots* (Massey, 1602, lost). 'pd at the apoyntment of the companye the 18 of aprell 1602 unto charlles massey for a playe Boocke called malcolm Kynge of scottes the some of . . . v^li; Lent unto Thomas downton the 27 of aprell 1602 to bye a sewt of motley for the scotchman for the playe called the malcolm Kynge of scotes the some of . . . xxx s.'

182. *2 Fortune's Tennis* (Dekker, 1602, 'plot').[126] A fragmentary manu-script 'plot', British Museum MS Add. 10449. Fol. 4. It is headed 'The P - - ond Part of Fortun - - is.' Its date can be identified by the players it names, including Singer, Cartwright, Massey, Rowley, Taylor, and a 'Tho', who may be Hunt, Parsons, Towne or Downton. Cartwright and Taylor were not yet in the company when *1 Fortune's Tennis* was paid for in Sept. 1600; they were by Dec. 1602 when Munday's *Set at Tennis* (see 198 below), conceivably the play for which the plot was written, was paid for.

183. *Love Parts Friendship* (Chettle, Smith, 1602, lost). 'Lent unto Thomas downton the 4 of maye 1602 to bye A Boocke of harye cheattell & m^r smyth called the love pertes frenship the some of . . . vj li; Lent unto Thomas downton the 31 of maye 1602 to bye a sewt for ther playe called love partes frenshippe . . . l s; (paper from William Playstow for payments to the Master of the Revels) bookes owinge for / 5 / per mei Willplaystowe / baxters tragedy / Tobias Comedy / Jepha Judg of Israel & the cardinall / love parts frendshipp.'

184. *The Bristol Tragedy* (Day, 1602, lost). 'Lent at the a poyntment of Samewell Rowlye unto John daye the 4 of maye 1602 in earneste of A play called bristo tragedy as maye a pere the some of . . . xx s; pd unto John daye at the apoyntmente of w^m Jube & the Reste of the companye for A Boocke called Bristo tragedi the 23 of maij 1602 the some of . . . xxxx s written by hime sellfe; dd at the apoyntment of Thomas towne the 28 of maye 1602 unto John daye in fulle payment for his playe written by hime sellfe called bristo tragedie the some of . . . xxxx s; (paper from William Playstow for payments to the Master of the Revels) bookes owinge for / 5 / per mei Willplaystowe / baxters

---

[125] Malone suggested that 'Caffes' was Caiaphas, a necessary character in the Pilate story.
[126] Chambers (*Elizabethan Stage* II. 180) conjectures that *2 Fortune's Tennis* may have been Munday's *Set at Tennis*, for which he received full payment on 2 Dec. 1602, but the two titles are treated here as separate plays.

tragedy / Tobias Comedy / Jepha Judg of Israel & the cardinall / love parts frendshipp.'[127]

185. *Jephthah* (Munday, Dekker, 1602, lost). 'Lent unto the companye the 5 of maye 1602 to geve unto antony monday & thomas deckers I earnest of a Booke called Jeffae As may apere the some of . . . v^{li}; Layd owt for the companye when they Read the playe of Jeffa for wine at the tavern dd unto thomas downton . . . ij s; Lent unto Thomas downton the 8 of maye 1602 to bye cottes for the playe of Jeffa the some of . . . vj^{li}; Lent unto Thomas downton the 12 of June 1602 to by Rebatous & other thinges for the playe of Jeffa the some of . . . iiij^{li}; pd at the apoynt of Thomas downton unto the tayller for mackynge of sewtes for Jeffa the 25 of June 1602 some of . . . xxx^s; Lent unto the company 1602 the 27 of June to paye unto hime wch made ther propertyes for Jeffa the some of . . . xxv^s; Lent unto thomas downton the 5 of July 1602 to paye the cuter for the play of Jeffa the some of . . . xxij^s; (paper from William Playstow for payments to the Master of the Revels) bookes owinge for / 5 / per mei Willplaystowe / baxters tragedy / Tobias Comedy / Jepha Judg of Israel & the cardinall / love parts frendshipp.'[128]

186. *Tobias* (Chettle, 1602, lost). 'Lent unto Thomas downton the 16 of maye 1602 to geve harey cheattell in earneste of a playe called Tobyas the some of xx s; Lent unto thomas downton the 2 of June 1602 to geve harey cheattell upon his Boocke of tobyas the some of . . . xx^s; Lent unto Thomas downton the 26 of June 1602 to paye unto harey chettell in pert of payment of A Boocke called tobyas the some of . . . iij^{li}; Lent unto thomas downton the 27 of June 1602 to paye unto harey chettell in fulle payment of his Boocke called tobias the some of . . . xxv^s; (paper from William Playstow for payments to the Master of the Revels) bookes owinge for / 5 / per mei Willplaystowe / baxters tragedy / Tobias Comedy / Jepha Judg of Israel & the cardinall / love parts frendshipp.'

---

[127] In the absence of any other indication of what 'baxters tragedy' may have been, I assume it to be another name for the 'bristo tragedie', if only because *The Bristol Tragedy* was the play most likely have been sent to the Master of the Revels along with *Jephthah*, *Tobias* and at least one of the *Cardinal Wolsey* plays.

[128] In view of Hamlet's comment on Jephthah in 1600 it seems a little odd that the Admiral's should choose to stage a play two years later whose subject was already familiar to early audiences. But the purchase was of the complete book, so it may well have been staged elsewhere before the Admiral's bought it from Munday and Dekker. Such a biblical subject would add to the number that Alleyn bought at this time.

187. *Caesar's Fall* (Munday, Drayton, Webster, Middleton, 1602, lost). 'Lent unto the company the 22 of maij 1602 to geve unto antoney monday & mihell drayton webester & the Rest mydelton in earneste of A Boocke called sesers Falle the some of . . . v^{li}.'[129]

188. *Richard Crookback* (Jonson, 1602, lost). 'Lent unto bengemy Johnsone at the A poyntment of EAlleyn & w^m birde the 22 of June 1602 in earneste of A Boocke called Richard crockbacke & for new adicyons for Jeronymo the some of . . . x^{li}.'[130]

189. *The Danish Tragedy* (Chettle, 1602, lost).[131] 'Lent unto Thomas downton the 7 of July 1602 to geve unto harye chettell in earneste of A tragedy called A danyshe tragedy the some of . . . xx s.'

190. *The Widow's Charm* (Wadeson?[132] 1602, lost). 'Lent unto thomas downton the 9 of July 1602 to Lend unto antony the poyete in earneste of A comody called the widowes cherme the some of . . . x s; Lent unto antony the poyet in pert of payment of A comody called widowes Charme the 26 of aguste 1602 the some of . . . v^s; Lent unto w^m Birde & w^m Jube the 2 of sepmbre 1602 to paye unto antonye the poyet in perte of payment of A comody called A widowes Charme the some of . . . x s; Lent unto antony the poet the 11 of septmbre 1602 in perte of payment of A comody called the widowes charme some of . . . v^s.'

191. *A Medicine for a Curst Wife* (Dekker, 1602, lost). 'Lent unto Thomas downton & edwarde Jewbe to geve unto Thomas deckers in earnest of A comody called A medysen for A curste wiffe. 19 of July 1602 . . . xxxx^s; Lent unto Thomas downton the 31 of July 1602 to paye unto [hary chettell] Thomas deckers in perte of payment of his comody called a medyssen for a curste wiffe . . . the some of . . . xxxx^s; Layd owt more for the company in perte of payment for A Boocke called

---

[129] No other entry for this play is on record, but Munday, Dekker, Drayton, Middleton and Webster were paid £3 on 29 May 'in full paymente for ther playe called – too shapes – ', the title added by another hand than Henslowe's to fill the space. Chambers and others think this must be the same play.

[130] Ten pounds was a large sum to pay 'in earneste' for a playbook plus some 'adicyons', particularly since no further entry for *Richard Crookback* appears in the *Diary*. Presumably Alleyn was negotiating with Jonson and the playbook was complete, though it has not survived in the Jonson canon. A new play about Richard III is not unlikely for this time.

[131] Chambers (*Elizabethan Stage* II. 181) conjectured that this was *Hoffman* (202 below). It could have been the story for which as a revenge play *Hoffman* was the sequel.

[132] The enigmatic 'antonye the poyet' is unlikely to have been Antony Munday, although he did turn from writing plays to pageants and history in his later years, dying in 1633. I wonder if it can have been Antony Wadeson, who may have written the nameless *Look About You* (39) in 1595 and who definitely wrote its sequel about the 'humorous' Earl of Gloucester (172) in mid-1601.

medsen for a curst wiffe the some of . . . x s unto thomas deckers;[133]
pd at the A poyntment of the company the 1 of septmbre 1602 in
perte of payment for A comody called A medysen for A curste wiffe
to thomas deckers some of . . . iiij li; pd at the A poyntment the of
company the 2 of septmbre 1602 in fulle payment for A comody
called A medysen for A curste wiffe to thomas deckers the some of
. . . xxx^s; pd unto Thomas deckers the 27 of septmbre 1602 over &
above his price of his boocke called A medysen for A curste wife some
of . . . x s.'

192. *Samson* (Chettle, 1602, lost). 'Lent unto Samwell Rowley & edwarde
      Jewbe to paye for the Boocke of Samson the 29 of July 1602 the
      some of . . . vj^{li}.'

193. *Phillip of Spain.*[134] 'pd unto my sone EA for ij bocke called phillipe of
      spayne & Longshanckes the 8 of agust 1602 the some of . . . iiij^{li}'
      [old].

194. *Felmelanco* (Robinson, Chettle, 1602, lost). 'Lent unto umfrey Jeaffes
      the 9 of septmbre 1602 in pert of payment unto m^r Roben sone for
      A tragedie called felmelanco ther some of . . . iij^{li}; Lent unto thomas
      downton the 15 of septmbre 1602 to paye unto harey chettell in perte
      of payment for his tragedie of felmelanco the some of . . . x s; pd
      at the a poyntment of thomas downton to harey chettell in fulle
      payment of his tragedie called felmelanco some of l s.'[135]

195. *Joshua* (Samuel Rowley, 1602, lost). 'pd unto Samwell Rowley the
      27 of Septmbre 1602 for his playe of Jhosua in full payment the some
      of . . . vii li.'[136]

196. *The Chester Tragedy* (*Randulf Earl of Chester*) (Middleton, 1602,
      lost). 'pd at the apoynt of w^m Jube the 21 of octobre 1602 unto m^r
      medelton in perte of payment For his playe called ~~felmelanco~~

[133] From this date (27 Aug. 1602) onwards payments are recorded on behalf of Worcester's at the
Rose, who must have been the company that actually performed the play. Henslowe has no note
about any transfer of costs or plays between the Admiral's at the Fortune, who paid for the
play's first instalments, and Worcester's. From the time Henslowe paid Heywood and Smith for a
play called *Albere Galles* on behalf of Worcester's it is not always clear which company bought
which play.

[134] *Longshanks* was one of the old plays revived by Alleyn, so it is likely that this otherwise unknown
play about Mary Tudor's husband was another of his revivals.

[135] Between the entry about *Felmelanco* of 15 Sept. and the undated 'full payment' comes an entry for
£718 as the total for 1602 of 'ther billes for tayllers & others', and another of 32s for 'the new playe
of the earlle of harfurd'. This may record the purchase either of an unnamed play from Herford's
Men, or of a play about the earl, the queen's cousin. It has not been listed here.

[136] The only entry for this play, it appears to be yet another biblical story written by Rowley for the
company, not a new playscript he was selling. Two months later, on 22 November, Rowley shared
£4 with Bird for 'ther adicyones in docter fostes'.

Chester tragedie the some of . . . iiij^{li}; Lent unto Edward Jube the 9 of novmbre 1602 to paye unto m^r mydelton in fulle paymente of his playe called Randowlle earlle of chester the some of . . . xxxx s.'

197. <u>*As Merry As May Be*</u> (Day, Smith, Hathway, 1602, lost). 'Lent unto Edward Jube the 5 of novmbre 1602 to geve unto John daye in earneste of A Boocke called mery as may be for the cort the some of . . . xxxx^s; Lent unto Thomas downton the 17 of novmbre 1602 to paye unto Johne daye & m^r smythe & hathwaye in fulle paymente for A Boocke called as merey as may be the some of . . . vj^{li}.'

198. <u>*The Set at Tennis*</u> (Munday, 1602, lost). 'Lent unto Edwarde Jube the 2 of desembre 1602 to paye unto antony mondaye in fulle payment for a playe called the seeat at tenes some is . . . iiij^{li}.'

199. <u>*The Four Sons of Amon*</u> (1602? lost). 'Layd owt for the companye the 10 of desembre 1602 unto Robart shawe for A boocke of the 4 sonnes of amon the some of . . . xl s, Memorandum that I Robert Shaa have receaved of m^r Phillip Henshlowe the some of forty shillinges upon a booke Called the fower sones of Aymon wch booke if it be not playd by the company of the fortune nor noe other company by my leave I doe then bynd my selfe by theis presentes to repay the sayd some of forty shillinges upon the delivery of my booke att Cristmas next wch shall be in the yeare of our Lord god 1603 & in the xlvjth yeare of the Raigne of the queene per me Robt Shaa' [old?].[137]

200. <u>*Friar Bacon and Friar Bungay*</u> (Greene, 1591, quarto). SR 14 May 1594, 'the history of Fryer Bacon and Fryer Boungaye'. Q1 'THE | HONORABLE HISTORIE | of frier Bacon, and frier Bongay. | As it was plaid by her Majesties servants. | Made by *Robert Greene* Maister of Arts. | LONDON. | Printed for Edward White, and are to be sold at his shop, at | the little North dore of Poules, at the signe of | the Gun. 1594.' 'Lent unto Thomas downton the 14 of desembre 1602 to paye unto m^r mydelton for a prologe & A epeloge for the playe of bacon for the corte the some of . . . v^s' [old].[138]

201. <u>*1 The London Florentine*</u> (Chettle, Heywood, 1602, lost). 'Lent unto Thomas downton the 17 of desembre 1602 to paye unto harey chettell in earneste of A playe called london florenten the some

---

[137] This looks like an old playbook that Shaa was selling, since its price is the same as those for which Alleyn was paid in 1600–02. On 6 Jan. 1624 Henry Herbert re-licensed it as 'an Old Playe' for Prince Charles's Men.

[138] For the Queen's Men's old play to be performed at court meant it had been revived during the 1602 season. Conceivably it could be counted as one of the many Alleyn had previously been famous for, revived after he returned to the stage in 1600.

of . . . x s; pd at the apoyntment of the company the 20 of desembre 1602 unto Thomas hewode in pert for his playe called london florentyn the some of . . . xxxx^s; Lent unto Thomas downton the 22 of desembre 1602 to paye unto harey chettell in fulle payment for his playe called the London florentyn the some . . . iij^{li}; pd for the company the 7 of Janewary 1602 unton Thomas hawode in full paymente for his playe called the London florantyn the some of . . . xx^s.'

202. *Hoffman* (Chettle, 1602, Q 1631). SR 26 Feb. 1630, '*A play called Hoffman the Revengefull Father.*' Q1 'THE | TRAGEDY | OF HOFFMAN | OR | A Revenge for a Father, | As it hath bin divers times acted | with great applause, at the *Phenix* | in *Druery-Lane.* | LONDON, | Printed by *I. N.* for *Hugh Perry,* and are to bee | sold at his shop, at the signe of the *Harrow* | in *Btittaines-burse.* 1631.' 'Lent unto Thomas downton the 29 of desembre 1602 to geve unto harey chettell in perte of paymente for A tragedie called Hawghman the some of . . . v^s.'[139]

203. *Singer's Voluntary* (Singer, 1603, lost). 'pd at the apoyntment of the companye 1602 the 13 of Janewarye unto John Syngger for his playe called Syngers vallentarey the some of . . . v^{li}.'[140]

204. *The Boss of Billingsgate* (Day, Hathway, 1603, lost). 'Lent unto Jube the 1 of marche 1602 to geve unto John daye & hathwaye in earneste of A playe called the bosse of bellengesgate the some of . . . xxxx^s; Lent the 7 of marche 1602 in perte of paymente for the playe called the bosse of bellensgate unto John daye & hathwaye the some of . . . xxxx^s; pd the 12 of marche 1602 for the company unto John daye & his felowe poetes in fulle payment for his playe called the bosse of belleingesgate the some of . . . xxxx^s.'

205. *The Siege of Dunkirk* (Massey, 1603, lost). 'Lent unto Edward Jube the 7 of marche 1602 to geve unto Charles masseye in eareneste of A playe called the sedge of doncerke wth alleyn the pyrete the some of . . . xxxx^s.'

[139] Chambers (*Elizabethan Stage* II. 181) identifies *Hoffman* with *The Danish Tragedy*, entered on 7 July 1602. Lukas Erne in *Beyond The Spanish Tragedy*, p. 39, suggests that *Hoffman* could have been designed as a sequel to the lost 'Danish tragedy', since like Kyd's play it starts with a revenge murder, and echoes *The Spanish Tragedy* in some characters' names. The incomplete payment must have been followed by others now lost, since the play was certainly staged. Its revival by the Cockpit company in 1630 goes with Beeston's acquisition of other former Fortune plays such as *The Jew of Malta.*

[140] John Singer's standing as a clown consorts with his skills as a musician, which may have led to his authorship of dances or jigs. He is not, however, noted anywhere but in this entry as a writer of plays. The price is that for a complete play, not a jig.

206. *2 The London Florentine* (Chettle, Heywood, 1603, lost). 'pd at the apoyntmente of thomas dowton the 12 of marche 1602 unto hary chettell in earneste of the 2 perte of the florentyn the some of . . . xx^s.'

207. *1 The Honest Whore* (Dekker, Middleton, 1604, Q 1604). SR 9 Nov. 1604, '*a booke called The Humors of the Patient Man, the Longinge Wyfe, and the Honest Whore.*' Q1 1604 'THE | Honest Whore, | With, | The Humours of the Patient Man, | and the Longing Wife. | *Tho: Dekker.* | LONDON | Printed by V. S. for John Hodgets, and are to | be solde at his shop in Paules | church-yard 1604.' 'Lent unto the Company to geve unto Thomas deckers & midelton in earneste of ther playe Called the pasyent man & the onest hore the some of 1604 . . . v^{li}.'[141]

208. *Richard Whittington* (lost). SR 8 Feb. 1605 Pavier entered '*the history of Ric. Whittington, of his lowe byrth, his greate fortune, as yt was plaied by the Prynces servants.*'[142]

209. *When You See Me, You Know Me* (Rowley, 1604, Q 1605). SR 12 Feb. 1605, '*Ent. N Butter (provided he get good allowance and procure the wardens' hands for the entrance): the enterlude of King Henry the Eighth.*' Q 'When you see me, | You know me. | Or the famous Chronicle Historie | *of king Henrie the eight, with the* | birth and virtuous life of Edward | *Prince of Wales.* | As it was playd by the high and mightie Prince | *of Wales his servants.* | By SAMVELL ROVVLY, servant | to the Prince. | LONDON, | Imprinted for *Nathaniell Butter,* and are to be sold | in Paules Church-yeard neare Saint | *Austines* gate. 1605.' Qq 1613, 1621, 1632.

210. *1 If You Know Not Me, You Know Nobody* (Heywood, 1605, Q 1605).[143] SR 5 July 1605, '*a booke called Yf you Knowe not Me you*

---

[141] With Elizabeth dying at Richmond on 24 March 1603 when all playing automatically stopped, the likelihood shrinks markedly that any more plays would be completed and bought for the company during this uncertain time. The plague epidemic that year kept the London playhouses closed until April 1604. The Admiral's in fact started travelling for Lent before the queen died, since the Canterbury records show a payment to the company 'becaus it was thought fitt they should not play at all in regard that our late Queene was then ether very sicke or dead as they supposed' (*REED Kent*, I. 241). On 5 May 1603 Henslowe drew up a summary of his company accounts, 'when we leafte of playe' (*Diary*, p. 209). It may be that the large 'earneste' of five pounds paid to Dekker and Middleton some time in 1604 for *The Honest Whore*, the usual amount for a complete playbook, was a consequence of the long closure, when giving advances on uncompleted plays was not seen as a sound investment, and complete playbooks were available.

[142] Never printed. At the opening of *The Knight of the Burning Pestle* (1607), Beaumont named various 'public' plays that seemed ripe for mockery, including 'The Legend of *Whittington*'.

[143] Heywood's pair of history plays have been usually ascribed to Queen Anne's at the Red Bull on the grounds that they later appeared with Beeston's company at the Cockpit. Heywood and Beeston were friends, probably from the time they worked together at the Rose in Worcester's company. Beeston wrote complimentary verses for *An Apology for Actors*. But the plague year following Elizabeth's death in March 1603 was a difficult time, and Heywood was as likely as Rowley to have

Know No body.' Q 'If you knovv not me, | You know no bodie: |
Or, | *The Troubles of Queene* ELIZABETH. | AT LONDON, | Printed for
Nathaniel Butter. 1605.' Qq 1606, 1608, 1610, 1613, 1623, 1632, 1639.
SR 21 May 1639, '*Tr. Butter to Flesher: If you know not mee you know
noe body, the first and second parts.*'

211. *2 If You Know Not Me, You Know Nobody* (Heywood, 1605, Q 1606).
SR 14 Sept. 1605, '*Ent. N. Butter: lic. Hartwell: a booke called the
second parte of Yf you Knowe not Me you Knowe Bodie, with the
buildinge of thexchange.*' Q 'THE | Second Part of, | If you know not
me, you | *know no bodie.* | VVith the building of the Royall |
EXCHANGE: | And the famous Victorie of Queene *Elizabeth,* | in the
Yeare 1588. | AT LONDON, | Printed for *Nathaniell Butter.* | 1606.'
In other copies, a cancel replaces the title-page, with 'THE | SECOND
PART OF | Queene *Elizabeths* troubles. Doctor | *Paries* treasons: The
building | *of the Royall Exchange, and the* | *famous Victorie in 1588.* |
With the humors of *Hobson* | and *Tawny-coat.* | AT LONDON, |
Printed for *Nathaniell Butter.*' Qq 1609 (with the cancel title-page),
1623, 1633.[144]

212. *The Whore of Babylon* (Dekker, 1606, Q 1607). SR 20 April 1607,
'*Ent. N. Butter and J. Trundell: lic. G. Buck: a booke called The Whore
of Babilon.*' Q 'THE | WHORE OF | BABYLON. | As it was acted by the
Princes | Servants. | *Vexat Censura Columbas.* | Written by THOMAS
DEKKER. | LONDON | Printed for Nathaniel Butter. | 1607.'[145]

213. *The Roaring Girl* (Middleton, Dekker, 1611, Q 1611). Not in SR.
Q 1611 'The Roaring Girle. | OR | *Moll Cut-Purse.* | As it hath lately
beene Acted on the Fortune-stage by | *the Prince his Players.* | Written
by *T. Middleton* and *T. Dekkar.* | Printed at *London* for *Thomas
Archer,* and are to be sold at his | shop in Popes head-pallace, neere
the Royall | Exchange. 1611.'

214. *No Wit/No Help Like a Woman's* (Middleton, 1611, Octavo 1657). SR
9 Sept. 1653, '*Ent. Mosely, several plays: No Witt, no Helpe, like a
Woman, by Tho. Midleton.*' Q 'NO HELP/WITT LIKE | A | WOMANS. | A |

written for the Fortune as the Red Bull. It is true that his two history plays could have been
composed to rival rather than add to Rowley's at the Fortune, but in the absence of any verifying
evidence we cannot be sure. The two plays are included here conjecturally.
[144] The 1633 edition has a much longer version of the final section than the earlier quartos. See MSR
edition, 1934.
[145] In 1611 Dekker wrote *If This Be Not Good the Devil Is in It* for Prince Henry's at the Fortune, but
they turned it down. Dekker then tried elsewhere, and it was taken up by Queen's Anne's Men at
the Red Bull. For the launch there he wrote a bitter prologue about the Prince's Men.

COMEDY, | BY | *Tho. Middleton*, Gent. | LONDON: | Printed for *Humphrey Moseley*, at the | Prince's Arms in St. *Paul's* Church- | yard. 1657.'[146]

215. *The Troublesome Statesman* (1623, lost). 'The *Troublesome Statesman*, a new P. perused and alld Jan 8, 1622–3; to be acted at the Fortune, by the Prince Palatine's servants, 1[li]' (Bawcutt, *Herbert*, p. 139).[147]

216. *Richard III* (Rowley, 1623, lost). "The Palsgraves Players—A Trajedy of Richard the thirde or the English Prophett with the reformation contayninge 17 sheetes written by Samuell Rowleye for the companye at the Fortune this 27th July 1623— 1[li] (Bawcutt, *Herbert*, p. 141).

217. *The Martyred Soldier* (1623, lost). '28 August for the Palsgraves Players. Under another name that itt may pass the better Att the Intreaty of M[r]. Gunnell who prevailed with mee to gett the consent of Mr. Biston to the Cockpitt itt bears the name of the Martir'd soldier this 28th of Aug[t]. 1623— 1[li].' (Bawcutt, *Herbert*, p. 144).[148]

218. *Hardship for Husbands, or Bilboe's the Best Blade* (Rowley, 1623, lost). 'A new Com: *Hardshipe for Husbands*, or Bilboes the best blade, containing 13 sheets, written by Sam. Rowley all[d] Oct. 29, 1623, for the Palsgrave's company' (Bawcutt, *Herbert*, p. 146).

219. *Two Kings in a Cottage* (Bowen, 1623, lost). 'For the Palsgraves Players November A new Tragedye called 2 kings in a cottage written by Bowen this 19th 1623— 1[li]' (Bawcutt, *Herbert*, p. 147).

220. *The Hungarian Lion* (Gunnell, 1623, lost). 'The *Hungarian Lion*, written by Gunnell, licensed for the Palsgrave's Company 4 Dec. 1623' (Bawcutt, *Herbert*, p. 147).

221. *The Duchess of Suffolk* (Drue, 1623, Q1631). SR 13 Nov. 1629, '*a play called The Duches of Suffolke, by Tho. Drue.*' Q 'THE | LIFE OF | THE | DUTCHES | OF | SUFFOLKE. | As it hath beene divers and sundry | times acted, with good applause. | Imprinted by *A. M.* for *Jasper Emery*, at the | Flowerdeluce in Paules-Church- | yard. 1631.' 'For the Palsgraves company. January The history of the Dutchess of Suffolk by M[r] Drewe being full of dangerous matter was much

---

[146] *The Almanac*, 1611, almost certainly an alternative title for *No Wit/Help like a Woman's*, was staged at court 29 Dec. 1611, and restaged for Prince Henry and his sister on 11 April 1612. See Chapter 5, pp. 196–97. This identification confirms it as Middleton's last play for the Fortune company.

[147] The loss of the company's resources, including their playbooks, in the midnight fire at the Fortune on 9 Dec. 1621, meant that the next years involved a struggle to retrieve copies. Some, such as *Tamburlaine* and *Faustus*, survived in printed versions. *Jugurtha* and probably others they re-copied from old manuscripts that survived and had re-licensed. At least two of the company sharers, Gunnell and Rowley, turned to writing new plays.

[148] Presumably a surplus play formerly in Christopher Beeston's hands, now secured by Gunnell and renamed as a new play to help fill the gaps in the company repertory after the fire. Herbert charged the fee for a new play although he knew it was an old one. Beeston may never have had it licensed.

reformed & for my paines this 2^d Jan. 1623 I had 2li' (Bawcutt, *Herbert*, p. 148).

222. *The Whore in Grain* (1624, lost). 'The *Whore in Grain*, a Trag: may be acted 26 Jan. 1624. 1^{li}. For the Palsgrave's Company' (Bawcutt, *Herbert*, p. 149).

223. *A Match or No Match* (Rowley, 1624, lost). 'For the Fortune—1624 A New Comedy called a Match or no Match written by Mr Rowlye this 6th Apr: 1624— 1^{li}.' (Bawcutt, *Herbert*, p. 150).

224. *The Way to Content All Women.* (Gunnell, 1624, lost). 'For the Fortune— The Way to content all Women or how a man may please his wife written by Gunnell this 17 Apr. 1624— 1^{li}' (Bawcutt, *Herbert*, p. 151).

225. *Honour in the End* (1624, lost). '*Honour in the End*, Com: conteyninge 12 sheets and half, allowed for the Palsgrave's company 21 May 1624 1*li*' (Bawcutt, *Herbert*, p. 151).

226. *Love Me or Love Me Not* (Drue, 1624, lost). '*Love me or Love me not*, a new Comedy by Drew, alld for the Palsgrave's Company July 1624, 1*li*' (Bawcutt, *Herbert*, p. 152).

227. *The Fair Star of Antwerp* (1624, lost). 'For the Palsg: comp:— A Trag: called the Faire Star of Antwerp 15th Sept. 1624 1^{li}' (Bawcutt, *Herbert*, p. 156).

228. *The Angel King* (1624, lost). 'For the Palsg: comp:— A new P call: The Angell King 15 Oct. 1624— 1^{li}' (Bawcutt, *Herbert*, p. 156).

229. *The Masque* (Gunnell, 1624, lost). 'For the Palsg: comp: A new P. call: the Masque 11th. Novr. 1624' (Bawcutt, *Herbert*, p. 157).

OTHER POSSIBLE PLAYS

Besides Heywood's two history plays, conjectured as possibly staged at the Fortune (210 and 211), no other plays with positive connections to the Rose and Fortune company survive amongst those printed without the company's name on them. Some plays printed very late, such as *Grim the Collier of Croydon* (1662) and *Lust's Dominion* (1657), may have been acquired from the Fortune company after 1625 by Beeston for the Cockpit or the Red Bull, as he did *The Jew of Malta* and *Hoffman*. Others may have gone to the press by some devious route without the company's permission, and thus appeared with no indication on the title-page of who performed them first. There is is *The Wit of a Woman*, printed by Edward Allde for Edward White in 1604, with a title-page giving no more than the name: 'A | Pleasant Comoedie, | *Wherein is merily shewen*: | The wit of a Woman. | LONDON | *Printed for* Edward White, *and* | are to be sold at the

little North | doore of Pauls Church at the Signe | of the Gun. 1604.'
I suspect that its writer intended it for a boy company rather than the
Rose or Fortune. It is in prose throughout, like almost all the plays written
for the boy companies after Lyly, and has parts for thirteen men, six of
them young and seven old, and seven women, two old and five young.

Plays more likely on internal evidence to have been written for the Rose
or Fortune might conceivably include *The Birth of Merlin*, issued in 1662
as 'THE | BIRTH | OF | MERLIN: | OR, | *The Childe hath found his Father.* |
As it hath been several times Acted | with great Applause. | Written by
William Shakespear, and | *William Rowley.* | Placere cupio. | LONDON:
Printed by *Tho. Johnson* for *Francis Kirkman,* and | *Henry Marsh,* and are
to be sold at the *Princes Arms* in | Chancery-Lane. 1662.' It has no obvious
connection to the Fortune, however. Of other possibilities, the idea that
the manuscript of *John of Bordeaux* was a sequel to Greene's *Friar Bacon
and Friar Bungay* and acted under the first play's name six times by
Strange's at the Rose in 1592, as W. L. Renwick claimed (Malone Society
Reprint 1936), is intriguing, but still gives it no obvious place in the
Admiral's repertory. *Wily Beguiled,* Q 1606 with five more quartos up
to 1638, was thought by Sykes to be part-written by Samuel Rowley, which
would have made it an Admiral's or Prince's play, but its epilogue
specifies performance in 'a circled round', which indicates that it was
not composed for the Fortune. Other signs suggest that it was probably not
for the Rose either, and its name does not appear anywhere in Henslowe.
A further possibility is *King Edward III,* for which Fred Lapides[149] made a
case that it was an Admiral's play, largely because it may have been
performed at Danzig in 1591 by a company with a licence from the Lord
Admiral. That would have been the old Admiral's company of those years,
without Alleyn. However, as Lord Admiral Howard issued passports to
several groups of players travelling overseas in time of war. The play's
absence from Henslowe's records and its putative Shakespeare associations
have made most scholars prefer to allocate it to the Pembroke's of 1592–93.
The last possibility is the manuscript play about Richard II known as
Thomas of Woodstock. MacDonald. P. Jackson has made a good case for its
being written after about 1604 by Samuel Rowley, which would make it a
Fortune play.[150] Nothing in the manuscript, however, or in the *Diary* or
elsewhere clearly identifies it as a play staged by the Prince's Men.

---

[149] THE RAIGNE OF KING EDWARD THE THIRD. *A Critical, Old-Spelling Edition,* ed. Fred Lapides,
Garland Publishing, New York, 1980.
[150] M. P. Jackson, 'The Date and Authorship of *Thomas of Woodstock*: Evidence and its Interpretation',
Research Opportunities in Medieval and Renaissance Drama 46 (2007), 67–100.

The players

Allen, Richard. 1597–1600. Not, as sometimes thought, a relative of Edward Alleyn. Loans from Henslowe summer 1598; contract as 'a hiered servante' for two years 25 March 1598: 'Richard alleyne came & bownde hime seallfe unto me for ij years in & sumsette as a hiered servante wth ijd syngell pence & to contenew frome the daye above written unto the eand & tearme of ij yeares yf he do not performe this covenant then he to forfette for the breache of yt fortye powndes & wittnes to this w^m borne Thomas dowton gabrell spencer Robart shawe Richard Jonnes'; he authorized payments for the company 17 Jan. and 7 April 1599, and 6 May 1600; lived in St Saviours (daughters baptised 1599 and 1601), d. 18 Nov. 1601; named in 'plots' of *Frederick and Basilea* (1597), and *Alcazar* (three roles, 1601); Henslowe made two loans to his widow, who married Thomas Marbeck of the Admiral's in Sept. 1602.

Alleyn, Edward. Sharer and later impresario 1594–1622. b. 1 Sept. 1566 in Bishopsgate. Co-owner with Henslowe of Rose, Fortune and Bear Garden. Will of 13 Nov. 1626 left £1,500 to his wife Constance (John Donne's daughter, m. 1623), books and household goods to the College, Executors to build ten almshouses in St Botolph's Without Bishopsgate, bequests of between ten and fifty pounds to friends and servant, the remainder to the College; d. 25 Nov. 1626. The College was endowed in 1619, with mortmain holding of Fortune and other properties.

Alleyn, John. Older brother of Edward, connected with Richard Jones and Robert Browne of the Admiral's and his brother Edward, in a deed of sale dated 3 Jan. 1589 of theatrical properties; in old Admiral's at Theatre 1590 (testified over quarrel Nov. 1590); d. May 1596.

Attewell, George. Strange's in 1591, when received payments for performances at court for 1590–91 season; with two other players William Smight and Robert Nicholls (not known to belong to any company) he witnessed a loan from Philip to Francis Henslowe on 1 June 1595; Admiral's? Pembroke's?;[1] d. 1598, since wife Catherine granted administration of the goods of George Attewell of St Leonard Shoreditch on 21 July; 'Mr Attowels Jigge' printed 1595.[2]

Barne, William. Boy player, Admiral's 1602, played Tarmia and a pygmy in 'plot' of *1 Tamar Cham*.

Bird, alias Borne, William. Pembroke's 1597, Admiral's, Prince's, Palsgrave's. A sharer, Henslowe lent him money along with Jones, Shaa and Downton to help repay his bond to Francis Langley after Pembroke's collapsed and he joined the Admiral's. A memorandum of 10 Aug. 1597 states that 'w^m borne came & ofered hime sealfe to come and playe wth my lord admeralle mean at my howsse called by the name of the Rosse setewate one the bank after this order folowinge he hathe Received of me iij d upon & A sumsette to forfette unto me a hundrethe marckes of lafull money of England yf he do not performe thes thinges folowinge that is presentley after libertie beinge granted for playinge to come & to playe wth my lordes admeralles men at my howsse aforsayd & not in any other howsse publicke a bowt London for the space of iij yeares beginynge Imediatly after this Restraynt is Recaled by the lordes of the cownsell wch Restraynt is by the menes of playinge the Ieylle of dooges'.[3] A series of loans from Henslowe and his wife to Bird March–Nov. 1598 noted *Diary* p. 76 and p. 77. Loan of 12s on 19 November 1598 for 'a long taney clocke of clothe . . . wch he sayd yt was to Imbrader his hatte for the gwisse' (p. 82), and 20s a week later to buy silk stockings for the Guise (*Massacre at Paris*, p. 76). From 1598 frequently represented the company in Henslowe's notes. On 26 November 1600 Henslowe lent Bird's wife £3 to get him out of the King's Bench prison where he had been put 'for hurtinge of a felowe wch browght his wife a leatter'; played Colmogra and Artabisus in 'plot' of *1 Tamar Cham*, 1602; named in company patents 1604, 1606, 1610, 1613; in 1617 he wrote to Alleyn about

---

[1] William Ingram (*A London Life in the Brazen Age: Francis Langley, 1548–1602*, Cambridge, Mass., 1978., p. 154) believes he may have been the clown in the Swan company of Pembroke's performing in 1596–98. He is not recorded as one of the members of that company joining the Admiral's in 1597.

[2] It exists in both manuscript and print versions, set to more than one popular ballad tune. It is described and music reprinted in Charles Read Baskervill, *The Elizabethan Jig and Related Song Drama*, Chicago, 1929, pp. 238–42.

[3] Bird was a fellow in the Pembroke's company at the Swan who brought down the Privy Council's 'Restraint' on all playing that summer. A majority of the ex-Pembroke's sharers, including Richard Jones and Thomas Downton, went with Bird over to the Admiral's.

a dishonest gatherer he had appointed, John Russell; dined with Alleyn on 19 April 1618 and several times later, and on 31 October signed the Fortune lease with other Palsgrave's men; wrote additions to *Faustus* with Sam Rowley 22 Nov. 1602 (*Diary*, p. 206); will of 17 Jan. 1624 left books to son Theophilus; also an actor; buried at St Leonard's Shoreditch on 22 Jan. 1624.

'Black Dick'. Possibly Admiral's boy, 1597; played 5 small parts in 'plot' of *Frederick and Basilea*.

Bradshaw, Richard. Named in Dudley's Men 1595; hired man at Admiral's c.1598–1601; a Bradshaw with no first name given is identified on 19 May 1598 as Gabriel Spencer's man (*Diary*, p. 83), and involved in a payment of thirty shillings to Drayton and Dekker for *Connan Prince of Cornwall* on 16 Oct. 1598; Henslowe sold him apparel, probably when he went on tour, on 15 Dec. 1600: 'Sowld unto Richard Bradshawe player the 15 of desembre 1600 j pownd & ij owences of coopere lace to be payde at to his Retorne a gayne to London next after the datte herof some of xiiij s & for the Aknoweledgement of this the sayd Bradshaw hath hereunto seat his hand . . . xiiij s Richard Breadshawe Wittnes Ed Alleyn; lent more unto Richard Breeadshawe player the 29 of aprell 1601 in mony to be payd at his next Retorne to London the some of . . . v^s June 13th 1601'. (See also *Diary* p. 287 for a bond for Bradshaw, Byrcot, Bird, and Robert Archer to pay Bird 50 shillings within a month of 2 March 1599, and a bond from W. Bird dated 8 January 1604 to recover 10 shillings from Richard Bradshaw if he himself did not pay it within the next month).

Bristow, James. Henslowe, *Diary*, p. 241: 'Bowght my boye Jeames brystow of William agusten player the 18 of desembre 1597 for viij li'; Admiral's 1597–1602; a 'James' is named in 'plots' of *Alcazar*, 1601, and *1 Tamar Cham*, 1602.

Browne, Edward. Admiral's 1599–1602; on 25 Jan. 1599 witness with Massey and Henslowe (*Diary* p. 45); played Crymm in 'plot' of *1 Tamar Cham*, 1602; a 'William Browne, son of Edward, player' baptised at St Saviours 1 Oct. 1596.

Browne, Robert. Possibly the 'olde Browne' who played in *1 Tamar Cham* along with Edward Browne in 1602. Of the three known Robert Brownes, he was probably the one who took companies to play in the Netherlands and Germany, not the one who ran Worcester's at the Boar's Head.

Cane, Andrew. The most famous clown of the Caroline years seems to have started with the Palsgrave's; listed by Herbert on 8 July 1622 as one of six 'Palsgrave's servants', but also 'the chiefe of them at the Phoenix [Cockpit]'; in a lawsuit of 1654 he cited himself along with Massey, Cartwright, Stratford, Price and Richard Fowler as signing a bond with Gunnell on 30 April 1624 to continue playing at the Fortune; in 1673 Henry Chapman in *The City of Bath Described* wrote that his book's Introduction was needed because otherwise 'a Pamphlet now a dayes, finds as small acceptance, as a Comedy did formerly at the *Fortune* Play-House, without a Jig of *Andrew Kein's* into the bargain.'

Cartwright, William (snr). Admiral's–Prince's–Palsgrave's 1598–1624, King's Revels in 1630s; dined with Alleyn 22 March 1618, 22 August 1619, 9 April 1620, 15 April 1621, 18 Aug. 1622; played Moor and Pisano in 'plot' of *Alcazar*, 1601, named in 'plots' of *Fortune's Tennis* 1600, and for 5 parts in *1 Tamar Cham*, 1602; not named in 1604 patent, but was in 1613; signed Fortune lease with six others 31 Oct. 1618; signed bond to Gunnell with five others (Massey, Stratford, Price, Cane, Fowler) to play at Fortune 30 April 1624; lived in White Cross St. near Fortune in 1623; Crosfield noted at Oxford in 1635 that he (or his son?) was a chief actor at the Fortune.

Clayton, Richard. A hired man with Palsgrave's at the Fortune in 1623, when living in 'Goulding Lane'; Gervase Markham's suit of 21 May 1623 against 'thirty-nine Defendants, chiefly Actors' cites him as a Fortune actor; buried 7 April 1634 at St Giles Cripplegate.

Colborne, Edward. Prince's man 1610 and 1612, named in Palsgrave's patent Jan. 1613; St Giles Cripplegate registered two daughters of 'Edward Colburne, player', 24 March 1611 and 3 June 1613, and a son on 23 Nov. 1616 (and perhaps other children born to 'Edward Coborne, gent' at St Giles subsequently).

Davies, Hugh. Admiral's 1602? Henslowe used him as witness 1594–1603; *Diary* 6 Nov. 1601 (p. 184) notes 'for the mending of hew daves tanye cotte the some of . . . x s wch was eaten wth the Rattes'.

Day, John. A son of John Day, 'player' (probably the writer), was baptised at St Saviours 3 June 1604, buried St Giles Cripplegate 2 Nov. 1617 as 'John Daye, servant to Thomas Doughten (Downton) Player'.

Dick. Boy player 1597; Edward Dutton's boy; played Basilea in 'plot' of *Frederick and Basilea* 1597.

Dob. (?) Admiral's 1598–1601; one of two 'young bretheren' and a ghost in 'plot' of *Alcazar* 1601; may also have been the owner of 'Fierdrackes sewtes for Dobe', 'Dobes cotte of cloth of sylver' in inventories of March 1598 (*Diary*, pp. 317, 322).

Downton (Dowten, Dowghton), Thomas. Strange's 1593, Pembroke's 1596–97, Admiral's 1597–Prince's–Palsgrave's; played at Swan with Langley and Pembroke's, leaving for Admiral's in summer 1597, binding himself on 6 Oct.1597 (*Diary*, p. 240) 'that he shold frome the daye a bove written untell sraftid [Shrovetide] next come ij yeares to playe in my howsse & in no other a bowte London publickeley yf he do wth owt my consent to forfet unto me this some of money a bove written [£40] wittnes to this EAlleyn Robarte shawe w^{m} borne John synger dicke Jonnes'; named on *Diary* wrapper as hired man 10 Aug. 1597, 25 Jan. 1599, loans 12, 16, 20 and 24 Nov. 1597, 25 April 1598; took on Hercules and probably other Alleyn parts in 1598; loan to fetch 2 cloaks out of pawn, 'the one wasse & embroidered clocke of ashecolerd velvet the other a blacke vellvett clocke layd wth sylke laces a bowt'; witnessed loans 12 and 19 Dec. 1597, 13 June 1601; bought 3 March 1599 'A payer of longe sylke stockenes of crymsone coller' from Henslowe, signed with Bird and Spencer for loan of £6 on 9 April 1598; in 1597 signed note with Bird, Spencer, Shaa, Jones, Juby, Towne, Singer, Humphrey and Antony Jeffes of Admiral's debt to Henslowe; on 10 July 1600 again for £300 with Singer, Shaa, Towne, Bird, Juby, Jones, Massey, Rowley and the two Jeffes; company payee 29 Dec. 1602, 7 Jan. 1603, 12 March 1603; named in 'plots' of *Frederick and Basilea*, *Alcazar* (Abdelmelec), and *1 Tamar Cham*, 1602 (Mango Cham and Tartar). Cited by William Wilson as leader with Juby of Palsgrave's 2 Nov. 1617. Gave bail on 28 March 1612 for Gunnell and on 9 April 1612 for William Stratford 'for hurting one Henry Saunders a porter at Hoggesdon'; named as a Groom of the Chamber at Prince Henry's funeral in November 1612; dined with Alleyn along with Cartwright and Gunnell 18 Aug. 1622. Lived in St Saviour's parish from 1597, and St Giles without Cripplegate when the company moved to the Fortune. St Saviours records son of 'musycyon' 27 Dec. 1592, another base-born son 25 May 1600; m. 1614, and again 1618 to vintner's widow, becoming vintner at the Red Cross tavern in Clerkenwell. Made will 5 Aug. 1625, which included a bequest in wife's control of £50 to his son Thomas, 'because my sonn hath bin a desperate sonn to me I give a desperate legacy'. Possibly one of the Duttons who were players from the 1560s.

Dover, —. As 'dover the tayller' (*Diary*, pp. 178, 180, 181), he made 'dyvers thinges' for two plays in 1601.

Drom, Thomas. Admiral's 1601, Nemesis in 'plot' of *Alcazar*.

Drue (Drew), Thomas. Actor with Queen Anne's 1613–18; lived at St James Clerkenwell; m. 1612, four children by 1618; probably wrote *The Duchess of Suffolk* and other plays for the Palsgrave's.

Dutton, Edward. Admiral's 1597, with a boy 'Dick'; played Philippo in 'plot' of *Frederick and Basilea* 1597; 3 children at St Saviours 1600–02, and 2 at St Botolph's Bishopsgate 21 Nov. 1604 and 15 Feb. 1609; in late 1599 in trouble along with Will Kemp for trespasses and contempts.

Fowler, Richard. A famous player at the Fortune and Red Bull in 1630s, began with Palsgrave's by 1618; last of the ten to sign the Fortune lease 31 Oct. 1618; named as one of nine Palsgrave's sharers by Herbert 1622; 24 April 1624 signed for Gunnell with five others to play at Fortune; children registered at St Giles Cripplegate 17 Feb. 1621, 26 Feb. 1623, 15 Dec. 1625; buried St Giles 11 Sept. 1643.

Frith, Moll. Performed herself on stage at the Fortune in *The Roaring Girl* in 1610.

Gedion. Admiral's 1602, in 'plot' of *1 Tamar Cham*.

Gibbs. Admiral's 1602, in 'plot' of *1 Tamar Cham*.

Grace, Francis. Prince's–Palsgrave's 1610–22. Signed Fortune lease 31 Oct. 1618; in Herbert's list of Palsgrave's 1622; dined with Alleyn 15 Aug. 1619 and 21 April 1621. Living in Golden Lane 1617–23; Alleyn paid for repairs to his house 30 Jan. and 24 March 1618. Will allocated his share in second Fortune to widow of creditor, sums for fellows and others to be distributed by Andrew Cane, also benefit of gathering place; buried St Giles Cripplegate 2 Feb. 1624.

Gregory, Jack. Boy player, Admiral's 1602; played Tarmia's son, Heron and Amazon in 'plot' of *1 Tamar Cham*.

Griffen. Boy player, Admiral's 1597, played Athanasia in 'plot' of *Frederick and Basilea*.

Grymes, Thomas. Supplier of apparel to the Fortune. In 1647 Dulwich College sued Tobias Lisle and Grymes for arrears of the Fortune lease, and Grymes responded that he was not a lease-holder but 'that he, having very great stock of Apparrell both for men and women, did furnishe the actors of the playhowse, and therefore they allowed him a part or share out of the playhowse'. This most likely post-dated demise of Palsgrave's.

Gunnell, Richard. Palsgrave's 1612–25, leaseholder of Fortune, builder in 1629 of Salisbury Court playhouse; named on Fortune lease 31 Oct. 1618; leased share in new Fortune 20 May 1622; took out bond with Cane, Massey, Cartwright, Stratford, Price and Fowler to play as Palsgrave's at Fortune 30 April 1624; dined with Alleyn 22 March 1618, 15 Aug. 1619, 9 April 1620, 15 April 1621, 26 May 1622, 18 Aug. 1622, 22 Sept. 1622; bailed by Downton in 1612; children registered at St Giles Cripplegate 15 Jan. 1614, 9 Sept. 1615, 20 April 1620, 17 Jan. 1622, 10 July 1624, 1 Feb. 1625; wrote *The Hungarian Lion, The Way to Content all Women* and *The Masque* for Palsgrave's after the Fortune's fire; Prynne in *Histriomastix*, 1633, p. 142, wrote of him 'the most of our present English *Actors* (as I am credibly informed) being professed *Papists*, as is the founder of the late erected new *Play-house*'. In 1635 Crosfield noted down as one of the Salisbury Court figures 'Mr. Gunnell a Papist' (*Diary*, p. 72); buried 7 Oct. 1634 at St Bride's; left Salisbury Court shares to wife Elizabeth, who remarried John Robinson, player.

Hearne, Thomas. Hired man Admiral's 1597–98; *Diary* p. 238 has 'M^r andom that the 27 of Jeuley 1597 I heayred Thomas hearne wth ij^d pence for to searve me ij yeares in the qualetie of playenge for five shellynges a weacke for one yeare & vj^s viij d for the other yeare wch he hath covenanted hime seallfe to searve me & not to departe frome my companey tyll this ij yeares be eanded wittnes to this / John synger / Jeames donston / thomas towne.'

Helle, John. Admiral's 1597; *Diary* p. 239 has 'lent John Helle the clowne the 3 of aguste 1597 in Redey money the some of . . . x^s / at that tyme I bownd hime by anew a sumsett of ij d to contenew wth me at my howsse in playnge tylle srafte tyd next [Shrove Tuesday] after the date a bove written yf not to forfytte unto me fortipowndes wittneses to the same / EAlleyn John synger Jeames donstall / edward Jubey samewell Rowley.'

Heywood, Thomas. Henslowe contracted him to Admiral's as player for two years 25 March 1598: 'Thomas hawoode came & hiered hime seallfe wth me as a covenante searvante for ij yeares by the Recevenge of ij syngell pence acordinge to the statute of winshester & to beginne at the daye above written & not to playe any wher publicke a bowt London not while thes ij yeares be exspired but in my howsse yf he do then he dothe forfett unto me the Recevinge of thes ij d fortie powndes I wittnes to this Antony monday w^m borne gabrell spencer Thomas dowton Robart shawe Richard Jonnes Richard alleyn'; wrote plays for Henslowe; joined Worcester's at the Rose when the Admiral's went to play at the Fortune; 4 children at St Saviours 1600–1605; after long career as writer of plays, buried 16 Aug. 1641.

Hunt, Thomas. Admiral's 1596–1601; Lady Elizabeth's 1611; loan from Henslowe October 1596; named in 'plots' for *Frederick and Basilea* 1597 (5 walk-ons), *Troilus and Cressida* 1599, and *Alcazar* 1601 (3 walk-ons); named by Alleyn dining with Palsgrave's 15 April 1621.

Jeffes, Antony. Chamberlain's, Pembroke's, Admiral's–Prince's. baptised St Saviours 14 Dec. 1578, younger brother of Humphrey; loans from Henslowe 11 April 1599, 2 Jan. 1602 ('to bye cloth for the playe of Judas'); 8 Aug. 1600 paid Henslowe for hire of boy James; Aug. 1600 listed with company owing Henslowe £300; named in 'plots' of *Alcazar* (Young Mahamet) and *1 Tamar Cham* (Linus and an 'olive cullord moore'); named in patents 1606 and 1613, and Prince's household 1610; received livery as a Groom of the Chamber for Prince Henry's funeral in 1612; m. 19 Feb. 1601 at St Saviours, 9 children baptised St. Giles Cripplegate 11 June 1602–23 March 1621; freeman of Brewers 1608, and called 'brewer' in entries 30 May 1610–23 March 1621; rented company house in Whitecross St. near the Fortune; d. 1648.

Jeffes, Humphrey. Chamberlain's, Pembroke's, Admiral's–Prince's–Palsgrave's; in list 11 Oct. 1597; loans from Henslowe 6 April 1598, 5 Sept. 1598 ('to by a payer of sylke stockenes'), 12 Dec. 1599; paid Henslowe 'hallfe sheare' from 14 Jan. 1598; Aug. 1600 listed with company owing Henslowe £300. Henslowe paid tailor £6 on 3 July 1601 'for mackynge of vmfry Jeaffes sewt in the vj yemen'; in 'plots' of *Alcazar* 1601 (Muly Mahamet Xeque) and *1 Tamar Cham*, 1602 (Otanes); named in patents 1606 and 1613; in Prince's household 1610; received livery as a Groom of the Chamber for Prince Henry's funeral in 1612; named as a Palsgrave's man in Pembroke's letter of 16 July 1616 along with Charles Marshall and William Parr; b. 1576; elder brother of Antony; daughter baptised St Saviours 25 Jan. 1601. Buried St Giles Cripplegate 21 Aug. 1618.

Jones, Jack. Boy player, named as Palmeda in 'plot' of *1 Tamar Cham* 1602; a John Jones had 3 children baptised at St Botolph's Aldgate, the last entry calling him a 'player'; his will 7 June 1628 gives five pounds to his eighteen-year-old daughter Mary 'whoe (as I hope) now liveth in

Virginia', and ten each to his two other daughters, his wife named as executrix.

Jones, Richard. Worcester's 1583, Admiral's 1589, 1594–97, Pembroke's 1597; on 6 Aug. 1597 signed for Henslowe 'to continew & playe wth the company of my lord admeralles players frome mihelmase next after the daye a bowe written untell the eand & tearme of iij yeares emidiatly folowinge & to playe in my howsse only knowne by the name of the Rosse & in no other howse a bowt London publicke & yf Restraynte be granted then to go for the tyme into the contrey & after to retorne agayne to London'; Admiral's 1597–1602; Priam in 'plot' of *Troilus and Cressida* 1599, De Silva and mute in 'plot' of *Alcazar* 1601; later in Germany and Poland.

Juby, Edward. Admiral's–Prince's–Palsgrave's 1594–1618. On Admiral's list 14 Dec. 1594; King in 'plot' of *Frederick and Basilea* 1597, Calcipius Bessa and Avero in *Alcazar* 1601, Pitho and a Moor in *1 Tamar Cham* 1602; in patents 1604, 1606, 1613, and Prince's household 1610; payee for Court performances 1604–15; signed Fortune lease 31 Oct. 1618; dined with Alleyn 13 Sept. 1618; George Buc consulted him about the authorship of *George a Greene*; m. 19 June 1597 at St James Clerkenwell; in St Saviours register with seven children baptised 3 June 1599–15 Sept. 1614; buried St Saviours 20 Nov. 1618; widow Frances took half a share (1/24) in the new Fortune lease 20 May 1622.

Juby, Richard. Boy player with Admiral's 1602; women in 'plot' of *Alcazar* 1601 (Abdulla Rais and Tavora), in *1 Tamar Cham* 1602 (8 parts incl. Chorus); son baptised at St Saviours 1 May 1602.

Juby, William. (? – possibly Edward) Admiral's 1599–1602; authorised payments for company 20 Jan. 1599–21 Oct. 1602.

Kendall, William. Admiral's 1597–98, Prince's, Palsgrave's up to 1614: 'Md this 8th of December 1597 my father philyp hinchlow hiered as A Covenauant servant willyam kendall for ij years after The statute of winchester w^{t} ij single penc A to geve hym for his sayd servis everi week of his playng in London x s & in ye Cuntrie v^{s}: for the wch he covenaunteth for ye space of those ij years To be redy att all Tymes to play in ye howse of the sayd philyp & in no other during the sayd Terme . . . wittnes my selfe the writer of This EAlleyn'. (*Diary*, p. 268–69); in 'plot' of *Alcazar* 1601 (Hercules, an English captain, the ghost of Abdelmunen and two walk-ons); son baptised at St Saviours 5 Jan. 1615; William Fennor: 'And let me tell thee this to calme thy rage, / I challenged Kendall on the Fortune stage; / And he did promise 'fore an audience, / For to oppose me. Note the accidence: / I set up bills, the people thronged apace, / With full intention to disgrace, or grace; / The house was full, the trumpets twice had sounded, / And though he came not, I was not confounded, / But stept upon the stage, and told them this, / My adverse would not come: not one did hisse, / But flung me theames: I then *extempore* / Did blot his name from out their memorie, / And pleasd them all, in spight of one to brave me, / Witnesse the ringing plaudits that they gave me.' *Fennor's Defence*, John Taylor, *Works*, 1630, p. 314).

Ledbetter, Robert. Admiral's 1597; Pedro in 'plot' of *Frederick and Basilea* 1597; travelled in Germany 1599 and after.

Lee (Leigh), Robert. Admiral's? Named with Richard Burbage in the 'plot' of *Dead Man's Fortune*; possibly with Strange's or the early Admiral's; in 1593 named as 'mercer' signed a bond to Edward Alleyn with Edward's elder brother John and Thomas Goodale; sold a play called *The Miller* to the Admiral's 22 Feb. 1598; in Worcester's 1602 and Queen Anne's 1604–1622.

Magett, Stephen. Admiral's tireman 1596, 1599.

Marbeck, Thomas. Boy player, Admiral's 1602; played 8 walk-ons in 'plot' of *1 Tamar Cham* 1602, incl. a child; b. 1577; m. Agnes, widow of Richard Allen, 1602; sister married Thomas Middleton.

Massey, Charles. Admiral's–Prince's–Palsgrave's 1597–1635? Contracted by Henslowe along with Sam Rowley 16 Nov. 1598 for one year to the following Shrove Tuesday: 'I hired as my covenente Servantes Charlles massey & samewell Rowley for A yeare & as muche as to sraftide [Shrovetide] begeninge at the daye A bove written after the statute of Winchester wth ij syngell pence & for them they have covenanted wth me to playe in my howsse & in no other howsse dewringe the thime publeck but in mine yf they dooe wth owt my consent yf they dooe to forfett unto me xxxx^{li} a pece wittnes Thomas dowton Robart shawe w^{m} borne Jubey Richard Jonnes'; witnessed Downton's contract 25 Jan. 1599; Henslowe loaned him 10s 3 Dec. 1600, signed debt to Henslowe with nine others March 1598, and £300 company debt with ten others 10 July 1600; in 'plots' of *Frederick and Basilea* 1597, *2 Fortune's Tennis* 1599, *Alcazar* 1601 (Zareo and Duke of Barceles), *1 Tamar Cham* 1602 (Artaxes and 3 walk-ons); in patents 1604, 1606, 1613, and prince's household 1610; paid 40s for play *The Siege of Dunkirk* 7 March 1603; in 1614 gave bail for John Shank over charge that he had bought stolen bands and cuffs at the playhouse; lessee of Fortune 1618, and of rebuilt Fortune; second in Herbert's list of Palsgrave's 1622; signed bond with Gunnell to play at the Fortune 30 April 1624; took half a share (1/24) in the new Fortune 20 May 1622; dined with Alleyn 20 Sept. 1618, 18 March 1621, 15 April 1621, 12 Aug. 1621, 21 July 1622. Wrote plays, notably in 1602 *Malcolm King of Scots* (*Diary*, pp. 199–200), and *The Siege of Dunkirk, with Alleyn the Pirate* (*Diary*, p. 208). A performance of one of his plays brought him 5 shillings from Alleyn on 19 Nov. 1624; m. 9 May 1596, and 4 April 1605; daughter 1610, and other children; in registers of St Giles Cripplegate 30 Dec. 1610–20 July 1625; in debtor's prison 1622; d. 3 Aug. 1625, in the same month as Downton and Stratford, and John Newton of Prince Charles's, all possibly of plague. The man named as Charles Marshall in Lord Chamberlain Pembroke's letter about Palsgrave's travelling in 1616 was probably an error for Charles Massey.

'Nick.' Boy player, Admiral's 1601–03; mentioned in Joan Alleyn's letter of 21 Oct. 1603; hose bought for him to tumble in before Queen, 25 Dec. 1601.

Parr, William. Admiral's–Prince's–Palsgrave's 1602–20; named for 6 walk-ons in 'plot' of *1 Tamar Cham* 1602; in patents 1604, 1613, and prince's household 1610; named with Marshall (Massey?) and Humphrey Jeffes in Pembroke's list of the travelling Palsgrave's 16 July 1616; ninth of the ten who signed lease of Fortune 31 Oct. 1618; dined with Alleyn 22 March 1618, and 9 April 1620.

Parsons, Thomas. Boy player, Admiral's 1597, 1602; noted by Henslowe as Downton's boy in 1599 (*Diary*, p. 107: 'Thomas downton boye Thomas parsons'); a Fury in 'plot' of *Alcazar* 1601, and 7 walk-ons in *1 Tamar Cham* 1602.

Pavy, William. Admiral's 1597–1602; Boniface in 'plot' of *Fortune's Tennis* 1600; Prince's 1608; buried St. Botolph's Aldgate 8 Sep. 1608. A note 31 March 1609 registers wife Elizabeth, and inventory of valuables £10 14s 7d.

Pedel, Abraham. Germany 1614–15, Palsgrave's 1623; living in Golding Lane in 1623.

Pigge, John. Alleyn's boy; Strange's 1593, Admiral's 1597–99; mentioned in letters between Joan and Edward Alleyn, 1593, and in inventory, 1598;

title role in *Alice Pearce* 1597, Andreo in 'plot' of *Frederick and Basilea* 1597, in 'plot' of *Troilus and Cressida* 1599.

Price (Pryor), Richard. Prince's–Palsgrave's 1610–1622. White Cross Street 1623, children registered in St Giles Cripplegate 1620–27. Named 'pryore' in Prince Henry's Household book in 1610, and granted cloth for the funeral procession in 1613. Signatory of the Fortune lease 31 Oct. 1618, dined with Alleyn along with Gunnell, Cartwright and Parr 9 April 1620, took half-share in new Fortune 20 May 1622, signed bond with Gunnell to play at Fortune 30 April 1624. Buried 16 April 1628.

Proctor. Admiral's 1599; named in 'plot' of *Troilus and Cressida* 1599.

Radford. 'the littell tayller Radford' is named for payments in the *Diary*, pp. 169, 180, 182, 184.

Rowley, Samuel. Admiral's–Prince's–Palsgrave's 1597–1624; contracted along with Charles Massey 16 Nov. 1598; player and writer; Heraclius in 1597 'plot' of *Frederick and Basilea* (as 'Sam'), in *Fortune's Tennis* 1600, a black-faced Moor, Pisano, a devil, and Death in 'plot' of *Alcazar* 1601, Ascalon and Crymm in 'plot' of *1 Tamar Cham* 1602; wrote *When You See Me, You Know Me* about Henry VIII in 1604; in patents 1604, 1606, 1613, and Prince Henry's household 1604 and 1610; Bentley (*Jacobean and Caroline Stage* II. 555) thinks he gave up playing and became a contracted writer for the company from 1613; for Palsgrave's as Henry Herbert noted he wrote *Richard III*, *Hardshifte for Husbands*, and *A Match or no Match* between 27 July 1623 and 6 April 1624; m. Alice Coley 1594; lived in parish of St Mary Matfellon, Whitechapel from 1601; will 23 July 1624 bequeathed Whitechapel and Stepney properties to daughters, with reversions to brother William, who also had his books; buried St Mary Matfellon 29 Oct. 1624.

Russell, John. Gatherer for Palsgrave's c.1617. Letter of complaint about him by Bird quoted in Bentley, *Jacobean and Caroline Stage* II. 558. Noted in Fortune lease of 31 Oct. 1618 as occupant of tenement of two rooms next to Fortune.

Shaa, Robert. Pembroke's 1596–97, bonded to Henslowe 6 Aug. 1597 by Richard Jones; Admiral's 1597–1602; Irish bishop in 'plot' of *Alcazar* 1601; took court payments for the company 1598, 1599 and 1600; in March 1602 received £50 from Henslowe to wind up his share; m. 19 May 1598 Mary Griggs, daughter of the Rose's builder; St Saviours registered son baptised 10 April 1603; 'Robert Shawe a man' buried 12 Sept. 1603.

Shanbrooke, John. In Prince Henry's c.1610–18; m. 1608, a son and two daughters registered at St Giles Cripplegate 1610–14; John 'Shamrock' and Thomas Downton gave bail on 22 March 1612 for Richard Gunnell, and Shanbrooke on 31 Aug. 1612 for Richard Grace; buried 17 Sept. 1618.

Shank or Shanks, John. In Pembroke's 1597? Probably joined Admiral's in 1603 to replace Singer as clown when he died; in Prince's in 1610, living near the Fortune at St Giles Cripplegate; in Palsgrave's patent 1613; in 1614 charged with buying stolen drapery at the Fortune, but cleared; he may not have been the John Shank who became the Globe's clown in 1614 and later a King's Men's sharer; Bentley (*Jacobean and Caroline Stage* II. 562–69) thinks he was the son of the King's John Shank, but that is unlikely since he lived near the Fortune; m. 12 Feb. 1610 at St Dunstan in the West; records register a daughter in 1612 and other children subsequently.

Singer, John. Queen's 1583 (in fatal affray at the Red Lion inn, Norwich, 15 June), 1588, Admiral's 1594–1603; in Henslowe list of 14 Dec. 1595; company payee for court performances 1595; Henslowe paid for 'his playe called Syngers vallentarey' on 13 Jan. 1603; St Saviours register notes 5 children 1 Aug. 1597–5 Oct. 1603; probably died late 1603; played clowns – Dekker in *Gull's Horn Book* says '*Tarleton, Kemp,* nor *Singer,* nor all the litter of Fooles that now come drawling behind them, never played the clownes more naturally then the arrantest Sot of you all shall.' Heywood praised him after his death in 1609 – 'John Singer, who playd the Clownes part at the Fortune-play-house in *Golding* Lane.' John Taylor, in *Taylors Feast* (1638), told an anecdote about his dislike of the smell of brandy.

Slater, Martin. Admiral's 1594–97; listed by Henslowe 14 Dec. 1594; 'marten slather went for (i.e. from) the company of my lord admeralles men the 18 of July 1597' (*Diary* p. 60); paid for company's court performances 1596; in 1603 indicted for receiving stolen clothing, but acquitted; m. 1 May 1594 at St Botolph Aldgate; in St Saviours parish Easter 1595–Easter 1602; despite his ten London children, from 1597 till 1625 seems to have preferred travelling rather than playing in one venue in London; involved in building of Red Bull 1604; owned several play manuscripts, five of which he sold to the Admiral's after he left in 1597.

Somerset, George. boy player, 3 walk-ons in 'plot' of *Alcazar* 1601; possibly the 'george' of the 'plots' for *2 Fortune's Tennis* and *1 Tamar Cham* (5 walk-ons); on 10 February 1601 his wife Frances consulted Simon Forman about the theft of a doublet from her husband which Thomas Towne eventually confessed he had stolen, and made reparation (see **Towne**).

Spencer, Gabriel. Pembroke's (1593? possibly the 'Gabriel' noted in *3 Henry VI*, 1.2.48) 1596–97, put in Marshalsea with Shaa and Jonson Aug. 1597; Admiral's 1597–98; named in *Diary* 11 Oct. 1597; b. 1576, so was twenty when he killed James Feakes with a rapier in 1596 and twenty-two when killed by Ben Jonson in a duel 22 Sept. 1598.

Stratford, William. Prince's–Palsgrave's 1610–23; arrested for injuring a porter at the Fortune in 1612, bailed by Downton; Groom of the Chamber at Prince Henry's funeral Nov. 1612; signed lease of Fortune 31 Oct. 1618, and bond to Gunnell to play at Fortune 30 April 1624; m. 9 May 1613 at St Giles Cripplegate, son and three daughters 1614–23; living at White Cross St. in 1623; children in St Giles register; buried there as 'Player' 27 Aug. 1625, the same month as Downton and Massey, all probably dying of plague.

Tailor, Robert. Admiral's 1600–02; named in 'plot' of *Fortune's Tennis* 1600, and 3 walk-ons in *Alcazar* 1601.

Taylor, Thomas. Possibly a player at the Fortune, because of a St. Giles Cripplegate entry about a 'Sonne of Thomas Taylor, player' buried 10 Jan. 1624; another son buried 21 Aug. 1625; named in Markham's suit as of Golding Lane, 21 May 1623.

Towne, Thomas. Admiral's–Prince's 1594–1612; Myron-Hamec in *Frederick and Basilea* 1597, Stukeley in *Alcazar* 1601, 3 parts in *1 Tamar Cham* 1602; ('Townes boy' was in 'plot' of *Alcazar* 1601); named in *1 Honest Whore* 1604 ('*Enter Towne like a sweeper*'); in patents 1604, 1606, and prince's household 1610; seriously assaulted by Thomas Gittons yeoman of St Giles at Golding Lane 20 Jan. 1602; according to Simon Forman, on about 10 February 1601 Towne stole doublet belonging to fellow-sharer George Somerset; Forman's notes say 'Yt was on of their own company that stole yt his name was Town a player & at laste confeste yt of himselfe, but the good was not had again, but recompence made for it.'[4] Buried St Saviours Southwark 9 August 1612; will 4 July 1612 left three pounds to Borne (Bird), Downton, Juby, Rowley, Massey and Humphrey Jeffes 'to make them a supper when it shall please them to call for it'; on his death the Prince's Men gave his widow £50 for his share.

Tunstall, James. Worcester's 1583, Admiral's 1590–94, new Admiral's 1594–97; on list 14 Dec. 1594; governor and friar in *Frederick and Basilea*

---

[4] Quoted in Barbara Howard Traister, *The Notorious Astrological Physician of London. Works and Days of Simon Forman*, University of Chicago Press, 2001, pp. 170–71.

1597; sons christened 16 May 1585, 20 April 1587 and 12 Jan. 1589; probably man who made will 8 Dec. 1599, living in parish of St Katherine Coleman, Aldgate, made wife Jane his executrix; inventory 22 Jan. 1600 valued assets at £17 17s; Henslowe commonly spelt his name 'donston' or 'donstall'; Guilpin in *Skialetheia* (1598) mocked a man 'With *Dunstons* browes, and *Allens Cutlacks* gate', though he probably meant St Dunstan.

White, William. A property man used by the company 4 Aug. 1601, 'pd at the apoyntment of the company unto w^m whitte for mackynge of crownes & other thinges for mahewmet the 4 of agust 1601 the some of . . . ls'. (*Diary*, p. 178).

'Will'. Boy player, Admiral's 1597, playing Leonora in 'plot' of *Frederick and Basilea* (1597).

Wilson, William. Friend of Alleyn, and possibly a gatherer at Fortune; letter by Wilson to Alleyn of late October 1617 refers to his imminent wedding, and appeals to Alleyn to get Downton and Juby to bring their fellows to perform on the day, 2 Nov., at St Saviours (printed in *Jacobean and Caroline Stage* II. 623).

Yarrington, Robert. Either the author, of more likely the scribe of Haughton and Day's *Two Lamentable Tragedies* (1601); Greg's conjecture that his name at the end of the manuscript from which the play was printed marked the scribe rather than the author was supported by the discovery of a 'Rob^r. Yarrington jun^r.' being made free of the Company of Scriveners in 1603;[5] he was too young to have been the Hand C who wrote the 'plots' of *2 Seven Deadly Sins* and *2 Fortune's Tennis*, but his name at the end of the quarto suggests that Henslowe used him as a scribe.

---

[5] See Bernard M. Wagner, 'Robert Yarrington', *Modern Language Notes* 45 (1930), 147–48.

Travelling

In these records of company travels it must be assumed that where two companies were linked in payments, for most cases the linkage was made by the accountants, not by the companies. In such cases the amount received by each company should be halved. The most anomalous case of payments to two companies is from Newcastle in May 1593, where it specifies 'to my lord admiralles plaiers and my lord morleis plaiers beinge all in one companye'. That may have something to do with the rarity of travel so far north, although Newcastle being a major port with its ships carrying coal to London may have been a factor in their travelling together. Lord Morley's players in the early 1590s seem to have made a habit of linking up with other companies, so they may have been jugglers and acrobats, or musicians, rather than a company of play-performers, adding their own skills to the plays the other group performed. While this book does not deal with the earlier Admiral's company, its travels are listed here, if only because Edward Alleyn probably travelled with them through the 1580s, and James Tunstall certainly did. The accountants' linkage of companies for their entries chiefly comes from the first company's records, though they may have registered a presence in their towns at the same time.

THE EARLIER ADMIRAL'S Dover 12 June 1585 'my Lord admiralles and my Lord of Hunsdons players' 20s, Coventry Nov. 1585 20s, Leicester 1585–86 'to the Lorde Chamberlens and the Lord Admiralles Playors more then was gathered' 4s, Folkestone 6s 8d, Ipswich 20 Feb. 1586 'my L. Admyralles players' 20s, July 1586 Rye 10s, Nov. 1586 Coventry 20s, 1586–87 Hythe 7s, Norwich 30s, Bath 10s, Plymouth 10s, Exeter 20s, Southampton 20s, Oxford town 20s, Leicester 'more then was gaythered' 4s, May 1587 Ipswich 10s, 1587 York 30s, Nov. 1587 Coventry 20s, 1588–89 Cambridge town 10s, 25 July 1589 Marlborough 7s 4d, 1589–90 Oxford 6s 8d, Winchester 10s, Maidstone 10s, Folkestone 6s 8d, Lydd 10s, June 1590 Rye 13s 4d, Ipswich £1, 'the second tyme' 10s, 1589–90 Canterbury ('the

Quenes players, and my Lord Admiralls players', 30s, 26 June 1590 New Romney 'for the benevolentes of the touneship xx.s', Aug. 1590 Bristol 30s, 17 Sept. 1590 Gloucester 20s, Dec. 1590 Coventry 20s, 1590–91 Oxford town 10s, Winchester 20s, Bath 16s 3d, Gloucester 30s, Canterbury 'the Quenes players, and my Lord Admiralls players' 30s, Faversham 10s, 1591 Southampton £1, Sept. 1591 Rye 10s, 1591–92 Folkestone 3s 4d, Faversham (10s), 1592–93 Faversham 10s, Folkestone 3s 4d, Norwich 20s, Ipswich 'the Lord Admyrals & the Lord Staffords' 20s, after 24 July 1592 Shrewsbury 'to my Lord strange and my Lord admyralls players' 40s, 7 Aug. 1592 Ipswich 'unto therll of Darbys players and to the Lorde admirals players' 20s, 19 Dec. 1592 Leicester 'more than was gaythered' 8s, 3 Feb. 1593 Shrewsbury 10s, April 1593 York 'to my lord Admorall & my Lord [Morden] players' 40s, May 1593 Newcastle 'to my lord admiralles plaiers and my lord morleis plaiers beinge all in one companye' 30s, 1593 Bridgwater £1, July 1593 Rye 13s 4d, 16 Oct. 1593 Lyme Regis 'to my lord admeras players' 5s, Nov. 1593 Coventry 13s 4d, 1593–94 Lydd 'the townes benevolence' 6s 8d, Bath 'the Lorde Admiralls & the Lord Norris players' 16s, 'more to the same players' 7s 9d.

THE ADMIRAL'S 1594–95 Oxford town 10s, Faversham 'by the appointment of Master maior' 20s, Maidstone 20s, Bath 13s 10d,[1] 1595–96 Gloucester 20s, 'geven for wine and suger for my Lord Admiralls players' 20d, Ipswich 13s 4d, Oxford town 10s, Bath 14s 2d, 21 Feb. 1596 Faversham 'by the appointment of Master maior' 10s, Aug. 1596 Dunwich 5s, Dec. 1596 Coventry 10s, April 1597 Newcastle 20s, 27 Aug. 1597 Ipswich 10s, Oct. 1599 Leicester 'to the Lorde Haywardes playars more then was gaythered' 10s, Oct.–Dec. 1599 Bristol 'to my Lorde Hawardes players playing before Master Mayor & Thalldermen' 30s, 1599–1600 Canterbury 'To the lorde Admiralls players, in rewarde for A Playe which they played before Master maior and manye of his frendes in the Court halle' 40s, Bath 'to the Lord heywardes players' 10s, Nov. 1600 Hardwick (Cavendish household accounts) 2s, 1600–01 Dunwich 6s, 2 March 1602 Faversham 20s, 1602–03 Faversham 10s, Canterbury 'paid to Thomas Downton one of ye Lo. Admiralles Players for a gift bestowed upon him & his company being so appointed by master maior & the aldermen because it was thought fitt they should not play at all in regard that our late Queene was then ether very sick or dead as they supposed' 30s, 1603 York 20s, Bath

---

[1] An additional note in the Bath accounts for this period includes 'the charges of twoe prisoners for 14 dayes which were founde with A counterfait licens of my Lord Admiralles'.

10s, 18 Aug. 1603 Leicester 10s, Nov. 1603 Coventry 'To the Earle of nottinghams players' 20s.

THE PRINCE'S 1604–05 Maidstone 20s, Faversham 10s, Winchester 20s, 17 July 1605 Oxford town 20s, 1605–06 Bath 23s 8d, 17 Oct. 1606 26s 8d, 1606–07 Bath 20s, 1606–7 Dover £2, Faversham 20s, Maidstone 20s, 14 Aug. 1607 Fordwich 10s, 5 Sept. 1607 Dover £2, Oct. 1608 Ipswich 'in Respecte that they shold not pleye within this towne att all' 40s, 1608–09 Shrewsbury 45s, 1609 Hereford 5s, June 1609 Coventry 'being 20 in number' £4, 1 Oct. 1609 Leicester 50s, 1609–10 Bridgnorth 20s, 1610–11 Winchester 'geven to the players of His Excellency Prince Henry' 20s, Carlisle 20s, 1611–12 Ipswich 'ij companies of pleyers the Quenes & Princes men' 54s 4d, 12 Aug. 1612 Howard of Naworth 10s, 1612–13 Ipswich £1 6s 8d, Barnstaple 'unto the Princes players and unto the Queens players' 40s.

THE PALSGRAVE'S 1613–14 Barnstaple 15s, 23 March 1614 Fordwich 6s 8d, Nov. 1614 Coventry 'to the Princes players' along with 'the Lord of Albignes players', i.e., Prince Charles's Men, 40s, 1 Jan 1615 Vavasour in Hazelwood £3 for 2 plays, 7 Nov. 1614 Coventry (with Prince Charles's) 7s 4d, 25 March 1616 Cambridge 'Dounton et Jubey were Charged themselves & all the rest of their companye presently to departe the universitye & playe noe moore at any tyme hereafter either in Cambridge or the Compasse of five myles',[2] 1616–17 Dover 'which was geven as a gratuity' 11s, Hythe 'given to the Players of the Palsgraves company, for that they went out of the Towne & dyd not play' 20s, 13 July 1616 Coventry 'to the Pallesgraves players' 40s, 19 March 1617 Fordwich 7s, 19 April 1617 Dover 'in gold' 11s, 4 June 1617 Norwich a restraint on duplicate warrants names as Palsgrave's Men 'Charles Marshall, Humfry Jeffes and William Parr', 30 Aug. 1617 Kendal 11s, Oct.–Dec. 1617 Bristol 'the Palsgraves Players' £2, 1618–19 Winchester 10s, 1619–20 Dover 11s, Fordwich 3s 4d, Sandwich 11s, Leominster 'to the King of Bohemya his players' 10s [and Ludlow],[3] 15 April 1620 Dover 'to the prince palatine, & King of Bohemia his players' 11s, 2 Dec. 1620 Dunkenhalgh (Sir Thomas Walmsley) 30s, Feb. 1621 Sandwich 11s, 10 March 1621 Fordwich 'to ye king of Bohemia his players' 3s 4d, 24 March 1621 Dover 11s, 13 Jan. 1622 Leicester 'to the

---

[2] The Cambridge town entry listed all the players concerned. Besides Downton and Juby it named 'William Byrde, Samuel Rowle, Charles Messey, Humphry Jeffe, Franck Grace, Willyam Cartwright, Edward Colebrande, Willyam Parrey, Willyam Stratford, et alii' (*REED, Cambridge*, I. 553).

[3] The fact that two local boys born in 1620 were baptised with the name 'Tamburlaine' does suggest quite strongly that the company had recently been playing Marlowe's plays there.

Fortune players having the kings Broad seale to their warrant as a gratuitye not playing' 30s, 1622–23 New Romney 'for a gratuitye' 5s, 26 Jan., 1 Feb. 1623 Dunkenhalgh (Sir Thomas Walmsley) 'the princes players 2 nights', 27 April 1623 Kendal 10s, 31 May 1623 Norwich 'The Company of the players of the Fortune howse in London doe under their handes protest against William Danyell who hath injuriously gotten their Letters Patentes', 1623 York 10s, 1625–26 Kendal 10s, 14 April 1626 Dover 10s, 4 Aug. 1626 Kendal 10s.

Performing at court

Admiral's–Prince's–Palsgrave's	Others
1594–95: Admiral's 28 Dec., 1 and 6 Jan. = **3**	Chamberlain's 26 and 27 Dec., 26 Jan. = **3**
1595–96: Admiral's 1, 4 Jan., 22, 24 Feb. = **4**	Chamberlain's 26, 27, 28 Dec., 6 Jan., 22 Feb. = **5**
1596–97: = **0**	Chamberlain's 26, 27 Dec., 1, 6 Jan., 6, 8 Feb. = **6**
1597–98: Admiral's 27 Dec., 27 Feb. = **2**	Chamberlain's 26 Dec., 1, 6 Jan., 26 Feb. Middle Temple (masque) 6 Jan. = **5**
1598–99: Admiral's 27 Dec. (*The Downfall of Robert Earl of Huntington?*), 6 Jan., 18 Feb. = **3**	Chamberlain's 26 Dec., 1 Jan., 20 Feb. = **3**
1599–1600: Admiral's 27 Dec. (*Old Fortunatus?*) 1 Jan. (*The Shoemaker's Holiday*) = **2**	Chamberlain's 26 Dec., 6 Jan., 3 Feb., Derby's 5 Feb. = **4**
1600–01: Admiral's 28 Dec. (*Phaeton?*), 2 Feb. = **2**	Chamberlain's 26 Dec., 6 Jan., 24 Feb., Derby's 1, 6 Jan., Paul's Boys 1 Jan., Blackfriars Boys 22 Feb. = **7**
1601–02: Admiral's 27 Dec. = **1**	Chamberlain's 26, 27 Dec., 1 Jan., 14 Feb., Worcester's 3 Jan., Blackfriars Boys 6, 10 Jan., 14 Feb. = **8**
1602–03: Admiral's 27 Dec. (*Friar Bacon and Friar Bungay?*), 6, 8 March (*As Merry As May Be?*) = **3**	Italians 29 Aug., Chamberlain's 26 Dec., 2 Feb., Paul's Boys 1 Jan., Worcester's 3 Jan., Hertford's 6 Jan. = **6**
1603–04: Prince's 4, 15, 21, 22 Jan., 20 Feb. = **5**	masques 1, 8 Jan., King's 26, 27, 28, 30 Dec., 1 Jan. (twice), 2, 19 Feb., Queen Anne's, 2, 13 Jan, Paul's Boys, 20 Feb. Blackfriars Boys 21 Feb. = **14**
1604–05: Prince's 23, 24 Nov., 14, 19 Dec., 15, 22 Jan., 5, 19 Feb. = **8**	King's 1, 4 Nov., 26, 28 Dec., 7, 8 Jan., 2, 10, 11, 12 Feb., masques 27 Dec., 6 Jan., Queen Anne's 30 Dec., Blackfriars Boys, 1, 3 Jan. = **15**
1605–06: Prince's 1, 30 Dec., 1, 4 Jan., 3, 4 Mar., = **6**	masque 5 Jan., King's undated = 10, Paul's = 2 undated, Queen Anne's 27 Dec. = **13**
1606–07: Prince's 28 Dec., 13, 24, 30 Jan., 1 Feb., 11 Feb. = **6**	masque 6 Jan., Blackfriars Boys 29 July, 1 Jan., Paul's boys 30 July, King's

Admiral's–Prince's–Palsgrave's	Others
	2 undated July–Aug., 7 Aug., 26, 29 Dec., 4, 6, 8 Jan., 2, 5, 15, 27 Feb., = **16**
1607–08: Prince's 19 Nov., 30 Dec., 3, 4 Jan. = **4**	2 masques 10 Jan., 9 Feb., King's 26, 27, 28 Dec., 2, 6 (2 plays), 7, 9, 17 (2 plays), 26 Jan., 2, 7 Feb. = **15**
1608–09: Prince's 3 undated = **3**	masque 2 Feb., King's 12 undated, Blackfriars Boys 1, 4, Jan., 1 undated, Queen Anne's 5 undated = **21**
1609–10: Prince's 28, 31 Dec., 7, 24 Jan., = **4**	King's 13 undated, Whitefriars Boys 5 undated, Queen Anne's 27, Dec., Charles's 9 Feb., masque 5 June 1610 = **21**
1610–11: Prince's 19, 28 Dec., 14, 16 Jan. = **4**	masques 1 Jan., 3 Feb., King's 15 undated, Queen Anne's 10, 27 Dec., Charles's 12, 20 Dec., 15 Jan., Whitefriars Boys 13 Dec., 2 Feb., 14 April = **25**
1611–12: Prince's 28, 29 Dec. (*The Almanac*, almost certainly Middleton's *No Wit/No Help Like a Woman's*) 5, 29 Feb., 11 April = **5**	masque 6 Jan., King's 31 Oct., 1 Nov., 5 Nov., 9, 19 Nov., 16 Dec., 26 Dec., 31 Dec., 1 Jan., 7, 12, 13, 15 Jan., 9, 19, 20, 23 Feb., 28 Feb., 28 March, 3, 16, 26 April, combined with Queen's 12, 13 Jan., Queen's 27 Dec., 21, 23 Jan, 2 Feb., Revels Boys 5 Jan., Charles's Men 12, 28 Jan., 13, 24 Feb., Lady Eliz. Men 19 Jan., 25 Feb., 11 March = **37**
1612–13: Prince's 2, 5 March (*1* and *2 The Knaves*) = **2**[1]	masques 14, 15, 20 Feb., King's 19 undated, Lady Elizabeth's 20 Oct., 25 Feb., 1 March, Whitefriars Boys Nov., 1, 9 Jan., 27 Feb. = **28**
1613–14: Prince's = **0**	masques 26, 29 Dec., 3, 6 Jan., 3 Feb., King's 1, 4, 5, 15, 16 Nov., 24, 27 Dec., 1, 4, 10 Jan., 2, 4, 8, 10, 18 Feb., 6, 8 March., Lady Elizabeth's 12 Dec., 25 Jan., Queen Anne's 5 Jan. = **25**
1614–15: Palsgrave's 3 undated = **3**	masques 6, 8 Jan., King's 8 undated, Lady Elizabeth's 1 Nov., Queen Anne's 3 undated, Prince Charles's 6 undated = **20**
1615–16: Palsgrave's = **0**	masques 1, 6 Jan., King's 21 Dec., 13 undated, Queen Anne's 17 Dec., 6 undated, Charles's 4 undated, Cambridge 12 March = **28**

---

[1] The performances of the two parts of *The Knaves* before the king in March 1613 are usually attributed (by Astington and Gurr, for instance) to Prince Henry's Men. This entry may, however, be an error for the newly named Prince Charles's Men. David Nicol, 'The Repertory of Prince Charles's (I) Company, 1608–1625', *Early Theatre* 9 (2006), p. 69, notes that Will Rowley took the payment for these court performances, being leader of Prince Charles's at the time.

Admiral's–Prince's–Palsgrave's	Others
1616–17: Palsgrave's = **o**	masques 25 Dec., 6 Jan., 19 Jan., 19 Feb., 4 May, King's 5 Jan., 11 undated, Charles's 28 Dec., Queen Anne's 3 undated, French 4, 5–11 March = **23**
1617–18: Palsgrave's = **o**	masques 6, 29 Sept., 6 Jan., 17 Feb., 19 Feb., King's 15 undated, 6 April, 7 April, 3 May, Queen Anne's 2 undated = **25**
1618–19: Palsgrave's 3 Jan. = **1**	masques 6 Jan., 8 Feb., King's 8 undated, 20 May, Charles's 1 Nov., 1 Jan. = **13**
1619–20: Palsgrave's = **o**	masques 6, 10 Jan., 29 Feb., King's 10 undated, Queen Anne's 2 Jan., Charles's 4 undated = **18**
1620–21: Palsgrave's = **o**	masques 6 Jan., 11, 13 Feb., King's 9 undated, Charles's 2 undated = **14**
1621–22: Palsgrave's = **o**	masques 2 Sept., 6 Jan., 6 May, King's 5, 26 Nov., 26 Dec., 1, 24 Jan., 5 Feb., Oxford 26 Aug., Charles's 27, 29 Dec., Revels 30 Dec. = **13**
1622–23: Palsgrave's = **o**	masque 19 Jan., King's 26, 27, 29 Dec., 1 Jan., 2 Feb., 4 undated, Charles's 6 Jan., Lady Elizabeth's 2 undated = **13**
1623–24: Palsgrave's = **o**	King's 29 Sept., 1 Nov., 26, 28 Dec., 1, 6, 18 Jan., 3 undated, Lady Elizabeth's 5 Nov., 27 Dec., 4 Jan. = **13**
1624–25: Palsgrave's = **o**	masque 9 Jan., King's 2 Nov., 26, 27, 28 Dec., 1, 12 Jan., March, Lady Elizabeth's 6 Jan, Cambridge 12 Feb. = **10**

Diary, p. 96. lent unto antony monday the 9 of aguste 1598 in earneste of A comedy for the corte called - - - - the some of . . . xs/m^r drayton hath geven his worde for the boocke to be done wth in one fortnight wittnes Thomas dowton.[2]

Diary, p. 102. Lent unto harey Chettell at the Requeste of Robart shawe the 25 of novembre 1598 in earneste of his comodey called tys no deseayt to deseve the desever for mendinge of Roben hood.for the corte . . . x^s.

Diary, p. 106. Lent unto Thomas Towne & Richard alleyn to go to the corte upon ester even the some of . . . x^s.

[2]· Henslowe left a blank for the play's name. The linkage here of Munday with Drayton in the second entry, affirmed by the single payment, suggests that the court play might have been *Mother Redcap*.

Diary, p. 137. Lent unto Samwell Rowley the 14 of desembre 1600 to geve unto Thomas dickers for his paynes in fay^eton some of x s / for the corte.Lent unto Samwell Rowley the 22 of desembre 1600 to geve unto Thomas deckers for alterynge of fayton for the corte . . . xxx s.

Diary, p. 207. Lent unto Thomas downton the 14 of desembre 1602 to paye unto m^r mydelton for a prologe & A epeloge for the playe of bacon for the corte the some of . . . v^s.

And other private shows:

Diary, p. 88. pd unto the carman for caryinge & bryngyn of the stufe backe agayne when they played in fleatstreat privat & then owr stufe was loste . . . iij s.

References

Acts of the Privy Council of England, ed. J. R. Dasent, 32 vols., HMSO, London, 1890–1907.

Astington, John H., 'The "Unrecorded Portrait" of Edward Alleyn', *Shakespeare Quarterly* 44 (1993), 73–86.

English Court Theatre 1558–1642, Cambridge University Press, 1999.

Baillie, William M., 'The Date and Authorship of *Grim the Collier of Croydon*', *Modern Philology* 76 (1978), 179–84.

Bartels, Emily C., 'Making More of the Moor: Aaron, Othello, and Renaissance Refashionings of Race', *Shakespeare Quarterly* 41 (1990), 1–15.

Spectacles of Strangeness. Imperialism, Alienation, and Marlowe, University of Pennsylvania Press, Philadelphia, 1993.

Barthelemy, Anthony Gerard, *Black Face Maligned Race: The Representation of Blacks in English Drama from Shakespeare to Southerne*, Louisiana State University Press, Baton Rouge, 1987.

Barton, Anne, *Ben Jonson Dramatist*, Cambridge University Press, 1984.

Baskervill, Charles Read, *The Elizabethan Jig and Related Song Drama*, University of Chicago Press, 1929.

Bawcutt, N. W., *The Control and Censorship of Caroline Drama. The Records of Sir Henry Herbert, Master of the Revels 1623–73*, Clarendon Press, Oxford, 1996.

Bayer, Mark, 'Staging Foxe at the Fortune and Red Bull', *Renaissance and Reformation* 39 (2003), 61–94.

Beckerman, Bernard, 'Philip Henslowe', in *The Theatrical Manager in England and America*, ed. Joseph W. Donohue, jr., Princeton University Press, 1971, pp. 19–62.

'Theatrical Plots and Elizabethan Stage Practice', in *Shakespeare and Dramatic Tradition: Essays in Honor of S. F. Johnson*, ed. W. R. Elton and W. B. Long, University of Delaware Press, Newark, 1989, pp. 109–24.

Bentley, Gerald Eades, *The Jacobean and Caroline Stage*, 7 vols., Clarendon Press, Oxford, 1941–68.

The Profession of Dramatist in Shakespeare's Time, Princeton University Press, 1971.

The Profession of Player in Shakespeare's Time, Princeton University Press, 1984.

Bland, Mark, 'The London Book-Trade in 1600', in *A Companion to Shakespeare*, ed. David Scott Kastan, Blackwell, Oxford, 1999, pp. 450–63.

Blayney, Peter W. M., 'The Publication of Playbooks', in *A New History of Early English Drama*, ed. John D. Cox and David Scott Kastan, Columbia University Press, New York, 1997, pp. 383–422.

Bossonet, Felix, *The Function of Stage Properties in Christopher Marlowe's Plays*, Francke Verlag, Berne, 1978.

Bowsher, Julian, M. C., *The Rose Theatre: An Archaeological Discovery*, Museum of London, 1998.

'The Rose and its Stages', *Shakespeare Survey* 60 (2007), 36–48.

Bowsher, Julian M. C., and Miller, Patricia, *The Rose and the Globe – Playhouses of Tudor Bankside, Southwark: Excavations 1988–91*, Museum of London, 2009.

Bradbrook, Muriel C., *The Rise of the Common Player*, Chatto & Windus, London, 1962.

Shakespeare the Craftsman, Chatto & Windus, London, 1969.

Bradley, David, *From Text to Performance in the Elizabethan Theatre: Preparing the Play for the Stage*, Cambridge University Press, 1992.

Briley, John, 'Edward Alleyn and Henslowe's Will', *Shakespeare Quarterly* 9 (1958), 321–30.

Bristol, Michael D., 'Theater and Popular Culture', in *A New History of Early English Drama*, ed. John D. Cox and David Scott Kastan, Columbia University Press, New York, 1997, pp. 231–48.

Brooks, Douglas A., *From Playhouse to Printing House. Drama and Authorship in Early Modern England*, Cambridge University Press, 2000.

Bruster, Douglas, *Drama and the Market in the Age of Shakespeare*, Cambridge University Press, 1992.

'The Dramatic Life of Objects in the Early Modern Theatre', in *Staged Properties in Early Modern English Drama*, ed. Jonathan Gil Harris and Natasha Korda, Cambridge University Press, Cambridge, 2002, pp. 67–96.

Burnett, Mark Thornton, *Masters and Servants in English Renaissance Drama and Culture. Authority and Obedience*, Macmillan Press, Basingstoke, 1997.

Butterworth, Philip, *Magic on the Early English Stage*, Cambridge University Press, 2005.

Calendar of State Papers, Domestic, 1595–7, HMSO, London, ed. Everett Green, 1869; 1598–1601, 1601–3, 1870.

Calore, Michela, 'Elizabethan Plots: A Shared Code of Theatrical and Fictional Language', *Theatre Survey* 44 (2003), 249–61.

Carson, Neil, *A Companion to Henslowe's Diary*, Cambridge University Press, 1988.

Cartelli, Thomas, *Marlowe, Shakespeare and the Economy of Theatrical Experience*, University of Pennsylvania Press, Philadelphia, 1991.

Cerasano, S. P., ' "More Elbow Roome, but Scant Better Aire": The Fortune Playhouse and its Surroundings', *Indiana Social Studies Quarterly* 35 (1982), 70–84.

'Revising Philip Henslowe's Biography', *Notes and Queries* 230 (1985), 66–72.

'The "Business" of Shareholding, the Fortune Playhouse, and Francis Grace's Will', *Medieval and Renaissance Drama in England* 2 (1985), 231–52.

'Edward Alleyn's Early Years: His Life and Family', *Notes and Queries* 232 (1987), 237–48.

'The Master of the Bears in Art and Enterprise', *Medieval and Renaissance Drama in English* 5 (1991), 195–209.

'Philip Henslowe, Simon Forman, and the Theatrical Community of the 1590s', *Shakespeare Quarterly* 44 (1993), 145–58.

'Tamburlaine and Edward Alleyn's Ring', *Shakespeare Survey* 47 (1994), 171–79.

'Edward Alleyn's "Retirement" ', *Medieval and Renaissance Drama in England* 10 (1998), 98–112.

'Cheerful Givers: Henslowe, Alleyn, and the 1612 Loan Book to the Crown', *Shakespeare Studies* 28 (2000), 215–19.

'The Patronage Network of Philip Henslowe and Edward Alleyn', *Medieval and Renaissance Drama in England* 13 (2001), 82–92.

'Henslowe's "Curious" Diary', *Medieval and Renaissance Drama in England* 17 (2004), 72–85.

'The Geography of Henslowe's Diary', *Shakespeare Quarterly* 56 (2005), 328–53.

'Philip Henslowe and the Elizabethan Court', *Shakespeare Survey* 60 (2007), 49–57.

Chalfant, Fran C., *Ben Jonson's London. A Jacobean Placename Dictionary*, University of Georgia Press, Athens Ga., 1978.

Chambers, E. K., *The Elizabethan Stage*, 4 vols., Clarendon Press, Oxford, 1923.

Chapman, George, *The Plays of George Chapman. The Comedies. A Critical Edition*, Gen. ed. Allan Holaday, University of Illinois Press, Urbana, 1970.

Clare, Janet, *'Art made tongue-tied by authority': Elizabethan and Jacobean Censorship*, Manchester University Press, 1990.

Clark, Stuart, *Vanities of the Eye: Vision in Early Modern Europe*, Oxford University Press, 2007.

Cook, David, and Wilson, F. P., *Dramatic Records in the Declared Accounts of the Treasurer of the Chamber 1558–1642, Collections* VI, The Malone Society, Oxford, 1961.

Cox, John D., *The Devil and the Sacred in English Drama, 1350–1642*, Cambridge University Press, 2000.

Dekker, Thomas, *The Dramatic Works of Thomas Dekker*, ed. Fredson Bowers, 4 vols., Cambridge University Press, 1953–61.

Non-Dramatic Works, ed. A. B. Grosart, 5 vols., London, 1884–86.

Dessen, Alan C., and Thomson, Leslie, *A Dictionary of Stage Directions in English Drama, 1580–1642*, Cambridge University Press, 1999.

Diehl, Huston, *Staging Reform, Reforming the Stage: Protestantism and Popular Theater in Early Modern England*, Cornell University Press, Ithaca, 1997.

Dillon, Janette, *Theatre, Court and City, 1595–1610: Drama and Social Space in London*, Cambridge University Press, 2000.

The Cambridge Introduction to Early English Theatre, Cambridge University Press, 2006.

Dollimore, Jonathan, 'Subversion through Transgression: *Doctor Faustus*', in *Staging the Renaissance: Reinterpretations of Elizabethan and Jacobean*

Drama, ed. David Scott Kastan and Peter Stallybrass, Routledge, London, 1991, pp. 122–32.

Dutton, Richard, *Mastering the Revels: The Regulation and Censorship of English Renaissance Drama*, Routledge, London, University of Iowa Press, 1991.

'The Birth of an Author', in *Texts and Cultural Change in Early Modern England*, ed. Cedric C. Brown and Arthur Marotti, St Martin's Press, New York, 1993, pp. 153–78.

Licensing, Censorship and Authorship in Early Modern England: Buggeswords, Palgrave, Basingstoke, 2000.

Eccles, Christine, *The Rose Theatre*, Nick Hern Books, London, 1990.

Eccles, Mark, 'Elizabethan Actors I: A–D', *Notes and Queries* 236 (1991), 38–49.

'Elizabethan Actors II: E–K', *Notes and Queries* 236 (1991), 454–61.

'Elizabethan Actors III: K–R', *Notes and Queries* 237 (1992), 293–303.

'Elizabethan Actors IV: S to End', *Notes and Queries* 238 (1993), 165–76.

'Middleton's Comedy *The Almanac*, or *No Wit, No Help Like a Woman's*', *Notes and Queries* 232 (1987), 296–97.

Edelman, Charles, '*The Battle of Alcazar, Muly Molocco*, and Shakespeare's *2* and *3 Henry VI*', *Notes and Queries* 247 (2002), 215–18.

' "Shoot at him all at once": Gunfire at the playhouse, 1587', *Theatre Notebook* 57 (2003), 78–81.

ed., *The Stukeley Plays*, Manchester University Press, 2005.

Edmond, Mary, 'On licensing playhouses', *Review of English Studies* 46 (1995), 373–4.

Erne, Lukas, *Beyond* The Spanish Tragedy: *A Study of the Works of Thomas Kyd*, Manchester University Press, 2001.

Farmer, Alan B., and Lesser, Zachary, 'Vile Arts: The Marketing of English Printed Drama, 1512–1660', *Research Opportunities in Renaissance Drama* 39 (2000), 77–165.

Fehrenbach, Robert J., 'When Lord Cobham and Edmund Tilney "Were att Odds": Oldcastle, Falstaff, and the Date of *1 Henry IV*', *Shakespeare Studies* 18 (1986), 87–102.

Feuillerat, Albert, ed., *Documents Relating to the Office of the Revels in the Time of Queen Elizabeth*, A. Uystpruyst, Louvain, 1908.

Foakes, R. A., *Illustrations of the English Stage, 1580–1642*, Stanford University Press, 1985.

'The Discovery of The Rose Theatre: Some Implications', *Shakespeare Survey* 43 (1991), 141–48.

Foakes, R. A., and Rickert, R. T., *Henslowe's Diary*. Cambridge University Press, 1961, second edn 2002.

'Henslowe's Rose/Shakespeare's Globe', in *From Script to Stage in Early Modern England*, ed. Peter Holland and Stephen Orgel, Palgrave Macmillan, Basingstoke, 2004.

Freeman, Arthur, *Thomas Kyd. Facts and Problems*, Clarendon Press, Oxford, 1967.

Garber, Marjorie, 'The Logic of the Transvestite. *The Roaring Girl*', in *Staging the Renaissance: Reinterpretations of Elizabethan and Jacobean Drama*, ed.

David Scott Kastan and Peter Stallybrass, Routledge, London, 1991, pp. 221–34.

Gasper, Julia, 'The Reformation Plays on the Public Stage', in *Theatre and Government under the Early Stuarts*, ed. J. R. Mulryne and Margaret Shewring, Cambridge University Press, 1993, pp. 190–216.

Gowan, Juliet Mary, ed., *An Edition of Edward Pudsey's Commonplace Book (c.1600–1615) from the Manuscript in the Bodleian Library*, University of London, London, 1967.

Grant, Teresa, 'History in the Making: The Case of Samuel Rowley's *When You See Me You Know Me*', in *English Historical Drama, 1500–1660: Forms outside the Canon*, ed. Teresa Grant and Barbara Ravelhofer, Palgrave Macmillan Press, Basingstoke, 2008, pp. 125–57.

Grantley, Darryll, *Wit's Pilgrimage: Drama and the Social Impact of Education in Early Modern England*, Ashgate, Aldershot, 2000.

Graves, R. B., *Lighting the Shakespearean Stage, 1567–1642*, Southern Illinois University Press, Carbondale, 1999.

Greenblatt, Stephen J., 'The Will to Absolute Play. *The Jew of Malta*', in *Staging the Renaissance: Reinterpretations of Elizabethan and Jacobean Drama*, ed. David Scott Kastan and Peter Stallybrass, Routledge, London, 1991, pp. 114–21.

Greenfield, Jon, 'Reconstructing the Rose: Development of the Playhouse Building between 1587 and 1592', *Shakespeare Survey* 60 (2007), 23–35.

Greenfield, Jon, and Gurr, Andrew, 'The Rose Theatre, London: The State of Knowledge and What We Still Need to know", *Antiquity* 78 (2004), 330–40.

Greg, W. W., ed., *The Henslowe Papers*, London, 1907.
   Dramatic Documents from the Elizabethan Playhouses, 2 vols., Clarendon Press, Oxford, 1931.

Gurr, Andrew, 'Who Strutted and Bellowed?', *Shakespeare Survey* 16 (1963), 95–102.
   'Intertextuality at Windsor', *Shakespeare Quarterly* 38 (1987), 189–200.
   'Intertextuality in Henslowe', *Shakespeare Quarterly* 39 (1988), 394–98.
   'Money or Audiences: The Choice of Shakespeare's Globe', *Theatre Notebook* 42 (1988), 3–14.
   (with John Orrell), 'What the Rose Can Tell Us', *Times Literary Supplement*, 9–15 June 1989, 636, 649; reprinted with additions in *Antiquity* 63 (1989), 421–29.
   'The Rose Repertory: What the Plays Might Tell Us about the Stage', in *New Issues in the Reconstruction of Shakespeare's Theatre*, ed. Franklin J. Hildy, Peter Lang, Frankfurt am Main, 1991, pp. 119–34.
   'Cultural Property and "Sufficient Interest": The Rose and the Globe Sites', *International Journal of Cultural Property* I (1992), 9–25.
   'The Loss of Records for the Travelling Companies in Stuart Times', *Records of Early English Drama Newsletter* 19 (1994), 2–19.
   'The Bare Island', *Shakespeare Survey* 47 (1994), 29–43.
   The Shakespearian Playing Companies, Clarendon Press, Oxford, 1996.
   'Traps and Discoveries at the Globe', *Proceedings of the British Academy* 94, 1997, 85–101.

'Maximal and Minimal Texts: Shakespeare v. the Globe', *Shakespeare Survey* 52 (1999), 68–87.

'The Authority of the Globe and the Fortune', in *Material London*, ed. Lena Cowen Orlin, University of Delaware Press, 2000, pp. 251–67.

'*Hamlet* and the Auto da Fé', *Around the Globe* 13 (2000), 15.

'Doors at the Globe: The Gulf between Page and Stage', *Theatre Notebook* 55 (2001), 59–71.

'Privy Councilors as Theatre Patrons', in *Theatrical Patronage in Shakespeare's England*, ed. Suzanne Westfall and Paul Whitfield White, Cambridge University Press, 2002, pp. 221–45.

'The Great Divide of 1594', in *Words that Count: Essays on Early Modern Authorship in Honor of MacDonald P. Jackson*, ed. Brian Boyd, Associated University Presses, 2004, pp. 29–48.

'Bears and Players: Philip Henslowe's Double Acts', *Shakespeare Bulletin* 22 (2004), 31–41.

The Shakespeare Company, 1594–1642, Cambridge University Press, 2004.

' "Within the Compass of the City walls": Allegiances in Plays for and about the City', in *Plotting Early Modern London: New Essays on Jacobean City Comedy*, ed. Dieter Mehl, Angela Stock and Anne-Julia Zwierlein. A Festschrift for Brian Gibbons, Ashgate, London, 2004, pp. 109–24.

'Henry Carey's Peculiar Letter', *Shakespeare Quarterly* 56 (2005), 51–75.

'The Work of Elizabethan Plotters, and 2 *The Seven Deadly Sins*', *Early Theatre* 10 (2006), 67–87.

'A Black Reversal', *Shakespeare* 4 (2008), 148–56.

'Did Shakespeare Own his own Playbooks?', *Review of English Studies* 59 (2008).

Haaker, Ann, 'The Plague, the Theater, and the Poet', *Renaissance Drama* 1 (1968), 283–305.

Hadfield, Andrew, *Shakespeare and Republicanism*, Cambridge University Press, 2005.

Hamilton, Donna, *Shakespeare and the Politics of Protestant England*, University of Kentucky Press, Lexington, 1992.

Hamline, William M., 'Scepticism in Shakespeare's England', *The Shakespearean International Yearbook* 2 (2002), 290–304.

Harbage, Alfred B., *Annals of English Drama, 975–1700*, 3rd edn by Sylvia Stoler Wagenheim, Methuen, London, 1989.

Harris, Jonathan Gill, and Korda, Natasha, ed., *Staged Properties in Early Modern Drama*, Cambridge University Press, 2002.

Harrison, William, *The Description of England*, ed. Georges Edelen, Folger Shakespeare Library/Dover Publications, Washington DC, 1994.

Hattaway, Michael, *Elizabethan Popular Theatre: Plays in Performance*, Routledge, London, 1982.

Hayes, Tom, *The Birth of Popular Culture: Ben Jonson, Maid Marian and Robin Hood*, Duquesne University Press, Pittsburgh, 1992.

Haynes, Jonathan, *The Social Relations of Jonson's Theater*, Cambridge University Press, 1992.

Honigmann, E. A. J., and Brock, Susan, ed., *Playhouse Wills, 1558–1642. An Edition of Wills by Shakespeare and his Contemporaries in the London Theatre*, Manchester University Press, 1993.

Hosking, G. L., *The Life and Times of Edward Alleyn*, Jonathan Cape, London, 1952.

Howard, Jean E., *The Stage and Social Struggle in Early Modern England*, Routledge, London, 1994.

Howard-Hill, T. H., ed., *Shakespeare and* Sir Thomas More: *Essays on the Play and its Shakespearian Interest*, Cambridge University Press, 1989.

Hoy, Cyrus, *Introductions, Notes and Commentaries to Texts in 'The Dramatic Works of Thomas Dekker'*, ed. Fredson Bowers, 4 vols., Cambridge University Press, 1980.

Hutchings, Mark, and Bromham, A. A., *Middleton and his Collaborators*, British Council, Tavistock, 2008.

Ingram, William, *A London Life in the Brazen Age. Francis Langley, 1548–1602.* Harvard University Press, Cambridge, Mass., 1978.

'The Globe Playhouse and its Neighbours in 1600', *Essays in Theatre* 2 (1984), 63–72.

Ioppolo, Grace, *Dramatists and their Manuscripts in the Age of Shakespeare, Jonson, Middleton and Heywood: Authorship, Authority and the Playhouse*, Routledge, London, 2006.

Jackson, MacD. P., 'The Date and Authorship of *Thomas of Woodstock*: Evidence and its Interpretation', *Research Opportunities in Medieval and Renaissance Drama* 46 (2007), 67–100.

Jowett, John, 'Middleton's *No Wit* at the Fortune', *Renaissance Drama* n.s. 22 (1991), 191–208.

Kastan, David Scott, 'Workshop and/as Playhouse: Comedy and Commerce in *The Shoemaker's Holiday*', *Studies in Philology* 84 (1987), 324–37.

'Workshop and/as Playhouse: *The Shoemaker's Holiday*', in *Staging the Renaissance: Reinterpretations of Elizabethan and Jacobean Drama*, ed. David Scott Kastan and Peter Stallybrass, Routledge, London, 1991, pp. 151–63.

Kastan, David Scott, and Stallybrass, Peter, ed., *Staging the Renaissance: Reinterpretations of Elizabethan and Jacobean Drama*, Routledge, London, 1991.

Kathman, David, 'Reconsidering *The Seven Deadly Sins*', *Early Theatre* 7 (2004), 13–44.

Kay, W. David, *Ben Jonson: A Literary Life*, Macmillan, Basingstoke, 1995.

Knapp, Jeffrey, *Shakespeare's Tribe: Church, Nation, and Theater in Renaissance England*, University of Chicago Press, 2002.

Knutson, Roslyn Lander, *The Repertory of Shakespeare's Company 1594–1613*, University of Arkansas Press, Fayetteville, 1991.

'The Commercial Significance of the Payments for Playtexts in *Henslowe's Diary*, 1597–1603', in *Medieval and Renaissance Drama in England* 5 (1991), 117–63.

Playing Companies and Commerce in Shakespeare's Time, Cambridge University Press, 2001.

'Two Playhouses, Both Alike in Dignity', *Shakespeare Studies* 30 (2002), 111–17.

'Toe to Toe across Maid Lane: Repertorial Competition at the Rose and Globe, 1599–1600', in *Acts of Criticism: Performance Matters in Shakespeare and His Contemporaries. Essays in Honor of James P. Lusardi*, ed. Paul Nelsen and June Schlueter, Fairleigh Dickinson University Press, Madison, 2006.

Kozusko, Matt, 'Taking Liberties', *Early Theatre* 9 (2006), 37–60.

Kyd, Thomas, *The Spanish Tragedy*, ed. Philip Edwards, Revels Plays, London, 1959.

Leggatt, Alexander, *Jacobean Public Theatre*, Routledge, London, 1992.

Leinwand, Theodore, *Theatre, Finance and Society in Early Modern England*, Cambridge University Press, 1999.

Levin, Harry, *Christopher Marlowe: The Overreacher*, Faber, London, 1954.

Levine, Nina, 'Citizens' Games: Differentiating Collaboration and *Sir Thomas More*', *Shakespeare Quarterly* 58 (2007), 31–64.

MacIntyre, Jean, *Costumes and Scripts in the Elizabethan Theatre*, University of Alberta Press, Edmonton, 1992.

MacIntyre, Jean, and Epp, Garrett P. J., ' "Cloathes worth all the rest": Costumes and Properties', in *A New History of Early English Drama*, ed. John D. Cox and David Scott Kastan, Columbia University Press, New York, 1997, pp. 269–86.

MacLean, Sally-Beth, 'Tour Routes: "Provincial Wanderings" or Traditional Circuits?', *Medieval and Renaissance Drama in England* 6 (1993), 1–14.

MacLure, Millar, *George Chapman. A Critical Study*, University of Toronto Press, Toronto, 1966.

McMillin, Scott, *The Elizabethan Theatre and 'The Book of Sir Thomas More'*, Cornell University Press, Ithaca, 1987.

'Sussex's Men in 1594: The Evidence of *Titus Andronicus* and *The Jew of Malta*', *Theatre Survey* 32 (1991), 214–23.

'The Rose and the Swan', in *The Development of Shakespeare's Theater*, ed. John Astington, AMS Press, New York, 1992, pp. 159–83.

'Professional Playwrighting', in *A Companion to Shakespeare*, ed. David Scott Kastan, Blackwell Publishers, Oxford, 1999, pp. 225–38.

McMillin, Scott, and MacLean, Sally-Beth, *The Queen's Men and their Plays*, Cambridge University Press, 1998.

Maguire, Laurie, *Shakespearean Suspect Texts: The 'Bad' Quartos and Their Contexts*, Cambridge University Press, 1996.

Marlowe, Christopher, *The Complete Works of Christopher Marlowe*, ed. Fredson Bowers, 2 vols., second edn, Cambridge University Press, 1981.

Doctor Faustus A- and B-texts (1604, 1616), ed. David Bevington and Eric Rasmussen, Manchester University Press (Revels Plays), 1993.

The Jew of Malta, ed. N. W. Bawcutt, Manchester University Press (Revels Plays), 1978.

Meads, Chris, *Banquets Set Forth: Banqueting in English Renaissance Drama*, Manchester University Press, 2001.

Melnikoff, Kirk, ' "[I]ygging vaines" and "riming mother wits": Marlowe, Clowns and the Early Frameworks of Dramatic Authorship', *Early Modern Literary Studies* Special Issue 16 (October, 2007) 8.1–37, http://purl.oclc.org/emls/si-16/melnjygg.htm.

Menzer, Paul, 'The Tragedians of the City? Q1 *Hamlet* and the Settlements of the 1590s', *Shakespeare Quarterly* 57 (2006), 162–82.

Middleton, Thomas, *The Collected Works*, gen. ed. Gary Taylor and John Lavagnino, Clarendon Press, Oxford, 2007.

Mowat, Barbara A., 'The Theater and Literary Culture', in *A New History of Early English Drama*, ed. John D. Cox and David Scott Kastan, Columbia University Press, New York, 1997, pp. 213–230.

Nakayama, Randall, ' "I know she is a courtesan by her attire": Clothing and Identity in *The Jew of Malta*', in *Marlowe's Empery. Expanding his Critical Contexts*, ed. Sara Munson Deats and Robert A. Logan, University of Delaware Press, Newark, 2002, pp. 150–63.

Nelson, Alan H., 'George Buc, William Shakespeare, and the Folger *George a Greene*', *Shakespeare Quarterly* 49 (1998), 74–83.

Nungezer, Edwin, *A Dictionary of Actors and Other Persons Associated with the Public Representation of Plays in England before 1642*, Yale University Press, New Haven, 1929.

Orgel, Stephen, 'Making Greatness Familiar', in *The Forms of Power and the Power of Forms in the Renaissance*, ed. Stephen Greenblatt, University of Oklahoma Press, Norman, 1984, pp. 41–48.

Orlin, Lena Cowen, "Things with Little Social Life (Henslowe's Theatrical Properties and Elizabethan Household Fittings)', in *Staged Properties in Early Modern English Drama*, ed. Jonathan Gil Harris and Natasha Korda, Cambridge University Press, 2002, pp. 99–128.

Orrell, John, 'Nutshells at the Rose', *Theatre Research International* 17 (1992), 8–14.
'Building the Fortune', *Shakespeare Quarterly* 44 (1993), 127–44.

Peele, George, *The Life and Works of George Peele*, ed. Charles Tyler Prouty, Vol. 2, *The Dramatic Works of George Peele, Edward I*, ed. Frank S. Hook, Yale University Press, New Haven, 1961.

Riggs, David, *Ben Jonson: A Life*, Harvard University Press, Cambridge, Mass., 1987.

Roberts, Sasha, ' "Let me the curtains draw": The Dramatic and Symbolic Properties of the Bed in Shakespearean Tragedy', in *Staged Properties in Early Modern English Drama*, ed. Jonathan Gil Harris and Natasha Korda, Cambridge University Press, 2002, pp. 153–74.

Robinson, Marsha S., *Writing the Reformation. 'Actes and Monuments' and the Jacobean History Play*, Ashgate, Aldershot, 2002.

Rutter, Carol Chillington, ed. *Documents of the Rose Playhouse*, Revels Plays Companion Library, Manchester University Press, 1984, rev. edn 2001.

Rutter, Tom, 'Merchants of Venice in *A Knack to Know an Honest Man*', *Medieval and Renaissance Drama in England* 19 (2006), 194–209.
'*Patient Grissil* and Jonsonian Satire', *Studies in English Literature* 48 (2008), 283–303.

Saeger, James P., and Fassler, Christopher J, 'The London Professional Theater, 1576–1642: A Catalogue and Analysis of the Extant Printed Plays', *Research Opportunities in Renaissance Drama* 34 (1995), 63–109.

Scott, Sarah, ' "Sell[ing] your selves away": Pathologizing and Gendering the Socio-Economic in *The Honest Whore, Part I'*, *Research Opportunities in Medieval and Renaissance Drama* 45 (2006), 1–22.

Shapiro, James, ' "Tragedies naturally performed": Kyd's Representation of Violence', in *Staging the Renaissance: Reinterpretations of Elizabethan and Jacobean Drama*, ed. David Scott Kastan and Peter Stallybrass, Routledge, London, 1991, pp. 99–113.

'The Scot's Tragedy and the Politics of Popular Drama', *English Literary Renaissance* 23 (1993), 428–49.

Shakespeare and the Jews, Columbia University Press, New York, 1996.

Shepherd, Simon, *Amazons and Warrior Women: Varieties of Feminism in Seventeenth-Century Drama*, Harvester, London, 1981.

Shepherd, Simon, and Womack, Peter, *English Drama: A Cultural History*, Blackwell, Oxford, 1996.

Skura, Meredith, 'Anthony Munday's "Gentrification" of Robin Hood', *English Literary Review* 33 (2003), 155–80.

Smith, Emma, 'Author v. Character in Early Modern Dramatic Authorship: The Example of Thomas Kyd and *The Spanish Tragedy'*, *Medieval and Renaissance Drama in England* 11 (1999), 129–42.

Sofer, Andrew, *The Stage Life of Props*, University of Michigan Press, Ann Arbor, 2003.

Somerset, Alan, 'Cultural Poetics or Historical Prose? The Places of the Stage', *Medieval and Renaissance Drama in England* 11 (1999), 34–60.

Spikes, Judith Doolin, 'The Jacobean History Play and the Myth of the Elect Nation', *Renaissance Drama* n.s. 8 (1977), 117–49.

Stallybrass, Peter, and Jones, Annie, *Renaissance Clothing and the Materials of Memory*, Cambridge University Press, 2000.

Stern, Tiffany, *Rehearsal from Shakespeare to Sheridan*, Clarendon Press, Oxford, 2000.

' "On each Wall And Corner Poast": Playbills, Title-pages, and Advertising in Early Modern London', *English Literary Renaissance* 36 (2006), 57–89.

Stevens, Andrea R., ' "Assisted by a Barber": The Court Apothecary, Special Effects, and *The Gipsies Metamorphosed'*, *Theatre Notebook* 61 (2007), 2–11.

Stone, Lawrence, *Family and Fortune: Studies in Aristocratic Finance in the Sixteenth and Seventeenth Centuries*, Clarendon Press, Oxford, 1973.

Stone Peters, Julie, *Theatre of the Book, 1480–1880: Print, Text, and Performance in Europe*, Clarendon Press, Oxford, 2000.

Streitberger, W. R., ed., *Jacobean and Caroline Revels Accounts, 1603–1642*, Collections XIII, The Malone Society, Oxford, 1986.

Teague, Frances, *Shakespeare's Speaking Properties*, Bucknell University Press, Lewisburg, 1991.

Thomson, Leslie, 'A Quarto "Marked for Performance": Evidence of What?', *Medieval and Renaissance Drama in England* 5 (1990), 225–43.

Traister, Barbara Howard, *The Notorious Astrological Physician of London. Works and Days of Simon Forman*, University of Chicago Press, Chicago 2001.

Tribble, Evelyn, 'Distributing Cognition at the Globe', *Shakespeare Quarterly* 56 (2005), 135–55.

Vaughan, Virginia Mason, *Performing Blackness on English Stages, 1500–1800*, Cambridge University Press, 2005.

Waage, F. D., 'Meg and Moll: Two Renaissance London Heroines', *Journal of Popular Culture* 20 (1986), 105–17.

Wagner, Bernard M., 'Robert Yarrington', *Modern Language Notes* 45 (1930), 147–48.

Webster, John, *The Works of John Webster*, ed. David Gunby, David Carnegie and Antony Hammond, 3 vols., Cambridge University Press, 1995–2007.

Weimann, Robert, *Author's Pen and Actor's Voice: Playing and Writing in Shakespeare's Theatre*, Cambridge University Press, 2000.

Whitney, Charles, 'The Devil his Due: Mayor John Spencer, Elizabethan Civic Antitheatricalism, and *The Shoemaker's Holiday*', *Medieval and Renaissance Drama in England* 14 (2001), 168–85.

 Early Responses to Renaissance Drama, Cambridge University Press, 2006.

Wickham, Glynne, Berry, Herbert, and Ingram, William, *English Professional Theatre, 1530–1660: A Documentary History*, Cambridge University Press, 2000.

Wiggins, Martin, 'A Choice of Impossible Things: Dating the Revival of *The Battle of Alcazar*', in *Shakespeare et ces contemporains: Actes de colloque 2002 de la Société Française Shakespeare*, ed. Patricia Dorval, Montpellier, 2002, pp. 185–202.

Winkelman, Michael A., *Marriage Relationships in Tudor Political Drama*, Ashgate, Aldershot, 2005.

Womak, Peter, 'Imagining communities: Theatres and the English Nation in the Sixteenth Century', in *Culture and History 1350–1600: Essays on English Communities, Identities and Writing*, ed. David Aers, Wayne State University Press, Detroit, 1992, pp. 91–145.

Index

Index

WITHDRAWN